A SOCIAL HISTORY OF ETHIOPIA

The Northern and Central Highlands from Early Medieval Times to the Rise of Emperor Téwodros II

Richard Pankhurst

Institute of Ethiopian Studies
Addis Ababa University
1990

FOR HELEN

CONTENTS

PART TWO
THE GONDÄR PERIOD

LIST OF ILLUSTRATIONS

St. James and St. John, from a 15th century Ethiopian volume of Psalms and Canticles in the Bibliothèque Nationale, Paris, Ethiopien-Abbadie 105.

INTRODUCTION

In introducing the present essay on the Social History of Ethiopia, it should be emphasised that the country, which today covers an area as large as France and Spain combined, has always been one of immense geographical and other contrasts. High mountains, which in the Sämén range tower more than 4,600 metres above sea level, give way to flat lowlands which in the 'Afär depression sink below sea level. Temperature, which, geographically, is no less varied, ranges from the icy cold of the mountains, with frost, and in places even snow, through the temperate highlands - the site of most of the country's historic settlements - to the torrid lowlands, with the Red Sea and Gulf of Aden ports reckoned as among some of the hottest places in the world. Differences in rainfall have been no less dramatic, the torrential downpours of the highlands contrasting with minimal precipitation in the parched almost waterless lowlands. It follows that vegetation was equally varied, with tropical jungles, particularly in the west, deserts and semi-desert scrublands, mainly in the east and south, and fertile - but largely deforested - regions in many areas of medium elevation.

The population of the country, not surprisingly, came to terms with such greatly varying environments in different ways, with the result that the world's principal types of economic activity were all represented - with agriculturalists, many of them practicing plough agriculture, in the extensive highlands, pastoralists in the even more widespread lowlands, and hunters and gatherers in the vicinity of the many rivers, lakes and forests. (This three-fold division is, however, far from rigid, for there was often much overlapping, particularly in the highlands where the supposed "agriculturalists" devoted much of their time to the upkeep of cattle which many farmers and peasants regarded as their principal source of wealth).

Ethiopia - like so many countries on the African continent - is in no less measure a land made up of varied ethnic - and linguistic - threads. It comprises members of no less than four broad language groups: Semitic, mainly in the north, but with pockets in the south (Guragé and Adaré), Cushitic, mainly in the south, but with pockets in the north (Beja, Agäw, Saho, and 'Afar), Omotic (Wällamo, Käfa, Gemerra, etc.) in the south-west, and Nilo-Saharan in the far west, near the Sudan border. The situation was, however, historically far from static, for there were over the centuries major movements of population, notably in the ancient and medieval period when Tegrés moved from north to south; in the sixteenth, seventeenth and early eighteenth centuries when Oromos migrated from south to north; in the nineteenth century when there was once more a movement, mainly of Amharas, from north to south; as well as throughout the centuries to and from sundry national or provincial capitals. For this and other reasons bilingualism, and indeed multilingualism, may well have existed throughout this period.

The religious pattern - in which the world's three main monotheistic faiths are all represented - was no less varied. For centuries Christians of the Orthodox faith predominated in the all-important northern and central highlands, Muslims were no less dominant in most of the lowlands, particularly to the east, as well as at the great commercial centre of Harär, but were also of paramount importance as merchants throughout the region as a whole. Followers of traditional local faiths preponderated in the south-west (the source of much of the country's exports of gold, ivory, civet and slaves), but also, we may assume, exerted some cultural influence in the north where they accounted for no small proportion of the slave population which, we may surmise, was by no means instantly assimilated to the locally dominant faith or faiths. The Fälaša, or Judaic Ethiopians, who constituted the smallest of the country's four religious groups, were located mainly in the north-west. Though their faith was in many ways distinct - both from other Ethiopians and from the Jews of other lands - their social life had much in common with Ethiopian Orthodox Christians, with whom they shared the Ge'ez Old Testament, whose scribes often wrote out their sacred writings and whose Church schools they sometimes attended. They also had some cultural affinities with the nearby Qemant who represented an intermediary faith between Judaism and an ancient Ethiopian religion often referred to as a form of Animism.

Such immense variations of physical and human geography coupled with those of language, culture and religion, inevitably resulted in the existence within the confines of the present-day Ethiopian region of many differing customs and ways of life. There ensued much cross-fertilisation of cultures and traditions, which still requires detailed study. Any comprehensive examination of so rich, and geographically varied, a history obviously requires many detailed monographs - for it would seem impossible, within the compass of one small volume such as this, to do justice to the rich variety of Ethiopia's historic social and cultural experience, either on a country-wide basis - or over the time span of more than a few centuries. Further factual studies, when completed, will doubtless lead to works of greater synthesis and interpretation.

* * * * * *

The present volume, which is planned as the first of a series dealing with various aspects of the country's varied social history, is devoted by and large to the northern and central highlands, and covers the period from early medieval times to the reign of Emperor Téwodros II which is considered a turning-point in the country's history - and serves at the same time as a point of departure for the dramatic changes that were to characterise the late nineteenth and twentieth centuries. The region under review was important in that it constituted the core of the traditional Ethiopian State, and was over the centuries to exercise no small influence on other parts of the country. The area was at the same time distinctive - and formed a cohesive entity - in that it had a unique highland, and predominantly Christian, culture. The region is moreover of special interest on account of its indigenous chronicles and hagiographies, and the many descriptions by foreign travellers, which made it, at least until the middle or second half of the nineteenth century, by far best documented part of Ethiopia. It is thus an area that can be studied over a considerable span of time.

Since the northern and, central highlands in the period under review are so palpably better documented it would be impossible to devote anything like equal coverage to other parts of the country without adopting the arbitrary, and from the scholarly point of view surely misguided policy of suppressing available data on a region for which it is available, in the interests of geographical balance.

Even with the above strictly limited geographical confines generalisation is often hazardous. It has been possible within the time and space available to consider only some of the more important aspects of Ethiopia's complex social life. Moreover there were often many variations of practice from one district or village to another, for the communities under review were composed, it should not be forgotten, of individual men, women and children, who lived their varied lives as they could, or thought fit - in blissful ignorance of the foreign traveller's accounts, and other historical sources, upon which scholars base their accounts - and develop their interpretations - of traditional Ethiopian behaviour.

The present volume, conceived as a first installment towards a full Social History of Ethiopia, is primarily descriptive. It is intended to present a survey based on available sources, and thereby to lay a groundwork for other writers to develop more ambitious, comprehensive and interpretative, studies of old-time Ethiopian life. It is hoped at a later stage to publish companion volumes on the south of the country, as well as on the period from Téwodros to more recent times.

* * * * * *

I should like to thank friends and colleagues who made this publication possible. I am grateful to Dr. Taddese Beyene, the devoted Director of the Institute of Ethiopian Studies, for his kind help and encouragement, as well as to Margaret Last for typing part of the first draft, to Amanda Woodlands for generously devoting her time to putting most of the text on computer, to my children Alula and Helen for initially helping me wrestle with that machine, to the computer wizard Bruno Neeser for producing IBM-compatible diskettes, and to Tatek Samare for expertly preparing the final work for printing and assisting in computer-indexing. Special thanks are also due to Demeke Berhane and to the ever-enthusiastic Dr. Carla Zanotti for helping me identify manuscript illustrations at the Institute; to Dr. Vincenzo Francaviglia, Denis Gérard, Santha Faiia and Membere Wolde Ghiorgis for kindly photographing these and other works; to the dedicated Degife Gabre Tsadik and his staff for constant library assistance, and to Belai Giday for approaching local informants on my behalf. I am, as always, indebted to my wife Rita for innumerable comments, criticisms and suggestions.

RICHARD PANKHURST

Institute of Ethiopian Studies,
Addis Ababa University.

A Lalibäla-style Ethiopian processional cross, probably dating from the 12th century, housed in the Institute of Ethiopian Studies.

PART ONE

THE MIDDLE AGES

King Solomon, with a broad-sword and parasol - both symbols of honour, from a 15th century manuscript of the Psalms and Canticles in the Bibliothèque Nationale, Paris, Ethiopien-Abbadie 105.

I

CHILDREN

Education and Training

Early historical data on children in Ethiopia is so scant that it is almost as though they were neither seen nor heard. We can, however, catch occasional glimpses of a medieval educational system which must have existed for centuries.

Schooling, in the Christian areas, was entirely vested in the Church, and was carried out by the clergy. Education, which was almost entirely restricted to boys, was based on reading and the recitation of religious texts, starting with the Psalms of David. Such works were written exclusively in the classical language Ge'ez, which was more or less unintelligible to those untutored in that tongue. Many of the pupils were the children of their teachers or other churchmen. The story of the Šäwan saint Täklä Haymanot was in this respect not untypical, for, the author of a traditional life, relates:

> "it came to pass that when the child was seven years old, he learned from
> his father the Psalms of David, and all the Books of the Church, both of
> the Old and the New Testaments, and he learned the meaning of the laws
> that were therein"[1]

Confirmation that a sizeable proportion of students were drawn from clerical families is afforded by the early sixteenth century Portuguese traveller Francisco Alvares who observed that "the sons of priests" were "mostly priests". Writing specifically of the rural countryside, he added: "the clergy teach what little they know to their sons". This was apparent when he visited a large church in Angot, where, on inquiring why it had so many canons, he received the reply that "all the sons of canons" became canons, for fathers taught their sons, "each his own", and it was for this reason that the canons had so "increased in number". This was apparently fairly general, for he was assured that the number of clergy was also growing at the "King's churches".

Not all students, however, were children of the clergy. A party of Portuguese who visited the famous monastery of Däbrä Bizän on the northern edge of the Ethiopian plateau in 1520 reported for instance that they saw "some twelve to fifteen" orphan boys of from ten or fourteen years of age whom the priests were bringing up "for the love of God", for this, Alvares comments, was their custom.

Children of ruling families, and, we may assume, of the aristocracy, in many cases also received some church education, besides what was perhaps even more important for them: training in the arts of war and government. Occasional brief mention of a monarch's childhood is made in the chronicles. Emperor Susneyos in the late sixteenth century is thus reported in his youth to have studied "all the ecclesiastical books", as well as to have learnt hunting, swimming, riding, archery,

---

[1] Budge (1906) 51.

stone-throwing and musketry.[2] In the following century the rulers of the Gondär period were educated in a not dissimilar manner. The annals of Yohannes I for example state that:

"After his birth he was carefully brought up in wisdom and discipline, and taught the Holy Books, that is to say the Old and New Testaments. Later, having grown, he learnt to throw the spear and draw the bow, as well as riding and swimming".[3]

St. Matthew and St. Mark, the former writing, from a 17th century Ethiopian Manuscript of the Four Gospels in the British Library, Orient 481.

---

[2] Beckingham and Huntingford (1961) I, 120, 236; Thomas (1938) 76; Esteves Pereira (1900) 5.

[3] Guidi (1903) 1.

4

Such statements are echoed in subsequent chronicles. Iyasu I was thus given a "good education in the study of the Holy Books", and was taught to ride on horseback, while Bäkaffa was said to be so well instructed that he was "constantly" reading the Psalter and Scriptures. In the eighteenth century Iyasu II likewise "learnt the Holy Books" in addition to riding, hunting and the use of the bow, spear and rifle.

Though the majority of students were no doubt content only with a modicum of education others proceeded to advanced studies in theology and related subjects. Record of such schooling in the 'medieval period is sparse, but there is abundant evidence of it, not only in the vast corpus of fine ecclesiastical and other literature produced by church scholars of the time, but also in the itineraries of Ethiopian ecclesiastics who travelled to Europe as recorded by the Venetian savant Alessandro Zorzi. Embedded in his interviews with them are intriguing references to "universities" - presumably church schools of higher learning, one of which, we are told, was attended by "many scholars", while another embraced "every faculty".

Despite the existence of such learning, the use of writing was almost entirely restricted to religious matters, for, as Alvares notes of Ethiopians: "They are not accustomed to write to one another, neither do the officers of justice write anything. All the justice that is done, and what is ordered, is by messengers and speech."[4]

Children and the Slave Trade

The records of this period indicate that numerous Ethiopian children were captured as slaves. Some, as we shall see in later chapters, served in a domestic capacity within the country itself, while others were taken abroad. The ravages of slave-raiders on the northern periphery were described in the mid-seventeenth century by the Italian traveller Giacomo Baratti who recalls that Turkish soldiers in the area were frequently "pillaging the Christians". Noblemen's children, he adds, were also seen, who "by their Meen and Garb were distinguishable from the ordinary sort. These poor creatures were led to be sold in Turky and other places as beasts", and were "forced to renounce their Religion..... What a grief", he exclaims, "it was to their Christian Parents, to suffer such a loss, to have their sons and daughters amongst infidels". Extensive slave-raiding, and trading, it should be added, were, however, also carried out by Ethiopians themselves.[5]

---

[4] Guidi (1903) 58, 291, (1912), 33; Crawford (1958), 149, 151, 153, 163; Beckingham and Huntingford (1961), II, 514-5.

[5] Baratti (1670) 20-2.

II

THE PEASANTRY

The peasants, who constituted the overwhelming majority of the population, played an all-important role in the country's economic life, for they were the producers who in the last analysis fed the entire society. They receive, however, remarkable little attention in the records of early times.

Fertility of the Land

Medieval Ethiopian agriculture, if we can believe the scant documentation available, was on the whole fairly productive, for the soil in the inhabited areas - which were far less populated than in modern times - tended to be fertile, and the highlands in normal years were blessed by abundant rainfall. The peasantry nevertheless suffered from considerable exploitation, as well as from a succession of natural and man-made disasters.

The "great abundance" of agricultural production was first described in the early sixteenth century by an Ethiopian monk, Brother Thomas of Angot, who told the Venetian author Alessandro Zorzi that his compatriots spent "nothing" on food-stuffs, and gave them "freely to all." Not dissimilar testimony is afforded by Alvares, who, having ascended the plateau from Massawa, exclaimed that "in the whole world" there was "not so populous a country", or one "so abundant in corn and herds of innumerable cattle".[1] Proceeding inland he reports that at the town of Manadeley, in southern Tegré, there was "much cultivation of all kinds". The inhabitants told him indeed that they had that year:

> "gathered so much corn of all kinds, that if it were not for the weevil, there would have been abundance for ten years. And because I was amazed they said to me, 'Honoured guest, do not be amazed, because in the years that we harvest little we gather enough for three years' plenty in the country; and if it were not for the multitude of locusts and the hail, which sometimes do great damage, we should not sow the half of what we sow, because the yield is incredibly great; so it is sowing wheat, barley, lentils, pulse, or any other seed. And we sow so much with the hope that even if any of those said plagues should come, some would be spoiled, and some would remain, and if all is spoiled the year before has been so plentiful that we have no scarcity".[2]

Agricultural yields of this magnitude permitted the growth of a sizeable population, particularly in some of the provinces of the interior. In Angot Alvares found "much population on the skirts of the mountains", while on reaching Amhara he wrote of it as "a wonderful country". One stretch he passed through, measuring ten

---

[1] Crawford (1956) 169; Beckingham and Huntingford (1961) I, 131.

[2] Beckingham and Huntingford (1961) I, 189.

to twelve miles, was "all cultivated", with "not a span" that was not made use of, and was "sown with all sorts of seed" so that "fresh crops" were gathered "all the year round".

The fertility of the land, and the magnitude of agricultural production, also impressed observers of the next few hundred years. Early in the seventeenth century the Jesuit Manoel de Almeida for example reported that in Dämbeya north of Lake Tana he saw "fine fields of very rich and fertile soil", while near Fremona in Tegré he found both wheat and barley growing abundantly.[3]

Livestock

Livestock by all accounts was also plentiful. On approaching Manadeley the Portuguese saw "beautiful herds" of cows on the outskirts of the town, as well as in the nearby hills. Some of Alvares's compatriots "guessed" the number of cattle at "50,000 (and more)", but for his part he did not say a "larger number" for their multitude could "not be believed". Confirmation of the abundance of livestock was provided a century later by a Jesuit Father, Jerome Lobo, who observed that the number of cattle was "almost unlimited". Cows, he explains, were the country's "principal form of wealth", and there was "an extremely large number of them", some farmers having indeed "many thousands". A "delightful custom" had accordingly grown up whereby "whenever one gains ownership of a thousand cows, he gives a great banquet, inviting relatives and friends, and taking milk from all the cows, for only cows [i.e. not bulls] are counted in the thousand, they take a bath in it, which I appropriately used to call 'a fly or huge fly in the milk' when they were in it. This custom is so prevalent that when people ask how many thousand cows a person has, they answer that he has already bathed two or some other number of times, which means that he owns that many thousand cows".[4]

Tribute and Taxation in Cattle

Cattle-owners were subject to considerable taxation. The antiquity of this tribute is apparent from the existence, at least since the reign of Emperor 'Amdä Seyon (1313-1344), of officials with the title of sähafä lam, or "scribe of cattle", which was given to governors of provinces, such as Amhara, Angot, Damot and Šäwa which provided the monarch with sizeable numbers of livestock. Evidence that cattle were a major item of taxation in the sixteenth century is provided by Alvares who reports that the "great lords", who were "like kings", paid tribute in "cows and plough oxen". The province of Hadeya for example yielded a "great number" of cattle which he had seen at court, while the district of Bugna in Angot contributed 150 plough oxen. The people of Guragé, according to a subsequent Portuguese observer João Bermudes, likewise paid their local ruler every year "one thousand live cows", i.e. almost three a day.

---

[3] Beckingham and Huntingford (1961) I, 149, 255, (1954), 37, 45, 188.

[4] Beckingham and Huntingford (1961) I, 189; Lockhart (1984) 167.

Cattle had also to be supplied to various churches and monasteries. A hundred villages around the monastery of Däbrä Bizän for example were reported by Alvares to have each paid 50 cattle every three years, the institution thus receiving a total of 1,650 head per annum, or almost five a day. The monks were thus so well supplied that, though they themselves did not consume meat, they slaughtered "many cows" every feast-day. Alvares states that twenty-eight were killed on one occasion, and thirty on another, and he, as an honoured guest, was each time given "two quarters of the fattest cow that was killed".

This cattle tax differed from other forms of tribute, according to Barradas, in that it was paid directly to the Emperor rather than to the local lords. Its yield amounted to "not less than thirty thousand head", and would have been "much more" had the collectors been "more faithful" or if the monarch himself had not granted numerous exceptions. Most of the cattle collected were in fact given over to noblemen so that "not many" animals actually arrived at the court.

Tribute in livestock seems to have been shortly afterwards increased, or was at least put on a more regular basis, during the reign of Emperor Gälawdéwos (1540-1559) when a new form of tax was instituted. It specified, according to Almeida, that each cattle-owner had to pay one cow in ten every three years. Because of the "many cattle" in the country this tax is said to have yielded a "great" amount of tribute.[5]

In order to place tax collection on a more efficient basis, the Emperor "divided his kingdoms and provinces" in such a way that he received some of the dues every year. This tribute was popularly called "burning" because the cows chosen for the monarch were branded, or "touched with fire", its skin being "burnt with a mark like branding". The nature and importance of this tax was corroborated by Lobo, who declares:

> "Every three years there is a general 'burning' in all the kingdoms of the empire which means that the Emperor takes one of every ten cows and the one that he takes has a mark branded on her buttock with a branding iron. For that reason they call it tucus, meaning 'burn'".[6]

The name "burning", Almeida felt, was, however, even more appropriate because "the men who collect this tribute are usually captains and military men, and the Emperor, in addition to the lands he has given them, usually divides most of these cows among them. In collecting the tribute they use so much violence against the peasants that they ruin and consume them".[7]

---

[5] Huntingford (1965a) 54-5, (1965b) 65; Beckingham and Huntingford (1961) I, 91, 94, 173, 228, II, 436, (1954), 50, 88; Beccari (1912) 103; Whiteway (1902) 232; Lockhart (1984), 167.

[6] Lockhart (1984) 167.

[7] Beckingham and Huntingford (1954) 88. See also Ludolf (1684) 205-6.

Clothing

Throughout this period the peasantry, and indeed the greater part of the populace, were poorly dressed. The menfolk are said by Alvares to have worn little beyond a loincloth or simple pair of breeches, and were therefore often "bare from the waist upwards", though some people wore a sheepskin over their shoulders. There were, however, regional variations. In central Tegré men wore "small skirts" of cloth or tanned leather, not more than "two spans", or little over a foot, in size - just sufficient to "cover their nakedness", though not so if the wind blew or if they stooped or sat down, while many in Wällo merely covered their private parts with "a strip of ox-hide".

Peasant women were also very scantily dressed. Married women in the Adwa area had "very little covering", and spinsters displayed even "less shame". Some wore no more than a sheep's skin tied to their neck which covered only one side of them, and "not more", because they wore it loose, so that "at every little movement", Alvares says, one could see "from one side of the body to the other what man wishes". Married women in the country of the Bahr Nägaš, or most northerly province towards the sea, on the other hand, often wrapped themselves in "black (or coloured) woollen stuffs, with wide fringes". Girls and young women were more scantily dressed. Some even twenty or twenty-five years of age were nude above the waist, or wore only a sheepskin which covered no more than one breast. The women of Wällo were scarcely better dressed: many had only a single piece of cloth which only partially covered "what God has given them."

The above picture was fully confirmed by later writers. Almeida stated that the menfolk wore breeches made of "native cotton", while many women who had insufficient cloth for both a skirt and a *šämma*, or wrap, wore only one or the other, while their poorer sisters wore only dressed, or even undressed skins, many of which were however fairly soft. The late seventeenth century German scholar Job Ludolf, who had doubtless discussed this, as well as many other matters, with his learned Ethiopian informant Abba Gorgoreyos, gave a similar account, observing that the apparel of the common people was "mean and poor": the more impoverished went about "half-naked", or covered themselves with skins that "hardly" hid "their private Parts", and many boys and girls went "stark Naked" till "riper Years" caused them to "hide their Shame", yet, being by then "so accustomed to go Naked", they paid little regard to modesty.[8]

Peasants' Difficulties

Despite the fertility of the soil, and the abundance of cattle, the peasants were often far from well-off. They were in many cases so grievously exploited, Alvares suggests, that they had in fact little incentive to produce. There would thus have been, he claims, "much fruit and much more cultivation in the country, if the great men did not ill-treat the people, for they take what they have, and the latter are not willing to provide more than they require and what is necessary for them".

---

[8] Beckingham and Huntingford (1961) I, 143-4, 253, 320, II, 510, (1954), 60; Ludolf (1684) 388.

The subject status of the peasantry was no less apparent in relation to cattle, and caused Alvares to testify that "nobody from the common people may kill a cow (even though it is his own) without leave from the lord of the country".[9]

Locusts and Other Pests

The peasants also suffered greatly from frequent plagues of locusts which, Alvares reports, were "not general in all the kingdoms every year", but one year would be "in one part, and another year in another", and in some years would afflict "two or three provinces" simultaneously. The multitude of these insects, he says, was "not to be believed", for they covered the earth, filled the air, and darkened the light of the sun; and when they had passed it was as though the land had been "set on fire". At such times the people were "dismayed, saying, 'We are lost because the Ambatas [i.e. locusts] are coming'".

On one by no means untypical occasion, when Alvares and his companions were in Angot, they travelled for "five days through country entirely depopulated" by locusts. The thick millet stalks were "all cut and bitten, as if bitten by asses", the fields of wheat, barley and *téf* were "as though they had never been sown", and the trees were "without any leaves", with their tender twigs "all eaten". There was likewise "no trace of grass of any sort", so that if the travellers had not brought provisions for themselves and their animals they would all have "perished from hunger". Men, women and children were "seated horror-struck" among the locusts, but when the Portuguese priest asked them why they did not kill the insects, and thereby revenge themselves for the damage they had done, as well as to prevent them from doing any further harm, they replied, with resignation, that "they had not the heart to resist the plague which God gave them for their sins".[10] Instead they preferred to flee from the worst-affected areas. Alvares reports:

> "The people were going away from this country, and we found the roads
> full of men, women, and children, on foot, and some in their arms, with
> their little bundles on their heads, removing to a country where they might
> find provisions; it was a pitiful sight to see them".[11]

The extent of destruction habitually wrought by locusts was also later apparent to Almeida who noted that these insects were a "constant'" source of misery, particularly in Tegré.

Other pests, which took their toll of agricultural production, included an "immense quantity" of rats and mice, as well as large ants which, as Bruce noted a century and a half later, consumed "immense quantities " of grain.[12]

---

[9] Beckingham and Huntingford (1961) II, 515.

[10] Beckingham and Huntingford (1961) I, 132, 136-7, (1954), 46; Bruce (1790), III, 124-5, 196.

[11] Crawford (1956) 169; Beckingham and Huntingford (1961) I, 131.

[12] Beckingham and Huntingford (1961) I, 189.

The Exactions of the Soldiery

The peasants were from time to time also seriously affected by the exactions of the soldiers who, Almeida notes, were "always" going about the country, "eating, plundering and looting everything". They were "worse than the locusts", he argued, for whereas the latter only destroyed what was in the fields, the former also seized what had been gathered into the houses.

The peasantry were also obliged to provide food and shelter, not only for the soldiers, but for virtually any traveller passing through the area. Such supplies, according to Lobo, would usually be contributed by an entire village, each member of which had to supply whatever he was asked. The scale of hospitality demanded would depend on the station in life of the traveller and, in addition to his own meal, he might have to be given a cow to be divided among his servants. The peasant was "accountable" to the head of the village for such provisions, and anyone who failed to supply a guest with a supper was liable to "severe punishment". Similarly, if the traveller had any of his property stolen, the peasant responsible would be obliged to pay twice the value of the missing article.

The peasantry was likewise expected to transport baggage for court and other travelling officials free of charge. When officers were summoned to the Emperor's presence their belongings would thus be entrusted to the lord of the first village along the road who would then put them in the hands of his vassals. The latter would deliver the articles in question to the next village, and so on successively until they reached the capital or court. Such transportation was almost invariably carried out by the peasantry with "wonderful exactness and fidelity" as the eighteenth century French traveller Charles Poncet afterwards testified.

Such obligations, though naturally a great convenience to the nobles and other travellers, constituted "a heavy burden" for the peasants, Almeida says, for: "Big companies of men, soldiers and lords bringing many servants come daily to quarter themselves in the very small villages. Each one goes into the house he likes best and turns the owner into the street, or occupies it with him. Sometimes it is a widow or a married woman whose husband is away and then by force he gets at not only her food and property but her honour".[13]

The various exactions on the peasantry, however unjust, were apparently accepted by all concerned with little or no question. Early in the seventeenth century a group of peasants asked the Jesuit missionary Emanuel Barradas to intercede on their behalf with their governor Täklä Giyorgis, but when he tried to do so the chief replied, "with reason and justice" the missionary says, as follows:

"Father, these villains are like camels, they always cry, weep, and groan when they are loaded, but in the end they rise with the burden that is put on them and carry it".

---

[13] Beckingham and Huntingford (1961) I, 149, 255, (1954), 37, 45, 188.

11

`Barradas accepted this observation, but, pursuing the analogy, replied, "That is true, but it is also sometimes true that they fall with their burden, and then the owner loses both the camel and the load".[14]

There are, however, no records of peasant rebellions in this period.

---

[14] Beckingham and Huntingford (1961) I, 189; Lockhart (1984) 167.

III

THE SOLDIERS

Warfare was frequent throughout the medieval period. The country's rulers were "continually in the field", Lobo remarks, fighting either "domestic vassals in rebellion" or else enemies on the periphery of the realm. For this reason garrisons were often established in the frontier areas - particularly on the eastern borders, where there were frequent battles with the Muslim lowlanders. Conflict with Adäl during the reign of Emperor Dawit I (1380-1409) for example caused that monarch to establish two important camps in the East. One of these was at Ṭobya, in north-western Ifat, at a pass that led from the port of Zäylä' to the highland Christian districts of Mänz and Gishé. The other was at Ṭelq, in Fäṭägar, where the Emperor's court, according to the modern Ethiopian historian Taddesse Tamrat, remained for "many years" - and where two later Ethiopian monarchs, Zär'ä Ya'qob and his grandson Eskender, were both born.

Conflicts of one kind or another were, however, so common that "every year" many warriors spent "most of the year" making war. Such a multitude of people were involved that Almeida wrote of the Ethiopians that: "In war they are reared as children, in war they grow old, for the life of all who are not farmers is war".[1]

Mobilisation

Frequent wars led to the mobilisation of vast numbers of soldiers. This was accomplished with relative ease, for the ruling monarch did "not pay any of those who took the field", as the Italian traveller Francesco Suriano noted in the fifteenth century, but merely exempted them from taxation.

Soldiers on campaign were expected to bring with them all necessary provisions, which consisted mainly of grain or flour. The men were, however, entitled to loot extensively wherever they went. When they accompanied the monarch they did this with particular impunity for wherever he travelled "everything" was "free", the Portuguese warrior Castanhoso notes, which was a major reason why "everyone" followed him.

Military service was based in large measure on the system of land tenure. Vassals thus held - or were granted - fiefs on condition that they served as soldiers, and, if they failed to do so, their lands were forfeited to others. The Emperor, who did not have to pay his soldiers, was in this way able to assemble "a large army", Almeida says, "without much expense".

Vast numbers of warriors, and no less numerous camp-followers, were often mobilised. In the late fifteenth century the Emperor was said, by Suriano, never to take the field with "less than two hundred thousand or three hundred thousand people". Early in the following century Alvares reported that it was the custom of the

---

[1] Lockhart (1984) 160-;1; Taddesse Tamrat (1972) 152; Beckingham and Huntingford (1954) 76.

monarchs to call "100,000 men, if they want as many, to assemble in two days", and that he had seen for himself that the number of people accompanying Emperor Lebnä Dengel was "unbelievable". A generation or so later, Emperor Gälawdéwos, then aspiring to overcome the great Muslim warrior Ahmäd Grañ, was likewise reported to have been joined by "more than one hundred thousand souls".

St. George, showing a 17th century Ethiopian artist's idea of a horseman, and horse decorations, from a manuscript of the Four Gospels in the British Library, Orient 481.

The number of fighting men was, however, by no means always so large. Castanhoso, describing a critical moment in the struggle with Grañ, estimated that Gälawdéwos's army consisted of only 20,000 infantry and 2,000 cavalry, for "the remainder were camp followers and women". Later, in the early seventeenth century,

Emperor Susneyos was said by Almeida to have habitually put into the field "thirty to forty thousand soldiers, four or five thousand on horseback and the rest of foot". Even when they were fewer they nevertheless made "an excessively big camp", for the camp-followers and baggage train amounted to "many more than the soldiery".[2]

Constant experience in campaigning, it was generally agreed, made the Ethiopians "good troops", for, Almeida notes:

"they sit a horse well, are quite strong and healthy and are brought up and inured to toil, enduring hunger and thirst as much as can be imagined, and continue in the field for the greater part of the year, suffering all the discomfort and inclemency of sun, cold and rain with little food".[3]

Ethiopian soldiers are said to have fought impetuously, with the result that battles often began and ended with the first onset, whereupon one or other side fled, and their opponents then followed up the victory. Flight, according to Almeida, was "not much decried" because it was "a common and everyday thing".

Ethiopian Christians never willingly fought on Saturdays or Sundays, or during the great Lent fast - though they were sometimes obliged to do so if attacked by Muslim enemies. Mahfuz, the amir of Zäylä' in the late fifteenth century, for example made a point of attacking the Christians during Lent when they were weakened by lack of sustenance, and "scarce a Christian", Bruce claims, was therefore "able to bear arms". The soldiers at such periods would moreover usually be dispersed in their own lands, preparing for the great festivities for Easter.

The Emperor's soldiers came at times from many parts of the realm. This was notably - and demonstrably - the case during the reign of 'Amdä Şeyon (1312-1342) whose chronicler reveals that the monarch's army included contingents from a wide stretch of the country, including Tegré and Bägémder, Wag, Lasta and Angot, Gojjam and Amhara, and Damot, Šäwa and Hadeya. Several localities in these regions are also specifically referred to in Ethiopian soldiers' songs of the period.

Campaigning was also virtually never carried out during the long rainy season which made travel of any kind almost impossible. Ludolf's scholarly informant Abba Gorgoreyos wrote: "There is no making War in Ethiopia in Winter time; neither does the Enemy attack us, nor we them; by reason of the great falls of Rain and Inundations of the Rivers".[4]

---

[2] Crawford (1958) 45; Beckingham and Huntingford (1961) I, 320, II, 477, (1954) 76-8; Whiteway (1902) 94.

[3] Beckingham and Huntingford (1954) 76.

[4] Beckingham and Huntingford (1954) 78, (1961) I 192-3, II, 411; Huntingford (1965a), 2, 18-9, 81-2, 129-32.

Weapons

Warfare was traditionally based on two main weapons: the spear for attack, and the shield for defence. Limited use was, however, made of daggers and clubs which were employed when fighting at close quarters, while members of the nobility also carried swords "for appearance sake", but, according to Almeida, "rarely" used them. Coats-of-mail were also occasionally worn. Fire-arms, which were later to determine the outcome of many a battle, were extremely rare at the beginning of our period, but, as we shall see, became increasingly plentiful in later centuries.

Several different types of spear were in general use. Foot soldiers had two main kinds. The first, which had a narrow iron head, was usually thrown in the first encounter with such force that it could pierce shields and even coats-of-mail. The second, the head of which was broader, was retained for subsequent hand-to-hand fighting in which the soldier would brandish the weapon in his right hand, and hold his shield in the left. The swords of the cavalry also tended to be smaller, and shorter, than those of other warriors.

Shields, which were carried by both infantry and cavalry, were for the most part made from the skin of the wild buffalo, and were, Almeida says, "very strong and firm".

Coats-of-mail, and helmets, gradually came into increased use. In the sixteenth century there are said to have been only "a few", and only of poor quality, but early in the following century it was reported that "as many as 700 or 800" horsemen were so equipped.

The speed with which fire-arms gained currency is worthy of note. When the Portuguese diplomatic mission left Ethiopia in the mid-1520s there were, according to Alvares, no more than fourteen muskets at court, whither they had been bought from Turkish traders. By the early seventeenth century, however, Almeida reported that there were over 1,500 muskets in the country, though "not more than 400 or 500 musketeers" took part in any one expedition, and "most of them" had "so little skill" that they could not "fire more than once in any action" which was not surprising as gunpowder and bullets were "so scarce" that few had enough to practice "four shots now and again" in a year.[5]

Camp Life

A large part of most soldiers' lives was spent in camps, commanded by the Emperor and his courtiers, which were usually established on a level plain, the highest point of which might be occupied, Alvares states, by as many as five or six thousand tents and innumerable soldiers and camp-followers. One of Emperor Lebnä Dengel's camps was so crowded that the people looked "like a procession of Corpus Domini in a great city." The "tenth part of them" were "well-dressed people, and nine parts common people, both men and women, young people, and poor, some of them clothed in skins, others in poor stuffs." The poor people carried with them pots for

---

[5] Beckingham and Huntingford (1954) 76-7, (1961) II 492, 516.

16

making wine and porringers for drinking, and, if they moved short distances, they also took their dwellings with them. The rich, on the other hand, brought "very good tents", while the "great lords and gentlemen" each moved with "a city or a good town of tents", and were accompanied by muleteers, and loads, "without number or reckoning." The camp as a whole might thus comprise at least 50,000 mules, and "from that upwards" to perhaps 100,000. The size of a typical camp was confirmed by Almeida, who, a century or so later, stated that it might consist of as many as "eight or nine thousand hearths".

Camps throughout this period - and later - were almost invariably arranged in an orderly manner so that, the Jesuit explains: "The Emperor's tents, four or five very large tents, are placed in the centre. A handsome open space is left and then on the left hand and on the right, before and behind, follow tents for two churches that he takes with him, those of the Queen and great lords, who all have their allotted places, then those of the captains and soldiers in accordance with the command to which they belong, those from the vanguard in front, and behind those from the rearguard, some of those from the wings on the right and others on the left." The whole camp, when disposed in this way, occupied a vast space, and constituted "a splendid sight, especially at night with the great number of fires that are lit"[6]

The methodical arrangement of the camp was one of its most enduring features, and one which greatly facilitated the army's efficient movement and operation. This was later vividly described by Ludolf, who, drawing on earlier Portuguese accounts as well as on information gleaned from Abba Gorgoreyos, explained that it was the camp-master's duty to locate a suitable site well supplied with wood, grass and water, which done:

"he fixes a Pole in the Earth with the Royal Banner at the Topp; upon the sight whereof, they that measure for the Nobility, set up their Masters Lodgings. After them the Common Souldiery, and others that follow the Camp either for Victuals or else upon business. And thus in a few hours' time the whole Camp appears in the same Order as it was before. For every one knowes his place and his proportion, there being never any alteration in the Order, but the same Streets and Lanes, the same distance of Tents, so that were it not for the variation of the Prospect, other Mountains, other Rivers, and another Face of the Country, you would think your self still in the same place. When the Cryer has once proclaim'd the day of Removal, they presently [i.e. quickly] know how to pack up their Baggage, and in what order to march without any more ado; who are to march in the Front, who in the Rear, who on the Right, who on the Left; so that all things are done without Noise or Tumult".[7]

Camps such as this were to be formed for several centuries.

---

[6] Beckingham and Huntingford (1954) 79, 188.

[7] Ludolf (1684) 214-5.

IV

THE NOBILITY

The Feudal System

Nobles played a major role in the Ethiopian feudal system. Deeply involved in government, as well as in the collection of tribute, they also served in time of war both as commanders and combatants. In return for their services they were allowed to appropriate a sizeable amount of the tribute due to the State, and enjoyed many of the privileges of absolute rule. However, being themselves subject to an overlord in the person of the Emperor or provincial ruler, they were often subjected, like the peasants and members of other classes, to many of the uncertainties, and indignities, of arbitrary government.

Despite their importance in State affairs nobles for the most part receive only passing mention in medieval records, whose authors, perhaps not surprisingly, tended to concentrate on the more prestigious figure of the monarch. It is nevertheless clear that many "great lords", as Alvares calls them, were rich, powerful and privileged.

Nepotism

Though in a sense a separate class - and thus distinct from the monarchy - many nobles were in fact connected - by blood or marriage - with the ruling house, while others, as we shall see, owed their position - and importance to local - and often hereditary - influence.

The significance of family connections in the appointment of officials was particularly evident during the reign of Emperor Zär'ä Ya'qob (1433-1468) who appointed his son-in-law, 'Amdä Mäsqäl, as his *Behtwäddäd*, or principal courtier, but, believing him disloyal, placed the government of almost the entire country, as we shall see in a later chapter, in the hands of his daughters and other female relatives.

The importance of nepotistic considerations, which in one way or another imbued the entire governmental structure, were no less graphically evident during the reign of Emperor Lebnä Dengel (1508-1540), who, during the war with Ahmäd Grañ, made his son-in-law Dégälhan the head of his army. When events turned against the Emperor, however, the latter is reported, by Grañ's chronicler, to have said to his wife, Wäyzäro Amätä Wätin,"Your brother, the King, placed me at the head of the army, but I have neither the strength nor the energy to fight. If I am killed, you will be left a widow, and your children will be orphans. Intercede then for me with the King so that he sends me again to you - but do not let him know what I have said". Amätä Wätin, according to this account, duly spoke to her brother, in secret, telling him that if her husband was killed she would be left a widow and her children would be orphaned. Though the above account cannot of course be confirmed there is no gainsaying the fact that at this time, when the fighting had become desperate,

Dégälhan, the son-in law, was duly replaced by another - and more dependable - officer, Eslam Sägäd, who was duly killed in battle.[1]

Tribute and Fiefs

Nobles serving as provincial and other governors received considerable tribute. They passed on much of this to their overlord, but retained a sizeable portion for themselves, as well as for their followers and dependents. Much of the taxes received by the nobility were extracted from the peasantry, and consisted of cattle and other livestock, farm produce, including grain, and various labour services. Taxes on traders were, however, also a major source of income, for they provided the nobles with sizeable quantities of silks, brocades and other costly goods imported from abroad, as well as fire-arms, of major importance throughout this period, and bars of salt from the 'Afär depression which were widely used as money. The demand for this mineral was in fact so great that many lords, according to Alvares, sent their servants to the vicinity of the mines each year with up to 300 or 400 mules to obtain supplies to meet their expenses at court. Not a few of the nobles were in consequence exceedingly wealthy, as evident from the Portuguese priest's statement that many "great gentlemen" had "very fine tents", which were so numerous that the entire camp looked like "a city or a good town of tents".

The nobility exercised considerable power in their fiefdoms where, as we have seen, Alvares reported that no one from the "common people" could kill a cow without leave from his lord. On leaving their fiefs the chiefs were likewise treated with great respect, and would be preceded by guards carrying whips which they would strike in the air, thereby making a "great noise" which caused the populace to keep its distance.[2]

Apparel

The nobles often wore sumptuous clothing, in many cases smartly fashioned of coloured silk, which differentiated them from the peasantry and the public at large. Lebnä Dengel's courtiers were thus described by Alvares as "dressed in white shirts and good silk clothes". Over their shoulders they wore lions' skins decorated with collars of gold adorned with jewels and false stones, and round their waist "girdles of coloured silk" with "fringes reaching to the ground". The Bahr Nägaš, or ruler of the northern province near the sea, was likewise said to have worn "rich clothes", including "a fine large burnous", while one of his subordinates, Ras Aredam, had "a very good silk cloth, and on his shoulders the skin of a lion". A "great gentleman" in command of Queen Säblä Wängél's soldiers, whom Castanhoso later saw in the 1540s, was similarly "clothed in hose and vest of red satin and gold brocade with many plaits", a French cape of fine black cloth all quilted with gold", and "a black cap with a very rich medal", while two other lords wore "tunics of silk garnished with silk" which reached the ground and trailed behind them like a woman's bridal dress. In the following

---

[1] Basset (1897) 179-80.

[2] Beckingham and Huntingford (1861) I, 114-7, 180-4, 248, 269, 320-1, II, 425-7, 515.

19

century Almeida likewise noted that the shirts of "some of the lords and richer men" were "made of taffety or satin and damask", and were worn with coats of "velvet or Meca brocade".

The women of the nobility similarly often wore bofeta or silk clothes over cotton underwear. Their top clothes were invariably "very wide and long", for "elegance", Almeida judged, "consisted in wearing a great deal of cloth and silk".[3]

Subordination to the Monarch

Though virtually all-powerful in relation to the peasantry and to the people at large, the nobles were almost entirely subordinate to the monarch. During the reign of Lebnä Dengel the "great lords", whom Alvares likens to kings, were thus "all tributary" to the sovereign who appointed and dismissed them at his pleasure "with or without cause". This seemed to create "no resentment", he says, or, if it did, this was kept secret, for he had seen "great lords turned out of their lordships and others put into them", and the persons thus appointed and dismissed "appeared to be good friends, though God of course knew what was in their hearts".

The nobility because of its subject status *vis-à-vis* the monarch was constantly at the latter's beck and call, and could not travel without his permission. "No great lord" could thus leave his land, or set out for the court, unless summoned by the King, and, having been commanded to appear, would "not fail to come for any reason". On departing he would not leave his wife, children or any property behind, but set forth in the expectation of never returning, for were he deprived of his governorship everything belonging to him would be taken away from him by his successor. For this reason chiefs leaving their fiefs carried off everything "without leaving anything, or at least without putting it in another lordship".

Court ceremonial sought to demonstrate the noble's dependence on his overlord. Whenever a chief was summoned to court he would thus travel "with great pomp" until he approached its neighbourhood when he would derobe, and remain "stripped from the waist upwards", perhaps for as long as "a month or two" until the ruler chose to call him. Throughout this time the noble would be treated as though he was "forgotten". He was permitted to visit the court to speak with other lords, but could not display any pomp or fine clothing, or be accompanied by more than two or three followers. On eventually receiving the King's order to attend him he would however appear "with great pomp, with kettle drums and other musical instruments sounding". Before reaching the monarch's presence, however, he was again expected to derobe, and would once more be "naked from the waist upwards". During this period people would say, "So and so is not yet in favour with our lord, for he still goes about stripped". On finally gaining access to his master - and receiving the latter's approbation, he once more went around dressed, and it would be said, "So and so is in our lord's favour". Only then would the reason for his summons be divulged. It was therefore no uncommon sight at court to see nobles undressed to the waist: Alvares recalls two occasions for example when he saw a Ras in front of the Emperor's gate naked to the waist "without a shirt".

---

[3] Beckingham and Huntingford (1961), 116, 122, 269, (1954) 60; Whiteway (1902) 17, 19-20; Thomas (1938) 75; Ludolf (1684) 388.

Chiefs returning to their fiefs were usually despatched quickly, but those dismissed might be detained for as much as five, six or even seven years. During that time they could "by no manner of means" leave without permission, and were indeed "so obedient", and "so much" in "fear of the King", that they never stirred from the court. Though accustomed to the company of "many people" they were now "neglected", and moved around with only "two or three men", for the "numerous attendants who had formerly accompanied them belonged to the lordships taken from them, and would have transferred themselves to the new lord.

Whenever the monarch travelled the chiefs through whose territory he passed had likewise to humble themselves. They did this once again by baring themselves to the waist, and, if in the presence of the monarch or the latter's consort, would show his subservience by leading the bridle of the mule or horse on which the master - or mistress - rode.

The subordination of the chiefs was apparent in the case even of the most powerful. Each of the two Behtwäddäd, or "beloved" ministers, was a "noble gentleman" and the "greatest lord at Court", with such a "multitude" of followers that they took up as much space as a city. Both noblemen nevertheless treated their master with the greatest possible deference. One, who brought the annual tribute from Gojjam, thus came before the monarch "stripped from the waist upwards", and when formally asked his identity, he humbly replied, addressing the King: "I... am the least of your house, and he who saddles your mules and puts the head stalls on your baggage mules. I serve in what other business you command". Notwithstanding this show of humility he and his fellow Behtwäddad were both soon afterwards arrested, and ignominiously dismissed.

Provincial rulers had no greater security of office. The governor of the important province of Tegré for example kept "a very large household", but during Alvares's visit was likewise replaced, and banished, at the monarch's whim. The Bahr Nägaš similarly lived in a "large house", and was "the lord of many lords, and of many lords and people", but he too held office only as long as the Emperor pleased. "For in our time, which was a stay of six years", Alvares writes, "there were here four Barnagais, that is to say, when we arrived Dori was Barnagais, he died, and at his death the crown came to Bulla, his son, a youth of ten to twelve years of age.... When they crowned him he was at once summoned to the Court, and while he was at the Court, the Prester John [i.e. Emperor] took away his sovereignty and gave it to a great nobleman... This man held it two years, and they took from him his lordship" which was then "given to another lord". Lesser chiefs were likewise entirely subject to the monarch, who removed and appointed them as he pleased. The nobles' lack of security of office, it should be emphasised, was very advantageous to the Emperor, for chiefs, both great and small, vied with each other in seeking his goodwill, and to this end presented him with "very large dues".[4]

The above state of affairs was no less apparent in the seventeenth century, by which time the contraction of the empire, resulting from Grañ's wars and the expansion of the Oromos, or Gallas, may well have led to greater competition for fief

---

[4] Beckingham and Huntingford I, 114, 116-7, 173, 271, II, 426, 430-4, 443-6; Whiteway (1902)18.

lands. Almeida reported that provincial rulers in his day were frequently appointed and dismissed, sometimes "every two years", and sometimes "every year, and even every six months". The "worst thing" about such frequent changes, he felt, was that fiefs seemed to be "sold rather than given", for:

"No one receives them except by giving for them an amount of gold which is more or less the income and profit the aspirant and applicant hopes to get from them. As there are always many applicants those who give most for them usually receive them. They give more than they can honestly derive from them, and so as not to be at a loss they fleece the people, disposing of the lesser offices and the governorships of particular places and territories to those who promise and give most in return for them. So it is all merely an auction".[5]

The result of this state of affairs, he believed, was that the chiefs, who exercised "absolute control over the lives and property of the whole population", were "generally speaking... all plunderers rather than governors".

Notwithstanding the privileged position of the nobles their insecurity of tenure continued to be "useful" to the monarch, for the gentry, fearing that they might lose their lands or hoping to acquire others, found it expedient to serve their lord both in peace and war. They also continued moreover to lavish presents on him, "for usually", Almeida says, "he who gives more gets more and he who gives less gets less".

There was, on the other hand, little to restrict the nobles's powers over the peasantry. Persons suffering from exploitation by their chiefs could theoretically appeal to the Emperor, but few, Almeida says, ever dared to do so, for it was as good as to declare oneself an enemy of the governor, and everyone was afraid that if angered he would find a pretext to destroy them. The time for poor people to make their complaints was supposedly when a governor's period of office had come to an end, but appeals for redress of wrongs were in practice even then often impossible, for chiefs in many cases obtained proclamations from the Emperor preventing them from being sued for anything that they or their servants might have done during their term of office. With such an exemption "all the robberies and acts of violence" of which they might be guilty were automatically "consigned to oblivion as though they had never been committed". Such indulgences were "so well established" that no one considered them "sinful", and anyone shocked by them was told that the practice was long-established and without it there would be "widespread rebellions".[6]

---

[5] Beckingham and Huntingford (1954) 72-3.

[6] Beckingham and Huntingford (1954) 72-3, 88-9.

V

MONARCHS

Monarchs, whose lives were the subject of a succession of royal chronicles, constituted the apex of the feudal system. They often wielded immense power, and, being supposedly appointed by the will of God, were treated throughout the centuries with immense deference and respect.

The *Fethä Nägäst*

The status accorded to the Ethiopian monarch corresponded very largely with his position as laid down in the country's traditional legal code, the *Fethä Nägäst*, or "Laws of the Kings", which proclaimed the Divine Right of Kings on Scriptural basis. The text thus recalled the words of Moses:

"Thou shalt in any wise set him king over thee whom the Lord thy God shall choose; one from among thy brethren shalt thou set king over thee: thou mayest not set a stranger over thee, which is not thy brother."[1]

The king, the *Fethä Nägäst* insisted, should receive obedience and respect as laid down in the Scriptures, for Christ had commanded, "Render... unto Caesar the things that are Caesar's; and unto God the things that are God's" (Matthew, XXII, 21), while St Paul, in his Epistle to the Romans, had written:

"Let every soul be subject unto the higher powers. For there is no power but of God: the powers that be are ordained of God.
"Whosoever therefore resisteth the power, resisteth the ordinance of God; and they that resist shall receive to themselves damnation.
"For rulers are not a terror to good works, but to evil. Wilt thou then not be afraid of the power? Do that which is good, and thou shalt have praise for the same.
"For he is the minister of God to thee for good. But if thou do that which is evil, be afraid; for he is the minister of God, a revenger to execute wrath upon him that doeth evil.
"Wherefore ye must needs be subject, not only for wrath, but also for conscience sake.
"For, for this cause ye pay tribute also: for they are God's ministers, attending continually upon this very thing.
"Render therefore to all their dues: tribute to whom tribute is due; custom to whom custom; fear to whom fear; honour to whom honour".[2]

---

[1] Deuteronomy, XVII, 15.

[2] Romans, XIII, 1-7. Guidi (1899) 467-75.

Court Powers and Ceremonial

The powers of the Ethiopian monarch were perhaps at their greatest during the reign of Emperor Zär'ä Ya'qob (1434-1468) who replaced his earlier provincial rulers by his own daughters and other female members of his family, and instituted an army of spies to seek out secret idolaters, with the result, his chronicle states, that "everyone trembled before the power of the king".

Court ceremonial, as described in the following century, was likewise designed to demonstrate the paramountcy of the monarch. When he gave audiences he was thus placed "behind a curtain", Brother Thomas reports, so that no one could cast their eyes upon him, and when he spoke it was often through a specially appointed spokesman who conveyed the royal words, or command, "with eyes lowered". When the King rode through the countryside everyone was expected to turn their faces toward the ground, and anyone looking at his face, it was said, would be executed on the spot. The sovereign was moreover generally preceded on his journeys, Alvares recalls, by "four lions bound with strong chains", while his retinue, like that of important chiefs, included officers with whips who ensured that he at all times received the full respect due from the public at large.

The Emperor's messengers, who to show their importance - and that of their master - sometimes carried drawn swords, were also treated with considerable deference. When visited by a royal messenger the Bahr Nägaš, for example moved to the highest place in the area, disrobed "from the waist upwards", and, on hearing the King's command, everyone "placed their hands upon the ground". After the message had been read the chief duly clothed himself again. The monarch's words were customarily heard "out of doors and on foot", and the person to whom they were addressed had to remain "naked above the waist" until they had been delivered. If the message expressed royal satisfaction the nobleman would then dress himself, but, if the contrary was the case, he would remain "naked as when he heard it", for he knew he was "in disgrace with his lord".

Subsequent political difficulties, due in part to the invasion of Ahmäd Grañ and the northward movement of the Oromos, or Gallas, rolled back the frontiers of the realm without greatly reducing the prerogatives of the throne in the areas still subject to its rule. The power of the monarch in the early seventeenth century thus "chiefly" rested, according to Almeida, on the fact that he was, as we have seen, "lord *in solidum* of all lands in the kingdom", and could give and take these away when and to whom he thought fit. Private persons, "great and small", had in fact "nothing except by the King's gift; and all that they held was by the monarch's "favour *ad tempus*".

Though nominally omnipotent the actual powers of the monarch in fact varied considerably from one part of the country to another. In some regions he still exercised complete jurisdiction, but there were others, chiefly in Tegré, "the lordship and government" of which he did "not take away from the families and descendants of their first owners". Such areas included Tämbén, Širé, Särayé, the country of the Bahrnägaš and "many other" neighbouring places in the north, as well as Dämbeya in the west, the governorship of which areas "never" passed from the descendants of their former chiefs. Even in such localities the sovereign's authority was, however, extensive, for he made appointments and dismissals within the ruling family "every two years and sometimes every year, and even every six months".

The monarch for his part remained jealous of the nobility, and to avoid dependence on men of noble descent, often gave preferment to slaves and others of lowly origin. This policy is said to have been extensively practiced by Emperor Susneyos who held that only those whom he had "created and made from dust and earth" could be relied upon to be faithful. Even if this was not fully the case such royal appointees seemed to Almeida more loyal than others.[3]

Royal Courts and Moving Capitals

Ethiopia, throughout most of this time, had no fixed capital, but was ruled by the monarch from a succession of temporary military camps which have aptly been described as "moving capitals."

Such camps were made up, according to the early sixteenth century Florentine trader Andrea Corsali, of "innumerable people," some on foot and others on horseback. This army or retinue was so large, he claims, that the monarch could not remain in any one place for more than four months nor return to the same place in less than ten years, because of the resultant exhaustion of supplies. This picture was confirmed a century later by Almeida who agreed that the Emperor's camp constituted the "royal city and capital of the empire," and deserved the name because of the multitude of people, and the good order that was observed in choosing the site, particularly during the rainy season, when a camp once set up could often not be moved until the abatement of the rains. Camp sites were wherever possible selected in localities with an abundance of wood, but the demand for timber and fire-wood was so great that neighbouring forests were usually denuded within a few years, with the result that the camp would soon be obliged to move elsewhere in quest of further supplies.[4]

Dress

The pre-eminence of the monarch was also expressed in the field of dress where a sumptuary law laid down that "no one but the King" or "a close relative or favourite", was allowed to wear anything, Almeida states, but "breeches" and a "piece of cloth" used as a wrap. The Emperors, their consorts and close members of their family, therefore wore luxurious and costly clothes not known outside their circle. Lebnä Dengel, when receiving the Portuguese mission of the 1520s, thus wore "a high crown of gold and silver", and was dressed in a "rich mantle of gold brocade", while his feet were covered with a "rich cloth of silk and gold". Sitting on "a platform of six steps very richly adorned'" he held in his hand a silver cross, and had in front of him "a piece of blue taffeta which covered his face and beard". Empress Säblä Wangél was later no less impressively described by Castanhoso as "all covered to the ground with silk, with a large flowing cloak". She had "a silk canopy" over her head, was "clothed

---

3 Perruchon (1989) 4-6, 75-6, 94-101; Crawford (1958) 169; Beckingham and Huntingford (1961) I, 122, 269-70, 286, II, 324, 337, 426, 433, 442, (1954) 72, 75, 88. See also Ludolf (1684) 234-5; Pankhurst (1985-7) passim.

4 Historiale Description (1558) 25; Beckingham and Huntingford (1954) 82-3.

in a very thin white Indian cloth and a burnoose of black satin, with flowers and fringes of very fine gold, like a cloak", and was "so muffled in a very fine cloth that only her eyes could be seen".

The old sumptuary law seems to have been relaxed in the late sixteenth century, with the result that increasing numbers of the nobility donned fine clothing. The sartorial pre-eminence of the monarch was, however, not affected.[5]

Dynastic Marriages

Despite Christian insistence on monogamy, this principle was in practice waived for Emperors who for dynastic and other reasons often had more than one wife. Alvares goes so far as to state that rulers until the reign of Emperor Na'od (1494 - 1508) "always had five or six wives," while Almeida a century later claimed that Ethiopian monarchs "always" had "many wives."

The monarch's principal spouse, or spouses, were never of the "imperial blood or family," for such women, who were known as Wäyzäros, were "all considered to be the daughters or sisters of the Emperors." Rulers, on the contrary, usually married the daughters of their vassals. Queens therefore tended to belong to noble rather than royal families. Monarchs, however, sometimes "paid no attention to noble birth but only to good character and charm, for they say the King gains nothing from his wife's noble birth while the great future in being chosen to be the Emperor's wife is sufficient nobility for her."

When a lowly woman was chosen she would be called to the court. There she would be made to live with one of the Emperor's female relatives so that the monarch "could inform himself more closely and positively about her good qualities." Once he was satisfied about them he would take her to church one Sunday to hear Mass and take Communion, after which he conveyed her to the palace where they would receive the *Abun*, or Patriarch's, blessing. The whole court would then celebrate.

Some royal marriages were also concluded, for political considerations, with the daughters or sisters of provincial rulers, both Christian and Muslim. The latter were usually converted, but, it is said, were also sometimes permitted to follow their original faith. Almeida, who, as a Jesuit, found this latter course of action reprehensible, claims that he was informed by Ras Se'elä Krestos, brother of Emperor Susneyos - with what veracity we cannot tell - that in the sixteenth century Lebnä Dengel "had some heathen wives and that, to please them, he had, like his ancestor Solomon, gone so far as to have idols in his palace so that on one side was the church of God and Our Lady the Virgin and on the other the house of the idol."

Queens, like wives in general, were supposed to be obedient to their husbands. Queen Säblä Wängél, consort of Emperor Gälawdéwos, was thus praised in the latter's chronicle for having put all her pride in obeying her husband.[6]

---

[5] Beckingham and Huntingford (1961), I, 241, (1961) I, 303-4; Whiteway (1902) 18.

[6] Beckingham and Huntingford (1961) I, 241, (1954) 68-9, 71; Conzelman (1895) 122-3, See also Pankhurst (1985-7) 48-9.

Royal Succession and Detention of Princes

The chief weakness of the monarchy throughout this period - and later - lay in the system of succession. Though the principle of primogeniture was to some extent operative the throne could normally be inherited by any of the ruler's male offspring. Because of the impermanency of Ethiopian marriages, and the royal practice of having several wives, the emperors tended to have numerous offspring. The resultant multiplicity of heirs was often a source of considerable intrigue and instability. Succession conflicts, Taddesse Tamrat observes, were in fact "endemic in medieval Ethiopia", and were particularly serious when, as a result of the machinations of the nobles, "infantile and immature princes were left to rule in preference to their more seasoned relatives". The Ethiopian Synaxarium recalls that when a king died, in the tenth century, the *Abun*, governors and generals of the royal army took counsel together, and agreed among themselves, saying, "The younger son will be far better for the kingdom than the elder".

The lack of any real law of succession was fully apparent to Alvares. Recalling that he was informed that "on the death of the Prester", i.e. Emperor, "the eldest born inherited" he added that "others say that he who appeared to the Prester the most apt and prudent, inherited; others say that he inherited who had most support". In the specific case of the accession of Lebnä Dengel in 1508, the *Abun*, or head of the Church, told him that he and the Dowager Queen Eléni had chosen that monarch "because they had all the great men (and all the treasure) in their hands", for which reason the Portuguese priest correctly concluded that "besides primogeniture, supporters, (friendship and treasure) enter into the question".

To minimise dissensions resulting from the multitude of heirs the practice developed of placing all unwanted princes in detention on an inaccessible mountain - in the sixteenth century Amba Gešen. Sons of the ruling monarch or of his immediate predecessor, and princes only recently detained, were closely guarded, but grand-children and other more remote descendants of earlier rulers were by contrast "not so much watched over".[7]

Coronation Ritual

Monarchs were usually crowned at the principal church in the area where they found themselves at the time of their accession to power. Emperor Zär'ä Ya'qob, however, reinstated an ancient tradition when he went in 1434 to be crowned at the ancient city of Aksum, and thus invested the monarchy, as Taddesse Tamrat notes, with the prestige associated with the country's old historical, religious and political capital.

Several subsequent rulers followed this tradition, among them Särsä Dengel (1563-1579) whose chronicle presents a graphic picture of the ceremonial. It states that the monarch, on reaching the vicinity of Aksum, sent a message to the priests

---

[7] Budge (1928a), p.667; Beckingham and Huntingford (1961) I, 193, 240-1, 243.

of the city, stating that he was "to celebrate the royal ceremonies in front of my mother, Ṣeyon, tabernacle of the God of Israel, as did my fathers [i.e. ancestors] David and Sälomon." He then made his way to the holy city where ecclesiastics, priests and deacons, received him with crosses of gold, and twelve fine parasols. The welcoming party included the superiors of all the convents of Tegré who sang the ancient Ethiopian hymns of Yaréd, chanting, "Be blessed, o King of Israel!" In front of the priests stood the "maidens of Ṣeyon," presumably part of the city's female population, who held a long cord as if to bar his way. There were also two old women with swords, one to the right and the other to the left, who, on the arrival of the ruler on horseback, cried out aloud, in an arrogant voice, "Who art thou? Of what family and of what tribe?" He thereupon replied, "I am the son of Dawit, son of Sälomon, son of Ebnä Hakim" [i.e. Menilek]. The women then questioned him a second time, again arrogantly, whereupon he cited his more immediate royal descent, declaring, "I am the son of Zär'ä Ya'qob, son of Bä'edä Maryam, son of Na'od." On the women asking the question a third time, he lifted his hand, and now, referring to more recent ancestors, declared, "I am Mäläk Sägäd, son of Wänäg Sägäd, son of Aṣnaf Sägäd, son of Admas Sägäd." He then severed the rope with his sword, whereupon the women cried out, "Truly, truly, though art the King of Ṣeyon, son of Dawit, son of Sälomon." After this the priests of the city began singing on one side and the maidens of Seyon began clapping on the other, and both groups continued doing so until the monarch entered the church compound, where he scattered on the ground a large quantity of gold for the churchmen there assembled.

A later account of the ceremony embodying a somewhat different series of questions, was later provided by Almeida. Stating that two women, each holding a silver cord, would bar the monarch's path, he reports that, when the monarch reached that place, a third woman would enquire, "Who are you?", to which he would reply, "I am the King." She would then declare, "You are not!", at which he would step back a few paces, before returning, at which point she would ask, "Whose King are you?" He would then answer, "I am the King of Israel," at which she would say, "You are not our King!" He would then once more retire a little, only to return again, when she would demand a third time, "Whose King are you?", whereupon, drawing his sword, he would cut the cord, proclaiming, "I am the King of Ṣeyon." At this reply she would exclaim, "Truly, truly, you are the King of Ṣeyon." Then the musicians would strike up with their kettledrums, trumpets and shalms, and the musketeers would fire a salvo.[8]

[8] Taddesse Tamrat (1972), 249-50; Conti Rossini (1907), 89-91; Beckingham and Huntingford (1954) 92.

VI

THE CLERGY AND THEIR INFLUENCE ON SOCIETY

Medieval Ethiopia, which abounded in churches and monasteries, had a considerable ecclesiastical population made up of priests, *däbtäras*, or lay clerics, monks, nuns and hermits. There were also several highly influential prelates, among them the *Abun*, or Metropolitan, who was traditionally an Egyptian Copt, the Aqabé Sä'at, an Ethiopian churchman attached to the palace, and the Ečägé, likewise an Ethiopian, who served as head of the monks.

Multitude of Churches and Monasteries

Testimony to the country's immense number of places of worship is provided by Alvares, who, travelling through the northern and central provinces in the early sixteenth century, noticed "many" churches and monasteries. A century or so later Lobo remarked that they were both so "numerous" that one could "nowhere give a shout without it being heard at least at one church or monastery and very often at many of both". Monasteries were in fact found all over the country. Most, Alvares notes, were placed - for safety - either on "high mountains" or else in "great ravines".

Churches and monasteries, though distinct from each other, were often associated, for every monastery housed at least one church, while many churches had monks attached to them. Alvares goes so far as to assert that he "never saw a church of priests which had not got monks, nor a monastery of monks which had not got priests".[1]

Priests, *Däbtäras* and Monks

The Ethiopian population of this time included "innumerable" priests, *däbtäras*, or lay clerics, monks and deacons. No estimate of the number of the clergy is available, but it was undoubtedly considerable. Debarwa, the capital of the Bahr Nägaš, for example had two churches, each served, Alvares says, by "twenty priests", while in Amhara the great church of Makanä Sellasé numbered "more than 2,000".

Several of the larger churches likewise had a "great" or "infinite" number of *däbtäras*, who enjoyed no small reputation. Popularly said to be descended from families who had come from Jerusalem with Menilek, son of the Queen of Sheba, they were on that account "more honoured than the rest of the clergy". Alvares, who refers to them as "canons" - a term which he also uses for priests - claims that there were 50 at the monastery of Abba Päntaléwon in Tegré, 150 at Aksum, 200 at Yemrehannä Krestos in Lasta, 400 at Makanä Sellasé, and 800 at an unidentified church in the Lalibäla area where there were no less than 4,000 at eight religious establishments.

---

[1] Beckingham and Huntingford (1961) I, 74-5, 119, 247, 256, II, 510; Lockhart (1984) 178-9.

St. Matéwos and St. Tadéwos, from a 15th century volume of the Psalms and Canticles in the Bibliothèque Nationale, Ethiopien-Abbadie 105.

A highly stylised representation of St. Mark, from a 17th century Ethiopian manuscript of the Four Gospels in the British Library, Orient 516.

The number of clerics in the sixteenth century may well have been growing. Alvares, on visiting a church in Angot, was informed that "at the beginning there were not so many canons, but that they had afterwards increased because "all the sons of canons, and as many as descended from them, were still canons... and so they had increased in number". An expansion in the number of clerics had also taken place in the king's churches where the monarch frequently transferred attendants to newly founded establishments. Emperor Lebnä Dengel for example had ordered 200 men to be taken to the church of Makanä Sellasé. Such reallocations were necessary, Alvares comments, for otherwise the clergy would "eat one another up".

Monks were even more "numerous", for they covered "the world, both in the monasteries as also in the churches, roads, and markets", and were seen "in every place". Däbrä Bizän monastery, overlooking the Red Sea, was variously reported as having 300 and 500 monks who lived at six separate centres. Alvares, however, believed that the figure did not actually exceed 200, though there were "always a hundred" at the main site, "most of them old men of great age, and as dry as wood". The number may have subsequently fallen, for Poncet two centuries later estimated that the monastery had only "a hundred" inmates. The Alleluya monastery at Däbrä Halolé, which Zorzi's informants described as a "very great" establishment with three "very great" churches, was likewise reported by Alvares to have had "many monks". One source quoted the figure of five hundred, and another of five thousand. Many churches also had a sizeable number of monks. Aksum for example had 150, while the two churches at Debarwa each had twenty-two. The number of ecclesiastics in the seventeenth century remained very considerable, Lobo going so far as to remark - possibly with exaggeration - that no less than "one third" of the population were devoted to the service of God.

Ecclesiastical gatherings, not surprisingly, often attained immense proportions. Emperor Lebnä Dengel on visiting the church of Makanä Sellasé in 1521 for example was greeted, Alvares says, by over 20,000 priests and monks, or, according to another version of his text, by no less than 30,000.[2]

Nuns and the Exclusion of Women from Monasteries

Nuns were also extremely numerous. Alvares, who saw a "great multitude" of them, believed that many were "very holy", but others "not so". Unlike monks they did not live together in convents, but resided either in ordinary villages or in monasteries of monks, without any special order of their own. They entered churches on entirely the same basis as other women.

Access to some holy places was entirely closed to women (including nuns), and even female animals and chickens were excluded. The situation at one of the churches at Debarwa was slightly different, for one woman was allowed to enter. She was the wife of the Bahr Nägaš, and was permitted to take one maid with her whenever she went to Communion - but she did not according, to Alvares, in fact use this privilege, and instead received Communion at the entrance. Monasteries, according to Lobo, often had separate churches for men and women.[3]

Wealth of the Clergy

The wealth of the clergy varied greatly from one religious establishment to another. Most of the principal churches and monasteries, according to Alvares, possessed "big estates". The ecclesiastics at Aksum were particularly fortunate, for they enjoyed "very large revenues", and, in addition, received every day after Mass a

---

[2] Beckingham and Huntingford (1961) I, 88-9, 119, 126-7, 160, 164-5, 203, 236, 247, II, 338, 360, 463; Thomas (1938) 79; Crawford (1958) 56, 125, 145; Foster (1949) 152; Lockhart (1984) 178-9.

[3] Beckingham and Huntingford (1961) I, 118-9, 126; Lockhart (1984) 179; Bruce (1790) III, 177.

collation of bread and wine. The nearby monasteries of Abba Päntaléwon and Abba Gärima were likewise well endowed. The priests at the former had "large revenues", and were "all respected men and well dressed", while the latter monastery, though "small" with only "small revenues", nevertheless received sixteen prized horses a year, as well as "many" other dues in food. Besides this they grew "much garlic, onions, and many garden plants", and had "an infinite number of very good vineyards" from which they made "great quantities of raisins". The two churches at Debarwa likewise had "much land", which they put to "good use", and were also provided by the Bahr Nägaš with ornaments, wax, butter, "incense in sufficient quantity," and "everything" else they needed.

The church of Yemrehannä Krestos was also reported to be in receipt of "much revenue" so that its canons appeared "well-to-do and honourable men", while the "royal churches" of the central provinces are said to have likewise had large revenues. One indeed possessed so much land that there was not "one span" in its vicinity that did not belong to it.

Such establishments maintained their great wealth throughout this period. In the seventeenth century the monastery of Abba Gärima was thus reported by Barradas to be in possession of many excellent lands. Some gave the whole of their revenues to the monks, while others paid only half, the remainder being allocated to the governor of Tegré. The monastery of Däbrä Bizän to the north, according to the same observer, also had large and good lands, not only in its vicinity, but also as far away as Širé.

Though most of the more important religious establishments were thus well endowed others were relatively poor. Many priests, and monks, were moreover obliged to spend much of their time labouring like peasants in the field. The monks at Däbrä Bizän, despite their large estates, were said by Alvares to have toiled on the land. They had in fact two sources of millet: that supplied to them by tenants, and that which they produced by their own labour. The latter was clearly important, for the monks, when asked by the Portuguese how they supported themselves, replied, "By the toil of our hands" - and the tools they used were reported to have been "rather poor". The monks and nuns of Jammadu Maryam were likewise reported to have had to work hard, sowing and reaping their own wheat and barley, for the monastery itself gave them but "little". This picture was confirmed by Brother Thomas who told Zorzi that many Ethiopian priests and monks undertook manual labour "like donkeys."

Church ownership of land was nevertheless at times regarded with jealousy. The rulers of the seventeenth century, who, as already suggested, were confronted with a shortage of fiefs, were as anxious to obtain the return of Church land, Barradas claims, as their forebears had been generous in giving it away. The question came to the fore during the reign of Emperor Susneyos (1607-1632) who in the course of his efforts to introduce Roman Catholicism seized a substantial part of the lands belonging to the monastery of Däbra Bizän, which did not regain them even after the subsequent re-establishment of the Orthodox faith. Once Church lands were seized by the chiefs and soldiers, Barradas comments, it was extremely difficult for the old owners to get them back.[4]

---

[4] Beckingham and Huntingford (1961) I, 116, 119, 160, 163-4, 166, 201, 203, 256, II, 511; Beccari (1903-17), IV, 234, 243, 226; Thomas (1938) 79.

Influence of the Hierarchy and Priesthood

The Ethiopian Church enjoyed immense prestige, and its hierarchy, which had great influence, was held in deep respect at both the national and local level.

The *Abun*, or Metropolitan, who in accordance with long-established custom came from Egypt, owned, or controlled, a sizeable amount of land. Alvares mentions two villages which belonged to the prelate, while Bermudes claimed that the latter's lands in Tegré yielded a tax of 3,000 ounces of gold a year. Highly revered by his flock he spent much of his time at the Emperor's court where he was in possession of "a great number of tents", for he would be visited by "endless people" who "came to seek him from all over Ethiopia to be ordained". His status was apparent from the fact that he was seated on a couch "covered with fine cloth" like that used by other "great people", and his establishment took up "as much space as a big country house." When travelling he rode on a "well caparisoned" mule, and was accompanied by many attendants, some on mule-back and others on foot, who took with them two tall standing umbrellas as large as those carried for the Emperor, though not as fine. Four men moreover preceded him with whips, thus obliging everyone to scatter before him, while crowds of children and youths followed him, wishing him long life and begging him to make them priests or deacons.

The wealth of the *Abun* was likewise remarked upon in the seventeenth century. The then encumbent, according to Almeida, possessed three or four large estates as *gult*, or land which paid him the annual tribute otherwise due to the Emperor. The prelate had in addition a number of lands in Tegré which were said to provide 40 to 50 *wäqéts*, or ounces, of gold, or the equivalent of 400 to 500 Portuguese *patacas*, as well as other estates in Dämbeya, which supplied him with sufficient provisions for the upkeep of his household. The prelate's lands in Gojjam, on the other hand, yielded little as they were near the Blue Nile, then subject to attack from the Gallas or Oromos. Some of the *Abun*'s tenants were exempted from labour service, and paid instead each year one or two *amolés*, or bars of salt then used in lieu of money. This assured the prelate an annual revenue of many thousand pieces.

The influence of an *Abun* varied greatly, and was in large measure a function of the length of time he had spent in the country. A newly arrived prelate would be hampered by his ignorance of the local language and customs, but a long-established one might become an astute master of court intrigue. Abunä Marqos, who had been in the country fifty years when Alvares met him in the 1520s, proudly declared, as we have seen, that together with the Queen Mother he had determined Emperor Lebnä Dengel's succession. The power of the *Abun* was also remarked upon at the end of the seventeenth century by Poncet who states that the Patriarch of his day, by coincidence also Abunä Marqos, had named "all superiors of the monasteries", had "absolute authority" over the monks, and received "great respect" from the then Emperor, Iyasu I.

The procurement of an *Abun* throughout this time was a difficult, costly, and sometimes hazardous affair, for which reason the country sometimes remained for a fairly long time without one. There was one period, in the early sixteenth century, when there was no Metropolitan for no less than twenty-three years. To obviate a repetition of this state of affairs the Patriarch of Alexandria subsequently sent two priests "so that one could succeed the other." Later, when the second of them, the said Abunä Marqos, became old Emperor Lebnä Dengel despatched 2,000 ounces of gold to Cairo to obtain another prelate, but the desired cleric's arrival was long delayed because of difficulties in Egypt.

The two principal Ethiopian ecclesiastics, who shared power with the Coptic *Abun*, were the *Aqabé Sä'at*, an important churchman attached to the palace, and the *Ečägé*, originally the prior of the great monastery of Däbrä Libanos, and later of the monks in general. The *Aqabé Sä'at*, or Guardian of the Hour - a functionary dating back at least to the fifteenth century reign of Bä'edä Maryam, acted for the Emperor in many matters of state. In Alvares's opinion the "second person" in the kingdom he was to all intents and purposes "a great lord", and travelled, like the *Abun*, with "a great many tents". The *Ečägé*, or head of the monks, was almost equally important, and, according to the same observer, was "the greatest prelate" after the *Abun*.[5]

Ordination of Priests, Deacons and Monks

Ordination, the most important event in a priest's life, was carried out exclusively by the *Abun*, without whom the act could not be performed. This created considerable difficulty at times when the country was without a prelate, as in the above-mentioned twenty-three year inter-regnum after which the people sadly complained to Alvares that there had been neither priests nor deacons to serve in the churches, and that "the servants being lost, the churches would be lost, and that when the churches were lost the faith would be lost".

Ordination was invariably carried out on a large scale. Alvares, who witnessed one ceremony in which "quite 5,000 or 6,000 people" received holy orders, has left a vivid description of it. A white tent was first pitched in a large uninhabited meadow, after which the *Abun* made his appearance on mule-back, accompanied by many followers. Without dismounting he made a speech in his native Arabic, which a priest then translated into Amharic. Its main theme was that if there was anyone there who had "two wives or more, even though one was dead", he could "not to become a priest", and, if he did, he would be excommunicated, and held to be "accursed by the curse of God". Having finished this speech the Prelate sat down on a chair in front of the tent, with three priests, each with a manuscript book, seated before him on the ground.The persons to be ordained then also sat down, squatting on their heels, in three long rows. At the end of each row one of the priests with a book examined them "very briefly, for each one did not read more than two or three words". Each examinee then went to one of a number of standing priests who had a basin of white ink and a kind of seal with which he stamped the flat of the man's arm. The successful candidate then made his way to the middle of the plain which was soon crowded, for "there were few who did not pass". When this examination was finished, the *Abun* went into the tent, which had two doors, and sat on a chair. The men who had been examined meanwhile fell into line, one in front of the other, and, entering through one door and going out by the other, passed before him. As they walked by he placed his hand on their head, and uttered a few words, thus complying with the rule, laid down in the

[5] Beckingham and Huntingford (1961) I, 70, 108, 235, 243, 262, 270, 286, 305, II, 333, 346, 355-7, 359 379, 419, 443-4; Whiteway (1902) 160; Crawford (1958) 79; Beccari (1903-17) IV, 243, 268, VI 161-2; Foster (1949) 122; Bruce (1790) III, 317; Perruchon (1893) 167.

Fethä Nägäst, that "when a bishop wants to ordain a priest, he shall impose his hands on his head". After this the *Abun* took a manuscript book in his hands, and read a sizeable piece from it. Then, holding a small iron cross, he made the sign of the cross several times. At the conclusion of this ritual one of the priests went out of the tent, and read from an Epistle or Gospel, after which the *Abun* said Mass, and gave Communion to no less than 2,357 priests. This number, Alvares learnt, was substantially lower than usual, for normally "about 5,000 or 6,000" were ordained, but there were "few" on that occasion, for not many people knew that the prelate was coming. Such ceremonies were carried out "almost every day, and always in great numbers", because candidates came "from all the kingdoms and lordships of the Prester".[6]

Marriage of Priests and *Däbtaras*, and Celibacy of Monks

Priests were allowed to marry once before ordination, but not afterwards. Strictly monogamous they observed "the law of matrimony", Alvares thought, "better than the laity", and lived in their houses with their wives and children in married bliss. A priest whose spouse died could not, however, marry again. Nor could his wife, who was expected to remain a widow or become a nun. A priest discovered to have had intercourse with another woman while his wife was alive was not allowed to enter church again; he forfeited his property, and had to become a layman. Widowed priests who married again had likewise to abandon their cloth. This did not, however, entail any disgrace, particularly if it happened in high circles. Emperor Lebnä Dengel's head chaplain Abuquer, on becoming a widower, was thus, according to Alvares, defrocked by the *Abun*, after which he married the monarch's sister Romanä Wärq. He thereafter no longer entered any church, but received Communion as a layman at the church-door among the women.

Däbtäras, by contrast, were entitled to marry like the laity. In some cases they lived together in a single enclosure, but ate separately, and their wives had houses outside where their husbands could visit them. Monks, and nuns, however, were, as in other countries, strictly celibate.[7]

Clothing

The normal clothing of the clergy was not dissimilar from that of other men, for both wore trousers and a tunic around which they wrapped a *šamma*, or toga. Priests and *däbtäras* attached to the richer churches were "very well dressed", Alvares says, but others wore poorer garments like those of the peasantry. The priest's vestment, however, was a fine affair, fashioned like a shirt, and the stole had a hole in the middle which was put over the head. Priests could moreover often be identified by the cross they carried in their right hand, as well as by their beards and shaven heads which contrasted with the shaved faces and hairy heads of the laity.

---

[6] Beckingham and Huntingford (1961) I, 120, II, 349-52, 356-7; Paulos Tsadua (1968), 43. For a later account of ordination, by Charles Poncet, see Foster (1949), 123.

[7] Beckingham and Huntingford (1961) I, 119-20, II, 511.

Monks frequently wore a distinctive garb, often made of coarse yellow-coloured cloth, but sometimes of tanned goat-skins. This dress consisted of a tunic and belt, a hood open in the front and at the top, and wide breeches. This apparel was often worn with a hat and a burnous, or a full, flowing cape which reached to the ground.

Nuns were similarly dressed, but without either a cape or a hat. Their heads were invariably shaved. When young they would wear skull-caps, but later would sometimes have a leather strap wound round the head.

The *Abun*, as befitted his high status, was always very finely dressed, sometimes in a delicate Indian white cotton robe with a blue silk hood, and a large blue turban.[8]

Reverence paid to Churches

Churches were highly venerated, and invariably places of great decorum. The need to enter them with respect, and orderly behaviour, was clearly established in the *Fethä Nägäst* which declared: "In church, people must attend mass quietly, with purity, with great attention to hear the word of God, with care, each one in his proper place, according to the positions of the heavenly spirits... The deacons shall ensure that everyone stays in his appropriate place, and shall watch the people lest some slumber, sleep, laugh, or deride their companions". This injunction was closely followed, and caused Alvares to remark, with admiration, that in Ethiopian churches "nobody" sat, entered wearing shoes, expectorated or spat, nor did they let any dog or other animal enter. This picture was confirmed a generation later by Castanhoso who remarked that Ethiopians always prayed standing, bowed frequently, kissed the ground, and then stood up again.

The "great reverence" paid to places of worship also found expression in the fact, noticed by Alvares and later observers, that no one would ride past a church, even if in a great hurry; the traveller would invariably dismount, and lead their mules or horses by the bridle until he had gone a good way on.[9]

Various Types of Church

Churches, though more imposing than most buildings, were often architecturally not dissimilar from them, for they were circular in the greater part of the country, and rectangular in Tegré and some other parts of the north.

Round churches, which were by far the most common, were divided by walls as well as in places often by curtains decorated with little bells, into three circular concentric sections. The outer, known as the *qené mahalet*, was occupied by laymen, and the second, the *mäqdäs*, by officiating priests, while the central section, the

---

[8] Beckingham and Huntingford (1961) I, 126-7, 175, II, 359, 511; Thomas (1938) 76, 80; Ludolf (1684) 388; Bruce (1790) IV, 61.

[9] Paulos Tsadua (1968) 82; Beckingham and Huntingford (1961) I, 120-1, 254 II, 511, 518; Whiteway (1902) 90-1.

qeddastä qedusan, or Holy of Holies, was the location of the *tabot*, or holy altar slab, and could be entered only by the clergy.

Portable churches were also in service at the Emperor's court, which, as we have seen, throughout much of the Middle Ages was largely itinerant. It was accompanied, Alvares reports, by two portable tent-churches which were erected near the tent of the monarch. One was dedicated to the Virgin Mary, and the other to the Holy Cross. They consisted essentially of the *tabot*, as well as sundry church paraphernalia, such as chalices, besides the tent which served as the Holy of Holies, and could easily be transported. When the monarch and court travelled "the altar and the altar stone", i.e. the *tabot* with its container or *mänbärä tabot*, would be carried, Alvares reports, on the shoulders of two groups of four priests who took turns to do so, while another cleric went ahead with a thurible, and a deacon proceeded ahead ringing a bell so that everyone moved aside to let them pass, and those who were on horses or mules dismounted as a sign of reverence. Next to these two tents, on the other side of the Emperor's tent, were placed "a very beautiful and good tent" in which were kept the church vestments, and another for the fire and grain used for the Communion service.[10]

Church Services

Priests and monks in a typical church service recited their prayers by heart, almost in the dark, for their candles, Alvares notes, produced but little light. Most of the clergy prayed or chanted "very loud", and did not "recite verses", but sang "straight on". The prayers consisted of the Psalms, supplemented by the recitation of appropriate pieces of prose. Services were conducted standing, and matins consisted of a single lesson which was shouted rather than recited in front of the principal entrance between the church's two outer sections.

Services on Saturdays, Sundays or major festivals were naturally grander than on other days. On great occasions the clergy donned their finest clothes, and on the completion of the ceremony proceeded through the outer circular section of the church, carrying with them four or five processional crosses in the left hand - because they carried censers in their right. The chief officiating priest with his two companions, Alvares reports, then entered the interior of the building, and brought out a painting of the Holy Virgin, which he placed before his breast, while his assistants, who stood on either side of him, held lighted candles. The remainder of the clergy then began to chant, and, walking and even dancing in procession, rang bells and beat drums in time. Whenever they passed in front of the painting they paid it great reverence before eventually taking it back into the church.

After this the priests, carrying crosses, censers and bells, made their way to a nearby small building, to the north of the church, where the *qwerban*, or host, was prepared. It consisted of round pieces of bread, "very white and nice", which were put in a small bowl taken from the altar. Having collected this bread the priests, ringing their bells all the while, returned to the church with the bread covered with a piece of cloth. The congregation, which had been standing all this time, then bowed their

---

[10] Beckingham and Huntingford (1961) II, 437, 442-3, 510, 518; Hyatt (1928) 117-8.

heads, and remained so until the bowl containing the Eucharist was placed on the altar at which point the ringing of bells stopped. Wine prepared from dried grapes were at the same time put in the chalice.

The priest who was to say Mass, which he invariably did with his head bare, then began an Alleluia which was once more shouted rather than recited, and all the congregation responded in chant. He then became silent, but continued his benedictions with a small cross which he held in his hand, and the entire congregation both inside and outside thereupon began to sing. One of the priests by the altar then lifted up a manuscript Bible while another taking a cross and a bell, rang it, and walked with his colleagues to the principal door where the latter read an Epistle to the populace standing in the outer chamber.

When he had finished he chanted a response which was followed by the rest of the clergy. The priest who had said Mass then took another holy book from the altar and gave it to a fellow cleric who was to read from the Gospels and who bowed his head and begged a blessing. He then walked forward with two of his companions, one with a cross and censer and the other with a bell, and duly read from the book, "as fast and as loud" as his tongue could move, with his voice raised. He then walked back to the altar, to the accompaniment of another chant, and gave back the book. The priest who had said Mass then took the censer and walked with it many times round the church, censing all the while, after which he returned to the altar, where he gave many blessings with the cross, and uncovered the sacramental bread. The officiating priest thereupon took a piece of it with both hands, and then letting go with the right, held it only in the left, and with the thumb of the right made five little marks, or hollows, one at the top, one in the middle, one in the lower part, and two others on the left and right, and at the same time spoke to consecrate it. After this he blessed the chalice. Then, taking the bread in his hands, he divided it in the middle. He took a small part of what remained in his left hand, as well as a portion of the wine, for himself, and placed the other pieces together, one on top of the other.

After this he gave the bowl containing the bread to the priest who read the Gospel and the chalice to the one who read the Epistle, and then administered Communion to the monks near the altar. He handed out small portions of bread from the bowl, which was held by a deacon in his right hand, and as often as he did this a sub-deacon took some of the wine with a spoon and presented a small amount to each person who had received the bread. As soon as the communicant had sipped this he stretched out the palm of his hand into which a priest with a ewer of holy water poured some of this whereupon the former washed his mouth and then swallowed the water.

This part of the ceremony completed the priests proceeded to give Communion to the laity, first to those in the inner and later in the outer circle of the church. Throughout this ceremony, as in other services, everyone was standing. On approaching to receive the Sacrament they raised their hands, with their palms upward to take the bread, and after this also the wine and the water. The officiating priest and those who had stood with him then returned to the altar where they washed the sacramental bowl with the water in the ewer, and then poured it into the chalice, after which the priest drank it. This done one of the ministers of the altar took a cross and bell, and, beginning a short chant, went to the main door, whereupon the whole congregation bowed and left in peace.[11]

Confession

Priests, according to Alvares, invariably heard confessions standing. A moie detailed description was later provided by Poncet who states that persons confessing prostrated themselves at the feet of the priest, who was seated, and accused themselves in general of being "great sinners and having merited hell", without descending to particular sins they had committed. After this the priest, holding the Gospels in his left hand, and a cross in his right, touched with the cross the eyes, ears, nose and mouth of the penitent, recited prayers over him, and making several signs of the cross over him, gave him penance and dismissed him.[12]

Two Sabbaths

Throughout the period under review it was customary for Ethiopians to celebrate two Sabbaths, namely the "Jewish" Saturday as well as the "Christian" Sunday. This two-day celebration, however, tended to be opposed by most of the *Abuns*, who, as Egyptian Copts, regarded it as contrary to the practice of the Church of Alexandria. Emperor Gälawdéwos in his famous Confession of Faith glossed over this as well as other Ethiopian deviations from Alexandrian practice by contending, as we shall see, that his compatriots did not celebrate the Sabbath after the manner of the Jews as the first day of the week, but rather as a new day on which Jesus rose from the dead.[13]

Easter

Easter, for the clergy and laity alike, was perhaps the most important religious ceremony of the year. Services began the evening before Palm Sunday when the priests would start their matins shortly after midnight, and keep up their singing and graceful dancing, with all their religious pictures uncovered, until daylight. They then took branches, which the congregation had previously prepared, into the church where, Alvares reports, they sang "loudly and hurriedly". They then came out again with a cross and palms which they distributed among their flock. Everyone then walked in procession round the building, after which they re-entered the church, and the priest with the cross said Mass while the others sang.

Throughout Holy Week long services were held in all churches. On Thursday at the hour of Vespers the clergy performed maundy, or the service of ritual washing of feet. The superior of the church, sitting on a three-legged stool, with a towel round

---

[11] Beckingham and Huntingford (1961) I, 74-5, 119, 247, 256, II, 510; Lockhart (1984) 178-9.

[12] Beckingham and Huntingford (1961) I, 88-9, 119, 126-7, 160, 164-5, 203, 236, 247, II, 338, 360, 463; Thomas (1938) 79; Crawford (1958) 56, 125, 145; Foster (1949) 152; Lockhart (1984) 178-9.

[13] Beckingham and Huntingford (1961) I, 118-9, 126; Lockhart (1984) 179; Bruce (1790) III, 177.

his waist, and a large basin of water before him, began by washing the feet of the clergy, and later of everyone else in the church. This done the priests started singing, and continued all night, the clergy, monks and deacons remaining in the building, without partaking of either food or drink until after Mass on Saturday.

On Friday at midday the clergy decorated the church with whatever crimson or other brocades they possessed, and erected a Crucifix covered with a small curtain. They then sang all night, and read the Psalms all day, after which they all threw themselves on the ground, prostrate, buffeted each other, knocked their heads against the walls, and punched themselves, weeping "so bitterly", Alvares says, "that a heart of stone would be moved to tears". This lamentation often lasted "quite two hours", after which two priests, each holding a small whip with five thongs, went to each of the church doors and began scourging the congregation who for this purpose had stripped themselves from the waist upwards, as they left the building. Some received only a few strokes, but others intentionally waited to receive many. Some old men and women remained being beaten for half an hour or so until their blood ran, after which they slept in the courtyard.

At midnight the priests began singing, after which they said Mass, and took Communion. They then recited matins, and before morning made a procession before saying another Mass at dawn. Such observances usually continued for no less than sixteen days, until the Monday after Low Sunday. Easter services were carried out, Castanhoso later confirmed, with "great decency", and were followed by a "very solemn procession" in which the churchmen carried so many and such large candles that he believed there were "more than in the whole of Portugal".[14]

Temqät

Another important ceremony took place at *Temqät*, or the Epiphany, when the priests and laity assembled by a river, spring or pool for a mass baptism which commemorated the Baptism of Christ. One such ceremony, which was attended by Lebnä Dengel's entire court, is described by Alvares who reports that the monarch had his tent pitched near a large reservoir of water in which "a great number of priests" waded, and throughout the preceding night "never stopped singing", thereby "blessing the water". At about midnight baptism by immersion began, and by sunrise was in full force. The water on that occasion was in a specially dug pool, or square-shaped reservoir, which was "very big and deep", and lined with planks covered with thick waxed cotton. The water flowed into it through a channel and thence into a pipe at the end of which a kind of bag had been placed to keep out soil or other impurities. Among the people in the water whom Alvares saw was the Emperor's chaplain, an old priest, who was "naked as when his mother bore him (and quite dead with cold, because there was a very sharp frost)". He stood in the water up "to his shoulders, or nearly so", and whenever anyone entered the reservoir to be baptised he put his hands on their heads, and pushed them under the water three times, saying "[I baptise thee] in the name of the Father, of the Son, and of the Holy Spirit", after which he made

---

[14] Beckingham and Huntingford (1961) I, 116, 119, 160, 163-4, 166, 201, 203, 256, II, 511; Beccari (1903-17), IV, 234, 243, 226; Thomas (1938) 79.

the sign of the cross as a blessing, and allowed them, most doubtless shivering, to leave in peace.[15]

Prayers in Time of Emergency

It was not unusual for the clergy - and laity - in times of emergency to recite special prayers. During a drought at Manadeley in southern Tegré, for example, Alvares heard "great shouts", and saw "many Christian people... entreating the mercy of God that he might give them water, for they were losing their flocks, and were not sowing their millet nor any other seed". They cry was *Egzi'o meherana Krestos*, or "O Lord have mercy on us".[16]

Pilgrimage

Many priests and monks, as well as members of the laity, went each year on pilgrimages, to holy places within the country or further afield to Jerusalem. The main local places visited, which were attended by vast throngs each year, were Aksum (and the nearby monastery of Abba Gärima) where Alvares found "more than 3,000 cripples, blind men, and lepers", Lalibäla, where he saw "infinite numbers" of worshippers, and Yemrahannä Krestos where he tells of "fully twenty thousand persons" receiving Communion.

Pilgrims bound for the Holy Land travelled thither more or less every year. Many assembled at Debarwa whence some travelled north-eastwards to the Red Sea port of Suakin where they embarked for Egypt, while others made their way northwards by way of Cairo. One land-bound party which Alvares saw consisted of no less than 336 monks and 15 nuns, and was accompanied by three tents (each doubtless with its *tabot*) which served as churches. The pilgrims gathered for departure around Christmas, after which they were entrusted by the Bahr Nägaš to a group of Muslims from Suakin and Rif on the Egyptian Nile who conducted them as far as Cairo. The pilgrims following this route were so laden, and spent so long in praying and taking Communion, that they did not cover more than about six miles a day. The journey therefore took them thirty-one days by land to Rif, and a further eight by boat down the Nile to Cairo. The expedition was, however, fraught with difficulties, and that year ended in disaster, for the party was attacked north of Suakin. Most of the old men were killed, and the young were taken as slaves: only fifteen pilgrims succeeded in escaping.[17]

---

[15] Beckingham and Huntingford (1961) I, 70, 108, 235, 243, 262, 270, 286, 305, II, 333, 346, 355-7, 359 379, 419, 443-4; Whiteway (1902) 160; Crawford (1958) 79; Beccari (1903-17) IV, 243, 268, VI 161-2; Foster (1949) 122; Bruce (1790) III, 317; Perruchon (1893) 167.

[16] Beckingham and Huntingford (1961) I, 120, II, 349-52, 356-7; Paulos Tsadua (1968), 43. For a later account of ordination, by Charles Poncet, see Foster (1949), 123.

[17] Beckingham and Huntingford (1961) I, 119-20, II, 511.

Fasting and Abstinence

The clergy, as well as the Christian population at large, were much given to fasting and abstinence. There was indeed, Ludolf believed, no country in the world where fasts were "more exactly obser'vd", for the people "kept themselves whole dayes without either Food or Drink". Days of Abstinence, which together amounted to about half the year, included a Lent of no less than 56 days, the Fast of the Apostles, 10 to 40 days, the Fast of the Assumption, 16 days, a Fast preceding Christmas, 40 days, the Eve of Nineveh, three days, the Eve of Christmas, one day, and the Eve of the Epiphany, also one day. Foods prohibited during such fasts comprised all animal products, namely milk, eggs and butter, as well as meat, and applied to all adults, Alvares says, even though they might be "near dying".

The principal diet during Lent and other periods of abstinence was bread and water. Fish and vegetables were permitted, but the former (which some of the more devout indeed refused to eat) was in most places difficult to find, while cabbages, the principle greens, were not abundant until after the rainy season, and were therefore not available in any quantity during the fasting period. Many monks, however, grew a vegetable like kale, the leaves of which they picked throughout the year, while others ate cress. Use was also made in a few areas of grapes and peaches, but this was very uncommon. Monks and nuns, and some of the clergy, carried the Lenten fast even further, for they ate, according to Alvares, only every second day, and always at night. Some old women, who had withdrawn from the world, also fasted in this way, and the aged Empress Eléni was said to eat only three times a week, on Tuesdays, Thursdays and Saturdays.

There were, however, significant regional variations. In Tegré and the country of the Bahr Nägaš it was thus customary to eat meat on Saturdays and Sundays during Lent, and on those two days, Alvares claims, they killed "more cows than in all the year". It was likewise allowed in the northern provinces, he says, for newly wedded persons to eat meat and butter throughout the fasting period. In the greater part of the country the fast was, however, strictly kept "by old and young, men and women, boys and girls, without any breech".

The intensity of abstinence surprised the Jesuits, among them Lobo, who confirmed that Ethiopians during Lent refrained from all meat and dairy products, even when seriously ill. During periods of abstinence moreover they ate and drank only once a day: in Lent after sunset, and on Wednesdays and Fridays not until three in the afternoon, a time which they told by means of the length of their shadows. Belief in fasting was so intense that it was not uncommon for Mass to be said late in the afternoon, as it was thought that the fast was broken by taking the sacramental bread and wine.

Severe fasting seems to have debilitated the population. One of the results was, as already noted, that Mahfuz, a Muslim leader in the eastern lowlands, often chose the fasting period to invade the highlands, and is said to have done so "every Lent for twenty-four years."[18]

---

[18] Beckingham and Huntingford (1961) I, 126-7, 175, II, 359, 511; Thomas (1938) 76, 80; Ludolf (1684) 388; Bruce (1790) IV, 61.

Penitence, and the Mortification of the Flesh

Many monks, and other devout Christians, practised extreme forms of penitence. A not untypical case reported by Alvares was that of a wandering monk accompanied by several novices whom he was taking to be ordained. On the evening of their meeting the Portuguese traveller invited him to share his meal, but the monk "excused himself for not wanting to eat", upon which the novices "came with water-cresses, and they boiled them without salt or oil, or anything else, and they ate these cresses without mixing in anything" . When Alvares inquired about this, they told him that "they did not eat bread". Though he had often heard that there were "many monks" who thus abstained he could scarcely believe it, and therefore watched the monk closely "night and day", but "never saw him eat any thing but herbs", that is to say, water-cresses, water-parsnips, nettles, mallows and kale - which latter he sometimes obtained from the monasteries he passed. Alvares, who tried to eat it, found it the "most dismal food in the world".

The mortification of the flesh was practiced in various other ways. Alvares, who met the monk again subsequently, recalls that on embracing him, he found that, though it was not even Lent, he was wearing a four inch wide iron girdle with thick points facing - and lacerating - the skin.

There were likewise "many monks" who during Lent refrained from sitting down, and spent the whole day on their feet. One such penitent, whom Alvares met in a cave, was standing in a wooden tabernacle, about his own size, "like a box without a lid, much plastered with clay and dung". This structure, which had been occupied by many previous inmates, had a ledge three fingers wide for the buttocks, two similar ones for the elbows, and a shelf in front for a book. The monk, not content with this penance, also wore a hair-cloth woven with ox-tail bristles and an iron girdle, and subsisted on food made only from herbs which was provided by two acolytes. Alvares later saw two other standing monks at Debarwa, who likewise lived only on herbs and sprouting lentils.

Many priests, monks and nuns also immersed themselves in cold water, and slept in it, Alvares says, "up to their necks". Unable to believe this when told of it, he and his companions went to Aksum to see for themselves, and were "amazed at the multitude of people" immersed in the water. They included "canons and wives of canons, and monks and nuns", al! of them sitting on stones which had been so arranged that they could crouch with their water up to their neck. The prevalence of this custom was confirmed by a Portuguese resident, Pero de Covilhão, who had been many years in the country, and stated that the practice was "general" throughout the land, and that there were also "many" hermits who lived alone in "the great forests", and in "the greatest depths and heights of the mountains".[19]

---

[19] Paulos Tsadua (1968) 82; Beckingham and Huntingford (1961) I, 120-1, **254 II**, 511, 518; Whiteway (1902) 90-1.

Circumcision, Baptism, Weddings and Funerals

The influence of the Church, and of Christianity, was so all-pervasive that the clergy were involved in the main events of a Christian's life, including circumcision, and, more especially, baptism, marriage and death.

Circumcision was almost universally practiced in Ethiopia, not only by Christians, but also by Muslims, Fälašas, or followers of a Judaic type of religion, and persons of local traditional faiths. The custom among Ethiopian Christians dated back to ancient times, and was carried out "by anybody", Alvares states, "without any ceremony", but was mainly women's work. The practice was attacked by most foreign missionaries, but was resolutely defended by the clergy, as well as by Emperor Gälawdéwos in his famous Confession of Faith, which, however, justified it, not on the basis of religious doctrine, but as one of the country's long-standing traditions. Circumcision was in fact so deeply ingrained that Almeida, who regarded it as a Judaic trait which should have long since been abandoned, later reported with sorrow and indignation that Ethiopians converted to Catholicism by the Jesuits could "not be persuaded to abandon it".

Baptism, unlike circumcision, was the direct responsibility of the clergy, and, Alvares states, was invariably carried out at the church door on the occasion of morning Mass, on a Saturday or Sunday. The infant was at the same time given Communion - and consumed "very small quantities" of the sacramental substance which it swallowed with water. The ceremony was carried out for male children forty days after birth, and for females after eighty days (Alvares mistakenly quoted the figure of sixty). The normal procedure was for a woman to hand the infant to the man who was to serve as godfather. The latter, holding the child under the arms, then raised it in the air, at which point the priest performing the baptism with one hand held a vase of water, which had previously been blessed, and poured it over the baby, while with the other hand he washed it all over, and pronounced in Ge'ez the words, "I baptize thee in the name of the Father, the Son and the Holy Ghost". He also put oil on the child's forehead, breasts and shoulder-blades.

The relatively long interval between birth and baptism in Ethiopia was criticised by foreign priests, such as Alvares who declared it "a great error", on the ground that the infant might die before being thus assured of Salvation, but the Ethiopians "many times" answered that "the faith of the mother", and the Communion she had received during her pregnancy, sufficed for the infant child prior to baptism. One of those unconvinced by this argument was the Jesuit Almeida who bemoaned that "many souls" over "many hundreds of years" had been "lost to Heaven through this error"!

Several different kinds of marriage ceremony were practiced, in all of which priests were in one way or another involved. Strictly religious marriages were carried out, according to Alvares, in the immediate vicinity of a church. In one such ceremony he had witnessed in both Šäwa and the country of the Bahr Nägaš the bride and bridegroom were seated on a couch beside a church from the front door of which the *Abun* gave his blessing. After this he walked round the bridal couple with incense and cross, and laid his hands on their heads, "telling them to observe that which God had commanded in the Gospels; and that they were no longer two separate persons, but two in one flesh; and that so in like manner should their hearts and wills be". Bride and groom then remained there until Mass had been said, after which he gave them Communion, and bestowed on them his blessing. One of the more secular marriages

45

described by Alvares took place near a settlement in an open space in which a couch had been placed.*

Priests likewise came to the fore at burials. After death the deceased was washed, and "much incense", Alvares says, was burnt. The body, wrapped in a shroud, was then carried away, and placed on a burial couch, after which the priests came, with crosses, holy water and incense, and recited brief prayers. They then at once set off with the body to the churchyard where they prayed and read the Gospel of St John. Burials normally took place on the same day as the death, and offerings were brought on the morrow.

It was the custom for mourners, according to Alvares, to shave their heads with a razor, to allow their beards to grow, and to dress in black. The rulers of the country paid particular attention to mourning ceremonies. On the death of King Manoel I of Portugal in 1521 for example, Emperor Lebnä Dengel issued a proclamation at his court "that all the shops should be shut where bread and other merchandise were sold, and also that all the offices should be closed". This closure, according to Alvares, "lasted for three days, during which no tent was opened", and this was the practice of the country for he adds: "The Ethiopians say that when any prince dies who is a friend of the King, they shut the shops for three days, and both men and women shave their heads and lament and whoso does not do likewise is punished."

Mourning for the dead continued, according to Almeida, for "many days". Relatives and friends of the deceased assembled with "many" female mourners "long before dawn", and continued "lamenting loudly" until "broad daylight". During this time they would "lament to the sound of the drum, striking together the palms of their hands, beating their breasts, and uttering heart-breaking lamentations in melancholy tones". In the case of noblemen or persons of substance the mourning ceremonial was particularly impressive, for the lamenters brought to the place of mourning the dead man's horse, if he had one, his pennons, if he was a captain, his shield, his sword, his rich clothing, his gold chains and his necklace, and displayed them to everyone, thereby calling forth many tears.[20]

Belief in Augury

Belief in augury was widespread, and caused Lobo to remark that a journey might be halted because people heard a bird singing on the left of their path, for it

---

* Alvares goes on to report that, when the bride and bridegroom were seated, three priests came and began chanting. Then, continuing their singing, they walked round the couch three times, and then cut a lock of hair from the head of the bridegroom and another from that of the bride, wetted them with mead, and placed the hair from the one on the head of the other whence the other lock had been removed, and vice versa. After that they sprinkled the couple with holy water, after which the wedding festivities and feasting began. Ludolf's informant Abba Gorgoreyos, commenting on Alvares's account, observed, "the cutting and exchange of hair between the bride and the bridegroom is not done in Ethiopia. It may, however, be a custom peculiar to some province which is unknown to me. Feasts and dancing they do have. The bride and groom do not leave the house for ten days, rejoicing with their neighbours". Ludolf (1691) 439.

[20] Beckingham and Huntingford (1961) II, 405, 437, 442-3, 510, 518; Hyatt (1928) 117-8.

was customary to interpret this as "such an evil omen" that they would not continue on their way until they heard "the same bird or another one singing on their right".[21]

Involvement in Trade

So many of the clergy were involved in trade that Alvares went so far as to remark that "the principal merchants" at many markets were "priests, friars and nuns". He was probably referring to clerics engaged in the sale of the often considerable produce of ecclesiastical lands. The clergy also constituted a major market for many articles, including incense and candles, and cloth for vestments, curtains and umbrellas, besides church paraphernalia of all kinds. Many imported spices, Brother Thomas claims, went for example to Aksum which he proudly described as "one of the greatest cities" and "another and greater Rome".[22]

Oaths and Excommunication

Ethiopians are said at this time to have made considerable use of oaths. Those in the name of St George, Lobo says, were in particular "much revered and feared". Priests and monks were likewise "very free" with the use of excommunication which, according to the same observer, evoked "great fear" on the part of the population.[23]

Religious Fortitude, and Apostasy

Ethiopians were generally considered ardent in their faith. Lobo, one of the Jesuits who attempted to convert them, described them indeed as "stubborn in their errors". He tells of "more than seventy monks", who, rather than embrace Catholicism preferred, as he puts it, "to enter hell ahead of time" by casting themselves from a high cliff, and being broken to pieces on the rocks at the bottom; and of "more than six hundred monks and nuns" who died in battle because they would not abandon their age-old beliefs and practices.

Notwithstanding such religious fortitude cases of apostasy were far more common than is sometimes supposed. Alvares, citing the case of one young nobleman who joined the service of the Muslim ruler of Adäl and later resumed that of the Emperor, comments: "here they think nothing of joining the Moors [i.e. Muslims] and becoming Moors, and if they wish to return, they get baptized again, and are pardoned and Christians as before".

Numerous conversions to Islam during the campaign of Ahmäd Grañ were later also reported by the latter's chronicler Šihab al-Din. Confirmation of the extent of apostasy at that time is provided by Bermudes who records that on the arrival of the

---

[21] Beckingham and Huntingford (1961) I, 74-5, 119, 247, 256, II, 510; Lockhart (1984) 178-9.

[22] Beckingham and Huntingford (1961) I, 88-9, 119, 126-7, 160, 164-5, 203, 236, 247, II, 338, 360, 463; Thomas (1938) 79; Crawford (1958) 56, 125, 145; Foster (1949) 152; Lockhart (1984) 178-9.

[23] Beckingham and Huntingford (1961) I, 118-9, 126; Lockhart (1984) 179; Bruce (1790) III, 177.

Portuguese expedition of 1541 many Christians, who had joined the Muslims "through fear", readily submitted to Christovão da Gama. One of them, a cousin of the Bahrnägäš, had thrown in his lot with Grañ when the latter had seemed victorious, but, on the latter's defeat, duly returned to the Christian camp.[24]

St. Mark, writing, from an early 14th century volume of the Four Gospels, in the Bibliothèque Nationale, Paris, Ethiopien 32.

[24] Beckingham and Huntingford (1961) I, 116, 119, 160, 163-4, 166, 201, 203, 256, II, 511; Beccari (1903-17), IV, 234, 243, 226; Thomas (1938) 79.

VII

TRADERS

Trade in a Subsistence Economy

Trade, because of the subsistence character of the economy, seems in medieval times to have emerged but slowly. By the late thirteenth century, however, Marco Polo reported that the country was "much frequented by merchants" who obtained "large profits". The existence of this class is further evident from the early fourteenth century chronicle of Emperor 'Amdä Ṣeyon which records that goods which the monarch had "entrusted to the merchants" had been seized by the Muslim ruler of Yefat, Säbr ad-Din, who had also imprisoned the traders concerned.[1]

Short- and Long-distance Trade

Medieval trade, which was conducted at innumerable markets throughout the length and breadth of the country, was both short-distance and long-distance in character.

Short-distance trade was centred entirely on local markets, usually held weekly, and based virtually entirely on barter. They were attended almost exclusively by the populace of the area, and buyers and sellers both consisted mainly of the peasantry. Articles dealt in, which were almost invariably displayed for sale in only modest quantities, consisted principally of local produce: grain, butter, and honey, perhaps a few lemons, *bärbäré*, or red pepper, and other spices, as well as cattle, horses, mules and other livestock, hides and skins, and sometimes raw cotton.

Long-distance commerce, though also mainly carried out at local markets, was on the other hand largely based on caravans, composed primarily of merchants, the majority of them Muslims, who were engaged in the import-export business and travelled far and wide. Such caravans linked the interior of the country northwards with the Red Sea ports of Massawa and Hergigo, or Arkiko, eastwards with those of Zäylä' and Berbera on the Gulf of Aden, and westwards with Sudan. Many caravans were also involved in the export of slaves, mainly to Arabia and Sudan, while others brought in large quantities of *amolé*, or salt bars, which were mined in the 'Afär depression, and served as "primitive money" over a wide stretch of the country.

Markets

Trade at most markets was based almost entirely on non-monetary exchange. This took the form, Alvares notes, of "bartering one thing for another, as for instance an ass for a cow". The individual whose product was of less value would make up the difference by giving the person with whom he was exchanging "two or three measures of bread (or salt)". Elaborating on this type of exchange, which was by then virtually

---

[1] Marco Polo (1954) 401; Taddesse Tamrat (1972) 85.

unknown in Europe, the Portuguese traveller explained that with bread people obtained cloth, and with cloth they obtained mules and cows, and whatever they wanted, including salt, incense, pepper, myrrh, camphor, and other small articles. Fowls and capons, and "whatever they need or want", was likewise found at these markets "in exchange for other things" for there was "no current money". Such barter operations, he notes, were carried out "quickly", and virtually without any talk.

Some of the larger markets were situated at the "chief towns", but others were located in the countryside. Debarwa, the capital of the Bahr Nägaš, for example, had "a great market and fair", every Tuesday, which was attended, by "300 or 400 persons". They included many old women and some young ones who went there to measure the wheat and salt sold. They also provided hospitality to travelling merchants who slept in the town on market-days, and after each fair they looked after unsold merchandise which they kept for the next week's fair.

Another market, at Durbit in northern Šäwa or southern Wällo, on the other hand was held, according to Brother Thomas,"in the open country". Its fair, which was likewise of considerable importance, was visited by merchants from Damot, Balé, Gojjam, Tegré and Agäwmeder. Goods sold included gold, silver, and jewels, as well as silk and other cloth. This market was unusual in that it was held, we are told, not weekly, but only "three times a year".

Important markets, in the days of moving capitals, were also found in the vicinity of the court where a square, Alvares reports, would invariably be set aside for trading purposes not far from the royal tent. Though some of the merchants at such sites, like the capital's population as a whole, were Christian the "greater number" were Muslims. The role of the two communities is clearly delineated by the Portuguese traveller who states that the Muslims were the "principal merchants" of cloth and large goods", whereas the Christians sold "cheap things", for the most part provisions. The Muslims, generally speaking, sold nothing to eat, for the courtiers and soldiers, as Christians, would not touch meat killed by Muslims or food prepared by them.[2]

Caravans

Merchants and other persons travelling long distances almost always did so, for reasons of security, in large groups, or caravans. Some of the largest were those which made their way to and from the coast. Traders travelling between Angot and Manadeley made the journey, according to Alvares, twice a week, so that one caravan left the market as the another arrived. Each caravan was under the command of a *Nägadras*, literally "head of the traders", and might consist of "1,000 persons and upwards". Despite their number such caravans were not infrequently attacked by the Doba people of the area, and in the ensuing skirmishes "many people" were often killed.

Caravans making their way from Debarwa to the port of Hergigo were often even larger. Alvares tells of one which consisted of around a thousand men on mules and "quite 600" on foot besides a few on horseback. At Dengel, an intermediate halt,

---

[2] Beckingham and Huntingford (1961) I, 105, 125, **II**, 442; Crawford (1958) 151.

they camped in a plain where people assembled every Monday night and Tuesday morning before going down to the coast. They went by caravan because the road was not passable "except by a big party, from fear of the Arabs and beasts of the country". The party was joined by "fully 2,000 persons" - which was said to be relatively "few" as many had failed to appear "from fear of lack of water".

Such caravans operated, however, only in the dry season, for during the rains, as the monks of Däbrä Bizän declared, "nobody" travelled in the three months from the middle of June to the middle of September, and after that month people had often to wait several more weeks until the rivers had subsided before beginning their journeys. Even in the dry season the absence of bridges made travelling in some places difficult. Merchants on reaching a river could in many cases cross it only by first constructing a raft, which might sometimes by supported by inflated skins.[3]

Salt Caravans

Many caravans travelling to and from the north were concerned mainly or exclusively with the transportation of *amolé*, or salt bars, which were mined in the 'Afär depression. One such caravan, which Alvares saw in southern Tegré, comprised 300 or 400 pack animals, "in herds, laden with salt", while others were making their way back to the mines in search of further supplies. While some large caravans belonged, as we have seen, to "great lords" who sent each year to obtain salt bars to meet their expenses at court, others were composed of smaller groups of merchants each of whom took with them "droves of twenty or thirty beasts", or else human porters who carried salt around "to make a profit from market to market".

A century or so later the roads from Tegré to Dämbeya were described by Almeida as "constantly full" of salt caravans. Many consisted of no less than a thousand porters, as well as perhaps 500 donkeys. The journey was particularly arduous for the latter, many of whom were often "crushed by their burdens" which were "usually far too great" for them. Numerous bars of salt were likewise broken on the long journey inland, and thereby lost much of their value.

Not a few donkeys moreover were lost on the journey, particularly in the more mountainous areas, where the path was sometimes rugged and narrow, as a result of which beasts of burden fell headlong down precipices, together with the salt they were carrying. One of the worst such places was on the mountain of Lälmalmo where "many" donkeys were "dashed to pieces" and their loads lost.

Another problem facing the salt merchants was that they were subjected to numerous, and very vexatious, taxes en route, as a result of which "nearly a third" of their load might be exacted "at different customs posts by way of dues".

The salt merchants and caravaneers were responsible not only for transporting the precious mineral, but also for mining it in the salt plains. This was arduous work, for it was necessary to enter the 'Afär lowlands at sunset, and cut as much salt as possible during the night, before the rising sun made the area unbearably hot, after

---

[3] Beckingham and Huntingford (1961) I, 72, 193-4, 469; Whiteway (1902) 201; Pankhurst (1961) 273-4.

which they, and their livestock - camels, oxen, mules and donkeys - all left, Lobo says, "hurrying to the mountain range for shelter". The life of the salt merchants was, however, a hard one, for besides having to endure thirst, which sometimes killed them, and heat, which "fries them even at night", they ran the risk of being attacked by enemies who lay in wait to .rob and kill them. Faced by "many hazards and enemies", those engaged in the salt trade thus risked their very lives, and only did so as they had "no other way to gain a livelihood".[4]

Difficulties of traditional transport. From E.A. De Cosson, *The Cradle of the Blue Nile* (London, 1877)

---

[4] Beckingham and Huntingford (1961) I, 181, (1954), 40, 44-5; Lockhart (1984)138.

Muslim Predominance in Trade

The foreign trade of Ethiopia was deeply influenced by its location in the Middle East where the Arabs had long since acquired a position of commercial dominance. The presence of Arab merchants in and around Ethiopia was reported by al-Ya'qubi as early as the ninth century. Ethiopian Muslims, some of whom were descended from Arabs or intermarried with them, gradually also became involved in trade, and, before long, were likewise engaged in commercial missions on behalf of the Christian rulers of the country. This development, according to Taddesse Tamrat, had already taken place by the early fourteenth century when Emperor 'Amdä Ṣeyon had "many" such Muslim traders in his service.

Evidence of the participation of Ethiopian Muslims in foreign trade, and royal business activity, is provided in a Ge'ez medieval work, the *Gadlä Zéna Marqos*, which indicates some of the countries they visited as well as the articles they handled. The text states that such traders "did business in India, Egypt, and among the people of Greece with the money of the King" who gave them ivory, and "excellent horses from Shawa, and red pure horses from Enarya" which the merchants exchanged in Egypt, Greece, and Rome for "very rich damasks adorned with green and scarlet stones and with leaves of red gold, which they brought to the King".[5]

Numerous Muslim merchants also traded on behalf of the Christian nobility. This was later explained by Almeida who noted:

"The great and rich men of this empire all have these Moors as their trade agents, and they carry gold to the sea for them and bring them silks and clothing. As they are not very scrupulous they usually profit by their management of other people's business, so that they get fat and rich on the pickings".[6]

Many Muslim merchants were also deeply involved in the slave trade, a highly lucrative branch of business from which Christians were barred by the country's legal code, the *Fethä Nägäst*. Testimony to Muslim paramountcy in this field is afforded by the *Gadlä Zéna Marqos* which reports that a group of Muslims converted to Christianity declared: "After having been baptized in the name of Christ... we no longer sell slaves". The exclusion of Christian merchants from the slave trade, an important area of commerce, inevitably placed them at a considerable, and long-enduring, disadvantage *vis-à-vis* Muslim competitors.

Muslim commercial predominance, which is apparent in the writings of Alvares, was confirmed in the following century by Almeida. Pointing to what he surmised was the principal reason for it, he notes that Muslim merchants at Massawa, the principal port for Ethiopian trade, were "better received and more welcome" than Christians, while at the ports of Arabia, which were also of major importance for the country's commerce, the latter were not allowed at all. The result was that Muslim merchants were "left in control of all the important trade of Ethiopia". This verdict was

---

[5] Taddesse Tamrat (1972) 85, 87-8.

[6] Beckingham and Huntingford (1954) 55.

subsequently endorsed by Ludolf. Noting that Ethiopian Christians were "no way addicted or expert in the Art and Intreagues of Merchandizing" he argued that "they that will not Travel into Forraign Parts must yield their gains to others", from which it followed that "the Chief Merchants in *Habssinia*" were "the *Arabians* who Inhabit the Ports of the *Red Sea*", and "especially, the *Mahumetans* scattered over the Kingdom".[7]

Christian Merchants and their Commerce

Despite the predominance of Muslims in long-distance commerce there was also no small Christian involvement in it. Not a few Christian merchants travelled down to the lowlands, particularly prior to the wars of Ahmäd Gran, and Christians even in later times were also actively engaged in the sale of farm produce and other provisions.

In the sixteenth century, during the era of "moving capitals", Christian merchants were prominent at the markets at court, where they were responsible for the sale of provisions - or, as Alvares puts it, "cheap things, such as bread, wine, flour and meat", and "priests, friars and nuns", as we have seen, were said to have been "principal merchants" at many markets.

Some Christian merchants were also involved in long-distance trade, but, however, often encountered many difficulties, particularly during the wars of Gran. The latter's chronicler. relates that his master, on arriving at the Šäwan market of Gendebelo, found a number of "infidel merchants with the riches belonging to the King of Abyssinia", but killed them, and seized their pack animals and all their goods.[8]

Armenians

In addition to the Arab merchants there were a number of Armenian and other foreign Christian merchants, who, because of their religion, gained the confidence of the Christian rulers of the country, and served as the latter's trade agents. Several Armenians in particular served a succession of monarchs as businessmen, and by extension as ambassadors. The best known of them in this period was Matthew, alias Abraham, who travelled to India and Portugal on behalf of Empress Eléni.[9]

Trade Routes and Ports

The country's principal trade routes throughout the Middle Ages led from the capital in Šäwa northwards to the twin ports of Massawa and Hergigo, and, of far less importance, Beylul; eastwards to those of Zäylä' and Berbera; and north-westwards

---

[7] Taddesse Tamrat (1972) 87; Beckingham and Huntingford (1961) I, 51-2, II, 442, (1954) 55; Ludolf (1684) 397; Pankhurst (1961) 338-55.

[8] Basset (1909) 65; Beckingham and Huntingford (1961) I, 126, 175, II, 442.

[9] Beckingham and Huntingford (1961) I, 264, II, 499.

through Sudan to Egypt. With the subsequent shift of Ethiopian political power to the Lake Ṭana area in the north-west the Gulf of Aden ports declined in significance while the route to Sudan, as we shall see, greatly increased in importance.

Massawa, which handled a major part of the country's foreign trade, was an island port off the Ethiopian coast, endowed with a good harbour suitable for shipping, and was the site, according to Barradas, of a "populous city". Its exports consisted of gold, civet, ivory, and slaves, as well as myrrh, wax, sheep and goats, and sundry provisions, such as wheat, durrah, honey and butter. Imports, which were more varied, according to Almeida comprised "clothing from India, carpets, silks and Meca brocades", as well as "drugs, pepper, cloves and a thousand other things". This is confirmed by Ludolf who states that imports included "garments of all sorts; velvet, silken; but chiefly Woollen and Fustian", as well as "spices, especially Pepper".

Hergigo lay on the mainland immediately opposite Massawa. It had inferior harbour facilities, but was relatively well supplied with water, which, according to Almeida, was carried across to the island port every day in two or three small boats. Hergigo was the place whither most northbound Ethiopian caravans made their way with articles for export which were then carried on small craft to the island of Massawa for shipment to Arabia, Egypt or India. Most goods imported at Massawa were likewise shipped to Hergigo before taken inland by caravans bound for the interior.

Beylul, further south on the 'Afär coast, was a port of only subsidiary importance. The Yamani ambassador Hasän ibn Ahmäd al-Haymi, who landed there in 1648, relates that he met there a "crowd of Abyssinian merchants", but tells of a caravan only thirty strong.

Zäylä', to the east, was a major port for the trade of the central, eastern and southern provinces, including Šäwa. A port of considerable commercial significance it was visited by many foreign ships, laden, the early sixteenth century Florentine trader Andrea Corsali reported, with "much merchandise", principally pepper and cloth from the East and incense from Arabia. These articles were taken inland by caravan to the Ethiopian interior, the land of "the churches of the Christians". This commercial picture was confirmed by Brother Antonio of Lalibäla who stated that Zäylä' was an "excellent port" visited by Moorish fleets from Cambay in India which brought many articles, including cloth of gold and silk. The port was the mart also for much produce of the interior. A seventeenth century Portuguese observer, Bernado Pereira, reported that every year caravans consisting of a thousand camels and other beasts of burden arrived there from the interior laden with grain, ivory and slaves.

Berbera, still further to the east, played a fairly similar role, for it provided commercial access to the sea for a vast stretch of the central and eastern interior. Described by the early fifteenth century Italian traveller Nicolo de Conti as the "gateway to Ethiopia" it was subsequently referred to by Brother Thomas as one of the principal ports for his emperor's trade. Goods shipped from the port, according to the early sixteenth century Portuguese traveller Duarte Barbosa, included gold, ivory and "divers other things", merchants of Aden in particular purchasing provisions, meat, honey and wax.

The western land route to Sudan over the centuries handled a vast, but not always well documented amount of Ethiopia's foreign trade. Alvares in the early sixteenth century reported that "white Moors from the Kingdom of Tunis" (which Beckingham and Huntingford equate with "Arab tribes in the northern Sudan") travelled along this route, bringing cheap "white burnooses" and "different kinds of merchandise".

Some Šäwan trade was also conducted along one or more southward routes, which, on the evidence of Brother Thomas, connected the area with Indian ocean ports such as Mogadishu or Malindi.[10]

Muslim Trade-based Settlements

Much of the long-distance trade of this period was based on a network of Muslim towns and villages, many of which were situated in the Christian highlands. Muslim communities in such areas were "separated", as Alvares notes, from the local Christian population, but, because of the lucrative business they conducted, paid "much tribute to the lords of the country in gold and silk stuffs".

Several of the principal Muslim settlements were fairly populous. One of the most important was Manadeley which Huntingford places 30 miles south-east of Mäqälé. Described by Alvares as "a town of very great trade, like a great city or seaport", it had "about 1,000 inhabitants, all Moors tributary to the Prester", as against only "twenty or thirty Christians" who lived apart and collected the toll charges. Goods exposed for sale included "all sorts of merchandise that there is in the world", which was brought by merchants of "all nations", notably "Moors" [i.e. Arabs] from Jeddah, Morocco, Fez, Bijaya on the Algerian coast, and Tunis, as well as Turks, "Roumes from Greece", and "Moors" from India, Ormuz and Cairo. Some the town's merchants traded on behalf of Emperor Lebnä Dengel. They claimed that he had "by force" thrust 1,000 *wäqéts*, or ounces, of gold on them, saying that he was lending them this money to trade with, and that each year they must give him a further 1,000 *wäqéts* in interest, so that his original deposit should "always remain alive".

Another Muslim settlement, referred to by Alvares as Acel, was situated further south in Wällo. Described by the Portuguese traveller as "a large town of Moors, rich with much trade in slaves, silks and all kinds of merchandise" it was the scene of "great intercourse between the Christians and Moors", for though the former lived "apart and alone", many of their womenfolk went to the Muslim town to carry water and wash clothes for its inhabitants. The place was also visited by traders from many lands, among them "white Moors" from Tunis who brought "cotton burnouses" and other merchandise. Trade was so profitable that the merchants of the town reported that they paid the Emperor "heavy tribute".

Wis, or Vis, a Muslim trading town in northern Šäwa, was no less important. First mentioned in the chronicle of Emperor Zär'ä Ya'qob it was described by Brother Thomas as a kind of "mercantile Venice" and a "warehouse and country of

---

[10] Beccari (1909) 106, (1903-17) XII, 67; Pankhurst (1982) 80; Beckingham and Huntingford(1954) 43, 181, (1961) I, 251-2; Ludolf (1684) 398; Peiser (1898) 13-5; *Historiale description d' Ethiopie* (1558) 32; Crawford (1958) 173-5, 167, 193; Longhena (1929) 159; Dames (1918) 24-5; Bruce (1790) III, 53, 55.

storehouses", one of which belonged to Corsali who had a plan, which never materialised, of printing books in Ethiopic. The place's significance was later corroborated in Grañ's chronicle which refers to it as "a large town" with a "considerable market without equal in Abyssinia". Its trade was so extensive that transactions were said to have been carried out only in gold.

The commercial centre of Gendebelu or Gendebelo, in eastern Šäwa, was also inhabited by Muslim merchants. Brother Thomas described it as "a great mercantile city" where "caravans of camels" unloaded their merchandise in "warehouses". Articles for sale, imported by way of Zäylä', included spices from Cambay, and "various things" from "the whole of India" which the Emperor's merchants purchased partly by barter and partly with "Hungarian and Venetian ducats" and "the silver coins of the Moors" [i.e. Arabs]. The town's commercial importance is confirmed by Grañ's chronicle which recalls that the place "belonged" to Lebnä Dengel, and was "inhabited by Muslims" who paid him taxes. When the Muslim warrior subsequently visited the town its Muslim population gave him a large amount of gold. This was at first offered to him for his wife Del Wänbära, on whose behalf he refused it, but he took it instead, as he said, for the Holy War against Ethiopian Christendom. The precious metal was accordingly used for the purchase of weapons. Perhaps for this reason the Muslims of the town enjoyed good relations with Grañ's army, and it was there that three bronze and iron cannon were subsequently carried from Zäylä' by camel. Yet another Muslim settlement, in eastern Šäwa, was at Amajah, near the Kässäm river, the population of which welcomed Grañ's forces, and prayed for the latter's victory.

Muslim merchants were probably also found in some of the principal Christian towns of Šäwa where they would have lived in their own quarters. One of the most important of these settlements was Bärärä or Berarä, just south of the Awaš river, where Corsali had another of his "warehouses". The place had a significant Muslim population which received Grañ warmly, asking him for soldiers to guard them against Lebnä Dengel's army, and informing him about the whereabouts of the great monastery of Däbrä Libanos and of the Emperor's riches at the town of Badeqé. The latter, the site of a palace belonging to Lebnä Dengel, also had some Muslim inhabitants who included a number of merchants, some of whom collaborated with Grañ, and brought him treasure bound for the Emperor.

From these and other places many Muslim merchants made their way over the years to the Emperor's court. There, as we have seen, Alvares reported that the "greater number" of traders were Muslims who were the "principal merchants", dealing especially in cloth and wholesale goods.[11]

---

[11] Marco Polo (1954) 401; Taddesse Tamrat (1972) 85.

VIII

HANDICRAFT WORKERS

The skill and status of Ethiopian handicraft workers, and the range and quality of their produce, reflected both the subsistence character of the economy and the hierarchical development of the society. Craftsmanship took place at four distinct levels: firstly, for the peasantry and others of humble station throughout the country; secondly, for churches and churchmen, many of them congregated at major religious centres; thirdly, for the rulers and their courts, mostly situated in the medieval period at "moving capitals"; and, fourthly and lastly, for the men and women who were clustered around the latter in military or other camps.

Rural Craftsmanship

Rural craftsmanship served primarily the peasantry, who, as we have seen, were largely self-sufficient. They and their families not only grew most of their own food, but also constructed their own houses, and made the greater part of their household furniture, agricultural tools and clothing. Self-sufficiency extended to the lesser gentry, for, Ludolf declares, "every one takes Care to supply his own wants either by his own or the pains of his Servants, which it is no hard matter to do, considering how little they have to use." Notwithstanding this attempt there were a number of articles in extensive demand which peasant families, mainly for lack of capital or expertise, could not produce.

Peasants for the most part lacked the equipment, and skill, required for smelting and the manufacture of ironware. They were therefore dependent on blacksmiths for a wide range of articles, including plough-shares and the blades of axes, hatchets, sickles and knives, as well as spear-heads, stirrups, bullets, needles, tweezers and even pectoral crosses.

Peasant households, which generally had no access to clay suitable for potting, had likewise in most cases little knowledge of pottery-work. They had therefore to make use of the specialised services of potters for such articles as cooking pots and clay *metads*, or plates for the preparation of *enjära*, or bread. *Jäbänas*, or coffee pots, might also be needed, though coffee-drinking was far from general as it had long been discouraged by the Church as an unChristian practice.

Many peasant families similarly lacked the equipment necessary for spinning, and more especially weaving. They were therefore not adept at such work, and had to rely on the specialised skills of weavers.

Ironware, pottery, and cloth were therefore produced in the main by specialised craft-workers: blacksmiths, potters and weavers, small numbers of whom could be found throughout the land.[1]

---

[1] Ludolf (1684) 391; Rüppell (1838-40) II, 180.

Blacksmiths

Blacksmiths tended to be regarded with distrust, fear, and at times even hatred. Oral tradition collected by the Jesuits in the seventeenth century claims that the fanatically Orthodox Christian Emperor Zär'ä Ya'qob (1434-1468) had gone so far as to kill "all" goldsmiths and blacksmiths as "sorcerers." This assertion is not corroborated in contemporary sources, but may contain at least some truth, for Almeida states that fear or hatred of these craftsmen in his day was still "so common" that it was "quite usual" to "suspect nearly all illnesses as coming from sorcerers" and to "attribute them to the blacksmiths." "Many" of the latter paid for their assumed guilt with their lives, as the relatives of their supposed victims killed them "on the suspicion of having caused their deaths by these devilish acts." Barradas, another Jesuit of the period, reports that the populace at large scarcely seemed to believe in the existence of natural diseases, but rather considered them the work of blacksmiths or possibly goldsmiths. It was sufficient for it to be thought that a particular smith was responsible for a person's illness: no proof was required; relatives and members of the public would at once threaten the unfortunate craftsman with death if the patient failed to recover. The blacksmith's trade, Ludolf asserts, was thus "abhorred", as was explained by his Ethiopian informant, Abba Gorgoreyos, who said, with a smile, that "the silly vulgar people could not endure Smiths, *as being the sort of Mortals that spit fire and were bred up in Hell*".

A sizeable proportion of the blacksmiths in the north-west of the country were Fälašas, or Judaic Ethiopians. In Dämbeya and some other regions of the north-west "many" of them, according to Almeida, were "great smiths," and lived by making spearheads, ploughshares and other articles. Ludolf agreed, observing that the Fälašas were "excellent smiths" and produced spear-heads and several other pieces of "Workmanship in Iron."

The Fäläša, like other groups differing from Orthodox Christianity, suffered for a time from persecution, and, according to traditions collected by the nineteenth century German Protestant missionary J.M. Flad, were driven to inaccessible or peripheral areas of the country, such as Sämén, Qwara and Čelga, where they nevertheless paid tribute to the Ethiopian state. "The craftsmen and artisans amongst them - masons, carpenters and smiths," he declares, were, however, "soon recalled by the Christian king and were well paid in his service." The result was that Fäläša villages soon sprung up in Sämén and in the neighbourhood of Gondär. "These work-people were joined by others, such as women skilled in pottery, and husbandmen, who established themselves in various parts of western Abyssinia, and supported themselves by their labour." After this "no more" was heard of "persecution and oppression in later centuries."[2]

Potters, Weavers and Tailors

Though Alvares and the Jesuits described fine Ethiopian pottery they provide no account of the craftsmen who produced it. This was perhaps not surprising, for

---

[2] Beckingham and Huntingford (1954) 54-5, 63, (1961) II, 337, 438; Beccari (1903-17) IV, 61; Ludolf (684) 390-1; Lockhart (1984) 170; Flad (1869) 9.

potters, as later evidence indicates, constituted an isolated, and largely despised, caste. They nevertheless turned out fine pottery of all kinds. Emperor Lebnä Dengel, thus travelled, Alvares reports, with as many as a hundred jars of mead which were "black, like jet", and "very well made". Other items at court included "many little round porringers of black earthenware", as well as little pots with lids. This picture was later confirmed by the Jesuits. Almeida reported that bowls of black pottery constituted "the dinner service" of poor and rich alike, and that "nothing better was seen even on the table of the Emperor himself", while Lobo agreed that even among the greatest in the land the "vanity of silver" was "unknown".

Weavers, who receive scarcely more attention than blacksmiths in the records of the time, also constituted something of a class apart. Their isolation from the rest of the community was increased by the fact that many of them belonged to a minority religious group, either Fälaša or Muslim.

Many Fälašas, Almeida notes, "lived by weaving," as was later confirmed by Abba Gorgoreyos, who, in a letter to Ludolf, patronisingly referred to them as the "weavers of our cloth." For this reason the German scholar went so far as to assert, though with obvious exaggeration, that the Fälašas were "the only persons" who employed themselves in "weaving Cotton."[3]

The participation of Muslims in weaving owed much, no doubt, to their involvement in trade, for cloth, whether imported or local, had, as we have seen, long been a major article of commerce, and one in which Arabs and local Muslims traded extensively.

Ecclesiastical Craftsmanship

The development of the Church, the founding of numerous religious establishments, some of them very wealthy, and the growth of a large class of clergy, created a demand for a wide variety of religious handicraft items. These included processional and hand crosses, ecclesiastical basins and plattens, sistra, bells and chandeliers of gold, silver or bronze, fine curtains and religious tents, priestly vestments, robes and turbans, ceremonial umbrellas and tallow candles, as well as church paintings, icons and scrolls, and religious manuscripts, many of them beautifully bound and illustrated. Some of these articles were made by monks specialising in handicraft activity, but others were the work of secular craftsmen, many of whom lived and worked in the vicinity of religious establishments.

The finest religious artifacts were produced at or in the vicinity of Aksum - where handicraft skills doubtless stretched back to the city's ancient days of greatness - and other great religious centres. Testimony of this is provided by Brother Thomas who claimed that "very fair and abundant" clothes of silk were made in the city, and that there was a "good" iron mine not far away. The latter statement was corroborated by Alvares who noted near the holy city "a very small village" which consisted "entirely of blacksmiths." Aksum was likewise the place, as Bruce afterwards learnt, where the

---

[3] Beckingham and Huntingford (1954) 54; Flemming (1890) 99; Ludolf (1684) 390.

"best parchment" was made, much of it by monks, and was also renowned for the manufacture of fine cotton cloth.[4]

Detail of a mid-15th century Ethiopian ecclesiastical painting on wood: the Virgin and Child, from the church of Daga Estifanos, Lake Tana, painted by the Ethiopian artist Feré Seyon, circa 1450.

---

[4] Beckingham and Huntingford (1961) I, 75-6, 149, II, 334, 338, 359, 444; Crawford (1958) 143; Girard (1873) 242; Bruce (1790) III, 133. The handicraft skill of the ancient Aksumites is evident *inter alia* in the minting of gold, silver and bronze coins, as well as - even more remarkable - bronze coins inlaid with gold.

Church Artists

Many church artists were to be found in the principal religious centres, among them Aksum in the vicinity of which "colouring materials," according to Brother Rufa'él, were unearthed for the use of painters.

Such artists, like other craftsmen, toiled anonymously without signing their work, and the names of only a few of them are preserved, often almost fortuitously. One of the earliest painters of whom there is record was a monk called Feré Seyon, who, as indicated in a contemporary inscription, painted a picture of the Virgin Child on a panel, now in the monastery of Daga Estifanos in Lake Tana, during the reign of Emperor Zär'ä Ya'qob (1434-1468). Mention is later made, by Alvares, in the following century, of two artists. One, a monk at Mäkäna Sellasé, had taught himself to paint, and was responsible for decorating the wall over the principal door with "two figures of Our Lady very well done, and two angels of the same sort, all done with the paint brush." The other artist was a Venetian, Nicolo Brancaleone, whom Alvares described as "a very honourable person and a great gentleman, though a painter." Brancaleone, he adds, placed his name on his pictures - a practice then virtually unknown in Ethiopia - and was popularly known as "Marcoreos." Confirmation of both statements was provided a decade or so ago by the discovery by an English art historian, Diana Spencer, of some of Brancaleone's pictures, which sure enough bore the signature *Marqoréwos Färänji*, i.e. Marcoreos the Frank.[5]

Craftsmanship for the Court and Army

The existence of a highly evolved State, with a large court and huge armies, often numbering tens or hundreds of thousands of men, as well as numerous camp-followers, constituted another major focus of demand for handicrafts. The court, with all its pomp and ceremony, was in constant need of many kinds of luxury goods, most of them made from gold or silver, or else from costly cloth or other imported materials. Such items of ostentation included gold, silver and gilt crowns, costly mantles and other articles of apparel made of brocade, silk shirts, and tents, besides decorated swords, spears and shields, ornamented saddles and finely wrought bridles and riding equipment. Though most soldiers brought their own weapons, clothes and supplies with them, the congregation of vast numbers of warriors also generated a considerable demand for spears and shields, which were often lost or broken and had to be replaced. Soldiers and their families, who tended to be better-off, and to dress better, than the populace at large, also exercised a significant demand for items of clothing of all kinds. At the town of Bärära, one of the early sixteenth century royal capitals in Šäwa, for example Emperor Lebnä Dengel employed a number of tailors, for the most part Muslims, who also made coverings for the royal horses.[6]

---

[5] Crawford (1958) 143; Chojnacki (1983) 21, 419 and fig 206; Beckingham and Huntingford (1961) I, 279, 332, II 340, 357; Spencer (1974) 201-20.

[6] Beckingham and Huntingford (1961) I, 302-5, 325-6; Basset (1882) 245.

Craftsmen in Moving Capitals

Throughout much of the medieval period the country, as we have seen, had no fixed capital. The monarch, his courtiers and soldiers were constantly on the march from one camp, or "moving capital" to another. Craftsmen, like other camp-followers, accompanied the court and army on their peregrinations. Alvares, who witnessed this, notes that "all who practise the smith's craft" had land allocated to them at camp. Their area was situated on either side of the market square, and took up "a very big space" like a "large village." The craftsmen also included some tailors. One of them, a certain Gäbrä Maryam, was a former Muslim and a renowned prize-fighter, who made braid and tassels of cloth.[7]

Craftsmen were in such demand that Emperor Lebnä Dengel (and many of his successors) took a keen interest in acquiring them from abroad. He wrote for example to King João of Portugal in the 1520s "as brother does to brother," saying:

"I want you to send me men, artificers, to make images, and printed books, and swords and arms of all sorts for fighting; and also masons and carpenters, and men who can make medicines, and physicians, and surgeons to cure illnesses; also artificers to beat our gold and sell it, and goldsmiths and silversmiths, and men who know how to extract gold and silver and also copper from the veins, and men who can make sheet lead and earthenware; and craftsmen of any trades which are necessary in these kingdoms, also gunsmiths."[8]

Some efforts was also made at about the same time to despatch a few Ethiopians abroad for training. An ambassador from Lebnä Dengel was sent to Goa with four slaves, two to be taught to be painters, and two others to be trumpeters - but whether they ever returned to their native country is not recorded.[9]

Artists in Royal Employ

Though Ethiopian artists were almost invariably churchmen some left the Church and entered the Emperor's service, as did most of the few foreign artists who settled in the country. The first of whom there is record was a *Färänj*, or Frank, who, according to the chronicles, painted an unorthodox picture of the Virgin and Child, for Emperor Bä'edä Maryam (1468-1478), thereby evoking some popular anger. In the following century a Venetian artist, Hieronimo Bicini, was reported by his compatriot Zorzi to have acted as "secretary" to Emperor Lebnä Dengel for whom he painted "many things." This artist, whose work appears to be no longer extant, was in possession of a large estate in Šäwa, and often resided with the monarch, and is said to have played chess with him "night and day."[10]

---

[7] Beckingham and Huntingford (1961) I, 319, II, 443.

[8] Beckingham and Huntingford (1961) II, 505.

[9] Beckingham and Huntingford (1961) II, 483-4.

[10] Basset (1882) 96; Crawford (1958) 162-3, 166-9.

IX

SLAVES

Slaves, who formed a sizeable section of the medieval Ethiopian population, receive only slight attention in the records of this period. They nevertheless played an important, if seldom fully recognised, rôle in the country's economic and social life, and constituted a major article of export.

The *Fethä Nägäst*

The status of the slave in Ethiopia was formally recognised in the country's code of law, the *Fethä Nägäst*, or "Laws of the Kings", which declares that though all men were basically free, as God had created them, the law of war caused the vanquished to become the slaves of the victors. The text therefore sanctioned the taking of slaves from among unbelievers, and declared that the children of slaves belonged to the owners of their parents. Both statements had strong Biblical sanction, for in *Leviticus* the Lord God was said to have declared:

"Both thy bond-men and thy bond-maids, which though shalt have, shall be of the heathen that are round about you; of them shall ye buy bond-men and bond-maids. Moreover, of the children of strangers that do sojourn among you, of them shall ye buy, and of their families that are with you, which they begat in your land; and they shall be your possession. And ye shall take them as an inheritance for your children after you; they shall be your bond-men for ever."[1]

Notwithstanding this clear sanction of slavery - and indeed of slave raiding - the *Fethä Nägäst* recognised that slaves were endowed, like other human beings, with souls and hence personalities. It declared in particular that a Christian slave was a son of the Church, and imposed on the master the obligation of providing his Christian slaves with facilities for religious worship. The duty was also laid on the master to compel non-Christian slaves to accept baptism, as well as to baptise any slave children born in his house. Christians were likewise forbidden from selling Christian slaves to non-believers. This prohibition, taken with the injunction that all slaves who were unbelievers should be baptised, was of major importance, for it tended to bar Christians from participating in the slave trade - and meant that this branch of commerce was open, as we have seen, more or less only to Muslims.

Other passages of the *Fethä Nägäst* recommended masters to free their slaves, for the love of God, and declared this a work of perfection and the most important form of alms-giving. Manumission was especially recommended in seven different circumstances: 1) if a slave had served his master's father and grandparent; 2) if he had been baptised by his master and wanted to become a priest or monk; 3) if he had been made a soldier by his master; 4) if he had saved his master from death, had fought for him, or had protected him from mortal peril; 5) if his mother had been

---

[1] Leviticus, XXXV, 44-6.

freed while he was in her womb; 6) if, after being taken prisoner in war, he returned voluntarily to his master; and 7) if his master died without heir. On the other hand the text stated that a master should not free any slave unable to provide for himself as a free man; and that a master's decision to free a slave could be reversed by a judge if it were shown that the slave had behaved to the master or the latter's children in an insolent or brutal manner, or had mal-administered their estate.[2]

Slavery, Slave Raiding and the Slave Trade

The population of medieval Ethiopia included innumerable slaves. Some, according to Alvares, ploughed and sowed the royal lands, while others, whom he described as "negroes," i.e. presumably darker-skinned, more "negroid-looking", people from the south or west of the country, carried baggage. The majority of slaves, to extrapolate from later evidence, were, however, probably in domestic service, and engaged for the most part in carrying water and fire-wood, as well as in cooking and other household chores. The Emperor's armies were likewise accompanied, Almeida states, by "many slave women."

Slave raiding and trading was extensive throughout this period. Christians, particularly in the east and north-east of the country, and persons of traditional local faith, further to the south and west, were constantly being seized as slaves. The Muslim ruler of Adäl in the east, who was engaged in frequent warfare with the Christian kingdom, received arms and horses, Alvares says, from the rulers of Arabia whom he presented in return with "many Abyssinian slaves."

There was also an extensive commerce in slaves, some of whom were castrated. The greatest number of eunuchs from Abyssinia, the fourteenth century Egyptian author Ibn Fadl Allah believed, were exported through the Muslim province of Hadeya, and came from "the country of the infidels", i.e. Christians or followers of local faiths. A merchant called El Hajj Faraj al-Funi had informed him that the castration of slaves had been expressly prohibited by the ruler of "Amhara," i.e. the Ethiopian Emperor, who regarded it as an abomination, and took active steps to prevent it, but the practice was carried out by rebels at Waslu who owed him no allegiance, and were the only people in the whole of Abyssinia who dared to do so. For this reason merchants often took their slaves there for castration, as this increased their price. The victims were then conveyed to Hadeya to recover, but the number who died of the operation was thought to be greater than those who survived. Trade in slaves was also carried out in other places, notably at Acel, one of the principal markets in Wällo, which was said by Alvares to have waxed rich from this trade.

Slave prices varied greatly from one part of the country to another. A slave on being taken to Damot in southern Gojjam could be purchased, Alvares says, for three or four *amolés*, though in the land where he was captured he might be valued at only one. Slaves from Damot were in particular "much esteemed" by the inhabitants of neighbouring Muslim countries, who would "not let them go at any price." The result was that Arabia, Persia, India, Egypt and Greece, the Portuguese priest claims, were all "full" of Ethiopian slaves.

---

[2] Guidi (1899) 298-9.

The slave trade continued to flourish throughout the period which followed. Slaves are reported to have come from many parts of the country. The Ottoman occupation of the port of Massawa in 1557 may well have contributed to an expansion of slave raiding, and trading, in the northern highlands, where in the late seventeenth century the Italian traveller Baratti, it will be recalled, described seeing Turkish soldiers returning to the coast with numerous Christian slaves. Slaves were likewise exported from the south-west, where the Jesuit Telles stated early in the seventeenth century that whenever the King of Jänjero bought rare goods from foreign merchants he would "give them in Exchange, ten, twenty, or more Slaves," for which purpose he sent his servants "into any Houses indifferently to take away the Sons, or Daughters of the Inhabitants, and deliver them to the Merchants." He did the same whenever he presented "a Slave or Slaves to any Person of Note", on which occasions he would order "the best and handsomest to be taken."[3]

Opposition to the Slave Trade

Though the *Fethä Nägäst* prohibited Christians from selling slaves, and thus from participating in the slave trade, this commerce was officially tolerated throughout this period, and indeed for many centuries to come.

Opposition to the trade is nevertheless said to have been voiced by Emperor Susneyos (1607-1632). Before going to sleep he was in the habit, according to the Jesuit Azevedo, of being read to by one of his learned men, Aläqa Krestos. On one occasion the reading touched upon the orders which King João III of Portugal had given his viceroy João de Castro prohibiting him from selling slaves to Muslims or Turks. The Emperor, impressed with his command (which coincided so closely with the *Fethä Nägäst*), immediately commanded that his subjects should have no dealings in slaves with either of these groups. He subsequently went even further, for he executed a rich Muslim trader found guilty of exporting slaves from Enarya, and had his head stuck on a pole in the market-place as a warning to others. Susneyos's governors and ministers of the court were later summoned, and instructed, on pain of severe penalty, to enforce the law, as God, he said, wished to protect the unfortunate Ethiopians then being transported in large numbers to Arabia, India, Cairo and Constantinople.[4]

---

[3] Beckingham and Huntiungford (1961) I, 96, 248, 251, 315-7, 319, II, 408, 455, (1954) 64; Gaudefroy-Demombynes (1927) 16-7, 32; Baratti (1670) 21-2; Tellez (1710) 200.

[4] Beccari (1903-17) XI, 421.

X

WOMEN

Ethiopian women, as we know from later times, played a major rôle in agriculture, handicrafts and trade, but their involvement in these fields is poorly documented for the Middle Ages. The records of this period nevertheless provide valuable glimpses of a number of women's domestic activities, as well as of their role in government, their clothing and jewellery, and their status in and out of marriage.

Grinding of Grain, Baking of *Enjära*, Cooking, Water-Carrying and Clothes-Washing

Women spent a large part of their time in and around the kitchen, and were actively involved in the grinding of grain as well as in cooking. Grinding, which was carried out entirely by hand and required "much labour", was exclusively "women's work," for, Almeida declares, "men, even slaves," would not undertake it "at any price." Flour was ground with the aid of two large grinding-stones: a roundish upper one, which the women manipulated by hand to crush the grain, and a wide lower one which rested on the ground. A woman could normally grind enough flour every day for 40 to 50 pieces of *enjära*, or pancake-bread. These were usually made more or less daily, because by the second day they were already dry, and were thereafter almost uneatable. Much flour was also utilised in the preparation of beer, which, Almeida says, "used up a great deal of meal."

Enjära, on the making of which women spent much time, was baked on wide earthenware pans, with lids of the same material. Bruce, who notes that they were "something less than three feet in diameter", subsequently wrote that they were fashioned out of "a light, beautiful potter's ware, which, although red when first made, turns to a glossy black colour after being greased with butter."

Cooking, which, as in most parts of the world, was also carried out solely by women, was likewise a "very great drudgery." It called for the service of "many slave women," as well as the consumption of "plenty of firewood."

Women, as Alvares observed at the Muslim village of Manadeley, in southern Tegré, were also much engaged in both the carrying of water and the washing of clothes.[1]

Camp-Followers

Innumerable women invariably accompanied the court and army. Emperor Lebnä Dengel's camp, according to Alvares, thus included many camp-followers, mainly women, who carried "pots for making wine and porringers for drinking," and was also the site of numerous tents assigned to the " kitchens and cooks", as well as

---

[1] Beckingham and Huntingford (1961), I, 251, (1954) 62-4; Bruce (1790) IV, 223.

to the *Amaritas*, or courtesans, who may be considered the Ethiopian equivalent of Japanese *geisha* girls.

Confirmation of the vast number of women to be found with the army was provided a century or so later by Almedia who believed that there were actually "more women than men in the camp." The Emperor was thus accompanied, he says, not only by the Queen, but also by "nearly all" the ladies of the court, "widows, married ladies and even many unmarried ones," as well as by the "wives of the chief lords and captains." Each of the ordinary soldiers likewise took with him at least one woman, and often several.

Such camp-followers had numerous duties. These included the grinding of flour and the baking of *enjära*, as well as the preparation and transportation of *ṭäj*, or mead, for the nobility, and *ṭälla*, or beer, for the soldiery. Many women also carried grinding stones, no fewer than three thousand of which, Almeida believed, might be taken on a single expedition, as well as large jars of honey for the making of *ṭäj*. Other women again served as tapsters, and had a busy time, for supplies of the drink were so quickly exhausted that "many" were constantly engaged in preparing fresh supplies. The *enjära*-makers attached to the army also had much to do, as each of them when travelling had, Bruce says, to carry a large baking pan on her back.[2]

Involvement in Government

Besides accompanying rulers on expeditions wives, and to some extent other female relatives, often played an important role in government, in numerous instances by moderating between the monarch and his chiefs and subjects. One of the most remarkable - if far from typical - cases of women's involvement in government was during the reign of Emperor Zär'ä Ya'qob (1434-1468), who, dissatisfied with the male officials he had earlier appointed, later set up a virtually entirely women's administration. The two principal officers of State, who replaced a kind of grand inquisitor considered unfaithful, were the monarch's two daughters, Mädhen Zämäda and Berhan Zämädä. The provincial administration was likewise entrusted to at least nine princesses who were respectively appointed governors of Tegré, Angot, Bägémder, Amhara, Damot, Šäwa, Gedem, Gañ and Ifat.[3]

Provincial Capitals and Trade

Large numbers of women congregated at provincial capitals. At Debarwa for example Alvares estimated that "a great part" of the 300 or so households were composed of women. Their number was so great in part because courtiers, soldiers and petitioners never came without their wives, and in part because some of the male inhabitants were so rich that, though Christians, they each kept two or three wives. The citizens in consequence included "many young women," for the most married women. There were, however, also a number of older women who earned their living,

---

[2] Beckingham and Huntingford (1961) I, 320, II, 437, **443**, (1954) 78-81; Bruce (1790) IV, 223.

[3] Perruchon (1893) 9-10, 13-4, 95.

as we have seen, by measuring wheat and salt in the market for visiting merchants, and also looked after unsold wares left over from one market day to another.

Women also themselves participated extensively in trade. Not untypical perhaps was a "sizeable village" near Lämalmo which consisted, according to Almeida, "almost entirely of market-women."[4]

Marriage, Divorce, and the Position of Wives

Christian marriage imposed certain obligations on women who were expected to obey their husbands as Sara in Biblical times had "obeyed Abraham, calling him lord."[5] This duty was enunciated in the *Fethä Nägäst* which also quoted the injunction of St. Paul:

"Wives, submit yourselves unto your husbands, as unto the Lord.
"For the husband is the head of the wife, even as Christ is the head of the church.....
"Therefore as the church is subject unto Christ, so let the wives be to their own husbands in everything."[6]

On the basis of this text the Ethiopian legal code instructed women to be "subject to their husband as to the Lord."

Marriage, though deeply influenced by Christian teaching, was essentially secular, and marriage contracts (except for a small minority of the population who took Communion with their marriage) were easily dissoluble. The two parties moreover tended to preserve their individual identities, wives keeping their pre-marital names, rather than adopting those of their husbands.

Among the higher classes furthermore it was customary for husbands and wives to retain their own property. This was especially the case among nobles and noblewomen whose lands after marriage were kept "wholly separate," so that neither party, Almeida says, would "interfere" with or give orders about what belonged to the other. Each spouse would likewise have his or her own servants, so that "neither the kitchen nor the table" was "common to both." If husband and wife ate together - in all probably accompanied by their respective servants and retainers - each would indeed bring their own food to the dining table.

Most marriages, particularly among the aristocracy, could easily be dissolved. This freedom, which contrasted with the then extreme rigidity of marriage in Europe, disconcerted observers such as Alvares who explains, with indignation, that spouses recognised from the outset that their marriages might only be temporary. Among persons of substance the two partners, he says, would thus enter into contracts, stating for instance, "If you leave me or I you, whichever causes the separation shall pay such

---

[4] Beckingham and Huntingford (1961) I, 105, (1954) 41.

[5] I, Peter, 3, 6.

[6] Ephesians, 5, 22-4.

and such a penalty." The amount to be forfeited would thus be laid down in terms of so much gold or silver, so many mules, cows, or goats, so much cloth, so many measures of corn. If either party separated he or she would, however, immediately seek to find a justification, so that "few", he believed, ever incurred the specified penalty: husbands and wives, he exclaims, therefore separated whenever they pleased. The gist of this account was later confirmed by Almeida who claims that both sides entered into marriage with the "tacit or expressed agreement" to dissolve it "as soon as" they "disagreed with one another."

The break-up of marriages was due, according to Almeida, either to one party's unfaithfulness or to "quarrels between the two." Conjugal disputes, however, were often "easily reconciled", for if either side proved to the other that adultery had been committed, they were "most often reconciled and became friends", provided, however, that "one of them paid the other out of his or her property." In cases of adultery they would thus "easily agree" that the guilty should pay the other "some oxen, cows, mules, pieces of cloth, etc."

Marriages usually broke up when the two parties became "so disgusted with each other" and quarreled so much that they wished to "separate entirely." The wife would then leave home, and place herself in the keeping of a judge. The two parties would duly appear before him, and he would either reconcile or divorce them. If he thought so fit, he might give sentence that "as they quarrel and have no affection for each other, she is free from such a husband and he is without obligation to such a wife, and that they can marry again whomsoever they please." Almeida, who considered this an "abuse" of marriage as he conceived it, notes that the possibility of divorce had "lasted for so many hundreds of years and was so rooted" that it was "a great obstacle" to the Jesuit missionary activity in which he was involved.

Despite such freedom, divorce among the population at large was not nearly as common as the above remarks may suggest. The peasantry, who constituted the vast mass of the population, had in particular "affection for their wives, Alvares says, if only because they brought up their livestock, as well as their children, worked with them in the fields, and at night when they returned from work provided them with a welcome. Many peasants therefore "married for the whole of their lives." Among the clergy marriage was likewise virtually permanent, for priests, who after ordination could not marry again, almost "never" separated from their wives.

Divorce, on the other hand, was widespread among the well-to-do. Alvares cites the case of a certain Ababitay, who had been married to seven wives, three of whom were still alive. Nobody objected to this, he says, except the Church, which had withheld the sacraments until the man had put away two of his spouses, retaining only his latest, the youngest. After this, to Alvares's surprise, Ababitay had been allowed into church like anyone else. Divorce in "high society," and especially among royalty, was even more frequent. One example the Portuguese priest reported was that of Emperor Lebnä Dengel's sister Romanä Wärq who was openly separated from her first husband, and living with her second husband Abuquer, the defrocked prelate referred to in a previous chapter.

Divorce among aristocracy and royalty was often accompanied by the payment of penalties. Not untypical was the case of Bahr Nägaš Dori who had separated from his spouse, to whom he had paid a penalty of 100 *wäqet*, or ounces, of gold, after

70

which he had married another wife from whom he also soon separated. She had then married his brother, who, in turn, soon left her and married another woman. Alvares, who reports this marital merry-go-round, comments that such events were not uncommon, and that no one should be "amazed," for such was "the custom of the country."[7]

Relations with the Church, Circumcision, and Scarification

Despite the prominence given to the "maidens of Ṣeyon" in the coronation ceremonial at Aksum mentioned in an earlier chapter, women were not only barred, as in other Christian countries, from the priesthood, but suffered from other disabilities. They were prohibited from entering the precincts of great monasteries (which also excluded cows, she-mules, hens, and "anything else", as Alvares says, that was female), and at the time of menstruation were not allowed to enter any place of worship.

Though underprivileged in matters relating to the Church, women played an important rôle in certain rituals, most notably circumcision, which, Ludolf noted, was normally practiced by "some poor woman or other". This was later confirmed by Bruce who stated that the surgeon, "generally" a female, effected the operation with "a sharp knife, or razor." In the case of the Fälaša, however, they sometimes used a sharp stone, or even "the nails of their little fingers" which were allowed to grow to "an inordinate length."

Female circumcision, which was likewise carried out by women, was also widely practiced, as recorded by Ludolf who recalls that it was a subject on which his Ethiopian priestly informant Gregory was "somewhat asham'd to discourse."

Scarification, which was likewise carried out by women, was also widespread, and took the form of making ornamental cuts on the face, most often on the nose, between the eyes or in their corners. Women, Alvares declares, were "very skilful" at this work which they did by placing a clove of garlic on the skin, cutting around it with a sharp knife, and widening the cut with their fingers. The wound would then be covered with a paste made from wax, and another of dough, after which it would be bandaged with cloth for the night, leaving a mark like a burn which endured for life.[8]

Clothing and Hair-Styles

Women's clothing varied greatly, on the basis of age, marital status, and wealth. Married women tended to cover themselves in cloth, whereas unmarried girls, according to Alvares, left the tops of their bodies bare, though they decorated them "gaily" with "little beads." Some women, on the other hand, wore sheepskins, which, as we have seen, often covered little more than one shoulder. Women of the aristocracy, on the other hand, wore many silk and other fine clothes, and considered

---

[7] Paulos Tsadua (1968) 80; Beckingham and Huntingford (1954) 65-6, (1961) I, 91, 105, 107-8.

[8] Beckingham and Huntingford (1961) I, 91, 110-1, (1954) 62; Ludolf (1684) 242; Bruce (1790) III, 341.

it necessary whenever possible to envelop themselves in "a great deal of cloth and silk." Women of royalty, whose finery attracted the especial attention of foreign visitors, were even more exquisitely dressed. Empress Säblä Wängél, whom the Portuguese met during the fighting with Grañ, was thus "all covered to the ground with silk," and was accompanied, according to Castanhoso, by a number of men who carried "a silk canopy that covered her and her mule." The Bahr Nägaš, whose country she was traversing, walked on foot beside her, naked to the waist, with a lion's skin on his shoulders, and his right.arm exposed, as he led her by the bridle, for it was the custom "whenever the Preste or his Queen makes a state entry, for the lord of the land to lead them... as a sign of submission". Two lords "like marquises" also walked beside her, holding her mule, while her ladies-in-waiting "muffled in their cloaks" rode nearby.

Many poorer women by contrast had only one piece of clothing, i.e. either a smock or a wrap, while the very poor made do with hides or skins. Such apparel was widely worn in Gojjam and Dämbeya, even by those who were not very poor, while the women of Tegré used shawls of sheep's or goat's skin which were, however, so badly tanned, Almeida says, that they resembled rough hair-shirts.

Women's hair was often arranged with considerable care, and was combed, according to Alvares, in two main styles, short and long. In the one it came down to the ears; in the other to the shoulders. It was often neatly plaited, and, Almeida says, not infrequently cooled, and disinfected, by the application of unrefined butter.[9]

---

[9] Beckingham and Huntingford (1961) I, 171, 253, (1954) 60-1; Whiteway (1902) 17-9.

PART TWO

THE GONDÄR PERIOD

Virgin and Child, an illustration from an 18th century volume of the Legends of Mary. Note representation of the patron for whom the work was produced at foot of painting. From the Bibliothèque Nationale, Paris, Ethiopien-Abbadie, 102.

INTRODUCTION

The establishment in 1636 of the great city of Gondär, the first truly fixed capital since early medieval. times, was an important "turning-point" in Ethiopian history. Gondär, which emerged as the country's political, religious, commercial and cultural centre, acquired a substantial urban population which was estimated by the Scottish traveller James Bruce in the late eighteenth century at no less than "ten thousand families," the equivalent, we may assume, of some 60,000 inhabitants.[1]

The rise of Gondär, in the late seventeenth century, witnessed a notable renaissance of Ethiopian civilisation which had an impact in and around the city on people in all walks of life.

The second half of the eighteenth century, however, marked the beginning of a time of decline in the country's fortunes. The ensuing period, a time of disunity, civil war and in some ways cultural regression, came to be known in Ethiopia as the era of the *mäsafent*, or judges, for it was thought to resemble that described in the Book of Judges, XXI, 25, when "there was no king in Israel: every man did that which was right in his eyes."

Notwithstanding the dissolution of the centralised State, as represented by the monarchy, the Ethiopian Church remained an important unifying factor in the highlands - and much of the country's social life continued as before.

A glimpse of 17th and 18th century Gondär, from an engraving in T. Waldmeier, *The Autobiography of Ten Years in Abyssinia* (London and Leominster, 1886).

---

[1] Bruce (1790) III, 380.

የይ.ም.ረ.ምጸፕ.ጸፕ.ኩኖ.እንደኪፈ.ሰመ

አዘዘረ.ው.ኩ.ልሳን.ከሱ.እን
ጋድቀ.ንበ.ኑ.ልቲ.ስብእ.ወ
ክልኢ.እ.ሞታ.ስ.ዕብራ.ኒ.ዋህ
ድቶ.ሶብ.እ.ም.ድ.ሳ.ረ.አ.ደ.ዑ.ወጠ

ኑ.ሐኒ.ጸ.ል.ው.ል.ወ.ህሳ.ፈ.ድ.
ዝር.ዎ.ሙ.ስ.እ.ጽ.ራ.ር.የ.ክ.ሙ
ሐ.ሠ.ረ.እ.ክ.ል.እ.ም.ዓ.ው.ድ.
ወ.ከ.ሙ.በ.ን.ፋ.ክ.ጋ.ያ.ል.ደ.ዘ.ረ.ው.ሐ.ሙ

The Tower of Babel, an illustration inspired by the Gondär castles, from an 18th century Ethiopic Book of Hymns in the British Library, Orient 590.

76

I

THE PEASANTRY

The peasantry in the Gondär period, as previously, constituted by far the largest, as well as economically the most important, section of the population.

Commercialisation of Agriculture around Gondär

Peasant life over the centuries probably changed only slowly, but the development of Gondär in the seventeenth and eighteenth centuries resulted in a certain commercialisation of agriculture in the area around the metropolis. Wägära, to the north-east, was thus described by Bruce as the "granary" of Gondär, while the district of "Chagassa," three hour's journey away, was "rich and well cultivated" for it depended on the capital, "the mart of its produce."

The Agäws south of Lake Tana, some of whom came a distance of a hundred miles, likewise arrived in the metropolis, sometimes "a thousand and fifteen hundred at a time," with cattle, honey, butter, wheat, hides, wax and other commodities. The Scotsman on one occasion passed a troop of Agäws near "Dinglebar," west of the lake, who were laden with honey, butter and untanned hides, and taking with them 800 head of cattle, all bound for the Gondär market. There was even some production of grapes for the city, notably in the regions of Drida and Karutta on the borders of Bägémder.[1]

Agricultural Production and Tribute

Notwithstanding some commercialisation in the Gondär area, there is no evidence of any significant change in farming techniques in the Ethiopian post-medieval period, certainly nothing comparable to the Agricultural Revolution then underway in Europe. One of the results of this was that foreign perceptions of Ethiopian agriculture inevitably changed. The French traveller Charles Poncet, writing at the close of the seventeenth century, was the last outside observer to write with enthusiasm of the Ethiopian agricultural scene. He exclaimed that the land was "so well cultivated" that there seemed no waste ground at all. "There is no country," he added, "better peopled or more fertile than Aethiopia. All the fields, and even the mountains (of which there are a great number) are well cultivated."

Bruce, looking at the situation three-quarters of a century later as a Scottish country squire, took a different view. Much more concerned than his predecessors with the commercially all-important question of productivity, he was far less impressed with Ethiopian farming. The peasantry in Bägémder, he reckoned, obtained no more than twenty-fold crop-yields, while in Tegré, where the land was less fertile, it was a "good harvest" which produced a nine-fold one, and ten-fold yields were "scarcely ever" obtained.

---

[1] Bruce (1790) III, 191-2, 195, III, 253, 284, 335, 394, 736, IV, 27; Jones (1788) **384**.

The peasantry, as in the past, moreover faced numerous disabilities. Many farmers had to contribute half their produce to landlords who in return furnished them with seed, but Bruce observed that it was "a very indulgent master" who did not also take "another quarter" for the risk he had run, so that the quantity that was retained by the husbandman was "not more than sufficient to afford sustenance for his wretched family." The peasants suffered furthermore from "the greatest" of all plagues, namely "bad government," which, the Scottish traveller argued, speedily destroyed all the advantages the peasants reaped from favourable climate and soil.[2]

A ploughing scene, from an 18th century Ethiopic Miracles of Mary in the British Library, Orient 24,188. Note the humped cattle and the traditional Ethiopian plough.

Abundance of Cattle

Notwithstanding reservations about productivity there was still no gainsaying the abundance of livestock. In Wägära, for example, Bruce saw "vast flocks of cattle of all kinds," mostly black, with "large and beautiful horns, exceedingly wide, and bosses upon their back like camels." Gojjam was likewise "full of great herds... the largest in the high parts of Abyssinia," while of Halay, in Tegré, he wrote: "All sorts of cattle are here in plenty; cows for the most part completely white, with large dewlaps hanging down to their knees, their heads, horns and hoofs perfectly well-turned; the

---

[2] Foster (1949 111, 127; Bruce (1790) III, 124.

78

horns wide... and their hair like silk." The herdsmen for the most part allowed their cattle to "roam at discretion through the mountains," but at times improved their pastures by setting fire to the grass and brushwood before the rains which produced an "amazing verdure."[3]

Tribute in Cattle

Considerable tribute in cattle continued to be collected throughout the early Gondarine period. The Armenian merchant Murad reported in 1696-7 that the tax on Agäwmeder, a district within easy access of the capital, yielded as many as 100,000 cattle a year. This tribute, however, subsequently decreased, after the decline of the realm, so that by the 1770's Bruce reported that the area provided the monarch with no more than 1,000 or 1,500 cattle annually.

Tribute in livestock was also despatched from other areas, including Wälqayt in Tegré and Hamasén in the far north. A competition which was to be remembered two hundred years later took place at some unspecified date in the eighteenth century, while the monarchy was still powerful, as to which of these two districts could contribute the largest tax. Däjazmač Nayzgi of Wälqayt supplied a large number of white, black and red cattle - but Däjazmač Mammo of Hamasén outshone him because he brought in addition a considerable quantity of gold, apparently obtained from trade passing through his district on the route to the coast. How the tax burden was divided between individual peasants is not, however, recorded.[4]

The Effects of War

The peasantry in the second half of the eighteenth century suffered frequently from the ravages of civil war. Bruce, who accompanied the army of Emperor Täklä Haymanot in 1770, describes many a scene of devastation. On approaching the Blue Nile, through which the soldiers of Ras Mika'él Sehul had passed, he found that "all the country was forsaken; the houses uninhabited, the grass trodden down, and the fields without cattle. Everything that had life and strength fled before that terrible leader, and his no less terrible army; a profound silence was in the fields around us, but no marks as yet of desolation." It was, however, not long before such signs were seen, and on the following page he records that on proceeding a little further he found "the houses all reduced to ruins, and smoking like so many kilns; even the grass, or wild oats, which were grown very high, were burnt in long plots of a hundred acres altogether; every thing bore the marks that Ras Mika'él was gone before, whilst not a living creature appeared in those extensive, fruitful, and once well-inhabited plains. An awful silence reigned everywhere around."[5]

Such scenes of destruction, it may be assumed, were by no means rare.

---

[3] Bruce (1790) III, 82-3, 125, 191, 196, 256.

[4] Van Donzel (1979) 94; Bruce (1813) VII, 90; Kolmodin (1912-15) 60-2.

[5] Bruce (1790) III, 434-5.

II

THE SOLDIERS

The rise, and subsequent decline, of Gondär had significant implications for the soldiery. The ensuing period witnessed constant struggles between the feudal lords, as well as frequent civil war. Large armies paying allegiance to a single monarch, as seen in the medieval period, were superseded by the smaller forces of provincial chiefs. The soldier's armament was also changing, for ever increasing numbers of fire-arms were being imported - and more of the palace guards were supplied with armour.

An Ethiopian rifleman kneels to fire. From an early 18th century manuscript Book of Prayers, now housed in the Institute of Ethiopian Studies, IES 315.

Size of the Army

At the close of the eighteenth century Iyasu I, the last of the great Gondarine emperors, is said by Poncet to have still had an "almost infinite number of feudatories." He could therefore raise "powerful armies," in "a short time" and at "a small expense," and was reported to have commanded a force in 1699 of no less than "between four and five hundred thousand strong." By the second half of the eighteenth century, however, Bruce was informed by the oldest officers at Gondär that the largest army remembered to have been in the field was a rebel army at Sarbakusa in 1771 which amounted to only about 50,000 men, and later "increased to above 60,000 men; cowards and brave, old and young, veteran soldiers and blackguards." Ras Mika'él, the seemingly all-powerful ruler of Tegré, was later reported to have brought with him a force of no more than "20,000 men," albeit "incomparably the best soldiers in the empire," with which he temporally subdued all his enemies.

The number of fire-arms on the other hand was substantially increasing. There were, by the late eighteenth century, Bruce calculated, as many as 7,000 muskets in the country, almost five times as many as Almeida had estimated a century and a half earlier. No less than 6,000 of these were in the possession of the soldiers of Tegré, which was not surprising as it was the province nearest the coast, with easiest access to imports from abroad. The soldiers of Tegré therefore included many men "very expert" in the use of match-locks.[1]

Royal Guardsmen

Despite the decline of central authority the Emperor's personal guards remained at times an important force. They consisted in Bruce's day of four regiments which were named after "houses", apparently buildings at Gondär to which they were attached. These included the *Anbäsa Bét*, or Lion House, the *Jan Bét*, or Elephant House, and the *Wärq Säqäla*, or House of Gold. Each regiment was commanded by a *šaläqa*, or colonel, and lesser officers in charge of respectively one hundred, fifty and twenty guardsmen. Every force was supposed to be composed of 2,000 men, but in fact usually amounted to only about 1,600. These soldiers, whose officers were "all foreigners," depended directly on the monarch from whom they received "great privileges," and, when their imperial master was powerful, would greatly "oppress the country." The guards, some 500 of whom were horsemen, possessed a total of about 2,000 muskets.

The royal cavalry, as we shall see, included two or three hundred "black soldiers," i.e. Šanqella, from the west of the capital. They wore coats-of-mail, and the faces of their horses were protected with plates of brass with sharp iron spikes about five inches in length which stuck out of their forehead. The horses' bridles were made of iron chains, and the body of the steed was covered with a kind of thin quilt stuffed with cotton, with two openings into which the rider put his thighs and legs, and which covered him nearly to his ankle. The stirrups were of the Turkish or Moorish type

---

[1] Foster (1949) 126, 129; Bruce (1790) III, 308, IV, 63, 11o.

St. George and the Dragon, showing the Ethiopian artist's conception of horseman's garb and horse decorations, from an 18th century manuscript of Prayers of Mary in the Institute of Ethiopian Studies. IES 73

which held the whole foot, rather than only one or toes as was then normal in Ethiopia. The "only hold" which the traditional stirrups provided was in fact "the outside of an iron ring", which they "grasped between their great and second toe", so that "they had no strength from their stirrups", while their foot was "always swelled", and their toes became "sore and galled." The new-fangled stirrups, by contrast, were hung high, enabling the horseman to raise himself up easily, and "stand as firmly as if he were upon plain ground." The saddles were likewise high in front and behind, as was customary also among the Moors.

Each rider was armed with a fourteen foot long lance with which he charged. It was made of "very light wood, brought from the Banks of the [Blue] Nile, with a small four-edged head, and the but end balanced by a long spike of iron." This spear was kept in a leather case which was fastened to the saddle by a thong. The horseman was also equipped with a small axe which he would keep in his saddle. His head would often be protected with a copper or tin helmet, with large crests of black horse tail, and a coat-of-mail type vizier which covered the face as far as the nose. Officers' helmets bore silver stars with yellow hair interspersed with the black.

These royal horsemen were so powerful, Bruce claims, that they could cut through "all the cavalry in Abyssinia." This was because every guardsman "sat immovable upon his saddle," and, thanks to the type and positioning of his stirrups, was "perfectly master of his person." The ordinary Ethiopian horsemen on the other hand were "most disadvantageously" equipped, for their heads and bodies were unprotected, their saddles were small and had "no support to them," while their stirrup-leathers were too long, and the riders, having no stirrups in which they could put their entire foot, were constantly afraid of their horse falling upon them.[2]

Mobilisation

The soldiers of the Gondarine monarchy were mobilised according to a well-established routine, first noticed by Poncet, whereby the monarch before beginning a campaign proclaimed the day of his departure, and ordered his tents "to be pitched in a great plain" within sight of the city. He then spent "three days in making a review," after which he undertook his campaign which, however, never lasted "above three months."

Three proclamations were usually made before the monarch marched. The first, Bruce recalls, was, "Buy your mules, get ready your provisions, and pay your servants, for, after such a day, they that seek me here, shall not find me." The second, generally made a week or so later, was, "Cut down the Kantuffa in the four corners of the world, for I do not know where I am going." The *kantuffa* was a tree with thorns which was liable to become caught in the soldiers' clothing. The third, and last, proclamation was, "I am encamped upon the Angrab, or Kahha [i.e. the two rivers around Gondär]; he that does not join me there, I will chastise him for seven years." The Scotsman was "long in doubt" as to reason for this mention of "seven years," until he recollected the Jubilee year of the Jews, for whom "seven years was a prescription for debts and all trespasses."

---

[2] Bruce (1790) III, 310-1, IV, 116-8.

Another proclamation cited by Bruce paid considerable attention to the soldiers' obligation to bring provisions, and declared: "That all those who had flour or barley in quantities, should bring it that very day to a fair market, on pain of having their houses plundered, and that all people, soldiers, or others, who attempted by force to take any provisions without having first paid for them in ready money, should be hanged on the spot."[3]

Camp-Followers

The soldiers of Gondarine times were accompanied, like those of the past, by numerous camp-followers of both sexes. They would include "women bearing provisions, horns of liquor, and mills for grinding corn upon their backs; idle women of all sorts ... mounted upon mules; and men driving mules loaded with baggage." Bruce, who on one occasion saw a force of 30,000 soldiers accompanied by as many as 10,000 women, says that the throng "presented such a tumultuous appearance" that it "surpassed all description."

The period of the *mäsafent*, in the second half of the eighteenth century, was one, as already suggested, of extensive warfare. This fighting seriously impoverished many areas, not least, the German explorer Edouard Rüppell noted, the province of Bägémder in which Gondär was situated. This was later confirmed by Menilek's chronicler, Gäbrä Sellasé, who states that as a result of the fighting all the province's cattle were killed and its ploughs burnt.[4]

Taking of Trophies

Fighting was not infrequently followed by acts of castration. Victorious soldiers, to show their prowess, would later take the foreskins they had cut, and display them as trophies before their commander, who was in many cases the monarch. himself. Such ceremonies, the chronicles reveal, were particularly frequent during the seventeenth and eighteenth centuries, notably during the reign of the great warrior Emperor Iyasu I (1682-1706), and were on occasion attended at Gondär by the redoubtable Empress Mentewwab, her son Emperor Iyasu II (1730-1755) and her grandson Iyo'as (1755-1769). The subsequent annals for 1769 likewise record, that, at the close of a successful battle, the warriors of Tegré threw down their trophies in front of Emperor Täklä Haymanot. They were so numerous, it is reported, that they "resembled a heap of grain in the fields of a rich man." The royal princesses and serving women marvelled, the chronicle claims, and "cried, in great astonishment, 'What is this?' as if they did not know, though they well knew."[5]

---

[3] Foster (1949) 129; Bruce (1790) III, 311, IV, 71.

[4] Bruce (1790) IV, 120-1; Rüppell (1838-40) II, 385; Guèbrè Sellassié (1830-1) I, 201,

[5] Guidi (1903) 181, 186, 224, 240, 258, (1912) 86, 154, 191, 195, 206; Weld Blundell (1922) 208-9.

Divination

Divination, Bruce suggests, was not infrequently practiced. It was, he claims, usually carried out with the help of a serpent which would be taken from its hole, and offered butter and milk, of which it was "exceedingly fond". If the creature failed to eat, ill-fortune was supposed to be "near at hand". Before an attack by a hostile army, serpents, it was further held, would disappear, and would nowhere be found. This belief was so firmly held, according to the Scotsman, that Fasil, the "cunning governor" of Gojjam, would "never mount his horse, or go from his home, if an animal of this kind, which he had in his keeping, refused to eat."[6]

St. Fasilädäs (*left*) and St. George (*right*), showing the two different types of stirrups known in Gondär in this period: one holding two toes, the other the whole foot. From an 18th century Miracles of Mary, in the Bibliothèque Nationale, Paris, Ethiopien-Abbadie 222.

---

[6] Bruce (1790) III, 733–4.

III

THE NOBILIITY

The nobles in the early Gondär period were, as in the past, almost entirely subordinate to the Emperor whose "great power" arose from the fact, the French traveller Poncet noted, that he was "absolute master of all the wealth of his subjects." Every "feudatory" under his command was therefore "obliged" to serve him in time of war at his own expenses and to furnish him with soldiers in proportion to the estate he gives. Whence it comes that this prince, who has an almost infinite number of feudatories, can in a short time and at a small expense raise powerful armies." Such "feudatories", according to the Frenchman, when appointed, were given a sign of office, which consisted of a headband of taffeta, bearing the name of the then monarch, i.e. Iyasus I, and his title "Emperour of Aethiopia, of the Tribe of Judah, who has always vanquished his enemies."

The rise of Gondär was followed in the fullness of time, as we have seen, by the decline of the monarchy. This enabled the nobles in the second half of the eighteenth century to usurp most of the power hitherto wielded by the sovereign. Several provincial chiefs became virtually independent, and established dynasties of their own. Nominally, however, emperors continued to reign - and, though little more than puppets of one provincial ruler or another, were treated, as in the past, with considerable ceremonial deference.

Because of the decline of the monarchy some of the more independent chieftains, however, were reluctant to humble themselves in the traditional manner before their by now only nominal overlord. Bruce, who took a royal message to the governor of Amhara, Däjazmač Gošu, recalls that the chief duly rose, and, "stripping himself bare to the waist," made a deep bow, so that his forehead touched the couch on which he sat, but "did not, as was his duty, stand on the ground, and touch it with his forehead". "Pride and newly-acquired independence" had thus "released him from those forms, in the observance of which he had been brought up from childhood."

Notwithstanding the relaxation of such observances the nobles of the period of the *mäsafent* maintained, and even strengthened, their own claims of superiority over the common people. Lords would appear before their vassals, Bruce says, like monarchs of yore with their head and mouth covered, nothing to be seen of them but their eyes.[1]

The Chiefs of Bägémder, Tegré, Gojjam and Šäwa

The principal noblemen of highland Ethiopia in this period were the rulers of Bägémder and Tegré who vied with each other in controlling the destiny of the Ethiopian state. The chiefs of Gojjam and Šäwa by contrast were then of only subsidiary importance.

---

[1] Foster (1949) 126;Bruce (1790) IV, 178, 204-5.

The significance of Bägémder lay in the fact that it surrounded the capital, Gondär, which thus depended on it for most of its provisions. The city, the country's main urban centre, was thus politically and economically at the mercy of the province's ruler. The result, according to Bruce, was that the government of Bägémder was entrusted to "none but noblemen of rank, family, and character", who were "able to maintain a large number of troops."[2]

Medallion-styled portrait of Ras Mika'él Sehul, the 18th century ruler of Tegré, an engraving from J. Bruce, *Travels to Discover the Source of the Nile* (Edinburgh, 1790).

Tegré, the oldest province in the empire, was at this time steadily resuming its ancient commercial and political importance. One of the principal reasons for this was that the region's relative proximity to the coast gave its rulers comparatively easy access to fire-arms imported from abroad. Bruce, who was well aware of this development, which had taken place within the memory of his older informants, recalls

---

[2] Bruce (1790) III, 254.

that all Ethiopian exports bound for the Red Sea had to pass through Tegré whose governor therefore had virtually "the choice of all commodities" intended for export. These included "the strongest male, the most beautiful female slaves, the purest gold" and the largest tusks of ivory. The control exercised by the ruler of Tegré over the import trade was, however, even more significant, for, Bruce explains:

> "Fire-arms ... which for many years have decided who is the most powerful in Abyssinia, all ... come from Arabia, and not one can be purchased without his knowing to whom it goes, and after having had the first refusal of it."[3]

Access to fire-arms contributed greatly to the rise of Ras Mika'él Sehul, the first of the great rulers of Tegré, who, extending his power westwards across the Täkkäzé river, made himself for a time the *de facto* ruler of Gondär.

Gojjam, though culturally no less important than the other provinces, was largely isolated from them by the great arm of the Blue Nile, and therefore had only tenuous links with Gondär and the main import trade routes. The rulers of the province were therefore seldom able to exercise any very decisive influence on state affairs.

Šäwa, though still nominally part of the empire, was by this time virtually independent. It was ruled by its own dynasty which had been founded, towards the close of the seventeenth century, by a local chieftain Abéto Nägassi. Contact with the northern provinces was restricted, Bruce insists, because the area had been cut off from them by the advance of the Gallas, or Oromos. Amha Iyäsus, the then ruler of Šäwa, was, however, a "loyalist," and a "friend to the monarchy," for "upon any signal distress happening to the king," he "never failed to succour him powerfully with gold and troops, far beyond the quota formerly due from his province."[4]

---

[3] Bruce (1790) III, 251-2.

[4] Abir (1968) 30-1; Bruce (1790) III, 255-6.

IV

THE MONARCH

Gondär and the Period of the *Mäsafent*

The Gondarine monarchy reached its zenith in the second half of the seventeenth century, during the reign of Iyasu I (1682-1706), the greatest of the Gondarine emperors. After his death, however, the powers of the monarch rapidly declined - though Emperor Bäkaffa (1721-1730) was said by Bruce to have temporarily "saved" the country from "aristocratical or democratical usurpation" by eliminating "the greatest part" of the local nobility. In the mid-eighteenth century, however, the Gondär monarchy finally disintegrated: the area under centralised rule contracted, and the nobles usurped much of the powers formerly wielded by the monarch. Emperors became little more than the puppet rulers.

Representation of Emperor Yekuno Amlak (1270-85) waited upon by Muslim ambassadors and slaves, from an early 18th century Ethiopian manuscript in the British Library, Orient 503.

Despite this decline many of the monarch's prerogatives appear to have been preserved. The emperors, as the very detailed chronicles of this period reveal, were, thus, as in the past, constantly appointing, dismissing or confirming the position of provincial governors and other officials. The practice of keeping the sovereign aloof from the court, let alone from the common people, was likewise retained. The King, Bruce explained, thus "sat constantly in a room of his palace, which communicated with the audience and council [chamber] by two folding doors or large windows, the bottom of which were about three steps from the ground. These doors, or windows, were latticed with cross-bars of wood like a cage, and a thin curtain, or veil of taffety silk, was hung within it; so that, upon darkening the inner chamber, the King saw every person in the chamber without, while he himself was not seen at all."

Notwithstanding the fragmentation of the realm in the later Gondarine period the governorship of many of the lesser provinces was still allotted at the pleasure of the King - or, more often, of the provincial potentate who had usurped his power. Appointment was thus based on "favour," and was often given, Bruce snidely says, "to poor noblemen," so that, "by fleecing the people," they might "grow rich and repair their fortune."

Despite the decline in his importance, the emperor continued to be surrounded with much pomp and circumstance. When riding, or receiving visitors, his head, and brow, would be "perfectly covered," and he would often cover his mouth with a hand, so that nothing could be seen but his eyes. His feet, in the absence of shoes, were also "always covered."[1] Deference to the monarch continued to be paid by all classes. His subjects, whatever their rank, were expected to appear before him with their breasts uncovered," and, on approaching, had to make an "absolute prostration." Bruce, who had many opportunities to witness the custom, recalls:

"You first fall upon your knees, then upon the palms of your hands, then incline your head and body till your forehead touches the earth; and, in case you have an answer to expect, you lie in that posture till the King, or somebody from him, desires you to rise."[2]

Though even powerful nobles were expected to prostrate themselves in this traditional manner, the monarch might waive this obligation as a sign of special respect. One such occasion of which there is record was in 1770 when a prince from Šäwa arrived to present himself before Emperor Täklä Haymanot. Two noblemen, Bruce recalls, had been instructed to stop him from throwing himself on the ground. The young man "ran forward, stooping, to the foot of the throne, inclining his body lower and lower as he approached," but he was seized, "just before the act of prostration," and "prevented from kissing the ground." Seeing this he "suddenly seized the King's hand and kissed it." The monarch tried to resist this, but, failing to do so, turned his palm for kissing, which was considered "a great mark of familiarity and confidence."[3]

---

[1] Bruce (179) II, 607, III, 254, 271-2, 277.

[2] Bruce (1790) III, 270.

[3] Bruce (1790) IV, 93.

The Detention of Princes

The detention of princes was resumed after the move of the capital to the north-west of the country when unwanted members of the royal family, from the reign of Emperor Fasilädäs (1632-1667) onward, were placed on the tall mountain of Wehni which remained a prison throughout the Gondarine period.

The position of the royal prisoners varied greatly from one period to another. It appears to have been particularly good during the reign of Iyasu I who paid a visit of inspection to the mountain, and, finding that his unfortunate relatives were suffering deprivations, increased their revenues. Bruce claims that the detainees by his day were in receipt of 250 *wäqéts*, or ounces, of gold a year, and 730 pieces of cloth.[4]

Emperor Iyasu I (1682-1706), from an early 18th century Book of Prayers in the Institute of Ethiopian Studies, IES 315.

---

[4] Bruce (1790) II, 430, (1813) VII, 76.

Illustration showing a monarch riding a finely caparisoned horse, an attendant holding an umbrella, a symbol of great dignity, above him. Note the stirrup holding a single toe, the guards with their rifles held over their shoulders (right), and men with spears (left). From an 18th century Book of Prayers in the Institute of Ethiopian Studies, IES 315.

The *Kwer'atä re'esu*

The supposed sanctity of the Ethiopian monarchy - and of its army - found expression, throughout the Gondär period, in a revered icon of Christ with the Crown of Thorns. This painting, which was possibly of Venetian or Flemish origin and dated from around the early sixteenth century, was known in Ge'ez as the *Kwer'atä re'esu*, literally "the striking of His head", a reference to St. Matthew XVII, 30; "they smote him on the head". The icon was considered so holy that emperors, at least since the time of Yohannes I (1667-1682), often took it with them, together with a *tabot*, when they went on campaigns, and courtiers on at least one occasion swore their allegiance to their ruler in its name. During Iyasu II's disastrous expedition to Sennar in 1744 the *Kwer'atä re'esu* was captured by the enemy but was later returned, whereupon "all Gondar", Bruce says, was "drunk with joy". The prized icon remained in Ethiopian royal possession until 1868 when it was looted by the British after their capture of Emperor Téwodros's capital at Mäqdäla, and its whereabouts is currently unknown.[5]

---

[5] Bruce (1790) II 642; Pankhurst (1979a) 169-87.

V

THE CLERGY

Religious life in the country in general changed little during this period, but the rise of Gondär, and the subsequent decline of the monarchy, both had some significant repercussions.

The *Abun*, the *Ečägé*, the *'Aqabé Sä'at*, and the Monks

After the establishment of Gondär, the *Abun*, the *Ečägé* and the *'Aqabé Sä'at*, like the Emperor, took up residence in the new capital, and their power and influence became increasingly urban and metropolis-oriented. The *Abun*, who had formerly accompanied the monarch on his peregrinations to a series of moving capitals, now resided primarily at Gondär. He was the principal ecclesiastical resident of the city, and it was there that he exercised his influence over state affairs. His power, like that of the monarch, however, later declined, as noted by Bruce who states that the prelate's status by the late eighteenth century had "much fallen in esteem." This development, due primarily to the weakening of central State authority, was intensified by the then incumbent's own personality. Like his predecessors for the past half millennium he was an Egyptian Copt with only limited knowledge of the Ethiopian scene, and was poorly regarded on account of his "little intrigues, his ignorance, avarice, and want of firmness." The result was that he had "no share" in the secular government, and went to the palace only on church ceremonies, or when he had a favour to ask or a complaint to make.

The position of the *Abun* in the church establishment, however, was not impaired, for he continued to be responsible for the ordination of priests, deacons and monks. Huge ordination ceremonies were held as in the past. Abunä Marqos at the close of the seventeenth century told Poncet that at one ordination alone he had "made ten thousand priests and six thousand deacons." Such proceedings were exceedingly profitable, for each newly ordained priest was obliged, Bruce says, to present the *Abun* with a bar of salt.

The ordination of deacons and monks was also carried out on a mass scale. Bruce, who claims on one occasion to have seen the entire Bägémder army ordained as deacons, states that "a number of men and children" would present themselves before the Copt, but would stand at a distance, "from humility, not daring to approach him." The prelate would then ask who they were, and they would reply that they wished to become deacons. Holding "a small iron cross in his hand," he would then merely make two or three signs, and blow with his mouth "twice or thrice, upon them, saying, 'Let them be deacons.'"

The appointment of monks was not dissimilar. The *Abun* while riding about the countryside might thus be confronted by a large group of bearded men who would assemble within 500 yards, and "begin a melancholy song." On his asking who they were, they would answer that they wanted to become monks, whereupon he would likewise ordain them *en masse*.

The acquisition of an *Abun* from Egypt, as in the past, often presented difficulties. A particularly serious problem arose in 1754 when Emperor Iyasu II raised 450 *wäqéts*, or ounces, of gold to meet the cost, and entrusted them to messengers bound for Egypt who were, however, detained by the Na'ib, or local ruler of the port of Hergigo, until the governor of Tegré and the Bahr Nägaš intervened on the monarch's behalf. The messengers were duly released, but the *Abun* on eventually arriving at Hergigo was seized by the Na'ib, and only freed when the Emperor despatched an expedition to the coast.

The *Ečägé*, formerly the head of the monks of Däbrä Libanos, and, unlike the *Abun*, a native-born Ethiopian, was by this time also resident in Gondär. He was the most important Ethiopian ecclesiastic, and was so influential in the city that he was, in Bruce's opinion, of a person of "great consequence," particularly in "troublesome times."

The *'Aqabé Sä'at*, who also resided in the city, continued to be important in this period, Bruce describing him as still "the first religious officer at the palace." The then incumbent, Abba Sälama, seems to have benefited greatly from the growth of the metropolis, for he had "a very large revenue," and even "greater influence." Though "exceedingly rich", he led, the Scotsman claims, the "very worst life possible," for, though he had "taken the vows of poverty and chastity," he was said to have "seventy mistresses in Gondär." Rumour, cited by the not altogether always reliable Bruce, had it that he seduced his women, "not by gifts, attendance, or flattery, the usual means employed on such occasions," but "under pain of *excommunication*."

The rise of Gondär also increased the influence of the monks of Wäldebba, who, because of their relative proximity to the city, superseded in importance those of the old Šäwan monastery of Däbrä Libanos. The holy men of Wäldebba were thus held "in great veneration," and , Bruce says, were "believed to have the gift of prophecy." Some were said to work miracles, and were "very active instruments" in stirring up the citizens of Gondär in times of crisis.

Many of the monks of this period, as previously, had the reputation of being extremely ascetic. Those of Däbrä Bizän, for example, lived in caves, and, according to Poncet, ate no flesh, and were "constantly intent upon God and the meditation of holy things." One aged sixty-five had for the previous seven years lived only on wild olive leaves, a mortification which caused him to spit blood "which incommoded him very much".[1]

The Multitude of Churches and Deference paid to them

Notwithstanding some changes in the religious scene at Gondär and perhaps a few other urban centres, the country remained essentially rural - and abounded, as in the past, in innumerable village-based churches. Bruce, whose amazement at their numbers is reminiscent of that of Lobo a century and a half earlier, thus declared that there was "no country in the world" with "so many churches," and added: "Though the

---

[1] Guidi (1903) 127-30, 143-7; Foster (1949) 123, 152; Brucce (1790) II, 647, III, 177, 201, 317-9. Though most of the buildings of the Gondarine religious establishment have long since fallen into ruins that of the *Ečägé* remains, and is today registered as house number 001 in *kebele* 11.

An Ethiopian artist's impression of the clergy, from an 18th century Life, Passion and Death of Jesus Christ believed to have been owned by Empress Mentewwab, in the Institute of Ethiopian Studies, IES 75.

country is very mountainous, and consequently the view much obstructed, it is very seldom you see less than five or six churches, and, if you are on a commanding ground, five times that number."

The vast number of churches in the country was scarcely surprising, for no Christian settlement, he notes, was without at least one, while many others had been built, by the rulers or nobility, for reasons of piety, or prestige. Kings and queens would thus have them erected, and endowed, wherever they intended to be buried, and many nobles emulated this practice, for "every great man that dies thinks he has atoned for all his wickedness if he leaves a fund to build a church, or has built one in his lifetime."

Churches, as in the past, were regarded with great deference. Poncet felt that the Ethiopians had "more modesty and respect" for their places of worship than was common in Europe, and never entered them except with bare feet, for which reason church floors were usually covered with carpets. Church-goers moreover were very quiet: one never heard them speak a word, or blow their nose, or saw them turn their head to one side. When going to church they likewise always wore clean clothes, and would indeed otherwise be refused admission.

The emperors of this period, like their predecessors, were also assiduous church-goers. Iyasu I was described by Poncet as having "a great stock of piety," while Bruce records that Täklä Haymanot, the emperor of his time, went to church "regularly." On such occasions, whether or not there was a service in progress, he kissed the threshold and side-posts of the door and stooped before the altar.

The religious discipline of former times may, however, have been weakening, for though people entering church continued to take off their shoes, and kiss the threshold, Bruce noted that when leaving one's footwear behind it was necessary in his day to "leave a servant there with them" - for otherwise they might be stolen.[2]

Ṭemqät at Adwa

The seventeenth and eighteenth centuries witnessed the development not only of Gondär, but also of several regional capitals. One such was Adwa which had its own distinctive religious life. Though largely traditional, this was in some ways also characteristically urban. During the Ṭemqät, or Epiphany, celebrations of 1770 for example the stream between the town and the church, Bruce recalls, was dammed several days prior to the event so that the water reached a depth of three or four feet, and on the morning before the feast three large tents were pitched - one may presume, for each of the city's churches, the tabots or altar slabs of which would spend Ṭemqät in it. Priests and monks assembled around midnight, and began prayers and psalms by the waterside which continued until dawn when the local governor, Wäldä Mika'él, made his appearance, with all the great men of the town dressed for the occasion in their finest clothes.

---

[2] Bruce (1790) III, 265, 313, 315, 317; Foster (1949) 117, 138. Poncet (Foster, 1949) described Ethiopian churches as "very neat", and adds that they made extensive use of incense which was offered "almost continually during the Mass and offices."

As soon as the sun rose three priests dressed in sacerdotal vestments arrived carrying large wooden crosses which they dipped in the water while some members of the crowd prayed and others fired their guns in joy. (Few such imported weapons would have been seen a century or so earlier). The priests then returned from the stream, one of them carrying a chalice full of water which he brought to the governor, and, taking as much of it as he could hold in his hands, sprinkled it on the chief's head, and offered him the cup to drink. On receiving it back he gave the nobleman his blessing. The three crosses were then brought to Wäldä Mika'él who kissed them. The ceremony of sprinkling the water was then repeated for all the great men of the town, after which some was sprinkled on the rest of their party. Two or three hundred deacons - a much larger number than seen in village ceremonies - meanwhile plunged into the deepest part of the river, while their elders assembled around it, and water was poured over them, "at first decently enough by boys of the town, and those brought on purpose as deacons, but, after the better sort of people had received the aspersion, the whole was turned into a riot, the boys, muddying the water, threw it round them upon everyone they saw well-dressed or clean." The governor thereupon retreated, and was followed by others, including the monks. The crosses were later carried away, and the brook was left "in the possession of the boys and blackguards, who rioted there till two o'clock in the afternoon."[3]

Mourning Ceremonies

Ethiopian society devoted considerable attention to mourning the dead. "When any Aethiopian dies," the French traveller Poncet reported, "you hear on all sides most doleful howlings. All the neighbours assemble in the house of the person deceas'd, and join in their bewailings with the kindred they find there. They wash the corpse with particular ceremonies; and after having wrapped it up in a new winding-sheet of cotton, they place it in a coffin in the middle of the hall with flambeaus of wax. Then they redouble their weeping and crying, to the sound of little tabors [i.e. drums]. Some pray to God for the soul of the deceas'd; others recite verses to his praise, or tear their hair and scratch their faces, or burn their flesh with flambeaus, in token of their grief. This ceremony, which is both frightful and moving, continues until the religious come to take away the body. After having sung some psalms and made use of incense, they begin their procession, holding an iron cross in their right hands and a prayer book in the left. They carry the body, and sing psalms all the way. The relations and friends of the deceas'd follow, and continue their cries, with drumming on the tabors. They all have their heads shav'd, which is the badge of mourning... When they pass by any church, the procession stops and some prayers are said there; after which they go to the place of burial. There they renew again their oblations of incense. They sing awhile the psalms, with mournful note, and put the body into the ground."

The deaths of important personalities were, not surprisingly, the occasion of even greater mourning. "When a prince or some person of eminent quality dies", Poncet recalls, "the Emperour for three months withdraws himself from business, unless it be very pressing". On the death of the Abun in 1699 Emperor Iyasu was "inconsolable", the Frenchman records, and put on mourning, which, as in France, consisted of purple clothes, and wore them for six weeks, during the first two of which he "bewail'd" the

---

[3] Bruce (1790) III, 324-6. See also Pankhurst (1982) 319-20.

cleric twice a day.[4] When the monarch's son, Prince Fasilädas, subsequently died in 1700 mourning took place all over the country. Poncet, who was at Aksum when the news arrived, states that the Bahr Nägaš, or ruler of the north, "order'd it to be made publick with sound of trumpet thro' all the towns of the government," whereupon:

> "Everyone put on mourning, which consists in shaving their heads; this is the practice thro' the whole empire, not only for men but also for women and children. The day following the two Governours, attended by all their militia and an infinite number of people, went to the church dedicated to the Blessed Virgin, where they perform'd a solemn service.... after which they return'd to the palace.... The two *Barnagais* seated themselves in a great hall... After that, the officers and persons of note, both men and women, rang'd themselves round the hall. Certain women with tabors, and men without, plac'd themselves in the middle of the hall and began to sing, as it were in parts, little songs in honour of the prince; but in so doleful a tone that I cou'd not hinder being seiz'd with grief and weeping for a whole hour that the ceremony lasted. There were some, who to testify to their sorrow, tore their faces till they were cover'd with blood, or burnt their temples with little wax candles. There were none in this hall but persons of quality. The common people stood without in the courts, where they gave such lamentable cries that it would have mov'd the hardest hearts."[5]

Persons of importance were buried in churches, the Frenchman explains; the rest of the population in common churchyards, where graves were marked with crosses. The mourning or burial party then retreated to the house of the deceased, where they met together for three days, night and morning, to bewail their loss and would eat nowhere else during that time. Mourning feasts were repeated on several subsequent occasions.

Ceremonies by the Gondär period also included the display of effigies of the deceased, as took place, the chronicles record, after the demise of Emperor Bäkaffa in 1730 and his son Iyasu II in 1755.

Another feature of mourning ceremonies first noticed by Bruce, was the practice whereby a close female relative of the deceased cut the skin of both her temples with the nail of her little finger which she allowed to grow long on purpose, and thereby made a gash as large as a sixpence. Though prohibited in Deuteronomy XIX, 1, this custom was so general, the Scotsman claimed, that one saw a wound or a scar "on every fair face" in the land.[6]

---

[4] Foster (1949) 124, 150.

[5] Foster (1949) 149-50.

[6] Guidi (1912) 32, 178; Bruce (1790) III, 350.

Expropriation of Church Land

The extent of Church ownership of land seems to have been a continued cause of tension. With a view to stabilising land rights an important church council convened by Emperor Yohannes I at Gondär in 1678 declared that Church lands should continue to belong to the Church, and lands of the *čäwa*, or soldiers, to the latter.

Difficulties over Church land are said to have erupted in the late Gondarine period, during the hegemony of Ras Mika'él Sehul of Tegré, when the power of the Abun was, as we have seen, on the wane. Ras Mika'él is said, by Bruce, to have considerably curtailed the extent of church property. The Abun's annual revenues from them were thus reduced from 400 ounces of gold to only 25, one-third of which was allotted to the Emperor's officers residing in the prelate's house. In line with Mika'él's policy a royal decree was issued at Gondär in 1771 ordering "that all lands and villages, which are now or have been given to the Abuna by the King, shall revert to the King's own use, and be subject to the government, or the Cantiba [i.e. Käntiba, or local ruler] of Dambea, or such officers as the King shall after appoint in the provinces where they are situated."[7]

St. Matthew, writing. Note pen, and inkwell (*right*). From a 17th century Four Gospels, in the Bibliothèque Nationale, Paris, Ethiopien-Abbadie 82.

---

[7] Guidi (1903) 37; Bruce (1790) II, 356, III, 114, IV, 78, (1813), III, 17, VII, 87.

VI

THE TRADERS

The Emergence of Gondär

Gondär emerged in the late seventeenth and early eighteenth centuries as a major commercial centre. It was the site of a flourishing market, which, according to Poncet, was held on "a wide, spacious place", near the principal palace, presumably that of Emperor Fasilädäs, where "all the merchants" met, and "everyone" had his "proper place". This fair lasted "from morning to night", and dealt in "all sorts of commodities".

The trade of the city, like that of many earlier commercial settlements, was largely dominated by Muslims. The latter, according to one of the earliest contemporary sources, the Yamani ambassador Häsän Ibn Ahmäd al-Haymi, had a sizeable Muslim population which lived on one side of the settlement in a kind of ghetto. The principle of urban segregation - for both Muslims and Fälašas, subsequently received official recognition at a church council held by Emperor Yohannes I in 1668. It decreed that Muslims "must remain separate and live apart" from Christians, and form "a separate village of their own. No Christian," it added, "may enter their service,-neither as slave nor servant; neither husband nor wife may live with them." This edict was later repeated after a further church council in 1678.

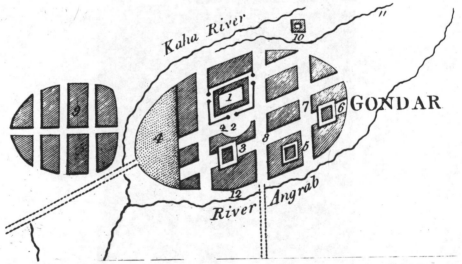

Plan of 18th century Gondär: 1) The palace complex surrounded by a wall; 2) The *Ašawa* area where troops assembled, gunpowder was sold, and executions were carried out; 3) The church of Hamar Noh, or Noah's Ark; 4) A "close quarter over a precipice" where merchants carried their provisions in time of trouble; 5) The church, and area, of Abbo; 6) Church of Däbrä Berhan Sellasé; 7) Regeb Bär, or Pigeon's Pass, a rocky area fortified in time of trouble; 8) Street of Abbo, called after the church of that name; 9) Muslim town by the Qäha river; 10) Emperor's palace by the Qäha river; 11) Stream of Rufa'él; 12) Angeräb river. From J. Bruce, *Travels to Discover the Source of the Nile* (Edinburgh, 1790).

The Muslims of Gondär were "tolerated," Poncet notes, but lived, as later evidence amply confirms, "in the lower part of the town in a separate quarter." Bruce, three-quarters of a century later, stated that they occupied "about 3,000 houses, some of them spacious and good," which would suggest that they constituted almost 20,000 inhabitants, or almost a third of the city's population which was estimated at "ten thousand families." The Scotsman spoke with some authority, for his caravan from the coast had been met at the Angäräb river, just outside the capital, by "many Mahometans" from the city, and he later resided in the Muslim quarter, in the "very neat" house of a Muslim merchant called "Mahomet Gibberti". The chief merchant of Gondär at that time was another Muslim, Nägadras Muhämmäd, who, to judge by his title, was the official in charge of trade. He was the "head", Bruce says, "of all the Mahometans" in Abyssinia, and the country's "principal merchant."

On the opposite side of the Qäha river stood what seems to have been an extension of the Muslim quarter, or, as Bruce calls it, another "large town of Mohametans." The Scottish traveller, who indicates this place in his plan of Gondär, states that it consisted of "about a thousand houses", and that its inhabitants were "all active and laborious people."[1]

Muslim Commercial Centres

There were also a number of important Muslim commercial settlements south of Gondär. One of the principal, "Tanguri," a "considerable village" north-east of Lake Tana, was "chiefly inhabited" by "Mohometans" whose occupation was "to go in caravans far to the south", beyond the Blue Nile. They thus passed through districts inhabited by Gallas, or Oromos, to whom they carried "beads and large needles, cohol, or Stibium, myrrh, coarse cloths made in Begemder, and pieces of blue cotton cloth from Surat, called Marowti." These merchants returned with "slaves, civet, wax, hides, and cardamom in large beautiful pods," as well as "a great quantity of ginger" from Enarya. They "generally" took "nearly a year" on the journey, which caused the Scotsman to comment that, in view of the time and "many accidents, extortions and robberies" encountered, the business was but a "poor" one.

Emfraz, a few miles to the south-east, also had a sizeable population, largely commercial. Poncet considered the place unusual in that it was "the only town in Aethiopia where the Mahometans have public exercise of their religion, and where their houses are mix'd with those of the Christians." Bruce, on the other hand, states that in his day at least the settlement consisted of two towns. One, situated on "a steep hill," with a "commanding" view of the lake, and "about 300 houses," was inhabited by Christians. The other, which lay on lower land, close to the Arno river, was the abode of Muslims, "many of them men of substance." They included merchants who travelled to "the myrrh and frankincense country" which stretched, the Scotsman believed, from the Dänkäli lowlands to Cape Gardafui. These traders also brought salt from the 'Afär depression, and did business with the Oromos south of the Blue Nile whom they supplied with myrrh and "damaged cargoes of blue Surat cloth" which they unfolded and cleaned, and then stiffened with gum before folding them "in the form of a book as when they were new." Further south lay the village of Dära which was on the road to Goggam and a halting place for Muslim merchants travelling further into the interior. One of the village's inhabitants was the afore-mentioned great merchant Nägadras Muhammäd. This settlement is indicated by Bruce on his map as "Vil. Turc," i.e. "Turkish village."

[1] Foster (1949) 121; Guidi (1903) 8, 37; Bruce (1790) III, 198, 362, 380-1, 405, 410, 416, IV, 57, 113; Peiser (1898) 41.

The western side of Lake Tana also had several Muslim trading settlements. One of the most important, situated by a ford on the Little Nile, was "Delakus" which Bruce describes as "more considerable in appearance" than most "small towns and villages in Abyssinia." It was inhabited "only" by Muslims whom he described as "a trading, frugal, intelligent, and industrious people."

Muslim merchants were likewise found on the trade route between Gondär and Sudan. At "Giesim," midway between the Ethiopian capital and Sennar, for example Poncet saw "a caravan of gebertas", or Muslim traders. There were also several Muslim settlements in the area, two of which were mentioned by Bruce. One was "Werkleva," four day's journey west of Gondär, the other, the frontier "town" of "Sancaho" which was inhabited by the "Baasa," a group of Šanqellas "converted to the Mahometan religion." Other Muslim commercial settlements were scattered along on the Gondär-based trade routes to the east. At one a day's journey from the capital al-Haymi thus found a mosque and Qoranic school, while another, further towards Däbareq, was referred to in the chronicles as Sälamgé - probably in fact Eslamgé, so named because it was inhabited by Muslims. Antalo, one of the principal Christian towns of Tegré, also had a significant Muslim population, and a Muslim presence may likewise be presumed at a customs post referred to in Iyasu's chronicle as Eslam Bär, literally Muslim Gate, which must have been inhabited, or run, by Muslims.[2]

Muslim Trade Agents

One of the consequences of the special Muslim position in trade was that Christian rulers in the Gondär period, as previously, often made use of Muslim agents to conduct their foreign commercial transactions. Several such functionaries are mentioned in the chronicle of Emperor Iyasu II which reports that when that ruler sent to Egypt to fetch a new Abun in 1754 he had resort to the services of an Egyptian called Giyorgis, as well as three Muslims, Ahmäd 'Ali, 'Abd Allah and 'Abd al-Qadir, who were almost certainly traders.

Muslim trade agents, or "factors," were no less important in Bruce's day. They were to be found, the Scotsman indicates, not only in Ethiopia, but also in Arabia. Some in the latter country had originated in Ethiopia, whence they had been taken in their childhood as slaves, but had later risen to some of the "principal posts" under the Sherif of Mecca and other "Arabian princes." The most powerful was "Metical Aga," a former "Abyssinian slave," who had become a minister, and confidant, of the ruler of Mecca. Though attached to an Arab court he was in close contact with the Emperor at Gondär as well as with the ruler of Tegré, Ras Mika'él Sehul. Of considerable influence on both sides of the Red Sea, the former Ethiopian slave was a "great friend and protector" of the British at Jeddah, but, as an ally of Ras Mika'él, seems to have also played a decisively important rôle in Ethiopian politics. He had not only arranged that the Ras should collect the Massawa taxes on behalf of the Ottoman Turks, but also "directed the sale" of gold, ivory, civet and other articles which the latter received in taxation, and also provided him with fire-arms. This remarkable cooperation had given Mika'él a near-monopoly of these weapons which had enabled him, as Bruce puts it, to depose two emperors and "subdue Abyssinia."

---

[2] Bruce (1790) III, 376-7, 385-6, 410, 416 IV, 19, map, V, 31; Peiser (1998) 35; Foster (1949) 110, 137; Guidi (1903) 158; Pankhurst (1982), 201-6.

One of Metical Aga's business associates was the afore-mentioned "Mahomet Gibberti" who travelled with Bruce to Gondär, and on several occasions provided him with valuable assistance. Muslim merchants such as Mahomet Gibberti operated at this time throughout northern Ethiopia. "Every great man in Abyssinia," the Scotsman says, had "one of these Gibbertis as his factor," while the Emperor had "many", for the most part "the shrewdest and most intelligent of their profession." Their principal role, like that of "Metical Aga", was to sell abroad such of the Ethiopian rulers' revenues as were paid in kind, and to purchase foreign articles, including fire-arms.[3]

Armenian Trade Agents

Besides the Muslim trade agents there were still a number of Armenian and other foreign Christians who served in a similar capacity. One of the best known was the Armenian Murad who traded and carried messages for several of the Gondarine monarchs. The significance of such "factors" - and particularly of the Armenians - was underlined by Bruce, who recalls:

"These men are chiefly Greeks, or Armenians, but the preference is always given to the latter. Both nations pay caratch, or capitation, to the Grand Signior [i.e. the Ottoman sultan] (whose subjects they are) and both have, in consequence, passports, protections, and liberty to trade wherever they please throughout the empire, without being liable to those insults and extortions from the Turkish officers that other strangers are.

"The Armenians, of all the people in the East, are those most remarkable for their patience and sobriety. They are generally masters of most of the eastern languages; are of strong, robust constitutions, of all people, the most attentive to the beasts and merchandise they have in charge; exceedingly faithful, and content with little."[4]

Trade Routes and Commercial Centres

The establishment and rise of Gondär had a significant effect on commerce, and, because of the city's location in the north-west of the country, greatly increased the importance of the old western trade route to Sudan. Ethiopian exports by that route at the close of the seventeenth century consisted, according to Poncet, mainly of slaves and ivory, while imports were made up of such varied items as "spices, paper, brass, iron, brass wire, vermilion, [mercury] sublimate, white and yellow arsenic, iron ware, *spica* [spikenard] of France, *mahaleb* [a kind of incense] of Egypt, Venice ware, which are several sorts of glass beads of all colours, and lastly black to blacken, which they call *kool* (kohl), and is very much esteemed... because they make use of it to blacken their eyes and eyebrows".

---

[3] Guidi (1903) 127-30; Bruce (1790) I, 275, II, 9, 131, III, 9-11, 198, 223, 225.

[4] Bruce (1790) II, 131.

The bulk of the country's trade, however, still probably passed by way of the Red Sea port of Massawa. Its imports, which had changed little since medieval times, were said by Bruce to consist of blue cotton, Surat and cochineal clothes, "fine cloth from different markets in India", coarse cotton cloth and unspun cotton, both from Yemen, and Venetian beads, glassware, and drinking, as well as looking-glasses, and once more *kohl* for darkening the eyes. Such trade was taken, as in the past, to the mainland port of Hergigo, which was by then a sizeable settlement, with a population, according to the Scotsman, of "about 400 houses".

The main trade route inland from Massawa led to Debarwa, the capital of the Bahr Nägaš. The inhabitants of the surrounding countryside were "partly Mahometans and partly Christians," both of whom, Poncet notes, brought provisions to passing caravans. Debarwa, through which all travellers from the Red Sea had to pass, was a place of considerable trade, and no less than "the bureau or general magazine of the commodities of the Indies." Like many other settlements of the period it was divided "into two towns," a "higher" and a "lower." The former was occupied by the Christians, who were then politically dominant; the lower by the Muslims, who were more important in commerce.

An alternative trade route inland led further south to the town of Degsa, which, according to Bruce, was "inhabited mostly by Mahometans." It likewise consisted of two adjacent settlements, "a high and a low." The Muslims, who, unlike their co-religionaries at Debarwa, were then politically paramount, were stationed at "the top of the hill", where they had "dug for themselves a scanty well," while the Christians had their abode at the bottom. Trade, the Scotsman claims, was based largely on the sale of children who were seized by Christian slave raiders and taken to the town which served as a "sure deposit" for them. They were there received by Muslim merchants who carried them to Massawa whence they were shipped to Arabia or even India. The route inland from Degsa led to the village of "Kaibara" which was "wholly inhabited by Mahometan Gibbertis", or merchants.

Adwa, the main emporium of Tegré, and the intermediate destination of most caravans bound for Gondär, was a place of even greater commercial importance. The Armenian merchant Murad reported in 1697 that it, together with nearby May Gwagwa, paid an annual tax of 1000 *wäqét*, or ounces, of gold, while three-quarters of a century later Bruce estimated that the city had "about 300 houses", which would suggest a population of almost 2,000 inhabitants, a sizeable proportion of whom were doubtless engaged in trade.[5]

Opposition to Usury

The rise of Gondär as a great commercial centre may well have led to a growth of money-lending, which was later prohibited by the church council of 1678. The decree specified that anyone lending silver or wheat should not receive interest.[6]

---

[5] Foster (1949), 105, 107, 113, 146-7, 151; Bruce (1790) III, 54, 63, 86-8, 107, 119; Fraenken and Cope di Valromita (1936) 81.

[6] Guidi (1903) 37.

VII

CRAFTSMEN

Pre-Gondarine Building Activity

The later years of the seventeenth century and the beginning of the eighteenth witnessed a considerable amount of building activity at a succession of short-lived capitals: Emfraz (also known as Guba'é or Guzara), 'Ayba, Wändegé, Qoqa, Gorgora, Dänqäz and Azäzo, all of which were the site of palaces, or castles, never previously seen in the country. Some of this construction work, at least as far as concerned palace-building, was carried out under the direction of foreigners - though the labour force must have been always primarily Ethiopian.

Emperor Susneyos's palace at Gorgora was built under the inspiration, and supervision, of the Spanish Jesuit Pero Paes, who, according to Belthazar Telles, "gave Directions for making Hammers, Mallets, Chizzels and all other Necessary Tools, handling them himself, and teaching the new workmen to dig, hew, and square the Stones for the Fabrick." He is said to have likewise taught "all the Joyners, and Carpenters."

The palace at Dänqäz, on the other hand, was erected for Susneyos, his chronicle states, by a Banyan, i.e. Indian, called 'Abdäl Kerim, who was also responsible for erecting the first stone bridge over the Blue Nile. The head workman for the palace was an Egyptian called Sädäqä Nesrani who was assisted by artisans from Egypt and "Rome", i.e. Constantinople, a name also sometimes applied to Greece. Many of the building workers, according to Almeida, were, however, Indian stone-masons brought over by Jesuits.

Another development of this period was the introduction - or more probably in fact the re-introduction - of mortar, around 1621, which took place when "an intelligent person from India discovered a kind of fine, light and as it were worm-eaten stone," similar to that used for the manufacture of lime in Gujarat. One - or more - of these craftsmen may later have been engaged in the construction of the great palace of Emperor Fasilädäs at Gondär, for the Yamani ambassador al-Haymi, who inspected it in 1648, reported that its "master-builder" had been an Indian.[1]

The Development of Gondär: Tent-Makers, Manuscript-Illustrators, etc.

The founding in 1636 of Gondär, the first long established capital for several hundred years, led to an immense increase in the demand for handicrafts in and around the city. Many skilled workers therefore emerged, or were attracted from the neighbouring countryside, or from lands further afield.

The craftsmen of Gondär and its environs included a sizeable number of Fälaša whom Bruce later described, doubtless with his customary exaggeration, as "the only

---

[1] Pankhurst (1982) 94-112; Tellez (1710) 206; Esteves Pereira (1900) 224-5; Beckingham and Huntngford (1954) 188; Peiser (1898) 37-9.

potters and masons" in the country. Fäläša potters, he claims, "greatly excelled," and "in general" lived "better than the other Abyssinians," who, however, attributed this to the former's "skill in magic" rather than to their "superior industry." Fäläšas were also to the fore as thatchers, and held an "exclusive" position in this profession. One of the roofs constructed by them was the split-cane ceiling of the palace of Emperor Iyasu II (1730-1755) which, the Scotsman asserts, was "gaier than it was possible to conceive." Some Fäläša craftsmen lived, like the Muslims, in a special quarter of the city, while others occupied several nearby "small villages," which were inhabited almost entirely by "masons and thatchers." Some of these villages were "situated out of the reach of marching armies," for they would otherwise have been "constantly raided, partly from hatred, and partly from hopes of finding money".

Though the first of the Gondarine castles was said, as we have seen, to have been designed by a master craftsman from India, an Ethiopian builder soon came prominently to the fore. He was a certain Wäldä Giyorgis who erected palaces for both Emperor Yohannes I and his son Iyasu I. This builder is described in one chronicle as a man "endowed with intelligence," and in another as "able, intelligent, and of good renown." Craftsmanship at the Gondär palaces was also carried out, according to Bruce, by a number of Greek artisans, whose sons were later involved in decorating the residence of Iyasu II. Its ornamentation included mirrors from Venice set in gilt frames, and wooden casings covered with ivory.

The existence of the court, and army, at and around Gondär, also led to the emergence of a class of tent-makers. Much of their work was carried out at Emfraz, south-east of the capital, where "a number of Mahometan tent-makers lived." Their responsibilities included loading the Emperor's tents and baggage, which they did with "surprising expedition," but though they conducted the mules and baggage to war they never participated in actual fighting.

The Gondär period also witnessed a resurgence of Ethiopian painting, in both manuscript illustration and church decoration, and constituted a "remarkable" and "new" era, as art historian Stanislaw Chojnacki has argued, of more "naturalistic" compositions in which many local motifs and scenes were introduced into religious themes. Royal and princely patronage of art at this time also found expression in the practice whereby a painter would place beneath his work, usually of the Virgin Mary or Crucifixion, a representation of the ruler or other noble who had commissioned the work. This custom, which became common during the time of Emperor Fasilädäs, flourished in the eighteenth century, and resulted in the painting of numerous pictures of the redoubtable Empress Mentewwab and her son Iyasu II*. Though Ethiopian artists generally speaking did not sign their paintings, some working on manuscripts in scriptoria of the Gondär period placed their names temporarily on unfinished sketches, probably as an indication as to who was responsible for their completion. Several such works were for one reason or another left unfinished, with the result that the identities of four eighteenth century artists, by name Sirak, Asäb Rufa'él Fanta, Wäsän, and Hezekiél, are preserved for posterity.

---

* The best contemporary picture of Mentewwab and her family is however perhaps that in British Library Orient 715, folio 134a.

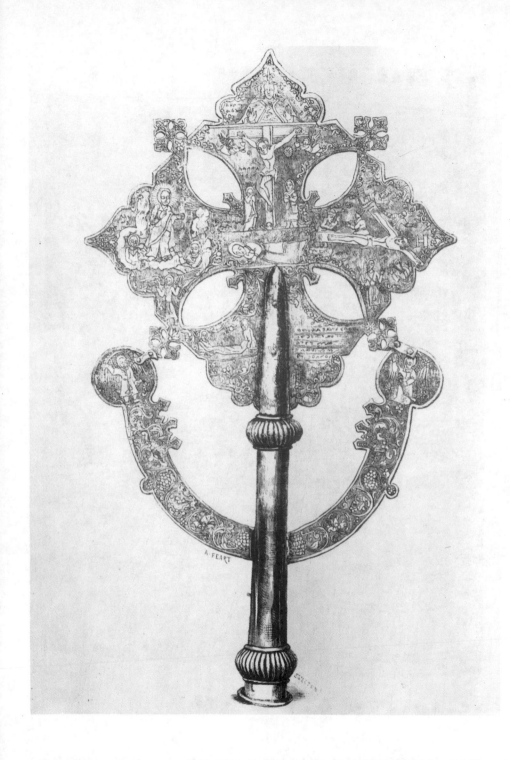

A fine 17th century processional cross from Gondär. From *Magasin Pittoresque* (1871).

Ethiopian art of the Gondär period. One of the Apostles asleep on the Mount of Olives, detail from a 17th century manuscript in the Church of Dima Giyorgis in Gojjam.

Though craftsmanship in the **countryside** probably remained largely unchanged, the Gondär period was thus a time when artisans and artists increased both in numbers and skill, particularly in and around the capital and several other urban or religious centres. This development contributed to a great flourishing of the country's culture.[2]

An example of Gondärine art. St. George, with two toes in the stirrups, killing the Dragon, from a mural at the Church of St. Gabriel at Kebran on Lake Ṭana.

Handicrafts in Šäwa

Gondär seems to have served as a point of diffusion for handicraft work in other parts of the country. Tradition, embodied in the writings of the modern Ethiopian historian Asmä Giyorgis, suggests that craftsmen from the metropolis made their way to Šäwa in the eighteenth century, during the reign of the local ruler Abbeyyé (1720-1745) who is said to have "received them well". These workers included "many" Fälaša who entered his service and whom he treated "respectfully". They made him axes and chisels with which the people of Šäwa cleared the forest of Yefat, as well as sickles, hoes and ploughshares which enabled them to cultivate the province more efficiently.[3]

---

2 Bruce (1790) II, 633-4, III, 123, 190, 195, 376-7, 380; Guidi (1903) 60, (1912) 89; Combes and Tamisier (1838) IV, 84; Chojnacki (1983) 242, 246-7, (1964) 10-1; Pankhurst (1984b) 107-12. One of many great churches built in the Gondär area this time was that of Däbrä Şähay at Qwesqwam, founded by Empress Mentewwab, whose gifts of manuscripts, church paraphernalia - and other treasures - were recorded in a contemporary chronicle: Guidi (1912) 101-8.

3 Bairu Tafla (1987) 513. See also Levine (1965) 33-4; Stitz (1975) 79.

Another example of Gondärine art. An illustration from an 18th century manuscript of the Miracles of the Virgin Mary at the Church of Giyorgis at Dima in Gojjam.

110

VIII

SLAVES

Slave-Raiding and Slave Troops

The move of the capital from Šäwa to Bägémder, which was near the borders of Sudan, led to extensive slave-raiding of Šanqella in the western frontier area. Some the first major raids were carried out during the reign of Emperor Fasilädäs, in 1641-2, 1651-2 and 1658-9, and in that of his son Yohannes I. Raiding was intensified by Emperor Iyasu I, who, having acquired a considerable number of fire-arms, succeeded in advancing far into Šanqella territory, and, according to his chronicle, on several occasions seized "many slaves, men and women." One account states that those he captured were "as numerous as the sands on the seashore." Slave-raiding expeditions were later also carried out by other rulers, notably Emperor Yostos.

With the expansion of the western trade route to Sudan in the late sixteenth and early seventeenth centuries slave exports to the west probably increased. Emfraz, one of the most important commercial centres in the north-west, was thus described by Poncet at the close of the seventeenth century as "famous for the traffick of slaves," while Bruce later claimed that "many thousand" slaves, "most of them Christians," were sold to neighbouring Muslim lands every year.

Gondär, whither most of the slaves were taken - though some were subsequently exported therefrom, was an important capital which soon acquired a sizeable population of Šanqella slaves. Most of them were too lowly in status to receive attention from the court chroniclers, and therefore scarcely figure in the annals of the period. Some were, however, employed, as we have seen, as palace guards, and are thus occasionally encountered in the records. Many of these men were succeeded, as was customary, by their sons, a fair proportion of whom were in all probability born of local women. Such descendants of slaves were referred to as *wellaj* (plural *wellajoč*), literally "relation" or "relations", though others, possibly of lower status, were known as Känisa or Känisot, the exact meaning of which is, however, obscure.

The *wellajoč*, like other slave troops in history, in due course gained considerable political power. First mentioned in the chronicle of Iyasu I for 1689 a group of them, described by Bruce as archers, played an important role after the death of Dawit III in 1721 in choosing his successor Bäkaffa, but later conspired against him, and were in consequence banished or executed.

Subsequent difficulties in the capital led to a temporary reduction in slave-raiding which was, however, resumed in 1741 by Emperor Iyasu II, who conducted several further expeditions during which, the chronicles state, he "led many men and women into slavery." Iyasu's son Iyó'as also despatched an expedition to the west,

111

from which, it is said, not one of its soldiers failed to return without prisoners, male and female.[1]

Slave troops were still of considerable importance in the second half of the eighteenth century when Bruce reported that "every department" of Gondär was "full" of them.[2] They were looked after with care, for, he explains:

> "The boys and girls under 17 and 18 years of age, (the younger the better) are taken and educated by the king, and are the servants in all the great houses of Abyssinia. They are instructed early in the Christian religion, and the tallest, handsomest, and best inclined, are the only servants that attend the royal person in his palace."[3]

The most important of these slaves constituted a force of "black" cavalry, once two hundred strong, which by the Scotsman's time had increased to three hundred. "All cloathed in coats of mail" and "mounted on black horses"," they were "commanded by foreigners entirely devoted to the King's will." The monarch, when alone, took a "great delight" in conversing with these slave warriors, and by "strict attention to their morals", by "removing all bad examples from among them," and by "giving premiums" to those who read "most and best" had made them in "firmness and coolness in action equal perhaps to any of the same number in the world." The "greatest difficulty was keeping them together, for all the great men used to wish one of them for the charge of his door." The guards, it appears, were great readers, for, according to Bruce, they had all time enough upon their hands, especially in the winter.[4]

Slave Descendants

Marriage between Šanqella or other slaves and the people among whom they lived in and around Gondär led to the emergence of a racially mixed population, which was distinguished, as the Italian scholar Ignazio Guidi later noted, up to the seventh generation.

The child of a "black" by an ordinary Ethiopian, often referred to as *qäy*, literally "red", was thus known, as we have seen, as *wellaj*, which Antoine d' Abbadie defined as a "mulatto". The child of a *wellaj* by a free man or woman was called a *qennaj* (and was a person of one-quarter slave origin); his or her child, who was of one-eighth slave descent, was known as a *fennaj*. The latter's child was an *amällät*, and his or her child an *asällät*, while his or her grandchild - who was of one-sixty-fourth slave origin -

---

[1] Basset (1882) 134, 136-8, 142,146-8, 150, 154, 157, 159, 175, 181, 191-2, 198, 202,; Béguinot (1901) 50-2, 54;, 62-3, 69-71, 73, 77, 95-6, 104, 110, 113; Bruce (1790) II, 416-7, 423, 545-7, 551, 553, 555, 558-61, 568, 592, 600, 632, 737,IV, 129, 327-8; Guidi (1903) 9, 47, 117-21, 128, 132, 142, 156, 160, 164, 166-74, 179-82, 186, 194, 196, 203-4, 209, 213, 218, 239-40, (1912) 76, 118-20, 122-5, 133-7, 149-50, 157-8, 163, 167, 170-1,180, 192, 194-5, 203, 209, 213; Foster (1949) 136; Bruce (1790) I, 393. See also Pankhurst (1976b) 13-40.

[2] Bruce (1790) II, II, 558.

[3] Bruce (1790) II, 551-2

[4] Bruce (1790) II, 552.

was spoken of as a *manbété*, an abbreviated form of the question *yäman bét näw?*, i.e. "Of whose house is he?" The child of a *manbété*, who was thus of one hundred and twenty-eighth slave descent, was referred to as a *däräba bété*, literally "My house [is] a hut", and one of the suburbs of the metropolis came to be called *däräbäbét*, doubtless because its population included many people of such partial slave descent.[5]

Mahbuba, an early 19th century Oromo woman from Guma who was seized as a slave during local fighting and taken by slave merchants to Cairo where she was purchased by a German nobleman, Prince Hermann von Pückler-Muskau. From *Le Monde Inconnu* (1882).

5 Guidi (1901) 559; Antoine d' Abbadie (1881) 648.

IX

WOMEN

The position of women, as far as the meagre records of this time suggest, remained basically unchanged throughout this period, but several interesting developments occurred at court.

Ownership of Land and Involvement in Land Sales

The establishment and growth of Gondär led to a substantial expansion of urban land ownership in which women, as well as men, were involved. By the late Gondarine period there is evidence of a significant number of women landowners in and around the city, as well as of noblewomen buying and selling land, giving estates to the church, and acting as witnesses for land sales. Records of such transactions, which illustrate the Ethiopian woman's traditional right to own land, are found in the marginalia of many manuscripts of this period, including several looted by the British from Mäqdäla in 1868 and now housed in the British Library. In one such document dating from the reign of Emperor Téwoflos (1708-1711) a certain Wäyzäro Mamité - who, to judge by her title, was evidently a noblewoman - asked the monarch's permission to build a church. Téwoflos replied that he would do so if the priests agreed. The latter then inquired about the dues payable to them, whereupon Mamité declared that she would pay twice the normal fee, and also give the church various lands, the details of which are specified in the text, for the upkeep of the clergy and the saying of Mass. In another record, written during the reign of Emperor Täklä Giyorgis (1786-1800), it is reported that one Wäyzäro Trengo, likewise a woman of high birth, had sold a third of her landed property for the then considerable sum of over seventy ounces of gold. A third text, dating from the same reign, mentions a transaction in which two other noblewomen, Wäyzäro Lehkut and Wäyzäro Emétu, gave certain estates to the Abun, the Etégé, or Empress, and various other important personalities. The same two women re-appear in a subsequent document of the reign of Emperor Egwalu (1801-1818) in which we find them giving further estates to the Abun, while retaining other land for themselves. Another document of the reign of Egwalu tells of a certain Wäyzäro Te'elmar presenting some of her father's lands to a church dedicated to St. Mika'él, while one written during the reign of Emperor Täklä Haymanot (1706-1708), records a land sale for which the witnesses included *wäyzäros*, or women of substance, as well as Däbtäras. Documents such as the above, which still await comprehensive study, indicate that noblewomen of the Gondarine period, unlike their sisters in much of the Middle East and many other parts of the world, including Great Britain, at that time, exercised considerable control over landed property.[1]

---

[1] British Library, Orient 518, f.15-6, Or. 529, f.197, Or. 513, f.216. For a recent detailed account of women's land ownership at Gondär see Crummey (1981b) 445-65, (1981c), also Pankhurst (1984a) 98-107.

Illustration of the Nativity, from an 18th century Life, Passion and Death of Jesus Christ at the Institute of Ethiopian Studies believed to have belonged to Empress Mentewwab, IES 75.

115

Participation in Expeditions

In the late seventeenth century it became customary, though perhaps only among the aristocracy, for women to participate in expeditions like men. One of the chronicles reports that they began to ride on mule-back, spear in hand with their belts tightened, and their *šämmas*, or togas, draped over their heads. This "unladylike" behaviour incurred the displeasure of Emperor Iyasu I who accordingly issue a decree, in 1691, ordering the practice to cease.

Noblewomen acquired increased prominence again some seventy or so years later during the paramountcy at Gondär of Ras Mika'él Sehul who insisted, according to Bruce, that female fief-holders who had previously mobilised their dependants for war, without joining them, should actually do so, in order to "compose a court or company" for his then consort Wäyzäro Astér.[2]

Wäyzäro Astér, consort of Ras Mika'el Sehul, who accompanied the latter on his expeditions. From an early 19th century engraving, inspired by a sketch by James Bruce, in M. Russell, *Nubia and Abyssinia* (Edinburgh, 1833.)

The bulk of women attached to the army in this period, as previously, were, however, not aristocratic fief-holders, but humble camp-followers. Mika'él's soldiers at the battle of Sarbakusa in 1771 were thus accompanied, according to Bruce, by "above 10,000 women." Some carried "provisions, horns of liquor, and mills for grinding corn, upon their backs," while about a hundred carried *gämbos*, or earthenware jars. There were, in addition, "idle women of all sorts," who were "mounted on mules," and after Mika'él's defeat, were, perhaps not surprisingly, "half dead with fear, crying and roaring."[3]

---

[2] Guidi (1903) 157; Bruce (1790) IV, 177.

[3] Bruce (1790) IV, 121-2, 191, 222.

State Banquets

The extent of women's attendance at State banquets in the Gondär period seems to have depended on political and other circumstances. At the close of the seventeenth century Emperor Iyasu I was reported by Poncet to have been visited "after dinner" by his consort, which may suggest that she - and probably other women - had not been present at the meal. The situation was, however, different during the Regency of Empress Mentewwab, for she was seated, according to the Armenian traveller Tovmačean, on a "high decorated platform" over which she presided with her grandson Emperor Iyo'as.

Bruce, who visited the Ethiopian capital only a decade or so later - and was, it should be recalled, not always too reliable a story-teller - claims that men and women at State banquets consorted together "with absolute freedom," and paid tribute "both to Bacchus and to Venus." His account of couples rising from their benches to make love, while screened by the šammas of fellow diners, is uncorroborated by other observers, and would appear essentially fictitious. This was indeed the opinion of the Swiss missionary Gobat who, writing on the basis of his residence at Gondär little more than half a century later, declared that he could "scarcely believe" that the feast of which the Scotsman had given "so disgusting a delineation, could ever have taken place, excepting among the grossest libertines of the country."[4]

Marriage

An attempt at limited marriage reform was made by the church council called at Gondär by Emperor Yohannes I in 1668, which laid down that no man should marry his sister-in-law, and no woman her brother-in-law.

The general pattern of marriage seems, however, to have undergone little change since medieval times. Many marriages, at least in the aristocratic circles frequented by Bruce, seem to have been unstable. The principle of permanent monogamous marriage, as laid down by the church, he felt, was not in fact binding, and, "like most other duties," was little more than a matter for discussion, "to be laughed at in conversation." As an example of the extent of divorce then prevalent among the Gondär nobility he claims to have seen "a woman of great quality" in the company of no less than "seven men who had all been her husbands, none of which was the happy spouse at that time." This, like several of the Scotsman's other anecdotes, should not be taken too literally, but probably contained some kernel of truth.[5]

---

[4] Foster (1949) 119; Nersessian and Pankhurst (1982) 86; Bruce (1790) III, 304; Gobat (1850) 474.

[5] Guidi (1903) 8; Bruce (1790) III, 292, 306. The early nineteenth century French Saint Simonian travellers Combes and Tamisier (1838), II, 105, later claimed that Ethiopians never married more than three times, and that Bruce's above account was therefore erroneous.

Clothing and Jewellery

The royal women of Gondär were often exceedingly well dressed, with many imported luxury clothes, as is evident both from descriptions and paintings of the period. Iyasu I's consort, Empress Mäläkatawit, for example was "covered all over," Poncet says, "with jewels, and magnificently cloath'd," while the monarch's sister was "mounted upon a mule richly accoutred," and was flanked on each side by two women who carried a canopy over her.

Among the common people it was not uncommon at this time, at least in Tegré, for women to be extensively decorated with beads, but, as Bruce learnt to his cost, these were subject to frequent changes in fashion. Recalling an attempt to use some beads, which he had obtained from Arabia, as articles of barter, he observes: "To our great disappointment, the person employed to buy our beads at Jidda had not received the last list of fashions from this country; so he had bought us a quantity beautifully flowered with red and green, as big as a large pea; also some large oval, green, and yellow ones; whereas the *ton* now among the beauties of Tigré were small sky- coloured blue beads, about the size of small lead shot, or seed pearls; blue bugles, and common white bugles, were then in demand, and large yellow glass, flat in the sides." The result of this change in fashion was that all his beads were "rejected, by six or seven dozen of the shrillest long tongues I ever heard." Some of the better-to-do Hazorta women near the Red Sea coast, according to the Scotsman, were by this time also making extensive use of beads which they placed in their hair, while wearing copper bracelets on their arms.

Another decorative practice, adopted by women at the time of their marriages, was to paint their nails, the palms of their hands, and their feet from their ankles downwards, with the yellow dye *moqimoqo* (*Rumex abyssinicus*).[6]

---

[6] Foster (1949) 120-1; Bruce (1790) III, 71, 107-8, 737.

PART THREE

THE EARLY NINETEENTH CENTURY

AZORO TISHAI AT ADOWE.

Wäyzäro Şähay, a noblewoman of early 19th century Adwa, seated on a couch, with servants or slaves in attendance. Note incense burning on the right. From G. Valentia, *Voyages and Travels* (London, 1809).

I

CHILDREN, EDUCATION AND LITERACY

Children's Work

It was the custom in the northern highlands for an infant immediately after birth to be taught to taste butter, often mixed with a little honey. As long as the child drew nourishment from the breast, it passed the night on the bosom of its mother, or, in the case of the aristocracy, on that of a nurse, for women of the upper classes, Gobat states, seldom looked after their offspring in person. The infant at the end of the first month had no other cradle during the day than the back of its mother, or nurse, who would take it by both its hands, and place it between her shoulders. In this way it soon learnt to cling with its feet around her sides, and lay its hands upon her shoulders to sustain its weight. She for her part secured the little one, by passing around her waist and about her neck, wide leather straps which served to support and partly to cover it.

An Ethiopian shepherd-boy, with traditional sheepskin cloak, an engraving from G. Massaia, *I miei trentacinque anni di missione nell' alta Etiopia* (Rome and Milan, 1885-95).

Children in the average home acted from the age of around seven as servants, or assistants, to their parents. Sons, until the age of about fourteen or fifteen, were generally occupied as shepherds or herdsmen for their fathers, though if the latter were in straightened circumstances their offspring might leave them at the age of eight or nine or so, and obtain support by tending other people's livestock. Daughters, like their mothers, were chiefly engaged in household duties, and, while very young, almost indeed as soon as they could walk steadily, began carrying large jars of water which in many cases had to be obtained at a considerable distance from the house. Later, when perhaps only eight or nine years old, they had to gather and carry fire-wood. At the age of fourteen or fifteen they began the task of grinding grain. Such menial work, however, usually came to an end after marriage, for, unless their families were extremely poor, the responsibility of grinding and carrying wood and water was passed on to young female relations - or slaves.[1]

Adoption Practices

In times of difficulty the upkeep of children was often entrusted to better-off kinsmen or even complete strangers. Adoption was sometimes induced by abandoning youngsters in the vicinity of the proposed foster-parent's house. During the rains of 1814, for example, when food supplies were scarce, "several" children were thus "dropped at the doors of respectable people" in Adwa, as Nathaniel Pearce, a British resident in the city, reported. He spoke from personal experience, for one dark and rainy night a little boy some four years old had been left at his house. He looked after the toddler for about six months, until one day the mother, who came from a village five miles away, called on him. She explained that her husband, the boy's father, had been killed in battle, and that she had therefore been unable to look after her offspring. In her distress she had placed the child at the Englishman's door, and had watched at a distance till he was taken into the house. She had then gone to another woman, to whom she had told the whole story, and who now came forward to bear testimony to its truth. The mother, having subsequently married again, and become relatively prosperous as a result of a good harvest, felt once again able to provide for her child whom she wished restored to her. Pearce, who declares that the little mite had by then grown fond of him, took the matter to the local elders. They ruled that it was entirely up to him whether he restored the infant or not, or at least that no one could force him to part with the child until he had been reimbursed for the maintenance he had expended. The mother had "abandoned it," the elders said, to the "mercy of the hyenas" from whose jaws he had delivered it. The poor woman, however, fell at his feet, and declared that she would "ever pray" for her son's benefactor. Pearce duly acceded to her request.[2]

Reminiscences of Shepherd Children

Valuable light on childhood preoccupations and attitudes of this time is embodied in the dictated correspondence of Akafedé Dallé and Otsu Aga, two Oromo slaves, as written down by Karl Tutschek, their tutor in Germany. Akafedé, recalling his life as a shepherd boy, and his relations with his parents, other elders, and members of his own age group, observed: "I used to make my father and mother very

---

[1] Gobat (1850) 470-1. For similarities in the upbringing of Fälaša children see Flad (1869) 27.

[2] Pearce (1831) II, 171-2

angry because as a shepherd boy whenever I saw my *hiria* [i.e. age group] go collecting sorghum heads I used to go with them and abandon the cattle. Whenever I went collecting the sorghum I never carried home a small quantity because my mother was fond of it, and I was more afraid of my mother than of my father. When she ate them she was pleased with me. One day I and a man from our village took the cattle to the *hora* [i.e. the spring]; when the animals drank and came up from the spring I saw the other boys asking permission from their brothers to go back to collect sorghum heads. I too asked permission from the man from my village. I said, 'Let me go and collect heads for my mother.' The man said I could go. He was not a bad man. So I went with the other children. When the children of the people to whom the heads belonged saw us they assembled and waited for us. When we came near to them they asked us, 'Where are you going?.' We replied that we were going to get sorghum heads. They replied, 'You can't take our sorghum unless you want to be beaten up. Try your luck another time!' After thinking for a while we egged each other on to go ahead with the plan. One of the farmers in the valley below was cutting sorghum. He called to us. 'Come here. Take some heads!,' he said. 'I have sown both white and ordinary sorghum. If you cut it for me you can take some heads.' Because we wanted the heads we cut the sorghum for him ...

"Some children collected too many heads, and when they could not carry them home, they threw some of them away, but those who were strong enough picked up what the other children had dropped. I walked behind and gathered what the others had discarded. After walking a while I came to a ridge called Hula. I could not climb this ridge. As I was tired I threw away some heads, and said goodbye to the other children. Those children who had thrown away some heads before then turned round and picked up what I had thrown away because their load had become light. We travelled along the ridge and came to a mountain called Tulu Tulam. At the foot of this mountain the children threw away the heads they had collected when I threw them away. I immediately picked up the heads they had thrown away as they had done when I threw them away. Having thus regained my sorghum there was nothing more for me to do that evening but to go home. The heads I brought home I divided between our relatives and neighbours."

The shepherd boys often got into scrapes of one kind or another, for Otsu recalls: "One day we went to the *hora*. When we became hungry we went poaching. While I was stealing *bäqqolo* [i.e. corn] the owners saw me, and caught and beat me. I threw away everything I had taken and fled. I began weeping because I was very angry. I arrived home in no time. The owner of the corn could not run fast because he was very irritated. He came in the evening, and accused me to my father. He said, 'Your son stole my grain today,' and then my father beat me. He beat me severely.'"

On another occasion, Otsu recalls, he secretly went out hunting, and because he had gone away without telling his father, incurred a further beating. Reverting to his love of hunting, the youngster observed, "In my country I had a good *bodé* [i.e. spear]. I and my brothers used to take a big dog with us and go hunting together." He later went on: "the children of the *tumtu* [i.e. blacksmiths] used to go hunting to kill *guge* [i.e. doves] and *weni* [i.e. colobus monkeys]. Whenever we killed a *weni* we used to quarrel amongst ourselves as to who had killed it. One would say, 'I struck it first.' Others would say the same. When we could not decide who had hit it first we would

Youngsters looking after cattle, from G. Massaia, *I miei trentacinque anni di missione nell' alta Etiopia* (Rome and Milan, 1885-95).

call a *mangudo* [i.e. elderly man] to arbitrate. Whenever we quarreled, and came near to breaking our heads, our mothers would punish us, exclaiming, 'Why are you bickering in this way?'

Akafedé shared his friend's passion for hunting, and declared,"When I was in my country I, together with the other children, often used to hunt partridges. One day while we were hunting them we came upon a wild cat. The big boys rushed shouting towards it, but the cat did not run away. It turned on the children and growled. The children stopped because they were afraid. There was nothing to do, but to go and bring a dog. At this point a boy came running across the field. He said, 'Why are you standing there instead of killing it? Give me a spear!' The children replied, 'If you go and strike this cat you will become our hero.' The boy did not take the spear that was offered him, but instead picked up a pointed stick and a club, and then advanced towards the cat. As he moved towards it the animal growled at him as it had done at the other children, but the boy was not afraid. He stood some distance away, threw the pointed stick at the cat, and pierced it in the ear. It immediately closed its eyes and rushed to attack him. When it came near, the boy struck at its feet with the club. The creature fell down screaming. The children who had earlier not dared to approach now came forward and helped to finish it off."[3]

The Slave Trade

The abundant records of this period show that many children continued to be captured in war or seized by raiders, and were then sold as slaves. "Young persons of both sexes," Pearce states, were often taken while attending their flocks. There were a "large number" of adventurers, according to the French Saint Simonians Combes and Tamisier, whose "sole occupation" was in fact to steal children. These men would hide in the forests or by springs to trap young girls coming to draw water or gather firewood. They would then ride off with the most comely, and sell them to local merchants who would subsequently dispose of them to travelling caravans.

A large proportion of the slave children were taken from the southern provinces. The Protestant missionary J.L. Krapf, describing the seizure of children from the Guragé area, states that though they slept beside their parents they would nevertheless be seized in large numbers. Kidnappers would break into the children's houses at night, place a large stick upon the necks of adult members of the family to immobilise them, and then run off with the youngsters. If the latter attempted to make an outcry a rag would be stuffed into their mouths. As a precaution against such attacks children were often made to sleep on beams across the upper part of their houses or had thick sticks placed over them, but the raiders had their ways of overcoming such obstacles. If they were unable to break into a house, or failed to get at the children within it, they would set fire to the building by night, having first dug a pit around it into which the inhabitants would fall in trying to escape, and the children would be seized amid the general confusion. Though most slaves were captured, some, as several observers report, were actually sold into slavery by their parents, particularly when the latter were destitute or unable to pay their taxes.

---

[3] Pankhurst and Adi Huka (1975) 39-47; Pankhurst (1976) 98-110.

125

Slave caravans invariably included large numbers of youngsters, many of whom, according to the English traveller C. T. Beke, were "children of eight or nine years at most." The British envoy Cornwallis Harris states that "caravans, consisting of from one hundred to three thousand individuals of all ages," passed through Šäwa "during the greater part of the year." "Three-fourths" of the captives were "young boys and girls, many of them quite children", nine-tenths of the girls being below ten years old.[4]

Church Education

Education, as in the past, was almost entirely restricted to boys, and even among them only "a small portion", according to Gobat, went to school. Most parents were said to have been reluctant to send their sons for study, lest they became monks - as many no doubt did. Many would-be students therefore deserted their homes to obtain education through their own unassisted efforts. Such youngsters often served during the day as domestic servants, and received their instruction at night. Others wandered the streets, begging for their daily sustenance. There were, however, a few wealthy philanthropists who made a habit of supporting children of poor parents, and of providing them with education. Teaching was essentially free, and when the French traveller Antoine d'Abbadie, who took some courses from Ethiopian churchmen, offered to pay for them, he was invariably told that learning was "not sold like base merchandise," and that the honour of the teaching body "expected that knowledge should be transmitted freely as it had been received." Education was, however, not universally favoured, and a nephew of the *Ečägé*, one of the principal churchmen at Gondär, went so far as to observe that it was "not so valuable an acquisition" as some supposed, for "knowledge corrupted the heart."

The sons of the nobility were in many cases sent to convents where they were taught to read the Psalms in the classical Ethiopian language, Ge'ez, and to commit them to memory. As soon as the youngsters had learnt to read, whether well or badly, they would usually leave school, and be instructed in the arts of war and government, after which they would be entrusted by their father with a district to govern. They would then be surrounded with servants, and, before long provided with a wife, would live the life of a nobleman and soldier for the rest of their days.

Some chiefs, however, received considerably greater education. Kasa, the future Emperor Téwodros, for example, "having learnt to recite Dawit," as a chronicler says, proceeded to a monastery for further study. His namesake, the future Emperor Yohannes IV, is likewise reported to have "studied the Books of the Old and New Testament, as well as the ecclesiastical and royal traditions," after which he too went to a monastery, and spent his time "listening to the interpretations of the Holy Books in order to build up his mind in the faith of the Holy Trinity." On reaching maturity he was instructed in martial arts, and was so proficient in these, his chronicler claims, that "when he threw the spear, he never missed anyone," and "when he aimed with his gun, he never missed wild animals, nor eagles, nor birds of the sky." Young Kasa, as a child of the mid-nineteenth century, also learnt how to repair fire-arms, "and acquired skill in fitting, unscrewing and repairing rifles and guns, as well as skill in

---

[4] Pearce (1831) II 9; Combes and Tamisier (1838) IV, 97-8; Isenberg and Krapf (1838), 179-80; Krapf (1867) 46; Johnston (1844) I, 310; Beke (1844) 20-1; Harris (1844) I, 310; Harris (1844) I, 223-4, III, 307-8. See also Pankhurst (1868) 82-92.

racing horses as fast as an eagle." The future Emperor Menilek, by contrast, was entrusted to a tutor, as his chronicle relates.

An Ethiopian priest with two of his church-school pupils, dressed traditionally in skin cloaks. One of the students holds a parasol respectfully to shield the master from the sun. From T. Waldmeier, *The Autobiography of Ten Years in Abyssinia* (London and Leominster, 1886).

Girls from noble families, by contrast, had virtually no educational opportunities, for they were taught, Gobat says, "little but spinning and culinary duties." A "few women of distinction" nevertheless succeeded in one way or other in learning to read. Most women, however, were married at an early age, often when only eight or nine years old, and, spending much of their time bearing children, seldom afterwards appeared in public, at least until after the death of their husbands.

127

Children in the Christian highlands went to two essentially different types of church school. The first, which may be considered essentially as primary schools, were small village establishments, usually run by a single priest or *däbtära*, i.e. lay cleric. The other schools, which were fewer in number, were larger, and academically more advanced, institutions comparable to secondary schools - or in some instances even to universities, where a number of teachers, priests, *däbtäras*, or monks, specialised in different subjects.

Village schools, concerned largely with the reading, and memorisation, of the Psalms, were found throughout the Christian highlands. They were generally held, according to Pearce, "in a churchyard, or in some open place near it, sometimes before the residence of the master." Students, in the latter case, would seek shelter during the rains in their teacher's dwelling, and would be "all crowded up in a small dark hut, learning prayers by word of mouth from the master, instead of a book."

Larger, more advanced, schools were attached to major churches or monasteries, in many cases located at provincial or other capitals. Students attending such establishments followed more specialised courses than were available at village schools. The church of Giyorgis at the Säwan capital, Ankobär, was thus attended in the late 1830's by sixty children who received instruction from six teachers. Krapf, who visited this school, found that ten pupils were studying reading; twenty, singing; and thirty, poetry. All declared that they hoped to go to Gondär to "take holy orders." At another of the town's churches a teacher called Arkälédes taught church chanting to no less than a hundred pupils.

Sizeable schools were also established in other major towns. At Adwa, for example, the British military expedition of 1867-8 found "five or six schools" where children learnt to read, and where "the Psalms, the Scriptures, the ceremonies of the church, and singing, were taught." Among the students were several blind boys who were instructed in "learning by heart." The great religious centre of Aksum also had at least one school of renown where many children, because of the city's status as a place of asylum, were left by their parents to study in times of war, as the German traveller Gerhard Rohlfs later reported. Gondär, as the capital of the empire, had an even larger number of students. Many flocked there because of the presence of the Abun, or Patriarch, by whom they were duly ordained. The city's church schools, however, also catered for many children of noble families who came, Rohlfs says, only to learn how to read and write, and for the most part eschewed higher learning.

Church school students, according to d'Abbadie, were usually diligent, but, like students in medieval Europe, had a hard life. They often lived in great poverty, had to beg for alms, and were in many cases little more than the servants of their masters. Students wishing to attend the more important schools often had to travel considerable distances. On leaving their home and family, they would put on their back a sack of grain or pease, which, the Italian missionary De Jacobis states, would be their entire subsistence for several months, after which they were obliged to beg. Journeys in search of education might at times entail no small risk, particularly in periods of civil war. Boys at Ankobär who hoped to make their way to Gondär for ordination nevertheless told Krapf in 1839 that they were not afraid of attack by the Gallas on the route, for their king, Sahlä Sellasé, would "charge a Galla Governor to take care of them." Because of civil wars in the north some students, according to Harris, were, however, "compelled to abandon their journey" and return to Säwa.

Church school students are reported to have been in many cases keenly interested in their studies. A youngster, on becoming "somewhat advanced in learning," Pearce reports, would often be "made to teach the younger ones." At the end of each lesson the students, d'Abbadie reports, would frequently disperse on the lawn surrounding the church, and memorise what they had learnt, at times attempting to compose poetry or hymns which they would later recite or sing to their master. The more enthusiastic pupils would likewise hold weekly study sessions at which one of them would read out portions of the Scriptures discussed in the previous week. Gobat, who had seen many such classes, reports that the group would "pause at every difficult passage" and diligently consult each other as to its probable meaning. In case of uncertainty the students would appeal to their teacher whose ruling would be considered as final.

Not all students, however, were well motivated. Some indeed were so unruly that their teachers had "great trouble" with them, and had to resort to various kinds of punishment. It was not uncommon, according to Pearce, for the master to stand over his students with a wax taper while five or six of them pinched the offender's legs and thighs. If they spared him the teacher would strike them with his candle which could cut as severely as a whip. The "correction considered most effective" was, however, that of having fetters placed on the delinquent's legs, sometimes for many months at a time. In one instance a thirteen-year-old boy, who had more than once contrived to remove his fetters and desert the school, was fitted with such heavy irons that he was unable to free himself. He became so enraged that he drew a knife and committed suicide by cutting his throat. It was on the other hand not unusual, according to d'Abbadie, for students fearful that they might run away from school, themselves to demand chains which were in no way considered dishonourable. Punishments might also be meted out by parents, particularly if they felt their children showed insufficient interest in their studies. Students playing truant might likewise be seized by fathers or mothers, and dragged to the church precincts where they were taught, and have their legs chained together.

Notwithstanding the severity of their schooling, and the hard punishments inflicted, many students became entirely devoted to their teacher. So far from criticising their master, d'Abbadie states, they would "worship him with a kind of veneration." On reporting in Gondär how his fellow students in Paris had once naughtily eaten their teacher's meal, and had left nothing on his plate, he was greeted with "such a deluge of reprobation" that he took good care "never to repeat the scandal." This picture was confirmed by De Jacobis who states that though it was not unusual for pupils to undertake the "most menial" service for their masters, their "filial affection" seemed to make this "sweet and easy."

Higher studies, according to d'Abbadie, comprised five main fields of learning, which could be compared to different colleges. These were consecrated respectively to the New Testament; the Fathers of the Church; civil and canonical law; the Old Testament; and astronomy. The latter branch of study had, however, then recently fallen into disuse: he was personally acquainted with its last teacher or professor at Gondär who had for many years been without a single student.

Study often involved great feats of memorisation, which, the Frenchman felt, were beyond the ability of most Europeans, for he had not heard of more than one of the latter who knew the entire Bible by heart, whereas no one could become a professor in Ethiopia without memorising both the entire text and the traditional interpretations, as well as variations in four or five manuscripts. Traditional Ethiopian scholars, he insisted, were highly intellectual, and in Gondär, Gojjam and elsewhere he had been able to hold discussions on religion, philosophy and even science which were "quite as sophisticated and subtle" as any he could have in Paris or London.

Students seeking to become learned men had, in fact, to embark on a remarkably extensive course of study. Having learnt to read, perhaps in a village school, they were required to commit to memory the Gospel of St. John, and to study several of St. Paul's Epistles and a number of the Homilies of John Chrysostom, after which they were assigned the task of learning by heart the Psalms of David, the *Weddasé Maryam*, or Praises of Mary, and several prayers, and were also supposed to memorise long lists of Ge'ez words, but few, Gobat believed, actually succeeded in doing so. After this they would sit at the feet of renowned masters who would explain to them the Scriptures and other texts, including the *Fethä Nägäst*, or traditional Ethiopian code of law. Such studies were, De Jacobis says, "perfectly despairing in length." The course thus embraced seven years on *zéma*, or chanting, nine years on *Sewasew*, or Ge'ez grammar, and four on *qené*, or poetry, or a total of twenty years, after which the student had still to face the *Qeddusan mäsähaft*, or sacred books of the Old and New Testament. There were in addition courses in civil and canonical law, astronomy and history, but "few students" had the courage to embark on them. D'Abbadie, no less impressed by the extent of church studies, quoted one old professor as telling him that he had learnt to read well in three years, after which he had consecrated two more to learning to sing liturgical songs, five to grammar and the composition of hymns, seven to the New Testament, and no less than fifteen to the Old as it required a "considerable effort" at memorisation. He had thus devoted to his education no less than thirty-two years.[5]

Fälaša Education

The education of the Fälaša was essentially similar to - and in all probability copied from - that of their Christian compatriots. Teaching among the Fälaša, as among the Christians, was thus in the hands of priests, *däbtäras* and monks, and was based, at the village level, on the study of Ge'ez and memorisation of the Psalms. Fälaša students desirous of following a religious vocation would, like Christian children preparing for the Church, also study the Ethiopic *Sewasew* in order to translate portions of the Ge'ez Bible, in many cases written out by Christian *däbtäras*, into

---

[5] Gobat (1850) 230, 318-9, 471-2; Antoine d' Abbadie (1868) 18-9; Pearce (1831) I, 330-1; Isenberg and Krapf (1843) 86, 145-6; Holland and Hozier (1870), I, 397; Rohlfs (1883) 269, 302, (1885) 205, 227; Herbert (1867) 81-2; Harris (1844) III, 295; Heuglin (1868) 261; Mondon-Vidailhet (1905) 2, 82; Bairu Tafla (1977) 39-40; Guèbrè Sellassié (1930-1) I, 76. Confirmation of the extraordinary length of traditional church studies is provided by Aläqa 'Enbaqom Qalä Wäld, a twentieth century scholar, who states that to master reading and writing may take two years, *zéma*, or music, in its various branches, eight and a half years, *qené*, or poetry, five, the Old and New Testaments, four or five years, the writings of the Church Fathers and rules of Spiritual Discipline, three years, computation of the church calendar and mathematic training, six months, history, at least one year, and arts and crafts, four years. "The average hard-working, intelligent student wishing to master all branches of traditional Ethiopian church education," he says, would probably take thirty years, though some "highly gifted individuals" might take "only twenty-five or even thirty-four." Imbakom Kalewold (1970) 1-2, 30-1. For another account of tradional education, by Mängestu Lämma, see also E.S. Pankhurst (1955) 244-67.

Amharic for gatherings on the Sabbath and other festivals. Though their community tended to live separately from the Christian population, Fälaša children wishing to become *däbtäras*, Flad reports, "for the most part" attended Christian schools. Classes for Fälaša, like those for Christians, were attended almost exclusively by boys. On asking why girls were not taught, he received the reply that it was "not becoming to instruct females."

Several Fälaša village schools were attended by sizeable numbers of students. At the village of "Oibga," for example, the German Protestant missionary Henry Stern met a teacher with over ninety students. Their graduation was often a great event, and it was the practice in some areas when a pupil had memorised the whole Psalter for his parents to give the teacher a Maria Theresa thaler, or other "small payment," with the result, Flad believed, that the earnings of the priesthood were "sometimes considerable." "Most" Fälaša *däbtaras* on the other hand went to Christian schools.[6]

Literacy

Literacy, which meant in effect the ability to read or write in Ge'ez or Amharic - for none of the other Ethiopian languages of the highlands were ever written - varied considerably from one region to another. In the Amharic-speaking areas "about one fifth of the male population," according to Gobat, had "some knowledge of reading." This skill was significantly less extensive in Tegré where most people were unfamiliar with Amharic, and where only about "one twelfth" of the menfolk could read. A visiting Belgian consul, Edouard Blondeel, nevertheless concluded that literacy in the country as a whole was not so different from that in Western Europe. The situation in peripheral areas, however, was far less favourable. At Degsa, on the northern edge of the plateau, for example, Salt states that there was no school, with the result that there were "only a few people who could read the church Bible", and those who obtained "this degree of knowledge" were "considered as priests; at least in their opinion."

A considerable proportion of the literate population were in fact churchmen of one kind or another. In Tegré, Mansfield Parkyns believed that the only persons who could read were "some, but not all of the priests, the scribes, and a very few among men of the highest rank," who, however, "rarely" understood what was written. The position was apparently not so different in Bägémder where Theophilus Waldmeier a generation later stated that reading was known only to the priests and *däbtäras*.

Proficiency in writing was far less extensive. "Few" people, according to both Pearce and Gobat, even learnt to write, while Salt observed that "not one in twenty could write the characters they read." Persons able to write were "chiefly occupied" in producing charms. One such man, whom Salt saw at Degsa, travelled around the country as "a physician as well as a priest." Charm-writing was a major, and often lucrative, occupation of *däbtäras*, who turned out amulets, Consul Plowden declares, against "every disease" known to man.

---

[6] Flad (1869) 30, 32, 35-6; Faïtlovitch (1905) 21; Veitch (1860) 32; Halévy (1877) 244-5.

Literacy among the Fälaša, who likewise used Ge'ez, seems, at least by the 1860's, to have also been fairly limited. In one of their larger villages, Gorgora "Eila," Stern could not find a single person able to read fluently, while in two other places, "Antonius" and "Atshergee," no one could "spell a single word.[7]

The Effects of War

The civil wars of the late eighteenth and first part of the nineteenth century appear to have led to a marked decline in education, literacy, and hence the demand for manuscripts. Locally written Bibles, Gobat reported in the 1830's, could "occasionally" be purchased for around 100 thalers, because people had given up studying, and books were therefore "no longer wanted." A generation later Plowden noted that manuscripts had "formerly" been "eagerly sought for", but by his day could "be found very cheap," for there were "scarcely any purchasers" as the number of persons that could read and write was "diminishing daily.["8]

---

[7] Gobat (1850) 472; Blondeel (1838-42) 64; Valentia (1809) II, 508-9; Parkyns (1853) I, 155; Waldmeier (1886) 16; Pearce (1831) I, 331, 391; GB House of Commons (1868) 110; Stern (1862) 212, 245, 259, 265, 268.

[8] Gobat (1850) 319; GB House of Commons (1868) 110. Gobat, quoted a Gondär priest of his acquaintance as stating that there were in the city (which then had a population of around 6,000) "about three hundred persons who can read." Gobat: 257. See Pankhurst (1982) 267.

132

II

THE PEASANTS

Classes in the Rural Economy

The agricultural population in the early nineteenth century consisted, according to Plowden, of three main categories: small peasants, farm labourers, and rich proprietors. The "small proprietors and peasantry" were by far the most numerous of the three groups, and indeed represented the backbone of the nation. Full of industry, as Salt noted, they bore, directly or indirectly, "the whole burden of taxation," as well as "most" of the exactions of the "large standing armies" which were frequently quartered on them. These peasants, according to the British consul, nevertheless appeared "attached to their way of life," and, though seldom wealthy," were "rarely in distress." Like mountaineers in other lands they manifested a love of liberty and impatience of restraint. Spending much of their time in the open air, and benefiting from the country's genial climate, they were "hardy in youth," but aged quickly.

The rich proprietors by contrast were relatively few in number. Like the peasantry they were despised and insulted by the soldiery, but made up for their "want of strength", Plowden says, by various "politic wiles" - and in this way probably succeeded in escaping most of the burden of taxation.

The agricultural labourers, who seem to have been fewer in number than the independent peasantry, differed from the latter in that they worked not for themselves, but for landlords who paid them a small daily wage, usually in kind. Many such labourers were employed in one way in specialised work, for they included diggers, grass-cutters and wood-cutters. The diggers, or *kofari*, were engaged to dig the land on steep slopes which could not be ploughed in the normal way. Cultivation took place on even very difficult land, where Salt saw "laudable attempts" being made even where these yielded "nothing but stones, weeds, thorny bushes and acacias." The grass-cutters for their part collected large loads of grass, or, during the summer, *téf* straw, for the landowners, and were provided in return with a small number of salt bars, the equivalent, Pearce thought, of about three Maria Theresa dollars a year. The wood-cutters, equipped with axes and bill-hooks, cut trees both for fire-wood and to clear land for tillage.[1]

Agricultural Implements and Practices

Agricultural techniques had probably changed little since medieval times. Farmers in the northern and central highlands made use of a small light plough drawn by two oxen. Bruce, in the late eighteenth century, suggested that this instrument was made entirely of wood, but Salt half a century later noted that an iron ploughshare was also sometimes used. The ploughman held the end of this implement in one hand, and in the other a large whip with which he directed his animals, who, according to Pearce, were "trained to be very steady." Cows were never put into the yoke, but were

---

[1] Plowden (1868) 134-5; Lefebvre (1845-8) III, 258; Salt (1814) 253; Pearce (1831) I, 342.

The ploughman tills the land with traditional Ethiopian plough pulled by two oxen. An engraving from R. Acton, *The Abyssinian Expedition* (London, 1868). Note the cattle's humps and traditional Ethiopian plough.

reserved for either milking or eating; oxen, on the other hand, were seldom killed unless unable to work. Fields on the sides of mountains too steep to plough were dug, as we have seen, by hand.

The typical Ethiopian ploughshare, as described in the early nineteenth century by the German Eduard Rüppell and the Frenchmen Ferret and Galinier, consisted of a piece of wood 30 centimetres long by 12 wide, roughly joined to a long tree-trunk at an angle which depended on the depth of the furrow which it was desired to cut. The ploughshare was usually covered with a piece of very poor quality iron. This bent at the least resistance it encountered so that its repair wasted much time for the peasant which, as Ferret and Galinier argued, could otherwise have been spent on productive work.

The peasantry were familiar with the idea of crop rotation, so that land which was considered exhausted was from time to time left fallow, or sown with different crops. Cultivation of *téf* and legumes, such as peas and vetches, were thus alternated for several years, after which fields were for a time left idle. Virtually no use was, however, made of manure, for which reason the land, Rüppell says, had in many places to be left fallow every other year. Some of the best yields were obtained from ground covered with stones, for they helped to retain moisture in the earth, and perhaps for that reason, Plowden states, were never removed.

When land had to be cleared for cultivation the peasants would begin by cutting down the trees and bushes, which they would then pile over the remaining stumps. These when dry would then be set on fire. After this the ground would be ploughed over two or three times, and thus made ready for cultivation.

Weeding, the next operation, was "one of the most irksome of toils," for "the luxuriance of the soil", Salt says, produced "a great number of weeds." To eradicate them the soil would often be turned over twice, after which the peasants would "pick out most carefully every root." If there were not sufficient men for this work, women and children would gather together, and, "forming a line along the field, and with singing, and much merriment," would "pluck forth all the weeds from the corn." Where the land belonged to a chief he would in many cases supervise operations in person. Having "mustered every soldier in his service" he would march at their head to his fields where they would "lay down their arms, form into a line, join in the chorus to a song, and, in general led by a female, march on plucking up the weeds." In this way, Pearce recalls, they would soon make their way through a number of fields, "throwing the weeds down as they pluck them, and leaving the farming-men, boys, and girls, to carry them to the borders of the field." Much of this work was carried out cooperatively, for "the Abyssinians always helped each other to weed their corn."

The labour of reaping, which was carried out with small wooden-handled iron sickles with tiny teeth, was on the other hand "entirely thrown on the females". When harvesting barley they would tie the stalks together in sheafs which they would take home and beat with small sticks - which Rüppell considered "a surprisingly laborious" way of handling cereals.

An agricultural labourer from Agamé in Tegré in traditional dress, carrying his hoe. An engraving from T. Lefebvre and others, *Voyage en Abyssinie* (Paris, 1845-8).

Threshing was carried out in the Biblical way, the grain being trodden by oxen, mules and horses. Winnowing, which was in many cases women's work, was then effected by throwing the grain in small quantities into the air, the husk being thus blown away by the wind.

Irrigation, though far from universal, was practised, Plowden notes, "whenever necessary" - or possible, and in view of the "numerous rivulets" was "an easy task." Small channels, as Salt noted in Tegré, would be dug from the higher parts of a stream to conduct water across a nearby plain which would be criss-crossed with small ditches to form "small compartments." Irrigation of this kind, based on ditches about two feet wide, was also used in some areas for the cultivation of cotton.

Two *sanga* cattle whose long horns were used for the manufacture of *wanča*, or drinking horns. From H. Salt, *A Voyage to Abyssinia* (London, 1814).

Burning was widely practiced by the peasantry for a number of reasons: to clear land for cultivation, to curtail the growth of bushes, and to destroy rats, mice, moles and insect pests, as well as to fertilise the soil. It was by no means unusual in the northern highlands, Rüppell states, to see the "splendid sight" of as many as twenty huge fires, some of which might take as much as an hour to pass on mule-back.[2]

---

[2] Bruce (1790) III, 115, 561; Valentia (1809) II, 507, III, 125, 230, 232; Pearce (1831) I, 200, 204, 343, 345-6; Rüppell (1838-40) I, 236 312, II, 155, 160-1; Ferret and Galinier (1847) II, 397; Lefebvre (1845-8) III, 255-6; Plowden (1868) 135-6; Salt (1814), p. 253.

The peasantry also devoted much time to animal husbandry, including the milking of cows, which was mainly carried out by men, and the watching of cattle which, as we have seen, was a task generally given to boys.

The Harvest Cycle

The harvest cycle varied greatly from one part of the country to another. It depended partly on the timing of the main rainy season, which started first in the south and gradually moved northwards, and partly on altitude and hence on temperature. The various crops moreover were sown and harvested at different times of the year. In the northern highlands of Tegré for example the peasants began to plough in the middle of April, when the small rainy season started, in order to open up the soil, Ferret and Galinier explain, to air and water. Sowing would then take place in April and May for durrah, *dagusa*, or finger-millet, and beans, in June for barley, wheat and lentils, and in the next two months, immediately before the main rainy season, for *téf* and broad beans. Other plants were sown at the conclusion of the rains, in October and November.[3]

Fertility of the Soil, Productivity, and Crop Yields

The fertility of the soil, though varying immensely, even within short distances, impressed foreign observers. Tegré, though in many places rocky, appeared to Salt, "highly productive," and capable of yielding "a very abundant harvest", while Parkyns observed that even "the most careless observer" could not but "fail to mark" the "extreme richness" of the soil, and the "great capabilities of the land." Dämbeya, according to the French Scientific Mission, was particularly fertile; Gojjam seemed to Combes and Tamisier "well cultivated and rich in pastures;" and the land of Šäwa was so good, Beke believed, that it could "produce everything."

Agricultural productivity likewise varied considerably from one area to another, because of differences in the climate and the fertility of the soil. Most highland areas produced only one main crop a year, but some lowland areas, as Salt and Pearce noticed, allowed for two, and where irrigation was practiced, as in the early nineteenth century by the governor's wife at Čäläqot in Tegré, no fewer than three harvests were obtained.

Crop yields were probably not so different from those seen by Bruce in the previous century. The meticulous German traveller Rüppell reported that wheat yields were six-fold on bad, eight on good, and as much as eleven on exceptional land, while the French Scientific Mission thought that they ranged, for both wheat and *téf*, from about eight to sixteen in the highlands, but could reach no less than sixty in the plains of Wägära and some river valleys.

The yields of various grains and cereals, as given by various travellers, were as follows:

---

[3] Ferret and Galinier (1847), II, 397-8.

Crop	Traveller		
	French Scientific Mission	Ferret and Galinier	Girard
Wheat	16	14 - 16	16
Téf	15 - 20	-	20
Dagusa, or Finger-Millet	45	24 - 45	50
Mašilla or sorghum	100	-	-
Barley	15 - 25	-	-
Lentils	-	18 - 20	-
Chick-peas	-	9 - 12	-
Broad beans	-	7 - 8	-
Oats	15 - 25	-	-

Notwithstanding satisfactory crop yields harvests were far from regular, and failures not infrequent. The peasantry was therefore inevitably much concerned with the question of crop yields, and this preoccupation entered the county's folk memory, as reflected in several Ethiopian folktales. In one a hard-working farmer sows ten *dawulla* of cereals, i.e. the equivalent of 40 to 50 litres, only to receive a harvest many months later of nine *dawulla*. When he bemoaned his fate a companion, who was a wit, declares that he has probably lost nothing, for the nine *dawulla*, if remeasured more carefully, might well turn out to be actually ten. In another story a farmer sows three *dawulla*, and reaps no more than four, whereupon his companion ridicules him, observing that if he had boiled the same amount of beans he would have obtained a similar increase - and would have saved himself the trouble of cultivating the land.[4]

Bärbäré, or Red Pepper

Many peasants produced *bärbäré*, or red pepper, which played an important rôle in the national diet. They dug and fenced small allotments which they sowed and then planted out with small seedlings. These they covered with reeds, and frequently sprinkled with water. When the plants were about a foot high they were transplanted elsewhere. A plantation of seedlings covering only ten or twelve feet in circumference was sufficient to fill a large field, which, according to Krapf, could earn its proprietor between two and four Maria Theresa dollars.[5]

Agricultural Taxes and Other Exactions

The peasantry throughout this period had to pay the gentry an inordinate number of dues, and were subject, as in the past, to frequent and often arbitrary depredations by the soldiers. The peasants, Plowden felt, were thus the victims of "bad government, military oppression, and the constant devastations of war," and had to bear "directly or indirectly, the whole burden of taxation and large standing

---

[4] Ferret and Galinier (1847), II, 397-9; Salt (1814), 253; Parkyns (1853) I, 119; Lefebvre (1845-8) I, 122, III, 256; Combes and Tamisier (1838) III, 262; Beke (1842) 86; Valentia (1809) III, 125, 232; Pearce (1831) I, 200; Rüppell (1838-40), I, 31, 312; Girard (1873) 290; Moreno (1948) 28-30.

[5] Isenberg and Krapf (1843) 435-6.

Winnowing. From T. Bent, *The Sacred City of the Ethiopians* (London, 1893).

armies."[6] The system of taxation constituted, in fact, a continual source of harassment and anxiety. Pearce, who had many opportunities to witness this at first hand, recalls:

> "The peasants or labouring people, in all parts of Abyssinia, never know when their persons or property are safe, on which account they are obliged to repair to the habitations of their chief on holydays, some presenting bread, butter, honey, and corn, and others a goat, sheep, or fowls, to keep in favour and to prevent him from sending his soldiers to live upon their premises."[7]

---

[6] Plowden (1868) 135-8.

[7] Pearce (1831) I, 340.

140

The extent of such depredations caused Plowden to observe that the position of the peasants could be expected to "improve," if they had a more peaceful government and "some security." Proof of this was apparent in the neighbourhood of towns, where "military license", as we shall see in a later chapter, was "in some degree checked by the priests," and where the "ravages of war" were therefore "less felt," as a result of which there were many "highly cultivated" fields. Such land was "eagerly sought for," and sold for "a good price," thus showing that "the sweets of tranquil labour" were "at least appreciated." It was no less significant that many of the peasants of Dabat had gone, according to Combes and Tamisier, to Bälässa where they enjoyed "greater security." In the greater part of the country, however, the peasantry suffered from "numerous imposts" which varied "according to the traditional customs of each village." Besides having to pay a "certain portion" of their produce in kind to the Ras, or other great chief, and sometimes a regular tax in money, they were expected to furnish oxen to plough the King's lands. The extent of the burden on the peasantry can be illustrated by the case of "Temmenon," a Tegré farmer who had been subjected, entirely without warning, to twice the usual tax. This, Parkyns reported, had almost reduced him to bankruptcy, with the result that he had been "obliged to sell his horse, mule, and several plough oxen." Even then the debt was still partly unpaid, and the poor man was living in "perpetual fear" of a visit from the soldiers.

Taxes on the peasantry were normally paid at *Mäsqäl*, the Feast of the Cross.[8] Such exactions were often fairly arbitrary, for, as Plowden noted, the governor had the "right to oxen, sheep, goats, butter, honey and every other requisite for subsistence," and had to be:

> "received with joy and feasting by his subjects whenever he visits them, and can demand from them contributions on fifty pretexts - he is going on a campaign, or has just returned from one; he has lost a horse, or married a wife; his property has been consumed by fire, or he has lost his all in battle, or the sacred duty of a funeral banquet cannot be fulfilled without their aid."[9]

A not dissimilar situation prevailed in Šäwa where Douglas Graham, a member of the British diplomatic mission, reported that King Sahlä Sellasé was "continually sending for cattle and honey and sheep in quantities," and added: "these offerings fall hard upon all classes, for should the Governor give entirely from his own means, he will find himself soon totally impoverished, and should he tax his people too roughly in the preparation of his gift, complaints will inevitably reach the royal ear, which are certain to strip the offender of government and remaining property." Some of the King of Šäwa's taxes were nevertheless basically reasonable. The Wahama tribe in the Awaš area, according to the British traveller Charles Johnston, thus for example paid Sählä Sellasé each year "one ox for every hundred head of cattle in their herds," which, according to Harris, amounted to only "three or four hundred" head on a herd of "many thousand." The problem was, however, that the monarch was "ever sending requisitions" for further livestock.

---

[8] Pearce (1831) I, 339-40; Combes and Tamisier (1838) II, 22; Parkyns (1853) 219-20; GB House of Commons (1868) 107; Rüppell (1838-40) II, 31; Plowden (1868) 135, 137-8.

[9] Plowden (1868) 137-8; GB House of Commons (1868) 107.

Taxation in fact played so major a role in the peasant's life that Plowdwn went so far as to declare that: "the prosperous or adverse condition of a village depends almost entirely upon the rapacity or moderation of its immediate chief." Conditions were at times so serious, when a harsh master was in charge, that some peasants would actually have abandoned their lands, Plowden believed, were it not for a law that empowered the local chief to seize them, and force them to cultivate their farms or give security for their share of the tax. Any attempted flight would moreover be opposed by other villagers, for, "though only three inhabitants should remain," they were expected to pay the whole sum at which the village was assessed. Notwithstanding such constraints one levy of taxes by Däjazmač Webé, the ruler of Tegré, was so onerous that "the greater part of the people" according to Parkyns, actually ran away from their villages.

The peasants also suffered, as in earlier centuries, from the obligation of having to provide hospitality to travellers of all kinds. It was customary for officials, state visitors from any province whether friendly or hostile, and anyone travelling under a chief's protection to be given free lodging for himself and his servants. Such travellers were supposed, Pearce claims, to find their own provisions, and it was also "a general custom", when a lodger killed a cow, sheep, or goat, "to give the skin to the owner of the house, with a piece of meat, and frequently to ask him to meals," though this "depended upon the good-will" of the lodger. Many travellers, however, expected to be fed without giving recompense in return. The worst offenders were travelling chiefs, who would "nearly ruin the inhabitants, by burning the doors of their houses, tables, cattle-pens, etc. for fire-wood," and by killing their sheep and drinking their beer. On such occasions, however, no one dared complain to the governor "for fear of having his premises burned altogether, and himself chained and brought into some unjust law-suit, which would inevitably drain him of his last farthing."[10]

Despite such abuses relations between farmers and travellers were often courteous. Parkyns relates that on one by no means untypical occasion he arrived at a village in Tegré only to find that all the inhabitants were at work in the fields. He therefore sat down under a tree to await their return as evening was approaching. Not long afterwards a number of villagers passed him, one of their number, "a very respectable but warm-looking gentleman," making a low bow and wishing him good evening. "I thought," he says:

> "their going straight in saying nothing rather impolite; but this was
> excusable, as no doubt they were much fatigued, and must have their
> supper before they could attend to us. However, I was not long left in
> suspense. Immediately on their entry there was a great bustle and moving
> of skins and other articles of furniture. Meanwhile one of the boys who
> had gone in with the others came out again bringing me a large bowl of
> new milk to drink, and before I had well begun my second turn, after each
> of my servants had had his, the respectable-looking man made his
> appearance more respectable than before, but not so warm-looking, for
> he had taken off his dirty breeches and sheepskin in which he had been
> working ... He politely ushered me into the house. The bustle we had
> heard had been occasioned by their placing skins, a couch etc. in the best

---

[10] GB House of Commons (186*0 107;Graham (1844); **Parkyns** (1853) I, 218-9; **Johnston** (1844) I, 477; Harris (1844), II, 203, III, 32; Plowden (1868) 137; **Parkyns** (1853) I, 219; **Pearce** (1831) I, 164-5.

hut, and removing some corn- jars and other utensils which had formerly occupied it. Having himself arranged the couch for me, he seated me on it and then going out brought us a good supply of provisions, serving me with his own hands, and putting into my mouth the very supper which no doubt was intended for himself; nor could I even induce him to sit down with me, though he must have been very hungry. He also gave us abundance of milk, and corn for the animals."[11]

Relations between the peasants and travelling soldiers, however, were often less cordial. Bands of the latter when in search of food would often form themselves into small parties, and then go "from farmer to farmer, living at free quarters, no one daring to deny them", unless they were "too exorbitant and unreasonable in their demands." On such occasions, Pearce says, the peasants would "give a general alarm, and raise the neighbouring villages to their assistance," with the result that "many lives" were "often lost on both sides." When news of such clashes reached the ears of the governor he would have both parties brought before him. If it were proved, on oath, that the peasant had offered the soldiers everything reasonable, such as a goat, bread and beer, the raiding party would be dismissed from service and their guns confiscated. Should they have killed any of the peasantry the man or men who had struck the fatal blow would be handed over to the relatives of the deceased. If, on the other hand, it was found that the farmer had refused to give the soldiers a supper or even lodgings he would be fined, in some cases more than he was able to pay.

Peasants and soldiers were often engaged in a seemingly unending battle of wits. The former, in an attempt to save themselves from the latter's exactions, would dig large underground pits, known in Amharic as *gwudgwads* which would be plastered inside with cow-dung and mud, and, according to William Coffin, a British observer, could hold as much as 300 to 400 gallons. Some of these pits would be dug in the vicinity of towns and villages, but others would be in open fields. When an invasion, or visitation by the soldiers was expected, the pits would be filled with grain, and other valuables. Their mouths would then be very carefully covered, first with spars laid close together, so that no earth might fall through, after which the area above them would be filled with earth to bring it to a level with the adjoining ground. Should the spot happen to be upon agricultural land the whole area would be ploughed over and over to conceal the mouth of the *gwudgwad*, or, if on other ground, it was made to appear like the land about it. If it was near a town or village, wood-ashes and rubbish might well be thrown over it to give it the appearance of a dunghill. The custom of burying grain, however, was so prevalent, and the soldiers "so well acquainted with the mode of finding these hiding-places," that these "scarcely ever" escaped observation. Armed clashes between the soldiers and the peasantry frequently resulted, and "more blood," Coffin declares, was in general shed in this way than in "regular battles." Tension of this kind continued throughout this period. Plowden a generation later noted that the peasants in the northern provinces had soldiers "constantly" quartered on them, "except in some districts that always turn out *en masse* to resist, and where the troops dare not venture."

Notwithstanding the miseries inflicted by the troops the northern peasantry would often follow the former's example by looting each other. "A whole province of

---

[11] Parkyns (1853) I, 218-9.

cultivators" in times when the military were "engaged elsewhere," might thus meet, Plowden records, "by accord," and "some thousands" of them would attack another province, "destroying, burning and bequeathing feuds to distant generations."

The situation in Šäwa by contrast tended to be more peaceful, with the result that the peasants, protected, Combes and Tamisier claims, by a "vigilant administration," had "nothing to fear from the looting of the soldiers," and therefore devoted themselves "with great energy to the cultivation of their lands, certain to harvest after having sown."[12]

The Effects of Warfare

The peasantry of the early nineteenth century suffered greatly from frequent civil war. Scenes of destruction were reported by many observers of the period. Pearce, who accompanied the forces of Ras Wäldä Sellasé, governor of Tegré, in 1810, describes for example how they burnt the town of Addi Gahso, after which, finding the corn in the neighbouring fields ready to cut, they spent five days destroying it. They then advanced "to the river Munnai, the finest country in that part of Abyssinia for corn and cattle" and "stopped a week to destroy everything." Only a few months later Wagšum Kenfu, the ruler of Lasta, advanced and burnt all the enemy"s "towns and villages," after which he carried off what cattle he could find: "five thousand bullocks, and a greater number of horses, mules, sheep and goats."

A decade or so later Rüppell reported that travelling towards the Täkkäzé in western Tegré he did "not encounter a single inhabited village," but "only the ruins of abandoned settlements." Gobat, writing of the country between Gojjam and Sämén where the "fiery banner" of civil war had waved for over 30 years, likewise observed at about the same time that while passing through a "champaign country" with a "rich and productive soil" he had not seen a "solitary village," and in a fifteen mile stretch found nothing but "a desolate waste," without a hamlet and "scarce a vestige of cultivation."[13]

The situation in Širé, hitherto "one of the richest and most productive" districts of Tegré, was not dissimilar. Lämma, the local governor, according to Parkyns, had pillaged and "entirely ruined" the area. The land was in consequence "nearly deserted," and:

"where once were prosperous villages with their markets and a happy and thriving people, the traveller now sees but a few wretched huts, vast tracts of fertile land lying uncultivated, and, of the few inhabitants that remain, many that were formerly owners of several yoke of oxen each are now to be found clubbing together to cultivate just enough corn to pay their taxes and keep themselves and their families from starvation."[14]

---

[12] Pearce (1831) I, 183-4, 206-7; Plowden (1868) 135; Combes and Tamisier (1838) II, 346.

[13] Pearce (1831) I, 69, 72; Gobat (1850) 151-2.

[14] Parkyns (1853) I, 223.

Conditions further north in **Rohabayta** were scarcely any better, for the "whole" neighbourhood had been "reduced to extreme poverty," and the "entire population" "scarcely" owned "as many cattle as one moderately rich man possessed prior to its oppression."

A similar tale was told of parts of the north-west of the country, notably Wägära. Rüppell reported that this province, once "the most cultivated and populated" in the entire empire, had been ravaged by sixty years of civil war, with the result that agriculture had been "destroyed", and the area "depopulated." Only a few herds of cattle were to be found, tended by nomad-like families who did not remain there throughout the year, but in the dry season withdrew to meadows near Lake Tana. This picture is confirmed by Combes and Tamisier who recall that the civil wars of the previous two generations had ruined the country, and much reduced its population. The peasants in particular had suffered "greatly" from the fighting between Ras Maryé and Däjazmac Webé . Farmers, "accustomed to see their harvests ravaged" and "their huts pillaged and burnt by the enemy," no longer sowed "more than a very little land." Many villages had been abandoned, and only their remains could be seen, so that what had once been a "fine country" was no more than a "desert."

The ravages of war varied greatly, however, from one part of the country to another, and were perhaps least felt in Säwa, which, as Gobat noted, had been spared the "hard-fought strifes and bitter contentions" which had "embroiled the northern provinces." By the third quarter of the century its ruler, King Sahlä Sellasé, had nevertheless embarked on a series of expeditions which had "very much extended the limits of his kingdom, especially to the south and west."[15]

Causes of Conservatism

The numerous exactions levied on the peasantry were serious, not only because they led to impoverishment and hampered production, but also because they stifled initiative, and therefore led to general agricultural stagnation. Plowden, who had many opportunities of talking with peasants in various parts of the country, states that the latter, though "ruder" than the soldiers, were on the whole "intelligent," and could be expected to have improved their methods of cultivation - if only they had "a more peaceful government and some security for property." They had, however, to be convinced that it was "better to cross a river by a bridge than to wade through a dangerous torrent; or that a mill for grinding corn is preferable to a slave-girl." How they were to be convinced of this, however, the good consul does not specify.[16]

Monkeys, Wild Hogs, Locusts and Other Pests

The peasantry also suffered grievously, as in former times, from the depredations of various pests, including monkeys, wild hogs, porcupines, addax, elephants, birds, and, particularly in the north of the country, swarms of locusts.

---

[15] Parkyns (1853) I, 272; Pearce (1831) I, 69, 72; Rüppell (1838-40), II, 72; Combes and Tamisier (1838) II,19, IV, 34; Arnauld d'Abbadie (1868) 149.

[16] Plowden (1868) 136.

Monkeys and wild hogs were particularly serious at the beginning of the rains when fields furthest from villages were "frequently" damaged by these animals, which, Pearce says, were "very numerous" near the mountains. The "larger plains" were alone exempt from such intruders. Monkeys were at times so brazen that Pearce on at least one occasion saw an assemblage of them drive the peasantry from the field. The beasts were only repulsed when reinforcements came from a nearby village, and even then, seeing that these had no guns, the animals retired but slowly. In certain areas, among them Širé, elephants were likewise a great nuisance, and would "pluck up the young corn and trample it, as if done on purpose and out of mischief."

To protect their crops, peasants would often appoint guards, armed with slings and stones, who remained in the fields both night and day. "It was also not uncommon" Rüppell reports, "for the cultivators to place sticks over hollows in the ground, which, when beaten, served like a drum to frighten away animal intruders, while at night large bundles of reeds would be lit and swung in front of them." High rustic platforms were often also erected so that the watchers could keep a look-out in safety, as Plowden says, from both the hyena and the lion.[17]

Locusts, against whom there was virtually no defence, were an even more formidable scourge. Gobat, who saw a "formidable army" of them at Addigrat in June 1831, recalls that "the first signal of their approach was a noise resembling the hum of many swarms of bees", but this rapidly grew in intensity, and before long resembled that of "heavy hail at some distance". On going out of his house to discover whence the sound originated he saw that "the air was teaming with locusts," which had "greatly obscured" the light of the sun. He found, however, that the insects were merely an "advance guard," for he "perceived, about a league distant, several faint clouds, as it were, rising from the earth." This "mist" soon afterwards became "so thick," that it "entirely hid" the sky and neighbouring mountains from view. As the insects approached the noise "fully equalled the roaring of the sea", whereupon:

> "terror and alarm filled every eye with weeping. The air was so darkened, that, we could scarcely discern the place of the sun; and the earth was so covered with these insects, that we could see nothing else. Children, running about the fields, at only a stone's throw, could scarcely be seen though the multitudes of locusts hovering about them."[18]

Festivals and Saints' Days

Agricultural productivity throughout this time was significantly curtailed by the fact that the peasantry in the Christian highlands was very religious, and abstained from work on the country's numerous Saints' days and other festivals. Plowden, a stern critic, comments that the peasants would have been "laborious", were it not for such "priestly devices" which forced "the whole population to be idle for a third of the year."[19]

---

[17] Pearce (1831) I, 280, 343-4; Rüppell (1838-40) II, 160-1; Plowden (1868) 136.

[18] Gobat (1850) 392-3.

[19] Plowden (1868) 135.

Commercialisation of Agriculture

Despite the decline of Gondär in the late eighteenth and early nineteenth centuries some commercialised agriculture continued to be practiced in the countryside around the old capital. Rüppell for example saw "countless herds of cattle" being brought from Wägära to the city, whence they returned at the beginning of the rains, while Combes and Tamasier report that there were many flocks in the neighbourhood which furnished the old metropolis with "a large quantity of milk products."

Commercialisation of agriculture likewise took place in several other areas, notably in Hamasén and Särayé on the northernmost plateau, which, as in the past, supplied wheat, durrah and other cereals for sale to Red Sea shipping at Massawa as well as for export to Arabia. The pastoralists to the north and east of Hamasén also produced butter which was taken to the port of Massawa for shipment to Jeddah.[20]

Standard of Living

Notwithstanding their hard work and the relatively plentiful rainfall in the highlands, the various extortions suffered by the peasantry meant that they lived but frugally. There would seem no reason to dissent from the reasoned opinion of Henry Salt that though the chiefs on the whole fared "well," the "lower class" but "rarely" obtained "sufficient, even of the coarse teff bread" of which their food almost entirely consisted.[21]

---

[20] Rüppell (1838-40) II, 137; Combes and Tamisier (1838) I, 105, 189, II, 22; Lefebvre (1845-8) II, Part II, 40; Ferret and Galinier (1847) II, 399.

[21] Valentia (1809) III, 153-4.

III

THE SOLDIERS

The Multitude of Soldiers

One of the effects of many decades of civil war was that the country by the middle of the nineteenth century was teeming with men under arms. Plowden considered that they constituted not only the most powerful class, but also the "most numerous" - the peasantry presumably alone excepted. The soldiers numbered "at least 200,000" men, and were accompanied by an even greater multitude of camp-followers, so that there were a total of perhaps "half a million idlers" who preyed on the population at large. The number of soldiers was scarcely surprising, for there were several provinces, such as Yäjju, where "every man capable of bearing arms" was a warrior, at least on his own land where he fought and ploughed alternately. All the servants of a chief moreover were soldiers, the two terms being in effect synonymous.

The vast majority of the soldiers, as in former times, were peasants who went to war whenever their overlords wished, and were expected as far as possible to provide themselves with both weapons and provisions. Soldiers, though seldom in receipt of regular pay, did not often suffer many deprivations. While on campaign, Plowden reports, they were either "fed by a tax in corn" which they themselves collected and therefore "soon doubled", or else took whatever they wanted from the peasantry. Frequent expeditions in search of spoil were likewise often conducted against "pagans."

While in service the soldiers were also provided by their ruler with frequent meals, each of which, according to Plowden, resembled a feast. There were in addition many palace banquets to which they were admitted "almost indiscriminately." At such carousals they would be "gorged with raw meat, and excited by huge droughts of mead," after which they would "recite their own warlike deeds," make "the most vaunting promises of future heroism," and "obtain rich gifts," but, though they were all armed, and often intoxicated, accidents and quarrels "seldom" occurred. The soldiers also enjoyed good promotion opportunities, for the bravest, or more fortunate, could expect to rise to high office, and benefit from the revenues accruing therefrom.

The soldiery, in the opinion of Parkyns, were, however, often recruited from "among the worst of the people", those who "preferred idleness in peace and plundering their neighbours in war to the more honest but less exciting occupation of agriculture." Roaming from one standard to another, though they had no uniform, they could "easily be distinguished," Plowden says, by their "air of military license." They were moreover almost invariably proud, and tended to "despise all other classes save the priesthood."

Each soldier who could do so kept a lad to hold his shield, a donkey to carry his provisions, a small tent in which to sleep, and "a wife to bring him water, make him bread and wash his feet after a march." Since he lived largely on loot, and was, in the more organised forces, entitled to a grain allowance for each dependant, the number of camp-followers a soldier had was seldom a burden. A soldier with a "good reputation for courage," Plowden claims, was moreover "everywhere respected": he

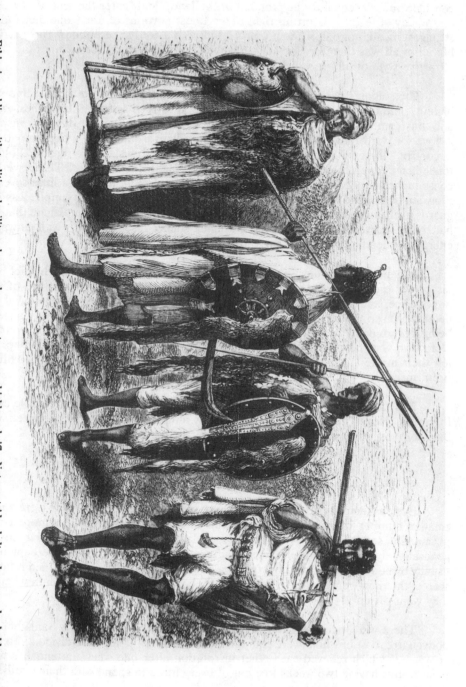

19th century Ethiopian soldiers, with traditional military dress and armament, spears, shields and rifle. Note cartridge-belt and gunpowder-holder on warrior to the right. From R. Acton, *The Abyssinian Expedition* (London, 1868).

149

would be "flattered and caressed by many Chiefs," who would strive to secure his services, and his name would be sung in ballads. He could therefore "with reason" consider himself "equal to the proudest in the land," and "enter the tent of any Chief on the day of festival, assert his right to the finest portions of meat, and demand the strongest mead; not only without reproof, but with a cordial reception." The warrior's life all in all was therefore "not disagreeable," and was moreover perhaps the "most attractive style of life" to which a soldier could aspire.

The soldier's passion for "individual distinction, leading to immediate and solid benefit," and the certainty that he might "by good fortune arrive at the highest rank," and thus command where once he had obeyed, were important in that they inspired a "love for war." Pride engendered by soldiering likewise induced "a fiery impatience of control," and an ambition that led to "unceasing rebellions and distraction." Soldiers tended, as a result, to be "proud, mutinous, and insubordinate." There were in consequence "frequent fights between rival bodies of men, though "a little severity," Plowden felt, would "soon ensure obedience." On one occasion, for example, Ras Ali's guards, refusing to march to battle, had laid on the ground, and complained that they had been starved for months, but the chief silenced soon them, "with unwanted energy", by leading a cavalry charge over them.

In general the soldiery was, however, not to be trifled with, for each chief owed his power entirely to the strength of his army. Warriors were fully aware of their importance, and changed masters "without ceremony." A military leader, faced with defeat, or even the increased reputation of a rival, was therefore "much in danger of being deserted by his army," and had therefore to treat his followers with courtesy. Defection was, however, so frequent that there was no punishment for soldiers who left their master's service - provided, Gobat says, that they did not run off with any fire-arms.

The soldiers of this time were, as formerly, accompanied by innumerable camp-followers. "Nearly half" the population of many military camps, Gobat estimated, were thus composed of women.[1]

Palace Guards

Besides the ordinary soldiers mobilised in time of emergency there were a much smaller number of palace guards, for the most part musketeers, in more or less permanent service. Unlike the soldiery at large they received a regular stipend, generally in kind. Guards in Tegré and Amhara, where fire-arms were plentiful, usually owned their own guns, but in Šäwa and Wällo, where these remained relatively scarce, the men were issued with rifles by their rulers, and handed them in whenever they went off duty.

There were, according to Johnston, "at least" 1,000 men in King Sahlä Sellasé's bodyguard, most of whom were equipped with fire-arms. They were divided into three companies which relieved each other in rotation after one week's attendance at the palace, thus having two weeks free out of every three to spend with their families. In

---

[1] GB House of Commons (1868) 103-5; Isenberg and Krapf (1843) 348; Parkyns (1853) I, 176; Gobat (1850) 413.

A 19th century Ethiopian soldier in his finest attire, with sword, shield and spear. From R. Acton, *The Abyssinian Expedition* (London, 1868).

return for their services they were given two double handfuls of grain, besides "one good meal a-day at the King's own table." The more privileged guardsmen were entitled to take their guns home with them, but the general rule was that after his term of duty was over each guard should deposit his weapon in an armoury attached to the palace where they were kept in the charge of the chief blacksmith Ato Habté. When members of the bodyguard grew old or had sons mature enough to attend in their place they became tenants of the king, and were only called on to serve when expeditions were in progress.

Guards played an important rôle, not only in defending the various provincial rulers, but also in suppressing occasional mutinies by other forces, and were therefore, Plowden reports, "generally favoured" by their masters.[2]

Traditional Weapons, Fire-arms and Horses

Ethiopian infantry and cavalry in the nineteenth century were primarily armed with spears and shields, but swords were also carried by persons of note. Fire-arms, which increased in numbers throughout the period, were in intense demand, and were acquired by any chief or man of property in a position to do so.

The diffusion of fire-arms, which depended largely on access to the coast, remained very uneven. The largest number of such weapons were found, as in the past, in Tegré. The matchlockmen of the province, according to Plowden, were "very skilful and brave," those of Agamé, one of its most easterly districts - with relatively easy access to the coast, being particularly renowned.

The largest number of horses, on the other hand, were to be found in the pastoral lands further south, and were of a "fine breed." The Galla, or Oromo, cavalry moreover by this time faced fire well, and, even when forced to retreat, would often "suddenly wheel round and inclose a rash pursuer." Possession of a steed was a sign of distinction, implying that its owner was a nobleman or man of substance, or else that he had distinguished himself in war, and had received one as a gift from his chief. Horses were used solely for fighting, or tournaments, and were never ridden for any distance. Soldiers who could afford to ride therefore invariably travelled to and from war on muleback. A soldier's horse, mule and weapons, however acquired, were (except in the case of some palace guards) invariably considered as his personal property.

Varying availability of fire-arms and horses had a significant regional effect on strategy. Amhara soldiers, who were short of rifles but had relatively numerous horses, thus preferred fighting in the open plains, and, according to Pearce, "seldom ever attempted to storm a mountain" when there were "one or two matchlocks" to defend its entrance. The men of Tegré on the other hand had "a few horse only and a great number of matchlocks" and therefore tended to chose mountainous areas in which to fight their battles.[3]

---

[2] Isenberg and Krapf (1843) 348; Johnston (1844) II, 75-7; GB House of Commons (1868) 103.

[3] GB House of Commons (1868) 103, 105; Isenberg and Krapf (1843) 348; Pearce (1831) II, 104-5, 214; Parkyns (1853) I, 343; Plowden (1868) 67.

Mobilisation and the Call to Arms

Though most of the inhabitants, as shown in the previous chapter, were engaged in agriculture, they were virtually all liable to military responsibility in times of war or other emergency. Every Christian agriculturalist in Šäwa was thus obliged, "on pain of forfeiting eight pieces of salt whenever summoned, to follow his immediate governor to the field." A "small bribe in cloth or honey," Harris says, would "sometimes obtain leave of absence," but the peasant was "usually ready and anxious for the foray," the more so as it afforded the chance of capturing a slave or a flock of livestock, besides obtaining honour in the monarch's eye - and resultant chance of political advancement.[4]

In times of emergency, or whenever it was desired to summon the population to arms, drums would be beaten in market-places throughout the area of mobilisation. The drummer began in very slow time, but gradually speeded up the tempo so as to end with very quick strokes. He repeated this over and over again until he had attracted a substantial audience, after which he cried out the ruler's decree in a loud voice, declaring for example:

"Clothe your servants, feed your horses, prepare your provisions, cut down and clear the regular roads of trees and bushes, in all quarters. I am not determined as yet which road I may take, but I march on such a day; take care that none remain at home. If the father is weak, the son must appear, and if the son, the father, on pain of your property being forfeited to the *wotada* (soldiers) and your persons to me. It is not my tongue that speaks to this effect but the governor's" (whose name was then cited).[5]

This speech would often be repeated several times, sometimes at every market-day for weeks, before the final day of mobilisation.

A chief, fearing that the enemy might be given warning and thus be enabled to prepare for impending attack, seldom let his soldiers, let alone the public at large, know the direction in which he intended to march. Proclamations directing the clearing of roads in directions entirely contrary to that to be taken were indeed not infrequently issued with a view to deceiving the enemy.[6]

Edicts, as in the past, often embodied threats of punishment for those who failed to respond to the call to arms. One such proclamation in Šäwa quoted by Captain Harris, in the 1840's, declared:

"Hear, oh, hear! Thus saith the King. Behold we have foes, and would trample upon their necks. Prepare ye every one for war. On the approaching festival of Abba Kinos, whoso faileth to present himself at

---

[4] Harris (1844) III, 168.

[5] Harris (1844) II, 22. See also I, 62.

[6] Pearce (1831) I, 62, II, 22-3

Yeolo as a good and loyal subject, mounted, armed, and carrying provisions for twenty-one days, shall be held as a traitor, and shall forfeit his property during seven years."[7]

Mobilisation, though an act primarily affecting the male population, was often actively encouraged by the womenfolk. During one early nineteenth century crisis in Tegré, for example, the latter are reported to have gathered together every evening, crying out, "at the highest pitch of their voices, 'To arms! To arms!'"[8]

Dress, and Decorations

Soldiers throughout this period wore the ordinary clothes of the country - uniforms being a thing of the future, but their dress, was, according to Parkyns, "usually cut in a somewhat smarter manner" than that of the population at large. Soldiers preparing for battle loved, in particular, to dress as far as possible in considerable splendour.

Different ways of plaiting the hair were often used to denote the number of men a soldier had killed, and persons with no such achievement to their credit, it is said, were denied the privilege of plastering their heads with butter.[9]

Military Reviews

Military manoeuvres were usually held at *Mäsqäl*, or Feast of the Cross, which occurred in late September, and marked the end of the rainy season, a time when the soldiers and their chiefs began to prepare for the ensuing year's campaigning. Parades were also sometimes held three months later at *Ṭemqät*, or the Epiphany, in January, by which time the rivers had largely subsided, and troop movement was thus much facilitated.

The soldiers' reviews were often most impressive. One held in front of Ras Wäldä Sellasé at Antalo in 1813 was described by Pearce as "fantastic", but was not without some danger, for the musketeers opened fire prematurely, with the result that one man was killed and a horse shot through the leg. Such accidents seem to have been fairly common at that time for soldiers often travelled around with guns containing shot which they could not unload, and, being reluctant to discharge them before the parade, actually fired them during reviews with real bullets. Orders were, however, later given by Wäldä Sellasé to prevent such untoward occurrences.

Annual *Mäsqäl* parades were also held at other provincial capitals. At Däbrä Berhan in Šäwa, for example, there was a yearly rally before King Sahlä Sellasé when, according to Johnston, "every tenant and slave capable of bearing arms" was "expected

---

[7] Harris (1844) II,155.

[8] Gobat (1850) 397. See also 417.

[9] Parkyns (1853) I, 176; GB House of Commons (1868) 103-4.

to be present." The ruler watched sitting "in a small cabinet" on the balcony of his palace, while about 6,000 warriors filed past on a large meadow-ground.[10]

The March

Soldiers on the march were usually under the direct command of their ruler or chief whose expedition they accompanied, and advanced day by day at his pace. The army would usually be led by the forces of the Fitawrari, or commander of the advance-guard, and would be flanked by those of a Qäñazmač, or officer in charge of the right wing, and of a Grazmač, in charge of the left wing. Notwithstanding this theoretical arrangement scarcely any order was usually apparent, for soldiers and camp-followers would seemingly press forward in "indiscriminate confusion," which, on reaching a precipitous pass or narrow ford, often occasioned accidents.

Princesses and other women of the court, anxious to keep themselves aloof from the ordinary soldiers, often began the march at dawn, or even earlier before the soldiers had struck camp, and were thus on the move before any "vulgar eye" might gaze on them. The Fitawrari would be the next to move, after which the soldiery, the camp followers and the beasts of burden would in turn all start their journey. The road to be followed could seldom be mistaken, for the line of people, from the old camp to the new, was usually unbroken.

Christian armies, as in earlier times, never marched on Sundays or other Church holidays, nor were battles fought on such days unless at the initiative of enemies of other faiths - as in the case in 1868 of the British assault on Emperor Téwodros's citadel at Mäqdäla.[11]

The Camp

Camps were arranged, as for many centuries previously, in a methodical manner which reflected both the hierarchy of state and the general order of march. The Fitawrari and his followers would thus be quartered perhaps three or four miles in front of the main camp, with their tents facing the direction of march. The King, or Ras, was "always stationed in the centre of the camp, in general upon the highest spot." His Bajerond, or head secretary, and his Blattengéta, or treasurer, placed themselves in front of his tent, a short distance away, while his household and horses were in the rear. To the sides of the royal or governatorial tent, and around the whole of the camp, were the *gojos*, or huts, of his personal soldiers. The chiefs, whose individual camps were sometimes in close proximity to each other, were located further off, and were surrounded in a rough circle by the huts of their soldiers.

Camps consisted of tents as well as rapidly constructed huts. Däjazmač Webé's camp, which was described by Parkyns, contained a great diversity of tents: "some bell-shaped, some square, like an English marquee; some white, and others of the

---

[10] Valentia (1809) II, 131; Pearce (1831) I, 138, 280, II, 18; Harris (1844) II, 74; Johnston (1844) II, 375; Isenberg and Krapf (1843) 113.

[11] GB House of Commons (1868) 103-4; Plowden (1868) 216-7; Pearce (1831) I, 63; Gobat (1850) 325.

155

black woollen stuff made principally in the southern provinces of Tigré". There were also "huts of all sizes and colours." The chief's personal establishment, which was in the centre of the camp, consisted on the other hand of "three or four large thatched wigwams," as well as a tent, the whole "enclosed by a double fence of thorns." Guards were stationed at the entrances, and the space between the two fences was divided into courts, in which soldiers or others craving an audience awaited the chief's pleasure. Most camps in Pearce's opinion presented a "somewhat orderly appearance," but could not be called "regular" - though Parkyns thought their sight was "by no means unpleasing."

A camp's duration varied greatly. Some served only for one or two days, while others lasted for weeks or even months on end. Soldiers returning from an expedition often, moreover, established themselves on their earlier sites, and might therefore leave some of their wooden structures for later use. Camps in enemy country, on the other hand, were almost invariably burnt to the ground before the army departed to prevent them falling into the hands of foes.[12]

Warfare, and Chivalry

Ethiopian soldiers in d'Abbadie's opinion were "very brave," and, if well led, fought with "great tenacity." The flower of the army, as in medieval Europe, was composed of horsemen. Regular battles, however, usually began with shooting by the riflemen, who would rush forward in a charge which would in most cases decide the outcome of the engagement, for the infantry, who were in the main badly armed, served mainly later to capture prisoners.

Fighting was for the most part conducted with considerable chivalry. Exchanges of civilities would "constantly" take place between hostile camps, messengers were respected, and prisoners, Plowden records, were "generally well treated, if of any rank, even with courtesy." A chief might thus send news to his adversary, if the latter was not in the field, of the defeat of his army, and the envoy bringing such bad news would almost invariably receive a handsome douceur. Messages, though couched in polite terms, might often, however, have an ironic core. Webé, when fighting against Däjazmac Säbagades, on one occasion for example sent the latter a seemingly polite message requesting him "to preserve the grass" in the neighbourhood of Adwa as he, Webé, would have "need of it for his horses when he had taken the country." Säbagades returned an equally ironic invitation to Webé and his men "to come to his country, as he was expecting them, and would not fail to prepare a great feast in their honour."

Cruelty, Plowden reports, was "rare", for "after a battle, as before," all was "good humour and laughter," and the vanquished generally shared the feast with the victors. Violence moreover was seldom offered to women who were captured, and ransom money was usually fixed with amenity. Severities were sometimes practiced against persons regarded as rebels, but in general the Ethiopian conqueror was "merciful." Much killing was, however, often carried out against the "pagan" Šanqellas and Teltäl,

---

[12] Pearce (1831) I, 211-2, II, 190; Parkyns (1853) I, 174-5; GB House of Commons (1868) 104.

but in their case the soldiers were persuaded that such ferocity was a "privilege of Christianity."

Fighting was still frequently followed by the castration of the dead. Foreskins were taken not only by and from "heathen" armies, but also, Plowden notes, in "battles of Christian against Christian." After an engagement these trophies would be displayed before the victorious commander, and often hung on the palace walls as a sign of triumph. The number of corpses thus castrated was often considerable. Pearce reports that on one occasion at Adwa, for example, the forces of Däjazmač Säbagades brought "one thousand nine hundred and seventy" foreskins.[13]

Battles

The decision to begin hostilities would be taken by the ruler or chief, in many cases after a council of war. Counsellors would sometimes be summoned to a formal assembly to hear their opinions, but on other occasions their views would be asked privately. The latter procedure was often followed by Däjazmač Webé as it had the advantage, Gobat notes, of enabling the chief to do as he pleased without being seen to reject the advice of others.

Once the decision to attack was taken, general instructions would be given to each chief who would be told where to position himself and his forces. Thereafter, however, each soldier fought largely as he pleased. The infantry, if we can believe Plowden - who had in fact participated in many an engagement - would thus advance or stand still as their courage led them; the horsemen would charge in large or small numbers when and where they thought fit; the matchlockmen would fire as they pleased; and each man, on seeing that he had killed one of the enemy, would shout his war cry, and proceed to collect and display his trophies, without waiting for the final end of the battle. Engagements often lasted only a few hours, seldom for more than a day. Fighting in many cases soon gave way to plundering which might begin whenever one side or the other gained the first "trifling advantage." It was therefore, curiously enough, "often very difficult to discover" which side had actually won. Another feature of the unstructured system of warfare was that soldiers, not being accustomed to rely on each other, were "absurdly subject to panics." It was thus not unknown for "a whole army" to run away from a single man who had charged into their camp at night shouting his war-cry. Notwithstanding this "desultory manner of fighting" there was often "considerable loss of life," for at the end of a campaign the soldiers would frequently "roam about their respective districts, arms in hand" exacting whatever they could obtain from the peasantry, who would seek revenge by slaying "remorselessly all fugitives of either side."[14]

---

[13] Antoine d'Abbadie (1868) 22; GB House of Commons (1868) 104; Parkyns (1853) II, 115; Pearce (1831)I, 71, II, 101.

[14] Gobat (1850) 441-2; GB House of Commons (1868) 103, 105; Parkyns (1853) I, 176.

Cavalry and infantry, with spears and swords, off to battle. From T. Lefebvre and others, *Voyage en Abyssinie* (Paris, 1845-8).

Looting

Looting, as already noted, was common practice, with the result, Plowden asserts, that there was "a constant enmity between the military and the population at large." Groups of soldiers would form themselves into bands, almost at random, and spend their time foraging, while the rest of their comrades remained in camp, looking after the baggage, if they had any, which was "seldom the case," Pearce says, unless they had acquired it by plunder. Raiding parties often came upon considerable quantities of supplies, for the soldiers, were "very expert in discovering hidden stores."

When provisions became scarce in the camp the ruler might himself consign a district for plunder. The drum would then be beaten, and the order for looting be given. Plowden, who witnessed one such expedition, explains that there was "no quarrel" with the people of the area to be raided, and that their head-man received only half an hour's warning. The looting was, however, so successful that the plunderers were busy for three whole days. Though the country raided was only a few miles square the grain collected met the army's needs for six months. The operation nevertheless involved much wanton destruction, for many houses were burnt to the ground, and four times as much grain was consumed by flames as actually taken away by the troops. For the soldiers, however, the expedition was deemed a great success. Their earlier cries of hunger gave way to songs of joy and merriment, and they ate "as much as they could manage, caring little when it might be finished." Faced with such depredations it is little surprise that the inhabitants often fled their homes, and took everything they could carry to the churches, or other places of asylum, for safe-keeping.

The fighting, and looting, of the first part of the nineteenth century, as many observers testify, resulted in considerable impoverishment of the peasantry and population at large. Rüppell noted in the 1830's that agriculture was increasingly neglected, communications were often completely interrupted, and the people were becoming progressively poorer. Arnauld d' Abbadie likewise remarked that while bands of marauding soldiers ravaged the country, trade was often carried out only with arms in the hand; peasants no longer occupied themselves with anything but fighting and pillage; cultivation was frequently left solely to women and children; abandoned lands were increasing in number; flocks were disappearing, and wild animals were taking the place of people. This picture was confirmed a generation or so later by the Swiss adventurer and scholar Werner Münzinger who declared that the "incessant commotions" from which the country had suffered had "paralysed" its productive power, for "trade enjoyed no security, and labour abandoned the plough to take to arms," while Parkyns observed, in more general terms, that civil war was "the perpetual scourge of Abyssinia" and "the principal cause of its poverty and barbarism."

A 19th century scene of looting, with houses on fire, and cattle and grain seized. From G. Massaia, *I miei trentacinque anni di missione nell' alta Etiopia* (Rome and Milan, 1895-95).

Despite the protection afforded by the Church to places of asylum, urban settlements at times also suffered from the ravages of the soldiery. In Gondär for example Gobat reported in 1830 that the city was "full" of men who were "plundering" the metropolis, while a subsequent Ethiopian royal chronicle tells of soldiers breaking into the city in 1840, eating up all the provisions, and thereby producing a "great famine" in which "many people perished of hunger."[15]

An early nineteenth century warrior with sword, shield and spear. From T. Lefebvre and others, *Voyage en Abyssinie* (Paris, 1845-8).

---

[15] GB House of Commons (1868) 103; Pearce (1831) I, 62-3, 206; Plowden (1868) 228; Gobat (1850) 253, 281-82, 386, 426; Rüppell (1838-40) I, 234, II, 52, 136, 332; Parkyns (1853) 1, 129; Arnauld d'Abbadie (1868) 142-3; Munzinger (1858) 35; Weld Blundell (1922) 492.

IV

THE NOBILITY

Acquisition of Power from the Monarch

By the early nineteenth century the government of northern Ethiopia, formerly vested in emperors claiming descent from King Solomon and the Queen of Sheba, had largely passed into the hands of the nobles and provincial chiefs. The latter, having usurped the powers hitherto wielded by the monarch, followed the latter's policy of distributing their lands among their followers or favourites who raised forces according to their rank and revenue. The tenure of such subordinates was, as in the past, still far from secure, for the ruler might, as Plowden says, "in a moment deprive any chief of all his power." Appointments to office with rare exceptions were not hereditary, and were indeed seldom of long duration.

Despite their usurpation of the prerogatives of royalty, provincial governors suffered, like the rest of the population, from the civil strife of the period. To gain the support of their followers chiefs were obliged in particular to grant away much of their land, and thereby surrendered a large proportion of their revenue. This expedient failed, however, to gain the full allegiance of their men, who, conscious that their masters had "no legal right to the sovereignty" they assumed, were always ready to "desert them, and seek a more munificent master." Though the basic structure of the old feudal system remained there was thus considerable instability, and frequent insubordination. A chief dismissed from office might, as formerly, become a hanger-on at the camp of his overlord, and await with patience for the latter's favour, but, "if of a more fiery temper" would "probably throw himself into some wild district" where he had family influence, and "set his master at defiance." *Šeftennät*, or more or less institutional banditry, was not uncommon.

Over half a century of warfare and turbulence had moreover cast a deep shadow over the land. Most of the inhabitants were "so crushed in their circumstances" and "so degraded in their characters," Gobat believed, that they were "incapable of forming any very expansive ideas of liberty" - such as those which characterised his native Switzerland.[1]

The disintegration of the monarchy led in particular to the emergence of several new regional centres of provincial power. Three which warrant special attention - and are comparatively well documented - were Tegré, Bägémder and Šäwa, whose rulers wielded virtually all the powers formerly exercised by the monarch, and, having to all intents and purposes no overlord above them, held almost total sway over sundry chiefs and nobles.

---

[1] Valentia (1809) III, 264; GB House of Commons (1868) 103; Gobat (1850) 445.

Tegré was divided into a number of districts, known as *šumät*, or lands whose rulers were "appointed." Some of the smaller of these estates were held by the Church, or occasionally private individuals, in the form of *gult*, a system of tenure in which the ruler ceded to the holder his own rights of tribute. The remainder of the land was held by chiefs, some of whom were hereditary, while others were chosen from among the governor's own followers.

Much of the province was divided into districts, known as *addi nägarit*, or "drum lands," so designated because their chief had the right of having drums played before him when he travelled in procession or marched to battle. There were said to have been once forty-four such districts - though Ludolf in the seventeenth century had listed no more than twenty-seven, or, if the country of the Bahr Nägaš were included, thirty-four. By the mid-nineteenth century the number had, however, shrunk to only seventeen, the rest, according to Parkyns, having been "cut up and apportioned out to the soldiers." Chiefs in charge of such districts were known as *balä nägarit*, i.e. "owners of drums". They often held the rank of Däjazmač, and even when, as in the case of the rulers of Agamé and Sälawa, this was not so, their status was not "a whit inferior," for they beat their drums "as loud as any one," and held "as high a place either in feast or field." Such chiefs often had the designation of their districts prefixed to their names, and might thus be referred to, for example, as Šum Agamé Wäldä Enka'él, i.e. Wäldä Mika'él, chief of Agamé.

Beside the *addi nägarit* lands there were a number of smaller districts, known as *addi embilta* or *addi qändä*, i.e. lands called after the names of the *embilta* or *qändä*, the musical instruments to which their chief had a right.[2] Estates belonging to the ancient nobility were known as *wäyzäro*, i.e. "princess's" land, while those given over to a group of soldiers, or more precisely cavalry, were called *färäsäñña*, i.e. "horsemen's" lands. All such lands were subdivided into smaller districts, or parishes, each under a *Čeqa šum*, or local tax gatherer, who represented the lowest rank in the administrative system.

On appointing a governor of any importance it was customary for the ruler of Tegré to issue a proclamation. Before it was read out drums would be beaten in his camp, as well as in the principal market-place. The drummer would gather a crowd by waving a stick or sheepskin over his head, after which he read out the decree in a loud voice. A typical proclamation stated that the master had made a gift "of such and such a country, from such a place to such a place (naming the boundaries), to Mr. Such-a-one, to be held by him as its chief, with the right to govern it, to exercise his authority, and punish offenders by imprisonment and flogging." Chiefs thus appointed exercised full judicial authority over the areas to which they were assigned, though the penalties of death and amputation had properly speaking to be referred either to the nominal emperor in Gondär or, more probably, to the ruler of Tegré himself.

District governors were entitled to a share in the taxes they collected, and had in addition "a certain quantity of cultivable land in each parish" which they could either use themselves or let to others. In the former case they would call on the inhabitants

---

[2] The *nägarit* is a drum, the *embilta*, a flute, and the *qändä* [*mäläkät*], a long horn.

to provide "one day's work for clearing and ploughing, one day for sowing, two for clearing the crop of weeds and two for gathering in the harvest." Land was also occasionally made available for a fixed rent, though it was "more common for the owner of the land to receive a proportion (sometimes half) of the crop." At the base of the hierarchy the Čeqa šum likewise took his share of the taxes he collected, as well as fines levied for various offences. He was also the recipient of numerous perks, for if villagers did not propitiate him with an occasional gift he could declare that they had no right to their land, which, Parkyns says, would accordingly be forfeited to his master.[3]

Bägémder

The nobles of Bägémder, most of whom claimed hereditary rule over their respective districts, were for the most part more powerful than those of Tegré. Many Bägémder chiefs, Plowden states, considered themselves equal by birth to their nominal ruler, Ras Ali Alula, and, "impatient" of any superior, were "in some instances sufficiently powerful to be nearly independent". Each chief holding the rank of Däjazmač, whether appointed by Ras Ali Alula, or as often as not only obtaining the latter's consent for the appointment after a successful contest with an immediate rival, was thus "entire master of all sources of revenue within his territory", and had "full power really of life and death", though this was supposedly "vested in the Ras alone".

The "feudal subjection" of these chiefs consisted in the obligation to send, from time to time, some presents to his superior, and to bear his shield", that is to say, to follow him with as large a force as they could master. These chiefs followed the Ras to war, and gave him "a portion of their revenues", but bestowed on their retainers districts and villages as they pleased, and allowed them to extract whatever they could from their fiefs.[4]

Šäwa

The provincial nobility of Šäwa on the other hand were completely subservient to the their local provincial ruler. "Scarcely a day passed," Johnston recalls, without "the most wealthy" being obliged to confess their dependence" or run the risk of being denounced as an enemy of the sovereign, which would be followed by confiscation of all property, or incarceration in Guancho [Gončo], the State prison, with a heavy fine." Such imprisonments were so taken for granted that they were not regarded as tyrannical. On the contrary all the neighbours and friends of the individual so punished would exclaim, with protestations of loyalty, "Our good King! Our good King! Alas! alas! to have such an ungrateful servant!"

The consequence of the ruler's "monopolising rule" was thus that the nobles of Šäwa, like its peasants, were in "the most abject state of submission." All officials were in the habit of making gifts or "oblations from time to time in kind" to the monarch,

---

[3] Ludolf (1684) 17; Parkyns (1853) II, 228-30. See also House of Commons (1868) 104.

[4] House of Commons (1868) 66, 114-5.

who was in addition "in the habit of requiring arbitrarily from those in charge of the districts, tribute in honey, clarified butter, cloth, or whatever else he may happen to require."

The ceremonial of Sahlä Sellasé's court, like that of the emperors of former times, reflected the society's almost unqualified dependence on the ruler. No nobleman returning after a long absence could for example "approach the throne empty-handed," and even the most powerful, when coming into the sovereign's presence, would "twice prostrate themselves" and kiss the dust in a "most abject and humiliating" manner, while "thousands of stern warriors" would "bend down with profound and slavish abasement."

Šäwa at this time was ruled by some four hundred *šumant*, or district governors, each of whom was obliged to appear before the ruler "with his contingent of militia, whensoever summoned for military service." There were also fifty *Abbagasoč*, or "fathers of shields," whose principal responsibility was to guard the frontiers. Appointment to a few of these posts was hereditary, but "the majority" were given, as was the case, it will be remembered, in medieval times, at the monarch's pleasure. This meant, according to the ever critical Harris, that appointments to office were in effect "purchased by the highest bidder" whose tenure was "extremely precarious." The amount of land any officer received depended moreover on the amount of tax he collected, and as he rose in the royal estimation so did he receive decorations and honours for such of his subordinates as might have "distinguished themselves by their zeal, activity or valour." Government appointments, "if not retained by fees and obligations" were, however, "constantly forfeited and resold." Frequent changes of office were at the same time also made "with the design of counteracting collusion and rebellion."

Provincial governors, though subservient to the ruler, tended, however, according to Harris, to be themselves "little despots," each of whom was actuated by a desire for "supreme" power, which, was nevertheless limited by that of their master. The "slightest error in judgment," or even the "mere whim of the monarch," might thus "involve them in destruction when least anticipated." Being "accountable for every event" their "assiduity in the management of affairs" often availed them nought. "Talents and bravery" were "sometimes displayed in vain," for "the caprice of the despot" could easily hurl a proud nobleman to "the deepest ruin and disgrace."[5]

"Armed," the British envoy says, "with the delegated authority of the despot, each governor, enacting the autocrat in his own domains," fashioned "his habits and privileges after those of his royal master." The lord's fields were thus "cultivated in the same manner" as those of the ruler, for the chief, like the monarch, was able to extort "many days" labour from the peasants. A "fluctuating tribute regulated by his will and caprice" was exacted in kind from all land-holders to meet the demands of the ruler. The latter also received "an inauguration fee" of "from four to six hundred" Maria Theresa dollars, and, unless propitiated by voluntary offerings, would be "ever sending requisitions for livestock and farm produce." Such burdens fell "heavily upon all classes." A governor, "trusting to his own resources," would thus be "speedily impoverished," whilst one who taxed "too roughly" was "certain to be stripped of

[5] Johnston (1844) II, 185-6; Harris (1844) III, 30-2

authority and property, on representation made to the throne." A deposed noble was, however:

> "never loth to climb up again whence he has fallen, and the humbled grandee, although impoverished and shunned by the servile crowd, strives again to ingratiate himself with the sovereign - frequently succeeds by long and patient attendance, and once more girded with the silver sword of authority, he attains the perilous and giddy pinnacle, where the weapon of destruction hangs over his head suspended only by a single hair."[6]

Village taxes in Šäwa, as in Tegré, were collected by a Čeqa šum, who was also responsible for ordering the populace of his area to plough the land of the King and nobility, to harvest their crops, and to construct such houses and other buildings as they might need. Chosen by the villagers from among their number, and appointed by the governor to whom he paid a fee of 20 bars of salt, or the equivalent of one Maria Theresa dollar, the Čeqa šum held office for twelve months, during which time he paid no tribute. He was also exempted in the following year, which was called the time of his rest, but had thereafter to contribute like any other villager. During his period in office, however, he had his perks, for the inhabitants gave him a banquet on every great festival, and treated him with great honour as befitting a local dignitary.[7]

Class Distinctions and Status Symbols

The exalted position of the nobility, and the spirit of deference with which they were regarded by the common people, found expression throughout the highlands in many fields of social life. These included the use of different forms of speech in addressing or referring to persons of rank, and different types of clothing and ways of wearing it, besides a number of sumptuary laws designed to exclude the lower orders from access to certain highly prized luxury goods.

The hierarchical character of the society permeated many aspects of language. The populace thus paid "great respect to their superiors," Gobat records, and was "rarely heard to speak reproachfully" of them. Servants, who were likewise "strongly attached" to their masters, made it a point to swear by the latter's names, and continued to do so even long after their death.

Status was also reflected in grammar, for the use of pronouns and the conjugation of verbs in Amharic served to indicate rank and respect. Persons speaking to their equals would employ the second person singular, for verb as well as pronoun. A child addressing a parent, or a wife a husband, would on the other hand use the second person plural, while in their presence they would refer to them in the third person plural. Someone speaking to a superior, or anyone whom they wished to honour, would use the third person plural for the verb, while in his absence use would be made of the plural pronoun also. The situation in Tegré was somewhat different for singular pronouns and verbs were employed only when talking with considerable

---

[6] Harris (1844) III, 32.

[7] Isenberg and Krapf (1843) 281.

familiarity or when addressing children. On most other occasions the second person plural was adopted, except, significantly enough, when speaking of a governor in his absence when the third person plural was almost invariably used.

Sumptuary laws were widely operative. "No male above eight years of age, from the lowest-born to the son of a Ras," Hormuzd Rassam states, was thus allowed to wear "any covering resembling a shirt," unless it had been presented to him in the first instance by the sovereign who would invest him with a garment of silk, after which he was entitled to wear a shirt of "any material, from the finest velvet or embroidered silk down to the commonest calico." The wives of those so honoured were likewise entitled to appear before the Emperor "with their bosoms uncovered." The nobles in consequence often wore highly coloured dress, while the rest of the population were very simply, and indeed, as in former times, often scantily, dressed. The drinking of *ṭäj*, or honey wine, was, as we shall see, likewise restricted to those of the highest rank.

The exalted position of the nobility was also demonstrated in other ways. It was thus customary in Tegré, as we have seen, for governors to have drums beaten before them as they marched in procession or to battle. Ceremonial swords also for a time served as status symbols. Early in the century the chiefs on state occasions had such weapons carried before them in scarlet bags, but this custom by the 1840's was "seldom" any longer practiced. Nobles in Šäwa, on the other hand, continued to wear a silver sword as the emblem of their rank and authority. It was girded, Harris says, on none but those who enjoyed an exalted place in the royal favour, and the forfeiture of government and the loss of this "cumbrous badge" went in fact hand in hand.[8]

Master-Servant Relations

The importance of the nobility was also demonstrated by the fact that they always travelled with a multitude of dependants, or servants, whose number was considered a measure of their master's grandeur, and even the lesser nobility were scarcely ever seen without some followers. Pearce, who did not believe there was a people "so fond of displaying their dignity" as the Ethiopians, notes that "a chief of any power" when he went to court, or to church, or made any visit, would invariably be accompanied by "a whole body of armed men." Anyone with "a little landed property" yielding an annual revenue of merely a hundred Maria Theresa dollars a year had "five or six shieldsmen close behind him, and perhaps a matchlock or two in front of him." Even a poor man, with a single servant or soldier, would expect the latter to follow with his spear and shield wherever he went, be it only within his own premises or compound.

Servants were likewise omnipresent at meal-times, when, as a sign of respect, they stood around their master's doorway. This served to show that they were truly in attendance on him, and not, as Parkyns says, "merely eating his bread and idling their time away."

---

[8] Gobat (1850) 475; GB House of Commons (1868) 104; Rassam (1869) I, 199; Parkyns (1853) I, 341, II, 227-8; Harris (1844) II, 267-8.

The women of the nobility, who were "fond of shewing themselves off," were likewise always accompanied by a considerable retinue. When travelling to or from church, or paying or returning visits, they would be "mounted," Pearce says, "on a mule, with a soldier on each side to steady them, a whole train of spearsmen following behind, and a great number of their female attendants running in front."

The servants of the nobility, who provided the latter with innumerable services, varied greatly in status and remuneration. Many enjoyed the master - or mistress's confidence, were relatively well paid and themselves employed slaves or servants, while others performed only the most menial of tasks, and were no better off than the latter.

One early nineteenth century servant of whom there is record was a converted Muslim messenger in the service of Ras Wäldä Sellasé, and was perhaps for that reason called Gäbrä Wäldä Sellasé. He received no less than 40 Maria Theresa thalers and as many pieces of cloth a year, as well as a mule, and had been assigned a piece of land yielding 40 *gäbäta* of grain (i.e. something between 800 and 200 litres), six of which he sold on the spot for a thaler, or four thalers if carried to Adwa. This, with what he received on his missions, which, Lord Valentia was led to believe, was "much more" - especially when he was sent to settle any dispute about trade, enabled him to keep "four servants", perhaps in fact slaves, to three of whom he gave five pieces of cloth a year, and to the fourth, two pieces, besides their food.[9]

Hunting, and Chess Playing

Hunting was a favourite pastime of the nobility, particularly of its younger members, many of whom went every year on expeditions to prove their manhood - and to obtain the right to wear a special decoration. Those who killed a lion or elephant were entitled, Pearce says, to wear earrings, or a small stud in the right ear. The killing of leopard, wild buffalo, and rhinoceros, did not provide the hunter with any decoration, but were also highly regarded feats.

Many of the nobles, among them Ras Wäldä Sellasé of Tegré, were also great players of *säntäräj*, or chess, a game which served in a way to familiarise them with military strategy. Ethiopian chess was an old-fashioned type of the game, which differed from that in vogue in Europe in that the Queen moved only one square at a time, while the Bishop could jump over other pieces just like a Knight. Perhaps the most unusual feature of the Ethiopian form of the game was, however, that players moved simultaneously - until the first capture was effected, after which they played alternately as in modern chess.

Many aristocrats were likewise accustomed to play a highly sophisticated form of the board-game *gäbäta* played on three rows, each of six holes. The rest of the population played far less intricate forms of the game, in most parts of the country with a board of only two rows, though those with three rows were also found in some areas, particularly in northern Tegré and in the south-west among the Dorzé.[10]

---

[9] Pearce (1831) II, 193-4; Parkyns (1853) II, 384-5; Valentia (1809) III, 153. On the *gäbäta* measure of capacity see *Journal of Ethiopian Studies* (1969), VII, No.2, pp. 114-5.

[10] Pearce (1831) I, 217-20, II, 1-3; Pankhurst (1971a) 165-6, (1971b) 149-72.

V

PROVINCIAL RULERS

The monarchy by the early nineteenth century had declined to such an extent that the powers formerly wielded by the emperor had almost entirely passed, as we have seen, into the hands of a small number of provincial rulers, each of whom developed his individual style of government. The office of monarch still, however, existed, but its incumbent, though continuing to reside in the old capital Gondär, and to claim the title of *Negusä Nägäst*, i.e. "king of kings" or Emperor, was in fact little more than a puppet. He was, as Lord Valentia noted, "invariably in the power of one ambitious subject or another," and, receiving no revenue save that from "nearly independent" provincial rulers, was "incapable of securing a sufficient force to sustain himself or to prevent them wasting the resources of the country in mutual hostility." It was symbolic of the enhanced powers of the chiefs that several of them kept lions - hitherto symbols of monarchy. These beasts, according to Pearce, were often "perfectly" tame.

The powers of the monarchy decreased further in the third decade of the century, by which time the emperors had been "stripped of every appendage of royalty," Gobat says, "except the name," and would have long since have been "rifled" even of "this remaining shadow," had not the governors "felt the necessity of suffering them to retain it, in order to pave the way for their assuming the office of *Ras*" which could be legally accomplished "only by placing a new King on the throne."

A corollary to the disintegration in monarchical power was that the old custom of detaining members of the royal family on an *amba*, or flat-topped mountain, fell into disuse. Descendants of former rulers, according to Gobat, were by then "everywhere dispersed throughout the different provinces," where they were "generally the favorites of the people," and lived "pleasantly among them," but though "so much beloved" there were "seldom any popular combinations in their favour." Several members of King Sahlä Sellasé's family, were, however, in detention - on the mountain of Gonco, east of Ankobär - in the 1840s.

The decline of the monarch, coinciding as it did with a period of civil war, was regretted by many thinking Ethiopians, among them the court chronicler, Abägaz Sä'unä, who felt compelled to interrupt his text to ask how it was that "the Kingdom had become a laughing stock," and why its government had been snatched by rulers of whom it could not be said, "They are of such and such a race." Admitting that he failed to understand the reason for this sad "usurpation," he declares that he mourned and wept "without ceasing." The malady of the times was likewise recognised by a foreign observer Lord Valentia, who declared that the country during this period suffered from "all the evils that attend inefficient government." It was not surprising that many people's "only desire" for the future was, Gobat learnt, "to see the royal family restored to the peaceful possession of their throne and all Abyssinia rejoicing in its light."[1]

---

[1] Valentia (1809) III, 264; **Gobat (1850)** 444-5; Harris (1844) II, 29, 113-8, 369, III, 14-5, 284, 387, 389; Pearce (1831) II, 29; **Weld** Blundell (1922) 477. See also Arnauld d' Abbadie (1868) 129.

Tegré

The decline of the central monarchy, and the rise of powerful provincial rulers, was particularly evident in Tegré, which, because of its access to fire-arms had, as we have seen, long possessed military superiority over other parts of the country. The province, which had by this time become virtually independent, was described by Parkyns as a "feudal kingdom" governed by its own "absolute ruler." Three successive chiefs held sway over it in the first half of the century: Ras Wäldä Sellasé of Endärta, Däjazmač Säbagades of Agamé, and Däjazmač Webé of Sämén. Each of them wielded power comparable to that exercised by emperors of former times, but failed to establish a dynasty. Each of these rulers had his own capital or capitals: Wäldä Sellasé at Antalo and Čälaqot, Säbagades at Addigrat, and Webé at Adwa as well as sundry camps.

Ras Wäldä Sellasé, the first of these rulers, exercised all the functions hitherto associated with the monarch. His "common mode" of punishing conspirators was, like the emperors of former times, to deprive them of the lands they governed. He was often heard by the British envoy Henry Salt to declare, "Men are only saucy when their stomachs are full." This saying was in the latter's opinion "peculiarly applicable" to Wäldä Sellasé's dependants, who, "when ruled with a hand of power," made "admirable subjects," but, if left to their own, seemed to him "intolerably presumptuous and overbearing." Notwithstanding his rights of appointment and dismissal the Ras appears in fact to have changed his governors but rarely, and, as long as they paid their tribute, "never" thought of removing them. Wäldä Sellasé's prerogatives, like those of the emperors of the past, were immense, for he had "personal jurisdiction," over the entire province. "All crimes, differences and disputes, of however important or trifling a nature," were "ultimately referred to his determination," "all rights of inheritance" were "determined according to his will," and "most wars" were "carried on by himself in person." The court of Wäldä Sellasé was characterised, like those of the monarchs of former times, by considerable ceremony. Most visitors who came into his presence thus uncovered themselves to the waist, though others exposed only the breast, and afterwards replaced their garments. No one addressed him in public without first standing up and undressing to the waist, after which they were however often permitted to speak sitting.

The rulers of Tegré, as befitted their status, also received the lion's share of taxation. Wäldä Sellasé in particular is known to have accumulated considerable wealth. At his death in 1816 he is said to have possessed 75,000 Maria Theresa dollars, 50 *wäqét*, or ounces, of gold, and "a number of gold and silver ornaments," besides 15,500 cows, 4,100 plough oxen and 1,730 ploughshares. His successor Däjazmač Säbagades was likewise so well endowed with funds that he could on one occasion give his British courtier William Coffin 2,000 dollars for the purchase of fire-arms, while later in the century Däjazmač Webé' levied extensive taxes, and had a treasury said to contain 40,000 dollars. Taxes levied by the ruler of Tegré were of two categories. One, called *fessassy*, was paid in corn. The other, known as *wärqé*, literally "gold," or by extension money of any kind, was, according to Parkyns, mainly contributed in pieces of cloth which served as a medium of exchange. There was in addition a *mäšomya*, or "acknowledgment," which each chief paid in "cattle, honey, butter, arms or anything else" to establish tenure to his land.[2]

Three early or mid-19th century rulers: Dajazmač Webé (*top left*) of Sämén and Tegré. From H. Blanc, *I prigionieri di Teodoro* (Milan, 1872); Ras Ali Alula (*top right*) of Bägemder. From G. Massaia, *I miei trentacinque anni di missione nell' alta Etiopia* (Rome and Milan, 1885-95); Negus Sahlä Sellasé (*bottom*) of Šäwa . From C.E.X. Rochet d'Héricourt, *Voyage sur la côte de la Mer Rouge, dans le pays d'Adel et le royaume de Choa* (Paris, 1841).

---

[2] Valentia (1809) III, 155-6; Parkyns (1853) II, 227, 229; Salt (1814) 328-9; Pearce (1831) II, 95; Rüppell (1838-40) I 327; Stern (1862) 75; Lejean (1867) 131; Dufton (18670 131.

Bägémder

Bägémder, with its capital at Däbrä Tabor, differed from Tegré in that it was under the rule of a single dynasty, that of the Yäjju, founded in the late eighteenth century by an Oromo chief named Gwangul. The province was ruled for much of the early nineteenth century by his great-grandson, Ras Ali Alula, the chief of the northern and western provinces - including Gondär, who was virtually the "master and king" of the empire. Well versed in "all manly exercises" - shooting, riding, throwing a lance and running - he was, according to Plowden, "perhaps one of the best horsemen" in the country, with "no lack of personal courage", and "spent much of his time in the chase". "Careless of dress or personal ornament of any kind, but cleanly in his habits" he was "indifferent as to his personal comfort, and moderate in his meals". As for his approach to government, having come to power "at the early age of twelve years" he was, if we can believe the Englishman, "singularly tenacious of his opinion, very conceited, despising all men, and very hard to be moved to any emotion". For that reason perhaps he was not easily "excited to anger", and was "extremely patient", and "never cruel", though this was more for reasons of state, Plowden felt, than from "real compassion". This tolerance was not, however, without its disadvantages, for since Ali scarcely ever punished anyone there was "much disorder and license in his territories".

The ruler of Bägémder, who, like so many chiefs, "loved dependency and subservience, claimed the right, Plowden states, of "appointing all other Chiefs of Provinces, and officers of every kind, at his will and pleasure", the formality of consulting the Emperor "having been disregarded for many years". Ali's actual powers were, however, much circumscibed, for "amid the conflicts of the great families," whose names would "at any moment conjure into existence a numerous army for rebellion or rapine", he was "obliged to employ a subtle and tortuous policy", in order to retain his control of those "fierce warriors". His government having been "established by the sword", and being largely dependent on his military strength - and on the outcome of a continuous series of battles, he was obliged in making his appointments "to be attentive to the claims of the great families", who on account of their hereditary influence were either "rulers or rebels in their respective districts". Invariably "generous to his enemies" when they were in his power he was "always too merciful" to adopt "the doubtful alternative of destroying them".

Though dependent on the provincial nobles for much of his revenues Ali also reserved "a number of provinces", to provide for his household officers and troops. He paid the latter occasionally "an uncertain amount of money", as well as whenever possible a monthly allowance of corn which was obtained from his own granaries, though the men were "more often" given "a half-plundering license" to quarter themselves on the land. This latter expedient, however, was "not always patiently acquiesced in", so that there were sometimes "bloody struggles", in which the peasantry succeeded in expelling the soldiery, on which occasions "the weakness of the Ras", generally obliged him to overlook such an affair".[3]

---

[3] Trimingham (1952) 110; Plowden (1868) 401-3; GB House of Commons (1868) 66, 115. See also Combes and Tamisier (1838) II, 55-6; Arnauld d' Abbadie (1868) 183-4.

Gojjam

Gojjam, isolated from the rest of the country by the great curve of the Blue Nile, was largely independent, and was ruled in the first part of the century by two notable governors, Däjazmač Gošu Zäwdé and his son Däjazmač Berru Gošu who were said to have developed very different styles of running the country. Gošu, according to Beke, took but little interest in the day-to-day working of his administration. "Extremely devout" he wore "a number of talismans, charms, etc." round his neck, and spent "a considerable portion of his time at prayers, and in the perusal of the Scriptures and religious books". In consequence he did not "appear to devote his time to public affairs", and although "now and then" listening to a complainant applying for redress of wrongs, and holding "a few private conferences" with his chiefs, there was in general "no signs of business" at his capital". Life at his court was likewise fairly uncouth - "much inferior" for example, the Englishman felt, to that in Šäwa. Public banquets thus presented "scenes of the utmost noise and confusion, everyone pushing and scrambling, and bawling" without the "least regard" for the chief's presence while his ushers lay about the populace with their sticks "without mercy, making still more noise in calling them to order".

Berru Gošu by contrast differed from his father in being a resolute and active ruler. Beke, who "could not be struck by the difference" between the two men, recalls a characteristic occasion when the young man, acting as the supreme judge of his province, ruled that a case be decided in accordance with the *Fethä Nägäst*, or traditional legal code, whereupon the plaintiff expressed the fear that his opponent might not abide by it. "If he does not I will have his legs cut off", was Berru's "impressive answer, uttered not at all with temper, but quite as a matter of course". Notwithstanding such firmness the younger ruler of Gojjam is said to have enjoyed the "deep respect" of his subjects. He was also "on terms of extreme familiarity" with "a few of his principal people", and allowed them to play with him - but only as "a lion might do, giving now and then signs of what he could and would if provoked".[4]

Šäwa and its Sumptuary Laws

Šäwa differed from Tegré and Gojjam in that it was ruled by a single dynasty for over a century rather than by a succession of less closely related chiefs, and from Bägémder in that its ruler exercised unquestioned control over his subordinate chiefs.

The most important ruler of the Šäwan line was Sahlä Sellasé who claimed the title of *Negus*, or King. His powers, like those of the rulers of Tegré, Bägémder and Gojjam, were akin to those exercised by the emperors of former times. It was thus "no fiction of Shoan law," Johnston claims, that "everything" was the "positive property of the monarch," who, according to Harris, actually owned "all the best portions of the soil." The ruler could moreover give and take away at his pleasure "every kind of property," and, "without assigning any reason, dispossess the present holder and confer his wealth upon another, or retain it for his own use." He could furthermore "demand the services of all his people at all times, who must perform everything required of them, to build palaces, construct bridges, till the royal demesnes, or fight his enemies."

---

[4] Beke (1840-3) 257-8, 416.

All subjects, "from first to last, both rich and poor," were thus "the mere slaves of one sole lord and master. "Holding wealth and honour in one hand, poverty and wretchedness in the other," Sahlä Sellasé had thus in a sense made himself "the point upon which human happiness" turned. Since he could "at any moment reduce to a beggar the richest, and most powerful of his slaves" he had almost inevitably become the object of a "kind of demon worship" like that used to propitiate "spirits supposed to have the power of inflicting evil."[5] The society was in fact so dominated by the monarch, Harris argued, that the "essence of despotism" permeated it "to its very core," for:

> "the life as well as the property of every subject is at his [Sahlä Sellasé's] disposal. Every act is performed with some view to promote his pleasure, and the subject waits on his sovereign's will, for favour, preferment and place. All appointments are made at the King's disposal. All rewards and distinctions come from the King's hand."[6]

Dependence on the ruler was particularly apparent during famines, when food was "alone to be obtained from the royal granaries." It was "not therefore surprising," Harris claims, that those in dire need of help from the absolute ruler should "be mean, servile, and cringing," and that "they should, in their aspirations after power and place, mould every action of their life according to the despot's will."

Ethiopian rulers of the early 19th century were holding immense banquets for their numerous followers whose life centred largely around the palace and the court. This banquet scene shows King Sahlä Sellasé (left) presiding over a large banquet in the reception hall of his palace. Note minstrels, front left, clowns, centre, and attendant offering raw meat, right, as well as diners seated, and guards standing. From J.M. Bernatz, *Scenes in Ethiopia* (London, 1852).

---

[5] Johnston (1844) II, 185; Harris (1844) III, 33.

[6] Harris (1844) III, 33.

Sumptuary laws in Šäwa seem to have been particularly rigidly enforced. The possession of gold, and above all the wearing of gold jewellery, was monopolised by the King who, Krapf declares, would "severely punish" anyone obtaining the rare metal without his permission. "None except the highest chiefs and warriors of the land," Harris says, were exempted from this law. The manufacture of *täj*, or mead, was similarly a royal monopoly, and King Sahlä Sellasé alone had "the right of preparing the much prized luxury."[7]

The Arbitrariness of Personal Rule

Because of the highly personal, and often arbitrary, aspect of Ethiopian government the well-being of the populace often depended, and was perceived to depend, greatly on the character and policies of the ruler. This relationship was so significant in the era of the *mäsafent* that Abägaz Sä'unä went so far as to observe in his chronicle that "if a ruler is good the times are good, and if a ruler is a bad one the times are bad." In support of this thesis he cited the "Book of Wisdom" as stating that "A King among Kings said to a wise man among wise men, 'How is the goodness of a time (to be reckoned)?', to which the wise man replied, 'The times are indeed as art thou. If thou art evil the times are evil, and if thou art good the times are good.'"

A whole philosophy of government was distilled in those few words.

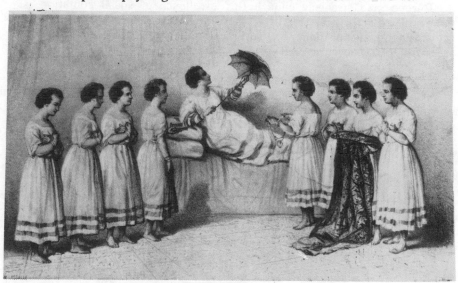

Provincial rulers, such as King Sahlä Sellasé and his consort Queen Bäzabeš, shown here with eight of her women attendants receiving gifts from a visiting French mission, kept considerable states, and were surrounded by numerous servants. From C.F.X. Rochet d' Héricourt, *Second Voyage sur les deux rives de la Mer Rouge, dans le pays des Adels et le royaume de Choa* (Paris, 1846).

---

[7] Harris (1844) III, 33; Johnston (1844) II, 170; Isenberg and Krapf (1843) 363.

The policies, and reputations, of the rulers of this period in fact varied considerably. In Tegré the "cruel administration" of Ras Mika'él Sehul thus gave way to what Henry Salt described, and lauded, as the "mild government" of Ras Wäldä Sellasé. A similar change of regime later took place in Säwa where the "severe and merciless" tyranny of Ras Wäsän Sägäd was followed by the more enlightened rule of his son Sahlä Sellasé. The latter, "most fortunately" for his subjects, was, in Johnston's opinion, a "sagacious monarch" and "a just and good man." His rule, like that of his forebears, was full of "petty restraints," but these could, in the Englishman's view, "readily" be excused when it was realised that Sahlä Sellasé was "superior" to the temptation of abusing his unlimited powers.[8] Elaborating on this view the traveller declares:

"The contemplation of such a prince in his own country is worth the trouble and risk of visiting it. During a reign of thirty years, save one or two transient rebellions of ambitious traitors, who have led, not the subjects of Sahale Selassee, but those of his enemies, nothing like internal dissension or civil war have by their ravages defaced this happy country; whilst gradually his character for justice and probity has spread far and wide, and the supremacy of political excellence is without hesitation given to the Negoos of Shoa throughout the length and breadth of the ancient empire of Ethiopia. To be feared by every prince around, and loved by every subject at home, is the boast of the first government of civilised Europe; and strangely enough this excellence of social condition is paralleled in the heart of Africa, where we find practically carried out the most advantageous policy of a social community that one of the wisest of sages could conceive - that of arbitrary power placed in the hands of a really good man."[9]

Though the picture thus conjured up was perhaps too rosy there is no gainsaying that conditions in Säwa were both more peaceful and more stable than in most of the northern provinces where civil war had long been rife.

Lepers and Mendicants at Court

Lepers, "many" of whom had been seen by Alvares in the sixteenth century, were not traditionally segregated in Ethiopia. Though prohibited in the *Fethä Nägäst* from serving as priests or judges, on the ground that to do so would cause their office to be despised, they were allowed to roam the countryside more or less at will.

Many lepers attached themselves to the courts of nineteenth century rulers. Däjazmač Webé thus used a leper monk from Gojjam as one of his messengers, while King Sahlä Sellasé is said by Rochet d'Héricourt to have treated such unfortunates with "especial charity". Johnston on entering the monarch's compound reports passing, "for about twenty yards, between two rows of noisy beggars, male and female, old, middle-aged, and young; who, leprous, scrofulous, and maimed, exhibited the most

---

[8] Weld Blundell (1922) 417; Valentia (1809) III, 155; Johnston (1844) II, 185, 190

[9] Johnston (1844) II, 189-90.

disgusting sores and implored chärity for the sake of Christ and the Holy Virgin". Such sights were also seen at other provincial capitals.

Lepers, as well as persons suffering from other serious diseases, were "great beggars", as Pearce notes. This was confirmed by Antoine d'Abbadie who heard the "plaintiff voice" of lepers, itinerant monks, and students, begging from door to door, in the name of the saint of the day, Saint Täklä Haymanot, or the Virgin Mary. They begged, according to Pearce, with great impunity. Often "very insolent" they would even abuse passing governors, who in accordance with the custom of the country, would never take any action against them.[10]

---

[10] Beckingham and Huntingford (1961) II, 514; Paulos Tsadua (1968) 21, 62, 250; Arnauld d'Abbadie (1868) 169-70, 547-8; Rochet d'Héricourt (1841) 307; Stern (1862) 121; Pearce (1831) I, 297; Pankhurst (1984c) 57-72.

THE CLERGY, THE CHURCH AND RELIGIOUS LIFE

The Multitude of the Clergy, their Education and Organisation

Observers of the early nineteenth century, as of previous times, were much impressed by the multitude of both churches and clergy. Ferret and Galinier remarked, in terms reminiscent of Bruce a century and a half earlier, that it was rare in the highlands to stop at the top of a mountain without seeing five or six churches, and almost as many monasteries. Pearce likewise declared that priests were "numerous beyond belief," while Dufton later in the century claimed that the religious community, consisting of "innumerable" priests and *däbtära*, constituted "nearly a quarter" of the population. Most churches were tended, according to Ferret and Galinier, by ten to twelve priests.

Most priests - other than the great church scholars discussed in a previous chapter - had, in the opinion of foreign observers of this period, only minimal education. Gobat claimed that many students preparing for the priesthood confined themselves to "learning to sing some of the church books," while Plowden felt that the learning of the clergy in general was virtually limited to the Old and New Testaments. To be admitted to the priesthood, candidates, according to Ferret and Galinier, needed only to know how to read, and be of good conduct, and over the age of eighteen. When they could fulfil these conditions they would present themselves before the *Abun* who would open a Bible and make them read out, or stammer through, a page, after which he ordained them, without really inquiring how much they knew. Priests were, however, said to have been "in general very polite," and as far as outward appearance went, were, "very good people." Some, Pearce agreed, had indeed "exceedingly good qualities," though many, he feared, were "despicable wretches."

Däbtäras, Plowden reports, were "often more learned" than the priests. Recruited from all ranks of society, Antoine d'Abbadie states, they were involved in many fields of church activity. Their principal function was to sing in church choirs, but they were also sometimes involved in church administration, taking the usufruct of church lands and paying and dismissing the priests who said Mass. *Däbtäras* had, however - for what it is worth - a poor reputation among foreign travellers, such as Plowden who declares that they were "generally cunning, debauched and mischief-makers." Monks by contrast, he believed, had "faith, and energy in their faith," for "many" of them often "risked their lives to visit shrines, not infrequently surrounded for many a weary day's journey by hostile tribes."

Opinions such as these, expressed by foreign missionaries often engaged in bitter conflicts with Ethiopian Orthodox Christianity, as well as by unfriendly or xenophobic outsiders only partially familiar with the culture, are interesting, but must be taken with more than average caution - for the clergy, as we shall see, were highly regarded by the population at large. An Ethiopian proverb nonetheless stated: "The worst of beasts, the scorpion; the worst of men the *däbtära*".[1]

Income of the Clergy and of the *Abun*

The clergy had "no pay", but, obtained their income, Plowden noted, partly from church ownership of land and partly in return for the services they rendered. Revenues from the land varied greatly from one church to another, but at any establishment were divided fairly strictly among the clerics attached to it. A church's income, according to Pearce, was thus "divided into equal portions" of which the *Aläqa*, or chief priest, received ten parts, the treasurer, three, and the others "according to their rank, one or more."

The hearing of confessions and granting of absolutions, was, according to Pearce, a not unprofitable business. The average priest might, moreover, have "two or three thousand" parishioners, each of whom would give him one or two *amolé*, or one-fifteenth of a Maria Theresa thaler, on St. John's or New Year's Day, thus providing a total income of almost 200 thalers a year. Priests after five or six years would thus have made enough money to maintain themselves for "the remainder of their lives," and would then probably "return to their native place," where they would purchase oxen, commence farming, and "live well" - so long of course as the country they lived in was at peace. Priests also obtained fees, often of some magnitude, for burial services. They "always" got "well paid" when "any great man" died, and even obtained part of whatever a poor man left behind, for which reason, Pearce cynically claimed, some actually prayed for people to die. Besides resident priests there were others who attached themselves to a church without any right to its income, but obtained their maintenance, either in return for undertaking some of their colleagues' duties, or else by outright begging. The size of the clergy's exactions also impressed Plowden who later observed that Father Confessors extracted what they could, according to the wealth of the penitent. The pious bestowed "rich offerings for their spiritual welfare," while the laity in general were "mulcted on the occasion of births, christenings, marriages, deaths, registers of sale and purchase, burials, and the like," so that the priests, "besides their continual feasting at the public expense," were "usually stocked with money," and on account of their numbers were often "compared by the Abyssinians to locusts."

Däbtäras, for their part, obtained their living in a variety of ways. Though one of their principal functions consisted in singing in church choirs, many abandoning the service of the Church, became legal advisers to provincial rulers, or, according to d'Abbadie, turned successfully to trade. The majority, however, devoted themselves in one way or another to, writing. Some earned their living by producing amulets and charms against disease and misfortune, and by the practice of medicine and occult sciences, while others were "hangers-on" at various churches. Many *däbtäras* claimed the ability of exorcising supernatural powers. One from Gojjam for example was said to have declared that he could "prevent the ravages of the smallpox," as well as destruction from both locusts and hail. Others, as we have seen, wrote out Ge'ez texts for their Judaic compatriots the Fälaša.

---

[1] Pearce (1831) I, 328, 336; Dufton (1867) 140; Ferret and Galinier (1847) II, 350-1; Gobat (1850) 319; GB House of Commons (1868) 109-10; Antoine d' Abbadie (1868) 17-8; Faitlovitch (1907) 14.

An Ethiopian priest, standing, and a monk, seated, both in traditional ecclesiastical dress. Note turban cap, fly-whisk and prayer beads. Engraving from H.A. Stern, *The Captive Missionary* (London, 1868).

Many monks by contrast lived in abject poverty, but some were quite well off. Those at the market town of Qorāṭa were said by Gobat to be "very wealthy", and were reported to have lent money - presumably to merchants or chiefs - at the rate of no less than 240% per annum.

The wealthiest churchman, not surprisingly, was, however, the Coptic Abun, or Metropolitan, who had "numerous" estates in different parts of the country, and also received a sizeable income, Pearce observes, in charges for ordaining priests and deacons, as well as for confirming the faithful.

One of the greatest beneficiaries of such fees was Abunä Qérellos who arrived from his native Egypt in 1815 after Ethiopia had been without a spiritual head for no less than fifteen years. This prelate, who, by all accounts, did little to justify the reverence paid to his office, immediately after his arrival "ordered a proclamation to be issued," Pearce states, declaring that "every man wishing to be confirmed a priest must first bring him four *amolas*, or pieces of salt each; those who wished to become deacons two pieces of salt each; and all the population, with their young children, that had not been confirmed by former Abunas, were to pay one piece of salt each. Persons were stationed at the gateway to receive the salt as the people entered, one at a time. More than a thousand priests and as many deacons were ordained the first day, and, as those who brought their children to be confirmed were departing, numbers were still arriving." As a result of these extortionate demands the Abun is said to have received no less than 1,000 *amolés* a day, a total of 730,000, or the equivalent of over 30,000 Maria Theresa thalers at Adwa prices or 100,000 at those of Gondär. These figures were, however, exceptional, for once the back-log of confirmations was overcome the prelate's income dropped to 1,000 *amolé* per month, though this still amounted to a value of 400 thalers per year, beside which he also received "a considerable quantity" of *amolés* in ordination fees from priests, or when they were appointed heads of churches. Qérellos's worldliness was deeply resented. Däjazmač Säbagades complained to the Patriarch of Alexandria in 1827 that previous Abuns had never behaved in this manner, and in a long indictment remarked that the prelate was demanding silver from those "who had no silver," and, claiming his right to "eat like a Ras," was threatening to excommunicate those who failed to meet his exactions. The validity of these charges was generally accepted, Combes and Tamisier going so far as to assert that Qérellos's rapacity had made ordination a "farce".

Though the subject of less opprobrium Qérellos's successor, Abba Sälama, who arrived in 1841, was also extremely wealthy. Besides receiving revenues from his extensive estates and fees from numerous ordinations, he is said to have engaged extensively in commerce, including, Antoine d'Abbadie goes so far as to claim, the slave trade.[2]

---

[2] GB House of Commons (1868) 109-10; Pearce (1831) I, 56-60, 65-6, 85, 199-201, 328-30, 332; Antoine d' Abbadie (1868) 17, 201 Gobat (1850) 343; Ferret and Galinier (1847) II, 351; Combes and Tamisier (1838) III, 190; Appleyard, Irvine and Pankhurst (1985) 21, 49. Hyatt (1926: 59) later went so far as to assert that the däbtäras "chief duty" was to chant, and that "no service" could "properly be held without their assistance,"

Church Ownership of Land

The Church throughout this period was a major owner of land, and, in the opinion of most foreign observers, held considerably more than it deserved. Stern, who, as a Protestant missionary, was admittedly greatly biased against the Ethiopian Church, declared that its priests, "partly by intrigue and partly by voluntary requests, had acquired a vast landed property," which, he believed "amounted to a third of all the landed property". Dufton, who was also unfavourably disposed to the Church, likewise quoted this figure, and went on to assert that the religious community "had through previous royal grants and private legacies, obtained possession of one-third of the landed property of the realm, which, being farmed out to the peasantry, was to its owners a vast source of wealth. This, he snidely claimed, enabled many to "live in idleness, and not infrequently drunkenness and debauchery."

Statements that the Church owned one-third of the land were much exaggerated, but there can be no gainsaying the observation of Heuglin, a more careful observer, that it possessed "a very large part of the land." The rights of the Church were, however, by then apparently beginning to be challenged, for some soldiers of fortune, according to Antoine d'Abbadie, were seizing religious fiefs to give them to their followers.[3]

The Procurement, and Arrival, of an *Abun*

Despite the improvement of international communications in the early nineteenth century the procurement of an Abun during this period, as previously, was a costly affair, and one which bore heavily on the population at large. When Ras Wäldä Sellasé took steps to import a Metropolitan in 1815 he proclaimed by the beat on the drum that every *Aläqa*, or village governor, throughout his dominions should collect from each of his tenants two Maria Theresa dollars in cash, cloth or salt, and ten to twenty thalers from each of the larger settlements. In this manner, Pearce says, no less than 10,000 thalers were collected, after which a group of priests were despatched to Egypt with several Muslim couriers, fourteen slaves and several fine pieces of cloth as gifts to the Egyptian ruler Muhammäd 'Ali.

The eventual arrival of the Abun was always the occasion of almost unbelievable popular excitement. When Abunä Sälama, for example, arrived in 1841 an "extraordinary emotion," the French Scientific Mission recalls, gripped the entire country. On landing at the port of Massawa the prelate was mobbed by a "large number" of Christians who had gone down to the sea to welcome him. The route he was to take, by way of Degsa to Adwa and Aksum, being known in advance, he was everywhere greeted by immense crowds. On reaching Taranta he was received by a son of the Emperor at Gondär while the governors of all the provinces to be traversed awaited him, with their soldiers, at the frontiers of their respective areas of command. In every parish he was welcomed by the priests, monks and laity attached to each church, after which they escorted him in procession as far as the next halting place.

---

[3] Stern (1868) 24; Dufton (1867) 140; Heuglin (1866) 256, 282; Antoine d' Abbadie (1868) 20.

At Gändäbta for example the whole population, headed by the clergy, was there to meet him. The crowd constituted a vast moving sea of heads. Suddenly, Ferret and Galinier recall, they heard the traditional ululation of welcome, *hili! li! li! li! li!*, whereupon all the horsemen dismounted as a sign of respect, and almost at the same moment the Abun himself appeared, mounted most colourfully on a beautiful, richly caparisoned mule which seemed to glory in its load as it slowly, proudly and majestically walked through the crowd. The prelate for his part was dressed in a robe of scarlet silk, yellow trousers, a white turban, and a luxurious burnous embroidered in gold. He was attended to the right and left by monks and priests from the various convents of Tegré, and behind them by provincial governors, superbly dressed in dazzling white, who were followed in turn by crowds of people of all classes and costumes: rich and poor, soldiers, farmers, and merchants, and in the middle of the human mass were women and young girls, as well as many children whom their mothers held high in their arms as if to reach the ray of glory emanating from the deeply revered visitor.

On reaching Adwa he was accorded another tumultuous welcome, for the city was "full of an inquisitive crowd impatient to greet the patriarch and to see his face. Rich and poor, priests and soldiers, farmers and citizens, women and children, obstructed all the streets, filled all the houses and gave an animated appearance to the normally silent town. There were perhaps even greater crowds at Aksum where the welcoming party included many *däbtäras*, anxious to see, and above all, the French Scientific mission says, to speak with their superior: to discover his ideas on the natures of Christ, and to fathom whether he would be a tolerant, persecuting or reforming prelate.

Further ceremonies occurred at Gondär, still the nominal capital of the realm, where Abba Sälama was greeted at a nearby village by a salute fired by the riflemen while many warriors on horseback carrying spears and shields formed a line on the road to receive him. As he appeared they bowed down to their horses' manes, after which they dashed off in many directions, and the crowd, bursting from time to time into a loud shout and the women ululating, followed him to the city.[4]

Respect Paid to the Clergy

Priests were invariably treated with great respect. They almost always carried in their hand a small cross. This they would frequently present to people to kiss, which the Christians would do with deep reverence. More important clerics when travelling would often be preceded by a long two-edged sword, and in some cases, by two, three, four or even more such weapons.

The clergy as a whole differed, however, from other classes in that they never carried weapons. They were nevertheless no strangers to fire-arms. Those at Däbrä Abbay, for example, kept "a great many gunners, with matchlocks of very large size," to defend them against attacks by the neighbouring Šanqellas, as well as to kill the numerous elephants in the area.

---

[4] Pearce (1831) II, 51; Lefebvre (1845-8) I, 291; Ferret and Galinier (1847) II, 63-4, 67-70; Bell (1842) 23. The Protestant missionary Joseph Wolff, who arrived some years earlier, and was mistaken for an *Abun*, described similar excitement: Wolff (1869) 341.

Administration of the Sacrament at a stone church in Tegré. From R. Acton, *The Abyssinian Expedition* (London,1868).

King David playing the harp, represented by the artist like an Ethiopian *bāgāna*, or lyre. From an early 19th century Psalter in the Institute of Ethiopian Studies, IES 1027.

The greatest reverence was, however, reserved for the Abuns, whose arrival in the country was, as we have seen, such a source of excitement and satisfaction. It was the more remarkable that Säbagades was obliged - and felt strong enough - to complain, as we have seen, to Alexandria about Abunä Qérellos whose offences are said to have included drunkenness, greed and murder, as well as abuse of his power of excommunication.[5]

Dress - and Marriage Rules

Priests, whose dress did not differ too markedly from that of the laity, for the most part wore a long open shirt, loose trousers, a skull-cap, and a turban. The shirt, which was the most distinctive part of their attire, had large wide sleeves and a collar, the ends of which hung down on each side to the waist and tapered to a point. These clothes were generally white, though a few priests dressed in yellow. This colour, Pearce recalls, was, however, "mostly confined to monks," or others who had "resort to the wilderness." Some priests also wore sandals, an article of apparel not known to the population at large.

Priests, as we have seen, were allowed to marry only once, before their ordination, after which marriage was prohibited. Many priests, according to Pearce, nevertheless thought it "not lawful" to marry at all, and "many thousand" who resorted to Wäldebba and other sacred places never in fact did so, though he feared that some were detected in adultery.[6]

The Influence and Power of the Priesthood

The priesthood by all accounts was influential and politically powerful. Pearce claims that Ras Wäldä Sellasé, the ruler of Tegré, once confided to him that if he alienated the clergy he would "not long be Ras."

King Sahlä Sellasé, who appears to have also appreciated the power of the Church, later wooed religious communities not only in his native Šäwa, but throughout most of Christian Ethiopia. Early in his career for example he paid for the erection of three churches in far away Tegré, and supplied them with *tabots*, or altar slabs. He is reported to have subsequently sent periodical gifts of money, and clothes, to Wällo for the monks of Lake Hayq in the hope of obtaining blessings from a congregation which, according to Krapf, had "the reputation of extraordinary holiness and heavenly-mindedness. The ruler of Šäwa also went out of his way to obtain church manuscripts from other provinces, and gave generous hospitality to visiting clerics from far and wide. There is record for example of his on one occasion sending fifty Maria Theresa thalers to a church in Gojjam to obtain two copies of the chronological work *Abušaker*. His generosity, according to Krapf, was in fact "known everywhere," so that priests, monks and other clerics flocked to Šäwa from all parts of the country. Among those who are mentioned as coming during a brief period in the missionary's diary

---

[5] Pearce (1831) I, 336, II, 176; GB House of Commons (1868) 103; Appleyard, Irvine and Pankhurst (1985) 49 et passim.

[6] Pearce (1831) I, 329-30, 336; Ferret and Galinier (1847) II, 351-2.

were three priests from Guragé, one from Qwara, and three monks from Lasta. The result of this policy was that "many people" in Lasta, Wag and Tegré observed that the Šäwans were the "best Christians" in the country, and their king the "best ruler." Sahlä Sellasé's "munificent donations" to churches and monasteries were also noted by Harris, ever a critic of all things Ethiopian, who states that the monarch in consequence stood "in high odour with the fanatic clergy," and was therefore enabled to benefit from their "influence over the priest-ridden population" which he ruled "principally through the church." The monarch, he claims, "never undertook any project without consulting some of its members," and was "in turn much swayed by their exhortations, prophecies, dreams and visions."[7]

Veneration of Religious Establishments

Religious establishments continued to be treated with deep veneration. On riding past a church it was thus customary, Pearce explains, for Christians to alight from their mule or horse. If the place of worship was in the vicinity they would go up and kiss its gateway, or a nearby tree, but if it was far away they would more often pick up a stone and throw it in a pile which was almost invariably found on pathways opposite religious establishments. On entering a church people would likewise "always bow and kiss the corners of the door-way," as well as any religious pictures shown to them.

Such customs were so deeply ingrained that people would use the expression, "I go to kiss the church of such a saint," or "I go to kiss St. Mikael, St. George, etc." Religious persons might indeed often kiss several churches in succession, and "to convey the idea that a man was truly pious," Gobat says, it might be said of him, approvingly, that he was "a kisser of churches."[8]

Church-Building, Libraries, and Manuscripts

Churches were built both by local communities and by provincial or other rulers. In either case much of the work was carried out by the populace at large, for when it came to church-building every Christian was ready, Pearce explains, to carry stones, earth or other materials without any thought of payment. A chief wishing to build a church, or even a residence for himself, would begin by purchasing or merely taking from the people, canes and grass for the roof, and would send his subjects to the forests to cut wood, after which construction was often carried out on a *corvée* basis. Ras Wäldä Sellasé for example, when wishing to have a building constructed, "called all the chiefs in turn, and, knowing the strength of their respective districts, tasked them as he thought proper; ordering every one to fell so many trees, take the bark off, and bring them before his tent by sunset." Many pious Christians who could afford it would also go to "great expense" to decorate churches with religious paintings, gold and silver objects and costly carpets and silks.

---

[7] Pearce (1831) I, 176-7, II, 209; Isenberg and Krapf (1843) 137, 141, 145, 149, 238, 446; Harris (1844) III, 25.

[8] Pearce (1831) I, 328, 336; Gobat (1850) 325.

Churches and monasteries were virtually the country's only repositories of manuscripts. One of the best collections was reputedly at Aksum, and was in the care early in the nineteenth century of a librarian called Abba Qälämsis. Many manuscripts were also housed in the churches of the imperial capital, Gondär, whence Emperor Téwodros II, as his chronicler records, was in 1864 to take no less than 981 to his mountain fortress at Mäqdäla - where they were looted four years later by a British military expedition launched against him. Also important was the library at the famous Šäwan monastery of Däbrä Libanos, which, according to the French Scientific Mission, contained five hundred manuscripts, "all dealing with religion" except for "a few" on the chronicles of the kings. On being asked if there were any books on medicine the monks "seemed very scandalised." If they found "a single one," they piously declared, "we would burn it. What are all the human cures compared with the miracles of our great patron saint Takla Haymanot!". Other sizeable collections of manuscripts were kept in important churches, among them that of Giyorgis at Ankobär which, Krapf reports, had a full seventy volumes. Detailed inventories of church libraries were included, and preserved, in the marginalia of numerous manuscripts - which still require detailed study.

Despite the existence of many fine collections of manuscripts church scholarship by this time was suffering from the effects of disunity and civil war. Books written by the monks with great labour, Plowden reports, had formerly been "eagerly sought for," but by the middle of the century were "neglected, almost forgotten." The art of painting was also "nearly lost," and ornamental missals might in consequence be "found very cheap."[9]

Annual Church Festivals, and Pilgrimage

The more important churches were thronged on occasion by vast numbers of the faithful. During the annual festival of Maryam Seyon at Aksum, wrote Pearce, "all Abyssinia" came to the city. In November 1817 for example the neighbouring plain was "crowded" with people from "all parts of Abyssinia," some of them from as far as Šäwa. The feast of Abba Gärima, which was held in the neighbourhood, likewise attracted "every class from all parts of the country" who were greeted by trumpeters, drummers and fifers. Women were not allowed into holy precincts, but "some thousands" assembled in different groups between it and the nearby church of Maryam Zacharias, while "gangs of young girls" danced and sang to the beat of a drum. The main celebrations began about two hours after sunrise when the *tabot*, covered with silks, was brought out of the church by priests "dressed in silks and rags of all colours," with "silver and gold crowns, and ornaments." Pictures and "all the various riches of the church" were also "brought out for the populace to do them honour." The priests gracefully danced and sang, while the women shouted and ululated, and the trumpeters made "all the noise" they possibly could.

---

[9] Pearce (1831) I, 148-50, 243; Ferret and Galinier (1847) I, 472; Lefebvre (1845-8) II, 274; Isenberg and Krapf (1843) 100; GB House of Commons (1868) 110; Mondon-Vidailhet (1905) 22, 49-50. For lists of manuscripts reported by early nineteenth century travellers see Combes and Tamisier, III, 347-51; Ferret and Galinier, I, 475-6, Isenberg and Krapf, 99-100, and Graham (1843) 666-70, and, for a subsequent Ethiopian record of holdings at Mäqdäla, Pankhurst and Germa-Selassie Asfaw (1979) 115-43.

Pilgrimages took place, not only to important religious centres within the country, but, as for many centuries previously, also to Jerusalem which was visited by many priests and monks as well as members of the laity each year.[10]

Saints' Days

Saints' days, which were celebrated monthly rather than annually as in Europe, were so frequent that Ferret and Galinier believed that no country had as many of them as Ethiopia. Such festivals were a time of much feasting, enjoyment and alms-giving when agricultural labour was suspended. The ban on working on Saints' days applied not only to agricultural labour, but also to most other other work, including building operations. It was indeed popularly held, according to Harris, that any structure erected on such a day would "infallibly entail a curse from above."

Beside holding monthly celebrations on Saints' days it was customary among the nobility, and "people of middling class," Pearce states, to hold a feast every year in the name of their patron saint," on which day they would also give alms to the poor, even though they might wring it from them "tenfold, before the year is expired, by arbitrary taxation." "Many people," Parkyns explains, would also make vows to their Patron Saint to slaughter on his principal day "a bullock, sheep or other votive offering, in order to consolidate his protection and favour for the remainder of the year." Each family thus had its Saint whose anniversary was "handed down from father to son as the family jubilee." On that day the different members of the family entertained their friends by some sort of merry making, "every man according to his means, and even servants considered it necessary among themselves to celebrate the saints' day of their forefathers."

The more important Saints' days were the occasion of colourful ceremonial which brought excitement into the dullness of people's lives. On such days the *tabots* of all the neighbouring churches were taken out, covered with silk or other coloured cloth, and carried on the heads of priests to honour the Saint celebrated that day. The priest carrying the *tabot* was preceded by the church's lower clergy, dressed in rich clothes, with crowns of gold, silver or brass on their heads, each ringing a bell and bearing a long stick with a cross at one end, and singing a joyful song. They were accompanied in front by trumpeters, and in the rear by the high-priest and other important clergy, followed by the populace at large. The women of the area meanwhile formed themselves into different parties, and sang, danced, and clapped their hands to the accompaniment of a drum beaten at both ends by a girl who carried it on a strap around her neck.

In large towns, or near any populous place, chiefs with soldiers mounted on horses and dressed in warlike apparel would also assemble to do honour to the *tabot*. While the latter was slowly carried along they rode about with great speed in all directions, and "many accidents," Pearce states, often occurred. The *tabots* of the various churches were then placed in small tents or huts constructed for the purpose, in which each group of priests administered the Sacrament to those who wished to

---

[10] Pearce (1831) II, 158, 243-4; GB House of Commons (1868) 110. See also Cerulli (1943-7) II, 193-211.

189

partake of it. Many chose to receive it from the hands of a cleric in the church dedicated to their favourite Saint, for it was widely believed that throughout one's life there was one such figure more helpful than the others.[11]

Mähabärs, or Church-sponsored Friendly Societies

Saints' days were the occasion also of the meeting of mähabärs, or church-sponsored friendly societies which usually consisted of twelve members, but sometimes more. The menfolk were generally in one mähabär, and the women in another, but when a husband or wife was absent, a spouse could attend instead. Pearce, who had himself participated in several such societies, states that the members swore to be brethren, and to assist each other in need - and "not to wrong each other's bed," though in this, he felt, they were not necessarily "very attentive" to their vows. Meetings were held once a month on Saints' days which were fixed when the club was first formed. Each mähabär had a priest who ate and drank free of charge. He it was who opened each meeting, on which occasion the members assembled to say the Lord's Prayer, and all repeated it together, after which he broke bread, giving first to the poor at the door, and then to all the members of the mähabär in rotation. Generally they dispersed very late, some of them in a state of intoxication, though "the higher class", Pearce believed, mostly had "the prudence not to get over-intoxicated." Some, however, often drank to such excess that they might fall off their mules on the way home, and, if there was no one to look after them, would be left to the mercy of the hyenas who ranged through most towns and villages all night. Many persons who loved eating and drinking in company would, if they could afford it, belong to several such mähabärs, each held on a different Saint's day.[12]

Church Festivals

The most memorable Church celebrations were those connected with the ending of Lent. Holy Thursday was thus "a sort of picnic-day," which was spent, Parkyns says, "entirely out of doors." On that occasion people took maize, millet, dried peas and any other grain, mixed them together, crushed them in a wooden mortar, and boiled them to produce a porridge which was eaten on that day and the following. On Good Friday the little boys and girls of the neighbourhood went round, knocking at all the houses to demand food, and crying out, "Mishamisho, mishamisho! May God give ye cattle in your yard, and children in your bosom; and may those you have already grow up in health and strength!" Everyone thus appealed to gave them something, but the youngsters made a point of being as grasping and impertinent as possible, and should anyone fail to meet their demands they made a sham corpse of a bundle of clothes, and, placing it on a couch, carried it in procession, pretending that they were mourning the miser's demise. At Gondär, Gobat likewise reported, the city that Friday morning was "all full of life and motion; masters were sending their servants to present their compliments to persons of their acquaintance; the streets were thronged with people rushing to and fro, coming and going to their churches".

---

[11] Ferret and Galinier (1847) II, 361; Pearce (1831) I, 337-9; Harris (1844) III, 353-4.

[12] Pearce (1831) II, 19-20.

On Easter Sunday the priests went around the town in procession, carrying crosses and church ornaments, and singing in praise of God, and of the person they were about to visit. At Adwa, for example, they visited "every respectable person in the town," Pearce recalls, or at least such as they "knew to be capable of giving them their fill of victuals and drink some days afterwards." On entering a house they handed the master and mistress, and then the servants, some green rushes, one of which they kept tied round the head throughout the day. The clergy then held out crosses for everyone to kiss, after which they recited the Lord's Prayer, and then proceeded to another house, and so on until they had visited every respectable man or woman in the town or parish. In return they would be invited, during the following month, by all those whom they had visited, and who would give them a feast, perhaps killing two or three cows for the occasion.

The festival of Saint Gäbrä Mänfäs likewise had its food associations, for everyone on that occasion ate peas which were made to sprout by soaking them for three days in water. Portions of peas were also given as presents to friends and neighbours. Some people claimed, according to Parkyns, that the sprouts represented the old Saint's white beard; others that they recalled his life of hardship when he lived on roots and berries.

The day of St. Yohannes, which coincided with the Ethiopian New Year and the beginning of Mäskäräm, the first month of the year, also had its distinctive ceremonies. Pearce recalls that the boys and girls gathered flowers to make nosegays which they took to the "higher sort of people", from whom they received in return a present, or were given "something to eat or drink". Parkyns, who confirms this picture, states that festivals began at dawn when people presented each other with bunches of wild flowers, saying *inkutataš*, literally, "Take this present," a phrase not, however, used on any other occasion. Such gifts elicited a present in return. Servants made a point of giving flowers to their master and mistress, and "in a great man's house" there was "a great deal of rivalry" as to who should be the first to do so, "for only the two or three earliest comers" were usually rewarded. A wife on being presented with flowers by her husband would reciprocate by giving him a new pair of trousers made from cotton spun with her own hand, and he might respond by presenting her with a new dress. The day was also important for persons believing themselves possessed by evil spirits, for it was then that they might choose a white or red sheep, drag it round them three times, and slaughter it "in the name of the Father, and of the Son, and of the Holy Ghost," after which they would place some of its blood on their forehead, and then depart, leaving the carcase on the ground without looking at it. They did this lest they should disturb the Devil who was supposed to have by then left his victim, and to be busy eating the mutton. The day's celebrations ended that evening with everyone, male and female, old and young, going down to bathe in a neighbouring river or lake.

Mäsqäl, or the Feast of the Cross, which took place toward the end of September, and more or less coincided with the end of the rainy season, was, according to Pearce, the "greatest holyday in the whole year", while Parkyns says it was the festival celebrated with "the greatest pomp and show." Pearce reports that the boys and girls at midnight began to "flock in gangs", singing and dashing about with long

An Ethiopian Palm Sunday service at Addigrat in Tegré. Note the manuscript book, crosses, censers and prayer-sticks. From R. Acton, *The Abyssinian Expedition* (London, 1868).

bundles of dried sticks, lighted like torches, while men, also carrying them, rushed into one another's houses, crying "*annkkerver, etc.,*" the meaning of which was "All bad things have gone out and good ones are coming in". In towns such as Adwa the festival, Parkyns recalls, was preceded by many days of desultory mock warfare between the young people of opposite sexes, the girls armed with gourds containing filthy liquids, and the boys with thorns or stinging nettles. When any of the opposing parties encountered each other they ritualistically exchanged insults, often using offensive language, after which the boys pricked and stung the naked breasts and shoulders of the girls who responded by throwing their smelly potions in the faces of their assailants.

The eve of *Mäsqäl*, which brought an end to such hostilities, was - by the early nineteenth century at least - marked at sunset by the discharge of fire-arms from all the principal houses. Bonfires were set ablaze, and people lit torches and paraded with them throughout the town. They also entered people's houses, and poked their lights into every dark corner, for example under beds and in stables and kitchens, as if looking for something lost, and would cry out, "*Akho, akhoky*! turn out the spinach and bring the porridge; Maskal has come."

Early on Mäsqäl morning, while it was still dark, the great men had huge piles of wood on high places near the towns set on fire. One or two oxen or sheep, according to the wealth of the officer, were then led three times around the fire, and slaughtered, their flesh being left on the spot to be eaten by the animals or birds of prey. The people that day rose early to see the fire, after which soldiers presented themselves before their master, and performed war-boasts, relating how they had served him and would do so again when opportunity arose. *Mäsqäl* celebrations at Adwa also included a regular fight between the different parishes, and on one of the days when Parkyns participated, those of Mika'él and Gabre'él, after a long contest, beat and put to flight that of Mädhané 'Aläm, or Saviour of the World.

Christmas, as in other Christian countries, was a day of much praying, singing and feasting. The ensuing *Ṭemqät*, or Epiphany, celebrations began on the eve of the holiday, a day of fasting, when priests and *däbtära*, bearing their *tabots* and church paraphernalia, went down to a neighbouring river or lake, on the banks of which tents were pitched to receive them, and where devout parishioners contributed "a store of comestibles of every variety," including large quantities of beer and mead. Feasting began that day at sun-set, and it was "fearful to behold", Parkyns comments, "with what vigour the half-famished divines set to work," for abundance was always awaiting them as the food was collected in the name of the *tabot*, and people thought they were "doing a very goodly act in providing vast quantities". The whole ensuing night was spent in alternate prayer, hymn singing, religious dancing, and drinking, after which, before sunrise, the Sacrament was administered, though many of the priests, he feared, were by then so inebriated that they were "not in a very fit state to partake of it." The chief priest then raised his hands over the water, and blessed it, whereupon the people would push themselves in to bathe. The great men and priests, however, did not immerse themselves, but were instead sprinkled with water, "to obviate the necessity of their mixing, even in such a ceremony, with the vulgar herd." At the conclusion of the ceremony the women danced and sang, while the men engaged in various sports, including *guks*, or traditional Ethiopian hockey. On the following day, which was dedicated to the Archangel Mika'él, there were further church ceremonies, as well as much feasting, in which the priests were always "well fed by their devout parishioners."

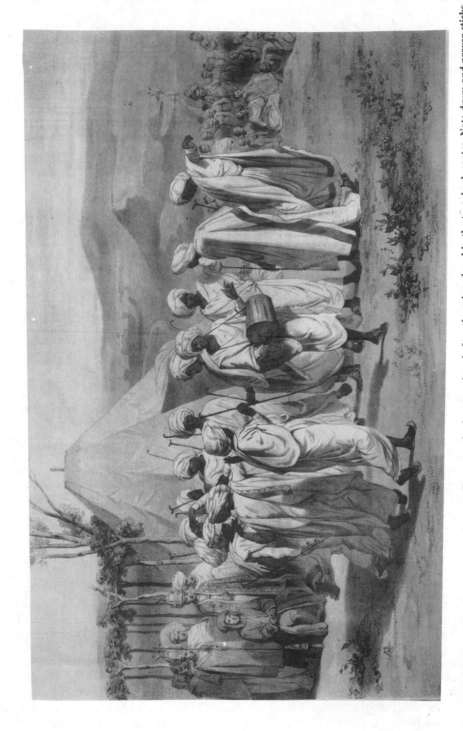

The **Ethiopian** priest's elegant dance, carried out on *Temqāt* and other occasions before the *tabot* placed in the tent, back centre. Note drum and prayer-sticks. From T. Lefebvre and others, *Voyage en Abyssinie* (Paris, 1845-8).

Other colourful festivals included that of Mika'él, in June, when King Sahlä Sellasé gave clothes to his slaves, and many people, according to Isenberg and Krapf, went from house to house begging for clothes; and the feast *Felsäta*, or the Assumption of the Virgin, in August, which was characterised at Ankobär, Harris says, by "customary skirmishes between the town's people and the slave establishment of the king." No less exciting were the celebrations of Däbrä Tabor, or the Transfiguration, when the Šäwan capital was as brightly illuminated as candles would allow. "Whilst boys, carrying flambeaux, ran singing through the streets, every dwelling displayed such a light as its inmates could afford."[13]

The Life Cycle

The Life Cycle had a significant religious dimension. Marriages, as we shall see, were largely secular, and carried out for the most part without the intervention of the clergy, but the latter invariably officiated at both baptisms and funerals.

(i) Baptism

On the day of a child's birth the parents were generally visited by a priest. His prinicpal duty on that occasion was to tell the father, who was in most cases illiterate - or at least unprovided with a calendar - the date of his offspring's baptism, which had to take place forty days after birth in the case of a boy or eighty in that of a girl. Strict adherence to this dating was considered essential, and a parent who failed to have his or her child baptised on the prescribed day was subjected, Parkyns says to "heavy penance," perhaps of several months' fasting.

Not long after the infant's birth the priests would return to the parental house with "all the pomp and ceremony of the Church," including crosses and incense, to purify the place from the impurity of childbirth by sprinkling the dwelling with holy water. This took place on the tenth day after the birth of a boy or the twentieth after a girl.

When the day of baptism arrived the family made their way to church where the priest received the child from the godfather. The cleric then placed his hand on its head, poured on it a little water, and then, taking some oil, made the sign of the cross on the child's head, hands, breast and knees, and concluded by tying round its neck a painted cord of red, blue and white silk - the sign of Christianity - which was later exchanged for a blue cord. The priest then returned the infant to its godfather, exhorting him to support and educate it, and look after its welfare, spiritual and temporal, as if it were his own child. The ceremony being thus concluded, the clergy then returned with the whole party to the house where the parents would have prepared a great feast in honour of the occasion.[14]

---

[13] Parkyns (1853) II, 74-8, 81-4; Pearce (1831) II, 219, 273, 277; Isenberg and Krapf (1843) 66; Gobat (1850), 205; Harris (1844) III, 349-50.

[14] Parkyns (1853) II, 38-9.

(ii) Funerals

Funerals were of considerably greater prominence than baptisms in traditional Ethiopian social life, and attendance at them was virtually obligatory. Anyone who failed to join in a mourning ceremony, Gobat explains, was indeed "not regarded as a friend."

Death was usually followed by three days of deep mourning, not only by relatives and friends of the deceased, but also by distant acquaintances, after which a series of commemorative feasts would be held over a period of several, and in some cases, many years. Funeral services, in the opinion of Pearce, who had participated in many in Tegré - including one for his only son - were "very affecting."

When someone became seriously ill, and was expected to die, friends and relatives at once assembled, and began crying and wailing. On news of the demise such lamentations were at once "recommencced with fury."

The burial ceremony itself took place only a few hours later, almost invariably on the same day as the death. The priests on that occasion began by reading out prayers for the soul of the deceased, whose body was at the same time washed, its hands placed across one another, upon the lower part of the body, and tied to keep them in that position, the eyes closed, and the two great toes also tied together. The corpse was then wrapped in a clean cloth, and sewed up, after which it was placed in a skin such as that on which most people slept. Coffins were in many cases made out of cane, but those for very important people were of wood, which, because of the shortage of timber, was often taken from the doors of their houses.

The body of the deceased was carried to the place of interment by bearers walking mournfully at a slow pace. The route from the house to the church was divided into seven sections, and on reaching each seventh the corpse was set down, and the priests offered up further prayers for the forgiveness of the deceased. At the churchyard itself each of the deceased's male neighbours brought tools and helped to dig the grave, and all tried to outstrip each other in the work. Even when a stranger died people would flock to assist in his or her burial, and many would join in the cry, as though they had been closely related to the deceased. When the grave was ready a priest would step into it, Parkyns recalls, and perfume it with incense, after which the body was lowered to its last resting place.

Though the burial itself involved no expense Pearce states that the clergy generally demanded an "exorbitant sum" from those who had property. He recalls seeing two clergymen quarrelling over the cloth of a poor dead woman, the only good article she had left. If a man died leaving a wife and child, he adds, the woman was sometimes drained of the last article of value she possessed in order to purchase food and drink for the priests, for she often had to make such contributions for no less than six months - lest the clergy failed to say the necessary prayers for her husband "which would disgrace her and render her name odious among the lowest of the populace."

Part of the funeral ceremony for Emperor Téwodros's consort Queen Teruneš who died in 1868, shortly after the fall of Mäqdäla. From R. Acton, *The Abyssinian Expedition* (1868).

The number of prayers for the dead varied greatly. If the deceased was of a wealthy family masses were performed daily, Parkyns says, for forty days, but if the relations were poor five were generally considered sufficient. They were performed on the third, seventh, twelfth, thirteenth and fortieth days. Such ceremonies were by no means cheap. The price of 40 masses, which were "bargained for by the priests," amounted at Adwa, by the eighteen forties, to anything between six and twelve thalers, "or more, according to the wealth of the family." The clergy also expected to be fed and provided with provisions on a number of occasions. They had thus to be given an "abundance of provisions," including a sheep, on the thirtieth day, one or two cows and "various other things" on the fortieth, and a feast to coincide with a midnight mass on the eightieth.[15]

Funeral ritual also included an immense amount of formal mourning. On the death of his son a large number of people, Pearce recalls, made their way to his house,

"striving who should get in first... Some brought twenty or thirty cakes of bread, some jars of maize [i.e. *mes*, or mead], some cooked victuals, fowls, and bread, some a sheep, etc; and in this manner, I had my house so full that I was obliged to go out into the yard, until things were put in order and supper was ready.... The bringers are all invited to eat with you; they talk and tell stories to divert your thoughts from the sorrowful subject; they force you to drink a great deal; but... when the relatives of the deceased become a little tranquil in their minds, some old woman, or someone who can find no one to talk to, will suddenly make a dismal cry, saying, 'Oh what a fine child! and he is already forgotten?' This puts the whole company into confusion, and all join in the cry, which perhaps will last half an hour."[16]

When commemorating the death of any person of substance, an even more considerable number of people would assemble in the vicinity of the deceased's residence. A sofa, symbolising his or her bed, was laid out, together with his carpets and other articles of grandeur. An effigy of the departed, frequently made, according to Parkyns, of cushions, covered with a white garment, was also made, and sometimes put upon one of his mules. His horses were then led before with his musket-men, and were followed by the whole of his household, with their shields and spears, having, Pearce says, "nothing but a skin around their waist, with their forehead and temples all torn, shouting and crying in a horrid manner." It was also customary for the churches of the area each to send a *däbäl*, or decorated umbrella, made of silk or carpet-like material, on a long pole, while the local church would provide all its *däbäls* and public ornaments to grace the funeral. On the death of Ras Wäldä Sellasé's brother Ato Debbeb in 1814 no fewer than three hundred and fifty umbrellas were thus displayed. Mourning was highly ritualised. Relatives and friends of the deceased wept and wailed, and rubbed their faces with their clothes. It was likewise customary, particularly in Tegré, for members of the bereaved family, both male and female, to

[15] Gobat (1850) 310; Parkyns (1853) II, 63-5; Pearce (1831) I, 83-5,125,189-97, 263-4.

[16] Pearce (1831) I, 189-90.

shave their heads and rub themselves "so severely on the forehead and temples," Parkyns reports, "as to abrade the skin completely," and produce a sore which took a long time to cure and was sometimes visible for life.

Funeral gatherings were often attended by professional singing women who sometimes received a handsome present as a reward for their services, though many went in the hope of being well fed at the feasting which took place after the ceremony. Each person in wailing took it by turn to improvise some verses in praise of the deceased. A son or daughter might exclaim, "Oh! my father, who fed and clothed me whom have I now to supply your place!" while his friends or relatives would refer to him as "Brother," and his wife and servants as "Master," each speaking of him according to the degree of relationship which existed between them. The professional singers meanwhile gave minute details of his ancestry, deeds, character, and even his property, Parkyns says, declaring for example, "Oh! Gabrou, son of Welda Mousa, grandson of Ita Garra Raphael, etc, etc, rider of the bay horse with white feet and of the grey ambling mule, owner of the Damascus barrel-gun ('baaly johar'), and bearer of the silver-mounted shield, why have you left us?" They thus entered "with astonishing readiness into every particular of the deceased's life and actions", while the by-standers, at the end of each verse, broke in with a chorus of sobbing lamentation, adapted to a mournful chant, "Wai! wai! wailaway" etc.

Funerals - after the advent of numerous fire-arms in the early nineteenth century - were also marked, as we shall see, by much firing of guns. After the death of Walda Sellasé's brother Ato Debbeb, Pearce who, at Antalo, thus heard much wailing as well as the firing of muskets in all parts of the town. "The multitude of people was so great," he says, "that it was impossible to pass the streets, and the walls and tops of the houses were covered with persons of both sexes, young and old. ... the noise was inexpressibly shocking. ... there was not an individual to be seen but with his face torn, and scratched, and covered with blood."

The funerals of the great and famous were in fact major events in which vast sections of the population participated. On the death of the Neburä Ed, the ecclesiastical governor of Aksum, in 1811, there was for example "great crying," Pearce says, "throughout Tigré." Ras Wäldä Sellasé himself joined in the ceremony for two days, giving 100 pieces of cloth, equal to a hundred Maria Theresa dollars, to the priests of the Trinity Church at Čäläqot, and another hundred to those of Axum, to offer prayers for the deceased.

The deaths of great personages sometimes differed from those of other mortals in that news of them was often concealed for reasons of state. Ras Wäldä Sellasé's demise at Čäläqot in 1816 was thus "kept secret from the people," Pearce recalls, for fear of the calamities that might follow. This gave time for many valuables to be placed for safe-keeping in a nearby monastery. When the death was finally divulged "the whole town was instantly alarmed," and hundreds of people, instead of attending the funeral, fled in all directions to bury their property to save it from the anticipated plunder. The priests, however, then came once again into their own, as we shall see, by making the town a place of asylum.[17]

---

[17] Gobat (1850) 310; Parkyns (1853) II, 63-5; Pearce (1831) I, 83-5,125,189-97, 263-4.

Asylum

Many religious centres served, as in medieval Europe, as places of asylum, and were rarely raided, except by Muslim or pagan foes. Localities where an Abun had resided, and had administered the Sacrament, were, according to Pearce, generally considered sacred. The most respected such place of refuge was Aksum, whose area of asylum had a circumference, according to Ferret and Galinier, of a kilometre. Within that circle the entire Christian population of the surrounding countryside would flee in time of trouble, and "even those who commit murder or the worst of crimes," Pearce says, were "safe from justice once they were within the sacred precincts. In times of disturbance Aksum, Ferret and Galinier state, thus attracted a "numerous population," for the rich would go there to place in safety their gold and valuable objects, the beggar his rags, the peasant his grain, and the soldier weapons for which he had no immediate need. Aksum's role as a place of asylum had a significant impact on the surrounding countryside which was well cultivated, the villages of the area being also richer and better built than those in the rest of Tegré.

At Gondär, the old imperial capital, the residences of the Abun and the Eçägé, and their environs, were likewise considered places of asylum. The latter, Gobat recalls, thus "always" afforded "a safe residence, even in the midst of the greatest troubles," for it was "entirely under the control of the priests," and "no governor" dared to enter it by force.

Throughout the Christian highlands it was not unusual for people to appeal to the clergy for protection in times of difficulty. During the disorders following the death of Ras Wäldä Sellasé in 1815 for example the people of Çäläqot, site of one of that chief's two capitals, proposed that the Abun should consecrate the settlement as a place of asylum. The prelate accordingly at once walked around the town at the head of all the clergy of the neighbourhood, with crowns of gold and silver and other church ornaments, to the beat of many drums. People from far and near thereupon brought their property to the city precincts for safety, and "even those who had committed murder," Pearce says, "came to the town where they were secure." Similar events were reported at Gondär a decade or so later when "most" of its inhabitants slept in the churches, Gobat noted in 1830, for fear of attack by the soldiers.

When a party of marauding soldiers subsequently appeared at Bahr Dar, Plowden was one of those who sought the clergy's protection. Following traditional Ethiopian practice he rushed to the local church, and tolled its bell, thereby signifying that he had taken sanctuary, whereupon a priest arrived to inquire what was the problem, and who was in need of protection. This was duly notified to the *Aläqa*, or head of the church, after which the news quickly spread through the town, the Englishman was able to return in safety to his house, and the soldiers "disappeared on hearing the bell," and came near him no more.

Such protection from the Church was beneficial not only to persons under threat, but also to life in the country as a whole. Fields in the neighbourhood of places of asylum, where "military license" had been "in some degree" checked by the priests,

200

and where the "ravages of war" were "less felt," Plowden states, were "highly cultivated," and therefore more prosperous than would otherwise have been the case.[18]

Attitudes to Drink, Tobacco, and Fasting

The Ethiopian Church displayed no objection to alcohol, indeed the priests throughout the country were described by Pearce as "great drinkers." They were, on the other hand, strongly opposed to smoking, with the result, he says, that no one who had smoked was allowed to enter a church. Despite such opposition many people took snuff, and not a few were addicted to smoking, which was, however,"accounted a sin."

Efforts to tighten fasts were made during this period by the bigotted Abunä Qérellos, who, though a Copt, is said to have insisted that fish should not be eaten in times of abstinence.[19]

Prayer, the Making of Vows, and Holy Water

Great importance was attached to both prayers and the making of vows. Besides individual prayer by the clergy and laity as individuals there were also mass prayers by communities in time of crisis. On the occurrence of an earthquake at Ankobär in the early 1840's, for example, a "hymn of entreaty," Harris recalls, "rose high in the mist from every church throughout the town; and bands of priests, carrying the holy cross, marched in solemn procession ... beating their breasts and calling aloud upon Saint Michael the Archangel, and upon Mary the mother of the Messiah, to intercede for them."

The making of vows was not infrequent, particularly on the part of women desirous of having children. It was the custom for such women to prepare wax candles, bread, beer and other articles in honour of the Virgin Mary or a favourite Saint, and take them to church on the day associated with that Saint. In many cases undertaking long pilgrimages for the purpose, they then offered their present to the resident priest who in return handed them a small bell to hold in their hand, after which they would "stand in one posture, repeating a prayer over and over, for several hours," until they were "entirely fatigued." They might do this "for several days successively," and, if they gave birth within the next year, they would probably call their child after the Saint they had thus petitioned.

There was also widespread belief in the curative value of *täbäls*, or springs of holy water, which, Pearce recalls, were "highly esteemed." Many, like that called after Gäbrä Mänfäs in Šäwa, were associated with specific Saints.[20]

---

[18] Ferret and Galinier (1847) I, 470-1; Pearce (1831) I, 164, II, 85; Gobat (1850) 157-8, 253; Plowden (1868) 42, 136, 261, 266; Krapf (1867), 450; Stern (1862) 177-8; Lejean (1872) 23; Arnauld d' Abbadie (1868) 161-2; GB House of Commons (1868) 107.

[19] Pearce (1831) I, 335, II, 175; Isenberg and Krapf (1843) 91.

[20] Harris (1844) III, 379-80; Pearce (1831) I, 290. II, 159; Isenberg and Krapf (1843) 311; Parkyns (1853) 82.

Prophesies, Omens and Auguries

There was widespread faith in prophecies, omens and auguries. Most people believed in, and were guided, Parkyns says, by the "revelations of seers," of whom there were many, professing the skills of soothsayers, fortune-tellers and predictors of the future, as Plowden recalls.

Decisions, both personal and public, were likewise often governed by omens or auguries. Some of those which exercised the greatest influence were connected with the sound of birds. Before starting on an expedition Ethiopian soldiers, like those of ancient Rome, would often listen for the voice of certain birds. If these were heard on the right an auspicious outcome, Parkyns says, would be anticipated, but if on the left it was believed that the journey would end in failure. Many wars or hunting expeditions, the success of which was "nearly certain," were postponed or abandoned "simply because a little bird called from the left." The singing of an unfavourably situated bird, according to Gobat, might even induce a commander to abandon an expedition underway. Hunters on the Märäb river were likewise often influenced as to the direction they should take by a bird's behaviour, and Parkyns had known parties "turn back from pursuing the fresh trail of a herd of buffaloes, and take an opposite direction, merely because its chirp was heard on the wrong side." One of the most notable birds of omen in Tegré was the *gaddy gaddy*, or black and white falcon, whose movement was closely watched by travellers. Should it fly away at their approach they would consider this an unfavourable sign, but if it remained perched, and looking at them, they felt that they could count on a prosperous journey.

Beliefs of this kind were held in other parts of the country. The Agäws of Lasta, according to Plowden, thus claimed a knowledge of the language of birds, and attached "great importance" to their twittering in regulating marketings, journeys and military expeditions. Not dissimilar practices were reported from Šäwa, whose ruler, Harris claims, never failed "to consult the omens" before setting out on an expedition. Priests and monks, the envoy goes on to assert, were likewise often referred to by its monarch, "and the accidental fall of the targe from a saddle bow, the alighting of a hooded crow in the path of a warrior, or the appearance of a white falcon with the tail towards him, " were "believed to augur unfavourably to success," whilst "the flight of a pair of ravens in any direction, or the descent of a falcon with her head towards the army," were "esteemed certain prognostications of victory." Journeys and hunting expeditions were thus not undertaken without the "receipt from on High of the desired omens of approbation," and, if these were wanting, people would "retrace their steps on any pretext, and patiently await the welcome sign." The sight of an "unclean hare" was likewise "sufficient to shake the stoutest nerves." An antelope bounding across the path augured "favourably to success in any undertaking," while a fox barking on the left destroyed "all hope of a happy result," but, if on the right, "a prosperous issue" might "with confidence be anticipated." The appearance of a white buzzard prognosticated "good or evil according to the position of the tail," and "the chief of all the numerous birds of ill omen" was the "Goorameila." Death or the most dire disaster was "certain to follow his portentous croak," and there was "no inhabitant throughout the realm" who had not "some tale to record in confirmation" of its "fatal character".

Belief in omens among the Oromos, on the other hand, was "almost entirely confined," Plowden states, "to the examination of the stomachs of slaughtered oxen and sheep." These were stretched out, and the lines of their fatty membranes, or *mora*, carefully examined. In one place the initiated might for example claim to discern evidence that the people of Jemma and Gudru would fight, while in another place they might see a corpse, or perhaps ten. On the day when an unlucky *mora* was found nothing could persuade the owner, however brave, to set forth in war.[21]

Belief in *Buda*, or Possessed Persons, and the Evil Eye

There was throughout the country a widespread belief in the evil eye, as well as in the existence of *budas*, or persons possessed by malevolent spirits. Fears of such forces resulted, according to Pearce, in "a great deal of hiding" from the evil eye. It was widely held that the latter could enter the bodies of people eating in the open air. A person of substance would therefore have his servants hold pieces of cloth around him, while the poorest members of the community would hide themselves under their *šämmas*, or togas. There were similarly fears of being seen drinking or exposing the naked body in public. When a chief such as Ras Berru raised a bottle to drink, or even opened his mouth to cough, officious servants would therefore rush forward to cover his face. When testing a horse it was likewise considered prudent, in the interests of man and beast alike, for both to avoid being seen by the general populace, for it was said that "the eyes of people are bad," and a "very good horse and a good rider" were "supposed to be in the greater danger" than others, for they attracted more eyes. Indeed, "without strong amulets, any too conspicuous act or appearance," Plowden says, was held to be "highly imprudent."

Popular belief in Šäwa, among Amharas as well as among Oromos and Guragés, held, according to Krapf, that there were no less than eighty-eight evil spirits known as *zar* (plural *zaroč*), each of whom had its own particular name. They were divided into two groups, each under an *Aläqa*, or head, who commanded forty-four spirits. One of these leaders was called *Mama* and the other *Warrer*. Persons wishing to free themselves from such spirits might smoke, sing, move their body or offer a hen, preferably a red one, in sacrifice. The bird would be slaughtered, and eaten by the organisers of the ceremony, its leader being accorded the bird's brain. Such customs, which were regarded as unChristian, seem to have earned the disapproval of King Sahlä Sellasé and were also opposed by the priests who had gone so far as forbidding Christians to smoke.

Illnesses were widely blamed on the evil eye. When anyone suffered from disease, or experienced any other misfortune, the person so afflicted and his or her neighbours often sought the cause in some supernatural power exercised by a *buda* or in "the influence of malignant eyes." Such suspicions, at first uncertain and vague, would, Gobat says, soon fix on a specific individual to whom they would "ascribe the origin of the evil," and who, in consequence, became "the victim of a secret and implacable hostility." *Budas*, as we have seen, were widely believed to have the power of turning themselves into hyenas or other animals at night. Such beliefs were so

---

[21] Parkyns (1853) I, 292-3, 344-5: Plowden (1868) 124, 295; Gobat (1850) 477; Harris (1844) II, 166, 331.

widespread, Parkyns testifies, that even Däjazmač Webé, though above most superstitions, expressed no scepticism about them.[22]

Conversions

Despite the great influence of the Church, and of the priesthood, many conversions from Christianity to Islam took place during this period, in several parts of the country, particularly on its periphery. One of the principal areas of conversion was in the vicinity of Massawa where the Bäläw and later the Habab abandoned Christianity for Islam. The conversion of the latter took place, according to Trimingham, around 1820. It was due, in Plowden's opinion, to the influence of Muslim neighbours with whom the Habab traded, as well as to the gradual and later the entire abandonment of the area by the chiefs who were "too much occupied in ceaseless wars with their neighbours." The process was encouraged, according to Lejean, by the Na'ibs of Hergigo whose religious fanaticism was compounded by Machiavellian politics, for they reasoned that if the tribe embraced Islam it would no longer refuse to pay them taxes, nor be able to count on the aid of their co-religionaries in the Ethiopian interior. Another explanation was given by Wärqé Käräbet, a foreign-educated Ethiopian of partial Armenian extraction, who declared that the tribe had adopted Islam when a monk had forbidden them from continuing to drink camel's milk, a major item in their diet. Evidence of the Hababs' late conversion is provided by the fact that "most" of the tribe in the 1840's still bore Christian names. The nearby Tegré people were Islamised at about the same time. The process had taken place, Antoine d'Abbadie states, under his very eyes, the whole tribe being converted, except for the chief who declared that "every king should die in the faith of his fathers." Another region in which Islam was then making inroads was Wällo, and particularly Wärra Himäno, - where there had been "many" Christians before Amadé Lebän, its early nineteenth century ruler, by "force and persuasion, converted a great number to the Mahomedan religion."

Not long after this the Egyptians overran Bogos in the north-west where they destroyed many villages, took at least three hundred slaves within a few months, and burnt down the principal church as a preliminary to converting the country. This move was, however, foiled, in part by the activities of an Italian missionary, Father Stella, and in part through diplomatic pressure from the British Government on the prompting of Consul Plowden. The advance of Islam at this time was so extensive that the Muslims of Ifat firmly believed, according to Johnston, that even Sahlä Sellasé had for a time considered changing his religion. He was reported to have sent for a Qoran and a Muslim scholar to expound it, and had only been prevented from adopting Islam, it was said, as a result of the coming of the zealous Protestant missionary Krapf who spoke to him of the possibility of obtaining help from Britain - which had then recently established itself in nearby Aden. Though unsubstantiated this rumour was doubtless symptomatic of the times.

Numerous conversions were also taking place on an individual basis. Two Christians of Adwa for example were reported in 1818 to have "turned Mahomedans," on which occasion, Pearce reports, no one objected, for "such fallings-off from their

---

[22] Plowden (1868) 124; Isenberg and Krapf (1843) 117-8; Gobat (1850) 477; Pearce (1831) I, 287-8, II, 339-42.

faith" were "occurring continually," and were "not thought shameful as formerly." Some such changes of religion were said to have been entirely opportunistic, as in the case quoted by Parkyns of a man who embraced Islam "for the sake of 150 piastres ... and a new garment."

Temporary switches of religion were also not uncommon, particularly among persons who travelled abroad. Most Ethiopians, Parkyns testifies, were "not difficult in matters of religion, except at home." Many Christians, "according to their own account," would, "rather die than swerve from their principles," but, on making their way abroad, would eat forbidden Muslim meat, and enjoy it "as if they had been born and brought up to it." There were moreover instances of them "turning Turk for the time of their sojourn in the land of Islam," but "returning to their Christianity ... as soon as they set foot in their own country." Even some pilgrims to Jerusalem "became Mussulmans for the road thither and back again," but "put on their Christianity" at the Holy City, and again on returning home.

Conversions from Islam to Christianity seem to have been relatively rare, but occasionally occurred, as at Adwa in 1818 when two young Muslim boys were beaten by their masters, as a result of which they "ran to the Abuna's premises, and turned Christians," as Pearce reports. The Muslims of the city "did all they could to get the boys back, but to no purpose."

Some conversions to European forms of Christianity were meanwhile also taking place as a result of the work of foreign missionaries who were becoming increasingly active in the early nineteenth century, and were then busy distributing printed Amharic Bibles. This activity won the hearts of some, such as a "poor man" of Gondär, who, according to Gobat, "ventured, though with trembling", to ask for a copy of the Gospel in 1830 "that he might be enabled to inculcate upon the minds of his children its holy precepts." Other missionaries, however, were less discriminating. Some, according to Parkyns, spent their time sitting in their tents, and handed out Bibles "indiscriminately" to anyone who, moved by curiosity, happened to enter. One man had thus been given two copies which "he sold the same evening for a jar of beer, and got drunk on the strength of it." Another recipient of a Bible was an Orthodox priest who visibly set little value on it. The missionary, seeing this, told him to be careful with the present as its cost even in England was around six dollars, whereupon the cleric replied, "I am unworthy of so costly a gift! Take back your Bible, and give me one dollar; it is enough for me." Genuine interest in the Bibles given away by the missionaries was so meagre, Plowden states, that many were used for "wrapping up of snuff, and such-like undignified purposes."

Many conversions were based on largely mercenary considerations. "Nine converts out of ten," Parkyns believed, were in fact "only converts to calico and Maria Theresa dollars." One of the consequences of this was that some of the principal converts on whom the Protestant missionary Gobat placed his hopes became disciples of the Lazarists only a short time afterwards. On the other hand one of the first young men to be taken abroad for study, Madhärä Qal Täwäldä Mädhen, after being enrolled in a Jesuit college in Paris, abandoned it in favour of a British Protestant missionary establishment.

The missionaries of this period had a mixed reputation. Gobat, the principal Protestant, was expelled from Gondär, where he was regarded as a heretic and almost as a non-believer, but was highly regarded in Tegré where he was always spoken of, as Parkyns concedes, "with the greatest respect and affection." Other missionaries, however, alienated the population by their lack of tact. On one occasion, on the outbreak of a fire, the people called on their Saints for aid, only to be reproved and ridiculed for their superstition by the European churchmen. On another occasion during one of the most solemn of Ethiopian fasts, some missionaries slaughtered an animal and offered its meat to the poor and hungry "as if to tempt them from the observance of the discipline of their Church." As a result of such behaviour, most missionaries in the opinion of Parkyns had "not left a single friend behind".

Notwithstanding such criticism there can be no gainsaying the genuine sincerity of many conversions, let alone the important long-term educational contribution of the European missionaries, both Catholic and Protestant, who were at this time beginning to take young Ethiopians abroad for religious and other studies, in Rome, Marseilles, St. Chrischona in Switzerland and elsewhere.[23]

Priest with sistrum and prayer-stick

[23] Plowden (1868) 7-8, 15; Trimingham (1952) 112, 157; Lejean (1865) 236, 238; Isenberg and Krapf (1843) 91, 94, 251, 362; Antoine d'Abbadie (1868) 16, 29; GB House of Commons (1868) 83, 85, 87, 90, 131, 140; Johnston (1844), II, 46, 143; Parkyns (1853) I, 149, 153-5, II, 92-3, 95; Pearce (1831) II, 245; Gobat (1850) 253; Pankhurst (1952) 245-6, (1962) 253; Lejean p.236 states that Habab, Bogos, Mensa and Marya were known as Kostan, a corruption of the term "Christian". On Mahdärä Qal see Dufton (1867) 79-81, 99, and Pankhurst and Ingrams (1988) 51.

VII

TRADERS

Muslim and Christian Merchants

Trade in the first part of the nineteenth century, as in the past, was largely dominated by Muslim merchants, and tended to be despised by the majority of the population which had little inclination to travel, except on campaign or pilgrimage. The prevailing attitude of Ethiopian Christians was summed up by Ras Wäldä Sellasé who told Henry Salt in 1811 that his co-religionaries were "little acquainted with commercial transactions," as they dedicated their lives "solely to war and agriculture," so that trade had "rested from a very early period in the hands of Mahometans." One of the results of this was that merchants, like trade, tended, Consul Plowden stated, to be "looked on with contempt by the military," though they were "patronized by the chiefs" whom the traders "conciliated" by "rare presents," in addition to their taxes. There were nonetheless a few wealthy Christian traders, the most prominent of whom in the early nineteenth century were Täsfä Haylu and Wäldä Sellasé of Gondär, Kidanä Maryam and Hagos Däräs of Adwa, and Kasa and Wändé of Qoräta.[1]

Caravans

Caravans played a major rôle in long distance trade, and were largely based on personal supervision by the merchants, or their agents, who accompanied their goods, and remained with them at the markets where they were offered for sale. The itinerant trader or agent was thus able to choose the articles in greatest demand, buy in the cheapest market, defend his goods if they were in danger from robbers, come to the best possible terms with extortionate customs officials, and sell most advantageously from point of view of price, place and time.

Caravans operated, Ferret and Galinier explain, on a well established pattern. The principal merchant about to make a journey would announce in advance the day of his departure, whereupon smaller traders, couriers, and persons with business in the area to be visited, would prepare to join the caravan, after which they would erect their tents beside that of the most important trader who in this way became the caravan leader. He it was who was responsible for obtaining armed escorts and guides, fixing the hour of departure, choosing camp sites on the journey, and settling disputes, as well as paying customs taxes and dividing their burden among all the members of the caravan. Each individual merchant was, however, responsible for his own transport, and traded as he thought best. In a typical caravan of the 1830's described by Rüppell the four richest merchants rode on mules; the rest walked on foot. Everyone was armed, mostly with either a sword or a spear and shield, but eight men had rifles.

Merchandise, which was generally kept in skin sacks, was invariably carried on the backs of mules, donkeys, horses and camels, or the shoulders of human porters, according to the wealth of the traders and the nature of the country to be traversed.

---

[1] Ferret and Galinier (1847) II, 411; Great Britain, F.O. 1/1 Salt, 4 March 1811; GB House of Commons (1868) 111; Lefebvre (1845-8) II, Part II, 30; Plowden (1868) 126, 392; Heuglin (1868) 55.

A group of Banyan, or Indian, merchants, who traded inland from the Red Sea port of Massawa. From T. Lefebvre and others, *Voyage en Abyssinie* (Paris, 1845-8).

If the land was mountainous, rich traders would load their goods on mules whose strength and sobriety rendered them invaluable for this work. Neither man nor beast could equal their ability in climbing rocky heights or precipitous cliffs. These sturdy animals were moreover far from expensive, for a good beast capable of carrying 45 kilos could be obtained at Gondär for only five or six Maria Theresa dollars. Traders crossing deserts or sandy regions, like those between Mätämma and Sennar or Aleyu Amba and the Gulf of Aden coast, on the other hand made use of camels. These remarkable animals could carry no less than 350 kilos, or almost eight times as much as a mule, and could be fed on almost anything available, barley, beans or brushwood, while subsisting for a week on a mere litre of water. There were, finally, human porters, many of whom were to be found in Gondär, Adwa and the other main towns. The average porter travelled 20 to 30 kilometres a day, and carried about 25 kilos, or about half as much as a mule, for two to three Maria Theresa thalers for a distance of 400 kilometres. Many merchants also employed their servants to carry loads, but slaves were usually better treated, for the master would reckon that they were worth 10 to 15 thalers per head, and if one died he would be the loser by that amount.

Caravans usually set forth at sun-rise, or shortly afterwards, and were so well organised that a party of two or three hundred mules could often be away, Plowden reports, in "less than half-an hour." If water and pasture were available the caravan-leaders would usually call a halt for the day at about noon. To avoid disputes with the population of the area to be traversed, camping-sites were often selected in uninhabited spots. In the absence of organised caravanserais the traders were obliged to bring everything they needed, including provisions and cooking equipment. On arriving at the halting ground they were often weary, but their servants had still not only to grind corn and make bread, but also to construct sleeping quarters for their master.

In establishing a camp the merchants' servants would begin by placing such stones as they could find in parallel rows, crossing each other at right-angles to form rectangles about five feet square. On these stones the packs would be piled close together to a height of about six feet, each owner's goods being carefully kept together. The loads thus arranged constituted a series of small compartments. These were then covered with sticks upon which ox-hides were stretched to form rooms for the protection and comfort of the caravaneers and their livestock. The skins kept out the rain, while the stones protected the merchandise both from damp and white ants and the packs gave privacy to the inmates. Thorn fences were sometimes also erected around the camp as a whole. While such work was in progress the children in the caravan would lead the mules to pasture where they would remain untethered until dusk when they were taken back to the camp and tied to a row of stakes facing the cells. Guards, who might be numerous in times of anticipated difficulty, then lit fires at each end of camp, and from time to time called out to each other, to cheer themselves and keep themselves awake, as well as to convince their masters that they were not asleep. If the presence of thieves was suspected the guards also from time to time hurled slingfuls of stones into the dark.

A traders' camp at night. Note tent, mule's harness and shield on the ground, standing guard with sword, spear and shield, and merchants in animated fire-side conversation. From T. Lefebvre and others, *Voyage en Abyssinie* (Paris, 1845-8).

Most caravans in this way normally fended entirely for themselves. There were, however, a few villages, notably two near Gondär, whose inhabitants, anxious to attract trade, prepared camping grounds for travelling merchants, and in return claimed the right, according to Rüppell, to sell the traders victuals and fodder.[2]

Markets, and Other Places of Sale

Most markets were held once a week on a specific day which varied from one village to another, thereby enabling travelling merchants visiting a succession of fairs daily to trade throughout any area for most of the time. Important centres, among them Gondär, Adwa, and Antalo, on the other hand, though having one or more main market-days also held a small additional market throughout the week.

Some of the most common articles for sale at country markets were, according to Salt, various types of grain, onions, red pepper and a few other spices, locally grown cotton, skins, cattle, donkeys, mules and horses and wrought and unwrought iron. The quantity of goods exposed for sale was usually, however, very modest. At one market attended by 700 people, Rüppell saw only a few cattle, sheep, goats and donkeys, two or three large earthenware jars and big dishes, a small quantity of iron, a little cane for weaving baskets, and some goats' hairs for making women's clothing, but most of these items were still unsold at the end of the day. Meat was not generally on sale. It could be purchased, according to Pearce, only at Gondär, Antalo, and on feast days, at Adwa. Elsewhere, and at other times, it was the custom for "the lower class of people to join together and buy a cow, which is killed and divided among them." Sale of meat was further limited by the fact that on feast days persons in the service of a chief would usually have livestock slaughtered for them.

Shops were non-existent, even in the principal commercial centres, though some commerce was carried out in merchant's dwellings. At Gondär "the interior and most secluded recess" of such houses served, according to Stern, somewhat like shops, though only the most "privileged purchaser" would be allowed in and then only as a "particular favour."[3]

Commercial Centres

A large part of the country's trade passed through, or was handled by, such major commercial centres as Gondär, Adwa, and Aleyu Amba, as well as many other markets great and small.

---

[2] Combes and Tamisier (1838) IV, 118-20; Ferret and Galinier (1847) II, 407-11; GB House of Commons (1868) 113; Rüppell (1838-40) II, 290.

[3] Pearce (1831) II, 16-7; Combes and Tamisier (1838) IV, 107; Valentia (1809) III, 12, 48, 54; Rüppell (1838-40) I, 330; Stern (1862) 238.

Gondär

The most important trading centre in the early part of this period was Gondär, still the imperial capital, which had the largest urban population in the empire, and exerted a significant commercial impact on the surrounding countryside. Trade in the 1830's was the capital's main preoccupation, Rüppell claims, and the merchants of the city were said by Stern to be, "next to the clergy and aristocracy," the "most wealthy and influential body in the land."

The Muslims, who included the city's principal merchants, as in the past occupied their own special quarter, in the valley near the Angeräb and Qäha rivers. This area was referred to as the Eslambét or Eslamgé, i.e. the "house" or "country" of Muslims. Early in the century Coffin stated that "many Christians" were "intermixed" with the Muslims, but later observers, such as Ferret and Galinier and Antoine d'Abbadie, assert that the area was inhabited exclusively by the latter. One of them, as in Bruce's day, held the position of *Nägadras*, or chief of trade. The Eslambét consisted, according to Rüppell, of some 300 houses out of the total of 1,000, and thus constituted almost a third of the total population, which was generally put at between 10,000 and 18,000. The merchants of Gondär, on account of their wealth and extensive trading connections, were rated by Arnauld d'Abbadie as the "most considerable" in the country. Many of them sent caravans southward to Gudru, Käfa and Enarya where they purchased slaves, coffee, civet and gold.

Two large markets were held at Gondär every week, on Mondays and Saturdays, on which days large numbers of merchants and purchasers or would-be purchasers flocked into the city from far and near. Many caravans came each year with textiles and other imported goods from Massawa and Sudan, as well as ivory, civet and slaves from the rich lands south of the Blue Nile. Supplies of all kinds were at the same time brought to the city from other lands. Herds of cattle and jars of honey came from Agäwmeder, iron from Wälqayt, timber from Gorgora by Lake Tana, wine from Qoräṭa, Yefag and Därita, salt from the 'Afär depression, fire-arms from Adwa, and civet, gold, ivory, ox horns and hippopotamus shields from various areas in the south or west. The quantity of supplies arriving was, however, very variable, and goods were sometimes scarce on account of civil war. Traders often found it inadvisable, Rüppell states, to invest in large stocks, for which reason articles often disappeared from the market overnight, so that prices sometimes fluctuated by as much as 100% or more from one week to the next. There were also considerable price variations due to changes in the value of the *amolé*, or salt bar, which served as "primitive money," for during the rains the swollen rivers rendered it virtually unobtainable at the very time when herdsmen around Lake Tana brought butter and other commodities to exchange for it. "Things have no fixed price at Gondär," Gobat complained, "everything is dear or cheap, according as the market of today is furnished."

The city's most important trade route, which led eastwards to Massawa by way of Adwa, was used by merchants throughout most of the year, but the largest number travelled between October and January, that is to say after the rainy season when the water in the Täkkäzé river had fallen, or again in June, prior to the outbreak of the rains. Before setting forth, each caravan elected as its chief the richest or most capable leader. The journey to the port, according to Rüppell, took about five months. In settled times the traders often divided up into small parties to avoid excessive concentration in one area, but in periods of insecurity they stuck together to defend themselves. Parties of over a thousand men were far from unusual. At the halting place of Däbareq for example Gobat in the 1830's saw no less than 1,200 to 1,500 people going towards the coast. On reaching Adwa the merchants from Gondär were usually joined by others from Amhara, Tegré and Šäwa bringing wax, coffee, ivory, gold, buffalo horns, hides, butter and mules bound for Massawa. Imports on this route, as noticed by Stern, included white, blue and red calicoes, coarse muslins, chintz, cotton velvets, cutlery, glass beads and Indian spices.

The other main trade route from Gondär ran westwards by way of Celga, Wähni, and Mätämma to Sudan, and thence to Egypt and North Africa. Traders left the Ethiopian capital in the dry season between October and May, for the route was virtually impassable at other times. A typical caravan, as described by Flad, consisted of 300 camels and perhaps 100 to 200 donkeys. Exports to Sudan included ivory and slaves, the latter estimated by Combes and Tamisier, possibly with exaggeration, at no less than 10,000 a year, as well as gold, civet, honey, wax, cattle, horses, butter, and coffee, while imports comprised Sudanese cotton and horses, besides a vast array of articles from more distant lands: cloth, coloured stuffs, carpets, beads, fire-arms, Maria Theresa thalers, copper, lead and other metals, sword-blades, gunpowder, sulphur, drinking-glasses, bottles, coffee-cups, stibium, antimony, leather, shoes and sandals, razors, nails, mirrors, beads, tin-ware, needles, pepper, cloves, dates, tamarinds, various types of incense and scent, and spikenard used in the preparation of medicine.

The southern trade route from Gondär, which served in a sense as an extension of the two above routes, was used by merchants who travelled each year in a large caravan which made for Yefäg where it was joined by merchants from Därita, while those bound for Šäwa hived off to the south. The main group, increasing in numbers through the addition of smaller traders who joined them on the way, then journeyed southwards to Gojjam where they halted to rest at Basso. They then forded across the Blue Nile, before dividing into separate parties to visit Bizämo, Gudru, Guma, Enarya, Käfa and Jänjero, where they exchanged salt, mules, and various imported goods, among them calicoes, muslins, chintz and velvets, pepper, glass-beads and trinkets, mirrors and knives, for such local products as gold, civet, ivory, ox and rhinoceros horns, skins, hippopotamus shields and slaves. The whole journey from Gondär to Enarya could take as much as ten months, after which the traders spent some three months doing business in the area, before returning to the capital.

Beside the three above main routes from Gondär, there were a number of subsidiary importance, among them one which led westwards to the country of the Šanqella, a source of gold, slaves and ivory, and another which ran south-eastwards to Šäwa, Harär and the Somali coast.[4]

---

[4] Stern (1862) 237-8; Rüppell (1838-40)I, 269, II, 80-2, 179-80; Arnauld d' Abbadie (1868) 161-2, 507-8; Antoine d' Abbadie (1898) 319; Ferret and Galinier (1847) II, 273-8, 416-24; Pearce (1831) I, 235; Plowden (1868) 127, 130; GB House of Commons (1868) 6, 112; Combes and Tamisier (1838) III, 343, IV, 90, 95-7, 104-5; Leiris (1934) 405; Gobat (1850) 149, 247; Lefebvre (1845-8) II, Part 26; Flad (1922) 65-6, 109; Pearce (1831) I, 78; Heuglin (1868), 227-8, 301 393, 408; Krapf (1867) 468-9; Rassam (1869) I, 167-8; Blanc (1868) 112-3; Massaia (1885-95) II, 97, 103; Arnauld d' Abbadie (1868) 241; Pankhurst (1968a) 355.

Smaller Markets in the Gondär Area

South of Gondär there were several markets of some importance. Perhaps the largest was at the town of Därita, site of a well frequented Monday fair. Its merchants are said by Combes and Tamisier to have rivalled those of the capital in sending caravans to Sennar and Massawa, and even further afield to Cairo and Arabia, as well as southwards, in quest of slaves, to Gudru, Käfa, Gomma and Enarya. One such trader, 'Ali Muz, did business in many of the southern provinces, and acted as the trade agent of Abba Bägibo, King of Enarya, for whom he travelled to Massawa to purchase imported goods. Other men of Därita whose identity has been preserved include Muhammäd Ibrahim who is known to have visited Limmu at least eight times, a certain Isma'él who was well acquainted with Enarya, and a man who had been to Bonga in Käfa.

Also of commercial significance was Qoräta, a place of asylum with a large market whither cotton, both raw and worked, from Qwara and the borders of Sennar, was carried by mule and shipped across Lake Tana. The town was described by Antoine d'Abbadie, probably with some exaggeration, as "the greatest city of East Africa, proud of its sanctuary and of its twelve thousand inhabitants." Lesser commercial centres in the area included those of Bahr Dar, site of a sizeable market on the southern side of Lake Tana, and Yefäg, where a fair was held in front of the Sellasé, or Holy Trinity church; as well as Mota, a notable place of asylum, and Bičäna, two major markets for cereals, cloth, cattle and horses, and Basso which was also visited by merchants from Sennar in search of slaves and civet.[5]

Adwa

The principal market town of the north was Adwa which Salt early in the century described as "the chief mart for commerce" on the eastern side of the Täkkäzé" river. "All the intercourse between the interior and the coast" was carried on by the merchants of Adwa, for which reason the Muslims of the city had "a greater degree of importance" than in any other part of the empire. Adwa, like Gondär, had a sizeable Muslim quarter, largely inhabited by merchants who were estimated by Arnauld d'Abbadie at "a little more than a third" of the town's total population which was generally held to number between three and five thousand.

The market at Adwa, which was held every Saturday, was attended, according to Ferret and Galinier, by 5,000 or 6,000 persons. Commerce was based partly on the produce of the area, and partly on goods carried up and down the trade route between Gondär and Massawa. Some caravans on this stretch of the journey were fairly large. Parkyns knew nineteen merchants of the city who travelled to the coast with a total of 800 mules, and reckoned that at least 1,200 animals were engaged in this trade, while Barroni, an Italian in British consular service, later reported the arrival at Massawa of some 500 merchants. On completing their business at the port the Christian traders in most instances returned home, but the Muslims, combining religion with trade, in many cases proceeded on pilgrimage to Mecca, after which they

---

[5] Combes and Tamisier (1838) II, 44-6, III, 228, 267, 335, IV, 64; Arnauld d' Abbadie (1980) 165, 270, (1983) 11-2, 141 Antoine d' Abbadie (1898) 31, 58, 104, 203; Rüppell (1838-40) II, 225; Blondeel (1838-42) Annexes 37 and 43; Bell (1842) 10; Lefebvre (1845-8) III, 112.

The port of Massawa, with two of the trading vessels upon which its early 19th century commerce depended. From T. Lefebvre and others, *Voyage en Abyssinie* (Paris, 1845-8).

visited one or more commercial centre of Arabia, and brought back all sorts of cloth and manufactured goods, including fire-arms, glassware and spices.

Caravans also reached Adwa from lands to the south, including Amhara, Wällo and Šäwa. "Large droves" of cattle from Wälqayt arrived, Salt reports, and were exchanged "very advantageously" for cotton cloth, a "considerable portion" of which came from the lowlands bordering on the Täkkäzé.[6]

Massawa

Massawa, the gateway to the sea of all northern Ethiopia, was the terminal, as in the past, of one of the principal trade routes from the interior. The port, an island, was dependent on the mainland for all sorts of supplies, including milk, cattle and goats, which, according to a British naval officer, Captain Weatherhead, were shipped across the intervening narrow stretch of sea in a small boat which travelled backwards and forwards all day. Drinking water was also supplied to the island in large quantities, at a price of one Maria Theresa thaler per twenty skin sacks, or a total of about 100 gallons. Numerous smaller vessels, according to the French Scientific Mission, were also engaged in the transportation to the island of water, as well as milk and other supplies, including sheep and chickens. Export articles from the interior consisted of slaves, gold, ivory, civet, butter, cereals, wax, and hides and skins, as well as small quantities of coffee, honey and gum, while imports were made up mainly of textiles, beads and trinkets, metals, tobacco, antimony, glass and chinaware, needles, scissors, knives and razors, swords and fire-arms, carpets, mirrors, pepper and sugar.

The market at Massawa was held every morning and evening, with a mid-day interruption, because of the island's intense heat, from noon to about 4 p.m. Trade, in the first part of the century, was dominated by Banyan, or Indian, merchants, who, according to Salt, were "very comfortable," and carried on a "considerable trade." The most important among them was a certain Currum Chand who often purchased an entire shipload of goods which traders would then receive from him on credit, take and sell in the interior, and pay for three months later in gold or other local produce. This practice, which was also followed by an Arab called Haji Häsän, had developed because none of the other Massawa merchants had sufficient capital to invest on any large scale.

Indian commercial paramountcy continued for several decades. In 1862 British consul Walker thus reported that there were 15 to 20 Banyans who seemed to "monopolise the whole of the trade." The "only men" with any money, they owned two large vessels which sailed to Bombay twice a year, and were responsible for the purchase of all the gold and ivory brought down from the interior. India was likewise responsible for a large proportion of Massawa's imports. Purchases from the sub-

---

[6] Salt (1814) 419, 424-6; Arnauld d'Abbadie (1868) 34; Parkyns (1853) I, 411-7; Great Britain, I.O., Political and Secret Letters from Aden , Baroni 11 September 1856; Rüppell (1838-40), I, 269, 289-91; Combes and Tamisier (1838) I, 204-5, IV, 93; Lefebvre (1845-8) II, Part II, 27, GB House of Commons (1868) 229-30; Ferret and Galinier (1847) I, 451-2; Pankhurst (1982) 225-6.

continent in 1852 were valued, according to Plowden, at 133,590 Maria Theres⁹ thalers, as against only 73,065 from Arabia and Egypt.[7]

Aleyu Amba

Aleyu Amba, the market for the twin Šäwan capitals of Ankobär and Angoläla, was the most important commercial centre of central Ethiopia, and the rendez-vous, Combes and Tamisier note, of numerous merchants, "almost entirely Muslim." Many came from Enarya and Käfa, while others travelled to or from the coast, making their way by caravan across the Awaš valley to Harär and the Somali country, after which they proceeded to the major port of Zäylä', or by way of Awsa, to the coast at Tajura. Articles on sale included gold, ivory, coffee, wax, hides and skins, cattle and cereals, which were sent down to the coast in return for imported goods, among them cottons and silks from India, brass wire, beads and glass trinkets, and old copper and zinc articles for the local manufacture of jewellery. Commerce was on a fairly large scale, Rochet d'Héricourt estimating that 1,500 to 1,700 camel loads of coffee were sold annually. Local trade was largely based on barter, though cattle were normally purchased for *amolé*, or, in some instances, Maria Theresa thalers.

The market of Aleyu Amba was held every Friday, enabling merchants also to participate in a much smaller fair held at Ankobär on the following day. This latter market, according to Johnston, was "almost exclusively" frequented by Christians who dealt in sheep, grain, butter and wood.

The settlement of Aleyu Amba consisted of around 250 to 300 houses whose inhabitants, according to Rochet d'Héricourt, were "very mixed," for they were made up of Amharas, Oromos, Ifatians, Somalis and Haräris, as well as people from Adäl, Argobba and Awsa. "More than three-fourths" of the population according to Johnston, were Muslims, and one quarter, Harris believed, came from either Harär or 'Afär. They consisted "chiefly", Barker says, of Haräri merchants who resided at Aleyu Amba until they had disposed of their merchandise, and were ready to return home with the slaves they had purchased. There were also "numerous retired slave merchants" who had earlier travelled to Guragé, Enarya, Jänjero and Limmu. The town was, however, not entirely Muslim for there were also "numbers of Christian Abyssinians," as well as several Persians. Merchants included Muslim businessmen, who invested most of their capital in slaves, Christian traders, who brought large supplies of cloth, cattle and corn, and, serving as the only money-changers, conducted their business beside high walls of *amolé*, and Muslim market-women. These latter, who constituted a large proportion of the throng, handled, however, only small stocks, sufficient merely for the probable sales of the day. They might thus sit all day offering, Rochet recalls, a thimble full of *kohl*, or antimony for darkening the eyes, a few lumps of gum and myrrh, a handful of frankincense, the blue and red threads of imported unwoven cloth used in decorating the borders of *šämmas*, or togas, and perhaps three or four lemons and as many needles.

A number of craftsmen would also be seen on market day: saddle-makers from Ankobär and iron-workers from the neighbouring artisans' monasteries who sold

---

[7] Salt (1814) lxix; Rüppell (1838-40) I, 196-7; Lefebvre (1845-8) I, 39-40; GB House of Commons (1868) 73-4, 230; Valentia (1809) III, 267-8; Pankhurst (1964b) 102-18.

spears, swords, hoes and ploughshares, while their womenfolk, who were potters, went around with their children hawking earthenware pots and dishes.[8]

Because of its commercial importance, and location on the cross-road of trade between the highlands and lowlands, Aleyu Amba was visited by merchants of widely different ethnic background. A colourful account is provided by the often xenophobic Harris who writes:

"the Dankali merchant exhibits his gay assortment of beads, metals, coloured thread and glassware. The wild Galla squats beside the produce of his flocks and the Moslem trader from the interior displays ostrich feathers, or some other article of curiosity from a distant tribe. The surly Adaiel brushes past in insolent indifference to examine the female slaves in the wicker hut of the rover from the south ... Squatted beside his foreign wares and glittering beads, we see the wily huckster from Harar, with the turban and blue-checked kilt ... The Christian women flit through the busy fair with eggs, poultry, and the produce of the farm ... Cantering over the tiny plain the wild Galla enters the scene of confusion, a jar of honey, or a basket of butter lashed to the crupper of his high-peaked saddle ... Caravans arrive every month during the fair season from Aussa and Tajura ... Bales of cotton cloth, and bags from Kaffa and Enarya in every direction."[9]

Markets such as these were important, not only from the purely commercial point of view, but also in that they were places where people - some of them from different cultures - met, conversed, exchanged ideas, and joked together.

Däbrä Berhan, Bollo Wärqé and 'Abd-al-Räsul

The great market of Aleyu Amba was complemented by a number of other Šäwan markets, among them Däbrä Berhan, Bollo Wärqé, 'Abd-al-Räsul and Rogé. Däbrä Berhan, which was also one of the capitals of Šäwa, did extensive trade in mules and horses, while Bollo Wärqé dealt in grain, donkeys and cattle. 'Abd-al-Räsul and Rogé by contrast were renowned slave markets which, like the slave trade in general, were entirely in Muslim hands. 'Abd-al-Räsul was frequented, according to Barker, by merchants from Tegré and the north, and handled an export of at least 3,000 slaves a year. Purchases of slaves, unlike that of other goods, were made almost entirely in Maria Theresa thalers.[10]

---

[8] Combes and Tamisièr (1838) III, 21; Johnston (1844) II, 50, 95, 101-2, 238-44, 249, 320; Harris (1848) I, 345, 365, 381-8, 395; Rochet d' Héricourt (1841) 299-301, (1846) 262; Barker (1906) 286-7, 296; Isenberg and Krapf (1843) 94-5. On the trade of Zäyla' and other Gulf of Aden ports, which largely paralleled that of Massawa, see Pankhurst (1968a) 418-24.

[9] Harris (1848) 381-2.

[10] Isenberg and Krapf (1843) 94-5, 111-3, 275; Beke (1845) 27; Barker (1906) 287, 289; Harris (1844) I, 388-9, III, 303; Krapf (1867) 50-1; Cecchi (1885-7) II, 490; Rochet d' Héricourt (1841) 300, (1846) 261.

Taxes, Market Dues and Internal Customs Posts

Merchants were subject to various taxes which were levied either by the provincial rulers of the lands in which they traded, or else by a special official called a *nägadras* to whom the chief farmed out the right to collect the taxes in return for a fixed yearly sum. The object of the latter was then, as Plowden says, to "screw" as much as he could from the merchants. The division of the revenue from trade between the chief and the *nägadras* was by no means uniform. At Adwa for example the governor besides the fixed rent from the *nägadras* received, according to Pearce, two-thirds of the duty on imported goods, slaves, ivory and civet, while the customs official kept all the tax on cotton. At Anṭalo on the other hand the governor took one-third of the tax on slaves, horses, mules, and ivory, and the entire tax on salt.

Persons with the rank of *nägadras* held office at the six most important commercial markets of the north, namely Adwa, Däbareq, Gondär, Säqoṭa, Däriṭa and Ajubay, as well as at Aleyu Amba in Šäwa. All but one were Muslims, the exception being the customs-man at Däbareq, the least important of the seven, who was a Christian. The names of two of these officials are preserved: Zeynu at Adwa who paid a "large" annual rent to Däjazmač Webé, and was described by Combes and Tamisier as a "crafty Muslim"; and a certain Abu Beker at Aleyu Amba, who was a Muslim from Argobba.

Merchants travelling across the country were obliged to pay taxes at a considerable number of customs posts, usually referred to as *kella*. There were no less than eleven tax stations, according to Rüppell, on the route from Gondär to Massawa, while traders making their way from Enarya to the coast encountered anything between eighteen and twenty-eight. "Custom-houses, or rather passes, have been established," Plowden reports, "on every spot where Nature ... has confined the road to some narrow defile, not to be avoided without an immense detour, if at all, and near some commanding elevation where a good look-out can be stationed at a brook fordable at one spot." Dues, which varied greatly from one *kella* to another, were mainly paid in kind. At one customs post in Tegré every porter-load was said, by Salt, to have paid two handfuls of pepper, and every donkey-load two pieces of blue cloth, while at another the tax on the latter was five or six *berellé*, or glass bottles, and some Surat cloth or other articles; at a third there was a tax of half a dollar or a piece of cloth and a handful of pepper on every donkey-load, and of a quarter of a dollar on every slave or horn-full of civet. Taxes, according to Ferret and Galinier, were, however, seldom paid in cash, but more often in such articles as pepper, red cloth, blue ribbon, silk or tobacco.

The existence of such customs posts, though of crucial importance for provincial rulers, was for the merchants a constant source of inconvenience and irritation. There were frequent quarrels, the French Scientific Mission reports, between traders and the tax-collectors, as a result of real or alleged smuggling of gold or civet, and disputes sometimes lasted several months, particularly when the officials were not too pressed for money or the merchants in too much of a hurry. "Very animated quarrels" were common, Ferret and Galinier confirm, and were in some instances brought to an end only through the intervention of the monarch, who was, however, in most cases too far away to give prompt judgment.

The difficulties which might confront a merchant travelling inland from Massawa across Tegré, to the great market of Basso in southern Gojjam, are graphically described by Plowden. He explains that the trader had first to pay a tax to the Ottoman governor of the port, after which he had to engage a guide, from among the Saho people living in the mountains inland, who, depending on the traveller's apparent wealth, might charge anything between half and ten Maria Theresa dollars.[11] Then:

> "arriving ... in Oubea's dominions he will be stopped four or five times before he reaches Adowah [Adwa], and on each occasion must arrange with those in charge of the tolls as best he can as regards payment, the amount being arbitrary, and the system in fact one of legalised plunder.
> "On arrival at Adowah he pays certain more regulated duties to the Negadeh Ras of the town, a douceur, moreover, being expected as the price of a friendly settlement of dues.
> "After meeting the exactions of several minor posts he will next have to pay at the town of Doobaruk, in the Province of Waggara, duties on the same scale with those of Adowah, generally about one dollar per mule-load of merchandize, and being then clear of the territories of Dejazmatch Oobeay, enters those of Ras Ali whose tolls commence at Gondar. Here the duties are nominally somewhat settled, though long disputes almost inevitably occur, and after three or more detentions and payments on a smaller scale in Begemder, he passes the Nile, and arrives in the domains of the chiefs of Gojam or Damot. These may be in a state of entire rebellion or of sulky submission to the Ras: as in the latter case they pay him a fixed tribute, he does not interfere with their toll-levying, and the merchant must disburse at some eight or ten more stages of his journey ere he can reach Basso. It is needless to dwell on the danger to the merchant in the case of revolted Chiefs, who plunder indiscriminately, and from whom, even if captured, the recovery of any property is hopeless."[12]

In addition to such taxes there were also market dues which were exacted on goods brought for sale. At Gondär for example every slave, horse or mule taken to market had to pay, according to Pearce, two drams of gold, or the equivalent of two dollars, every large tusk of ivory one *wäqét*, or ounce, and every porter-load six drams. A generation later Rüppell found that mule and donkey-loads paid ten Maria Theresa dollars, and porter-loads half as much. At Adwa, on the other hand, Pearce says that every mule or donkey-load of imports was subject to a tax of half an ounce of gold, or goods to that amount, and porter-loads or tusks two and half drams, while slaves or matchlocks paid half an ounce. Each porter-load of cotton was charged two pieces of cotton cloth, each equal to two dollars, as well as a pound of cloth. Gold was often subject to special taxation. Before being sold it had to be weighed by a special official who for every ounce collected two bars of salt at Gondär and Säqota, four at Antalo, or a quarter of a piece of cloth at Adwa.

---

[11] Pearce (1831) II, 11-3; GB House of Commons (1868) 68, 112; Ferret and Galinier (1847) II, 411-2; Blondell (1838-42) 42-4; Valentia (1809) III, 213-4; Rüppell (1838-40) II, 183-4; Heuglin (1868) 253; Lefebvre (1845-8) II, Part II, 27.

[12] GB House of Commons (1868) 68.

Persons exposing goods for sale were also often taxed, as at Aleyu Amba, where they had to make a payment either in kind or in salt, with the result that "during the day," Johnston recalls, "large heaps" of *amolés* and market produce accumulated "around the feet of the Governor" and appeared to be his "perquisites of office." Persons attending the market regularly, on the other hand, made "a fixed payment of one to three bars of salt a week," but the people of the town were "exempted from any imposition of toll."

Market taxes were sometimes allotted to specific courtiers or other personalities. At Antalo, for example, Pearce reports: "The duty on salt ... is distributed among the favourites of the household; the governor's or Ras's wives have a certain quantity, and others of his favourites and relatives a proportionate allowance ... The salt is considered a gift to one of the favourites about the Ras's person."[13] The Englishman spoke from personal knowledge, for he explains:

"I had myself, from the latter end of the year 1805 till 1808, six pieces of salt allowed to me every Wednesday, which was market-day... afterwards my allowance was raised to ten, till 1810, from which time... it was augmented to twenty; but shortly afterwards ... the Ras thought properly to order a yearly allowance ... of one thousand pieces of salt, instead of our receiving it weekly at the toll."[14]

Camels after a march. From H. Salt, *A Voyage to Abyssinia* (London, 1814).

---

[13] Pearce (1831) II, 12-45; Johnston (1844) II, 230.

[14] Pearce (1831) I, 12-5.

VIII

HANDICRAFT WORKERS

Blacksmiths and the Iron Trade

Blacksmiths were responsible throughout the nineteenth century for the manufacture in many parts of the country of a wide variety of articles of considerable economic and military importance. These included plough-shares and the iron parts of pick-axes, sickles and other agricultural implements, as well as knives and razors, spear-heads, daggers, swords, bullets and spare parts for rifles, besides tent-pegs, hammers, pincers, drills, nails, hatchets, saws and files, steels for striking fire, pans on which to cook bread, bits and stirrups for horses and mules, chains and rings, tweezers, scissors and needles.

Smelting was carried out over a charcoal fire with the aid of one or more pairs of home-made bellows fashioned from sheep or goat skins. Pearce, describing an operation in which several blacksmiths were involved, states that the latter would throw the ore into a large charcoal fire which they then blew with several bellows, each man working two such instruments, one in each hand. When the metal was completely hot it was "taken out of the fire with large awkward pincers, or thongs, and held by one man upon a large flat stone, while two or three others, with large, round or rather oval stones, strike it in turn, with all their might with both hands." This action was repeated until the metal was "free from all earthy matters, and fit to use."

The ore having thus been produced, a blacksmith wishing for example to make a sword, would obtain a piece of iron of convenient size, whereupon, Combes and Tamisier explain, he would heat and beat it until he had given it the requisite shape. The blade was then worked over with a file, after which it was again put in the fire and tempered, by thrusting it into water, and then finally sharpened on a stone. Spearheads and swords were produced in more or less the same manner, while needles were made by beating small pieces of metal into thin strips, which were then filed sharp at the ends, and pierced with a sharp-pointed piece of metal to produce the eye.

Though most blacksmiths made exclusive use of simple, locally made tools, a few had access to foreign files, which, as Combes and Tamisier noted in the 1830's, were then being imported via Massawa. A decade or so later the French Scientific Mission reported that though ordinary stones often served as an anvil, blacksmiths also sometimes made use of specially-made tools, such as hammers, pincers, chisels, files and shears. Such implements, according to a subsequent report by Girard, were imported from Europe.[1]

---

[1] Pearce (1831) II, 202-3; Combes and Tamisier (1838) IV, 67-72; Rüppell (1838-40) II, 225; Rochet d' Héricourt (1841) 297; Lefebvre (1845-8) III, 245-6; Girard (1873) 192.

Blacksmiths, Fälaša, and Belief in *Buda*

Many blacksmiths in the nineteenth century, as in the past, were Fälaša, as noted by both Dufton and Stern. The former recalls that Fälaša craftsmen who were often accused of being *budas*, or sorcerers.

The old idea that blacksmiths possessed supernatural powers found expression in the widespread conviction that they could turn themselves into hyenas at night. Salt, the first foreign traveller to notice this belief, reported in 1810 that "a very strange" superstition, "inconceivably strong throughout the country," held that "all workers in iron" were regarded as *buda*, with the power of transforming themselves into hyenas, "capable of preying upon human flesh." The prevalence of this belief was confirmed by Pearce who noted that blacksmiths were thought, "even by their nearest neighbours," to be capable of turning themselves into hyenas or other beasts, and that their "evil eye" was held responsible for "all convulsions and hysteric disorders," which were far from uncommon. The "greater part" of those believed possessed by blacksmiths' evil spirits, according to Parkyns, were women who had despised a *buda's* proffered love. The result of these beliefs was that the blacksmiths of Ethiopia, like the alchemists of medieval Europe, were "the terror of the countryside" as Combes and Tamisier aver. "Few people," according to Parkyns, would therefore "venture to molest or offend" any worker in iron. Blacksmiths, though feared, and, according to Combes and Tamisier, relatively well paid, suffered greatly. They were "not allowed the privilege of being in common society," Pearce states, and were even denied Christian burial, while Parkyns asserts that their trade, which was hereditary, was "considered as more or less disgraceful."[2]

Blacksmiths lived moreover in constant danger of persecution. The story is told of an iron-worker of Enčätkab in Sämén who had gained his living by making spear-heads and repairing rifles, but, having been accused of having relations with the Devil, was obliged to flee to Gondär. There too he was charged with sorcery, and forced to make his way to Tegré, Bägémder, Amhara and Gojjam, before eventually returning to Bägémder, where he sought refuge in a cave and lived as a beggar. Interviewed by Combes and Tamisier, he is quoted as exclaiming:

"Oh, if instead of being a blacksmith I had worked the land or adopted the occupation of a soldier, I would not have had to exile myself. I would still be in my native country, in the midst of a family which loved me; and here I live alone in a cave which wild animals will perhaps one day dispute with me. Oh! why was I born a blacksmith? My skill in that art made my entire life miserable."[3]

Other cases of victimisation were reported by Parkyns who states that it was not unusual for friends and relatives of a sick person "to procure charms with which to force the spirit by which he was supposedly possessed to declare his name and residence." They would then go in a body and apprehend a blacksmith who would be ordered to "quit his victim" - and to add force to this injunction the party would point

---

[2] Dufton (1867) 165; Stern (1862) 193; Salt (1814) 426-7; Pearce (1831) II, 286, 339-42; Parkyns (1853) II, 144-5, 160-2; Combes and Tamisier (1838) IV, 72, 76-7; Lefebvre (1845-8) III, 245.

[3] Combes and Tamisier (1838) IV, 73-6.

spears at his breast and threaten him with death. Such threats were by no means empty. A blacksmith accused by a soldier of being responsible for his illness was seized by order of Däjazmač Webé, and, after some investigation, "condemned, with part of his family, to be put to death." Prejudices against blacksmiths, though general, varied in intensity from region to region. They were thus more intense in Tegré and Amhara, Combes and Tamisier assert, than in Šäwa. Even in the latter province, however, it was not unusual for blacksmiths to live in isolated communities. There were two villages of blacksmiths, Morat and Zalla, in the vicinity of Fečče, where the inhabitants, as Soleillet later learnt, lived entirely apart from the population at large.

The prejudice against blacksmiths was, it is interesting to note, shared by both Christians and Fälašas, but did not, however, extend to armourers, who, the French Scientific Mission records, were never accused of sorcery. The charge was moreover confined to Ethiopian blacksmiths, and, Combes and Tamisier claim, was never directed against European ones.[4]

Weavers

Weavers, who likewise constituted a class apart, also tended to belong to a minority group, for the most part either Fälaša or Muslim. Fälaša involvement in weaving was reported by Flad who asserts that this trade in the north-west was "entirely confined" to members of the community except at Gondär where it was mainly carried out by Muslims. Fälaša weavers were predominant in Bägémder, where the missionary Stern, describing the village of "Atshergee," recalls that the Fälašas's looms, which were the clumsiest imaginable, stood under sheds at the entrance of the village, and formed both the means of their subsistence, and "a slight barricade against the inroads of wild beasts."

The majority of weavers in most of the north were, however, Muslims who were particularly important at Gondär, as well as throughout Tegré. Testimony to this is provided by several observers. Rüppell for example noted that weaving was "entirely" done by Muslims, and Combes and Tamisier that the latter enjoyed "almost the monopoly" in the field, while Dufton later remarked that "all the manufacturers of cotton cloths" were followers of the Prophet.

Most weavers made use, as Parkyns says, of "a very rough kind of handloom, placed over a hole in the ground", but a few seem to have had equipment obtained from Arabia. The more sophisticated frames, Combes and Tamisier assert, were probably imported by pilgrims of Därita or Aleyu Amba returning from Mecca.[5]

---

[4] Parkyns (1853) II, 158, 160; Combes and Tamisier (1838) IV, 77; Lefebvre (1845-8) III, 246; Soleillet (1886) 288.

[5] Flad (1869) 24-5; Stern (1862) 193, 267-8; Parkyns (1853) II, 41; Rüppell (1838-40) I, 367; Combes and Tamisier (1838) IV, 66; Dufton (1867) 92; Lefebvre (1845-8) III, 244-5

The Traditional Loom

The typical Ethiopian loom was simple, but efficient. It was made by striking two stakes perhaps as high as a man into the ground a metre or so apart, and keeping them firm by the attachment of a third piece of wood or pole tied horizontally to the top of them. Towards each end of the latter pole a string made of wool was lowered to subtend a thin piece of wood perhaps a span long which served as a kind of balance from each end of which two other strings held the reeds or comb-like devices. These latter were made of a couple of long, thin, horizontal pieces of wood or cane joined together by innumerable strings between which the weft passed. From each reed, a string or thong led down to a kind of stirrup made of a single flat piece of wood upon which the weaver's foot was placed, a peddling motion of his feet causing the two reeds to rise and fall alternately. Also subtended from the horizontal pole was a somewhat stronger reed made of two long horizontal beams joined at frequent intervals by vertical bars of thin twig-like pieces of wood or cane. This latter reed was used to strike, on beat, the weft threads. Perhaps a metre behind this equipment a couple of smaller vertical stakes were erected, also about a metre and a half apart, upon which would be fixed a second horizontal pole. This latter acted as a roller on which the woven thread was gradually wound as the work proceeded. To prevent it from unwinding, the upright pole nearest the weaver's right hand was shaped to fit into one of a series of holes cut in the corresponding end of the roller. As more and more cloth was woven, the weaver would wind up the roller, and secure its immobility by means of the locking device.

A weaver with traditional Ethiopian loom, placed in his garden in one of the central or southern regions. From G. Massaia, *I miei trentacinque anni di missione in alta Etiopia* (Rome and Milan, 1885-95).

Three other stakes were also stuck in the ground to hold the warp. The largest and strongest was placed several metres in front of the loom, a second, considerably smaller, stake some metres to its right, and the third, usually smaller again, immediately beside the loom on the weaver's right. The warp thread originated near the smallest stake to which it was tied and every now and then released by the weaver.

The thread, which was so placed as to form something of a circle, then passed round the two remaining stakes before entering the loom on the side opposite the weaver. By this simple expedient the warp was kept tight and prevented from sagging.

The shuttle, which was about a span long, was made of wood and shaped like a hollow canoe. In it the bobbin - a simple piece of bamboo - was fitted horizontally by means of a thin reed which ran through it to prevent if from falling out, while at the same time allowing it to rotate and the thread to unwind. From the bobbin the thread passed out of the shuttle by means of a small hole cut in one of its sides.

The weaver, who sat on the ground with his feet in a hole perhaps two feet deep, used both his feet and his hands. By a peddling motion of his feet he alternately raised and lowered the two reeds, thus shedding the warp threads, while with his hands he threw the shuttle from side to side, beat up the weft with the third reed, and from time to time released some of the warp at his right and rolled the woven material on the roller immediately in front of him. These operations were invariably carried out in the open air a few yards from the weaver's house, and at nightfall when the work came to an end the weaver took up his stakes, and rolled the warp around them. The whole contraption would then be replaced in its former position at daybreak for further labour.[6]

Potters

Potters, like blacksmiths and weavers, had, as we have seen, long constituted an isolated, and largely despised, class which consisted of both women and men. Like the blacksmiths and weavers again, a considerable proportion of potters in the north-west were Fälašas, as Rüppell records.[7] Stern, who described those he saw as "industrious," reports visiting two villages of Fälaša potters, at Gorgora Eyla and Atshergee. In the former, he recalls:

> "Men and women ... were busy moulding pots and pans and other useful domestic utensils. Lathe and moulds they do not require to give shape to their manufacture, necessity having taught them to dispense with every implement in carrying on their craft. Their dexterous fingers give form to the clay, and the sun and a good fire dry and temper it afterwards. The articles they make are very strong, and this, as the poor people naïvely told me, is a serious obstacle to their industry."[8]

Earthenware was used for the manufacture of all sorts of cooking and food receptacles, such as bowls, dishes, pitchers and jars of many shapes and sizes, as well as the *gullelat*, or clay centre-piece, often placed at the apex of churches or thatched houses. Such artifacts were usually red or black, the colour depending on the method of firing.

---

[6] Combes and Tamisier (1838) IV, 65-6; Lefebvre (1845-8) III, 244-5; Ferret and Galinier (1847) II, 394-5; Rochet d' Héricourt (1841) 298-9; Girard (1873) 243-4.

[7] Rüppell (1838-40) II, 181.

[8] Stern (1862) 265 . See also 193, 268. and Lefebvre (1845-8) III, 249.

Most potters, a majority of whom were probably women, worked only with their hands, and had no equipment whatsoever, though a few of the more sophisticated, according to Girard, used a horizontal potter's wheel, as well as a spatula or scoop.[9]

Typical Ethiopian pottery. From J. Borelli, *Ethiopie méridonale* (Paris, 1890).

Tanners

Tanning was widely practised, and, since it did not require capital equipment, was largely carried out - with considerable expertise - by the ordinary peasantry rather than by specialist craftsmen. "All the Abyssinians," Combes and Tamisier claim, thus knew how to make skin containers. There were, however, also a number of professional curriers, many of whom were Muslims as Rüppell notes. These and others turned out a wide range of goods, among them saddles, shields, scabbards, cartridge and other belts, tents, thongs, straps, bags and pouches, sleeping-skins, articles of clothing, and parchment.[10]

Flaying and Tanning

Flaying and tanning were carried out with considerable expertise. The hide of a goat would frequently be separated from the carcass with only the head removed. The first cut, according to Johnston, who had many opportunities to witness the work, would be a circular incision around both haunches and around the tail. The hide would then be stripped over the thighs, two smaller incisions being made around the

---

[9] Combes and Tamisier (1838) IV, 82; Girard (1873) 243.

[10] Combes and Tamisier (1838) IV, 77-8; Rüppell (1838-40) I, 367; Lefebvre (1845-8) III, 242.

227

middle joint of the hind legs to enable them to be drawn out. A stick was next placed to extend these extremities, and by it the whole carcass was suspended from the branch of a tree; by some easy pulls around the body, the skin was then gradually withdrawn over the forelegs which had earlier been cut around the knees to allow them to be taken out. After this, the head was removed, and the skin pulled inside out. The inside was then rubbed all over with a stone to remove any pieces of flesh which might remain.

The next stage depended on whether it was desired to remove or retain the hairs. In the manufacture of hides, i.e. skins without hair, the flayed skin was usually stretched in the sun to dry, this being done, according to Parkyns, by nicking pegs through them into the ground. Dried in this manner the skin became "hard and stiff," but was kept "in a dry place for a long time." To soften the texture, a mixture of clotted milk and linseed flour was spread on it, and allowed to soak in for a night. The skin was then taken, folded, fur outside, and trampled on and worked by the feet for a considerable time every morning until it became "as soft as a piece of rag." After each "pedipulation" it was covered with fresh grass pressed down on it by heavy stones, to prevent its drying till the process was completed. After this operation had been continued for some days, the number of which depended on the quality of the skin, the fur was easily cleaned of whatever dirt might have become attached to it, and the membrane of the skin was then peeled off, leaving it "quite white" and as soft "as chamois leather".

Skin bags were made in a somewhat different manner. The skins, Johnston states, were made into sacks by the apertures around the neck and legs being secured by a double fold of skin, sewed together by means of a "slender but very tough thong" which rendered the seams "quite air-tight", and the aperture around the haunches was likewise "gathered together." The skin bag was then "distended with air," and left for days until "slight putrefaction" commenced, at which stage rubbing with a rough stone soon cleaned its surface of the hair. After this a considerable amount of labour was required, for at least one day, to soften the distended skin by beating it with heavy sticks, or trampling upon it for hours together, the labourer supporting himself by clinging to the bough of an overhead tree or holding on to a wall. In this way, whilst drying, the skin was "prevented from getting stiff," and, further to ensure this, it was "frequently rubbed with small quantities of butter." When there was "no chance of the skin becoming hard and easily broken," the hole was opened to allow the air to escape. A "very soft flaccid leather bag" was thus produced, which, for several ensuing days, afforded an amusement to the owner when otherwise unoccupied by "rubbing it over with his hands." Such bags were used as containers for "almost all the produce of the fields," including cotton, grain and flour, which were kept or transported in them.

Tanning was also carried out, according to Johnston, by extending the skin loosely upon four sticks which raised it about a foot from the ground, thus forming a kind of trough into which was strewed the pounded bark of the *kantuffa* acacia (*Petrobolium lacerans*). The hollow was then filled with cold water, which in the course of a few days became a strong red infusion with which the whole surface was frequently washed, after which the leather was trodden on until it was soft. Another method, as described by the French Scientific Mission and others, was to soak the skins for six to eight days in a pot containing a mixture of cattle urine and the crushed astringent fruit of the *imboy* (*Solanum marginatum*), after which they might be rubbed

228

with the juice of lemons or washed in running water, before being stretched on stakes to dry, or covered with some milk, and again rendered supple by treading.

In the preparation of skins, where it was desired to retain the hair, as in the case of lion, leopard, fox, sheep or other pelts, the fur was placed on stakes, hair downwards, and left to dry in the sun for one or two days. The pelt, as the Italian geographer Antonio Cecchi later noted, was then covered with butter, milk, or linseed oil paste, and on the third day would be trodden over to render it supple.

Fine skins were produced in many parts of the country, notably at Gondär, as well as at Morät in Šäwa, whose inhabitants, according to Krapf, were also particularly "skilful" in this field.[11]

Woodworkers, and House-Builders

Wood-workers using the simplest of tools, mainly axes and hatchets, fashioned a considerable variety of household and other artifacts. These included doors, door-frames and other parts of the house, mortars for crushing grain, and items of furniture, such as beds, chairs and head-rests, as well as the wooden parts of ploughs and other agricultural tools and spears. Most of these articles were crudely produced by peasants with only minimal experience of woodwork, but there were also more skilled, and specialised, craftsmen who produced objects of greater sophistication, including rifle-butts.

Carpenters would begin by splitting trees with wedges, after which, the French Scientific Mission explains, they would "very cleverly" plane the pieces into boards with the aid of an adze. Though rustic labourers had virtually no equipment a few of the best-equipped carpenters in the more important towns used a number of imported tools, including adzes, chisels and saws for cutting, gimlets and wimbles for drilling holes, and the compass and carpenter's line for making accurate measurements. The use of such equipment was later confirmed by Girard who noted that some of the most fortunate craftsmen had carpenters' lines, braces and gimlets. Planes were also used by workers making butts for rifles and pistols, as well as relatively sophisticated articles of furniture.

House-building in some parts of the north-west was carried out by Fälašas, some of whom are said to have also repaired the mausoleum of the Abuns, or heads of the Ethiopian Church, at Jenda.

The construction of traditional houses was far from costly. The Englishman Coffin for instance built a house for no more than eighty Maria Theresa thalers. The break-down was:

---

[11] Johnston (1844) II, 369-73; Parkyns (1853) II, 13-4; Lefebvre (1845-8), III, 240-4; Isenberg and Krapf (1843) 255-6; Combes and Tamisier (1838) II, 46, IV, 77; Rüppell (1838-40) I, 367, II, 180-1; Cecchi (1885-7) I, 292-3. For examples of leatherware see Duchesne-Fournet (1901-3) II, Plates XIV and XXI.

Materials:

15,000 canes for covering	10 thalers
500 small spurs of wood	10 thalers
Large pieces of wood for doorways, etc.	20 thalers
1,600 loads of hay, carried by children	10 thalers
	-----------
	50 thalers

Labour:

4 builders' work for 12 days	8 thalers
One thatcher	4 thalers
Mixing of clay by men, women and children, and its carriage and that of stones to builders	8 thalers
	-----------
	30 thalers

Total:	80 thalers[12]

Basket-Making, and Carpet-Weaving

Basket-making, which needed skill, but no equipment, was carried out exclusively by women. This work was of considerable importance, for basketry was widely used, in the manufacture of containers for all kinds of foods, both solid and liquid, as well as both the *mäsob*, or basket-table, and the parasol. Basketware was sometimes rendered watertight, for the containing of liquids, by the application of the juice of the *qwalqwal* (*Candelabra euphorbia*).

Several rural areas of high elevation, where sheep and goats flourished, were noted for their use of wool. The population of the Sämén mountains for example included a number of weavers of small carpets which, according to Salt, were "much superior" to what might have been expected of rural handicraft work. Among the people of highland Mänz in Šäwa there were likewise many carpet-makers, who worked with goats' hair (and wool?), as well as tent-makers who made use of thick black woollen cloth.[13]

The Craftsmen of Gondär

Gondär, in the early nineteenth century, was still, as for the previous two hundred years, the country's principal handicraft centre. It was "the only town,"

---

[12] Combes and Tamisier (1838) IV, 82; Lefebvre (1845-8) III, 246-7; Stern (1862) 254-5; Girard (1873) 199; Pearce (1831) I, 243-4.

[13] Combes and Tamisier (1838) IV, 82-3; Parkyns (1853) I, 138; Salt (1814) 426; Valentia (1809) III, 162; Dufton (1867) 165; Stern (1862) 254-5; Isenberg and Krapf (1843) 255-6. For examples of basketry see Duchesne-Fournet (1901-3) II, Plates XIX and XX.

Gäbrä Sellasé, a carpenter of Gondär, in his finest attire. From T. Lefebvre and others, *Voyage en Abyssinie* (1845-8).

Combes and Tamisier declare, "where one finds ... the professions of the tailor, miller, baker and a mass of others unknown in Abyssinia." Other occupations represented in the city, according to Arnauld d'Abbadie, included weavers, curriers, leather-workers, harness-makers, blacksmiths and forgers of spears, swords and knives, saddle-makers and sandal-makers, parchment-makers, book-binders, scribes and copyists, goldsmiths and copper-workers, embroiders of women's shirts, priests' clothes and saddle cloths, makers of shields, and carpenters, turners who fitted wood in rifles, and makers of drinking vessels. Most of these craftsmen, as far as we can tell, were male, but the city's population also included numerous women who specialised in basketry and pottery.

The handicrafts of Gondär, in its hey-day, included some of the finest possible description, but, with the city's decline, deteriorated markedly in quality. By the 1830's the capital's silversmiths, who had once fashioned priceless crowns, were reduced, Rüppell states, to making neck-chains and finger-rings, and shamelessly adulterated their gold and silver with zinc and tin. Some blacksmiths still turned out iron bullets (which were preferred to lead as they could penetrate the stoutest shield whereas lead bullets only flattened themselves and bounced off), but armourers often soldered over holes in rifles so badly that if a weapon was over-charged the metal often sprayed out dangerously. The city's large tanned hides, which sold for a third of a Maria Theresa thaler each, nonetheless won the German traveller's unqualified praise, and were said by Combes and Tamisier to be demanded even by the Arabs. The carpets of Gondär were likewise highly regarded.

Other notable handicrafts were produced by jewellers, who, according to the French Scientific Mission, worked in gold, silver, tin, zinc and copper, as well as by horn-workers who made rhinoceros-horn sword-handles, and skilfully wrought goblets from ox horn. The city's tailors, a few of whom by the 1840's were using tools imported from Europe, likewise made a variety of articles, including ceremonial shirts and cloaks for the chiefs, ornate clothes for the higher clergy, fine burnouses for the well-to-do, and richly embroidered dresses for noblewomen, as well as colourful saddle-cloths for the horses and mules of the aristocracy. The city's shoemakers, who made skilful use of knives and awls, supplied those comfortably off with slippers unknown in the country at large.

The masons of Gondär were also highly regarded though they had, according to the French Scientific Mission, little equipment beyond a plumb-line. The city's builders were, nevertheless, so well regarded that King Sahlä Sellasé of Šäwa, when erecting the church of Mädhané 'Aläm at Ankobär, sent for carpenters from Gondär. Half a century later a master carpenter from the city was likewise to go to Šäwa with nine assistants who were employed by Menilek in constructing his palace at Entotto.

The carpenters of Gondär, who cut down trees and squared timber into planks, seem to have been relatively well equipped. They possessed, according to the French Scientific mission, such tools as saws, adzes, gimlets, braces and compasses. Veritable artists, they turned out chairs, beds, rifle-butts, and delicate objects of wood-work, some of the best of which were fashioned from the kosso tree (*Hagenia abyssinica*). Considerable use of wood was also made by another of the city's specialised workers - the charcoal-makers.

Gondär, as a religious as well as a political and commercial centre, also had many skilled artisans catering for the needs of the Church, such as calligraphers, artists and book-binders. Rüppell, who praised their craftsmanship, exclaimed that one could only wonder at the elegance of the tooled leather binding of Gondäré manuscripts. This work, according to the French Scientific Mission, was normally carried out by *däbtäras*, or lay clergy. Other craftsmen produced fine, and often intricate, church metalwork, mainly of silver, copper and zinc.

One other lesser-known category of craftsmen at Gondär deserves to be mentioned: the makers of small mirrors who fashioned these highly prized artifacts from glass and mercury which were imported separately by way of Massawa.

Much of the handicraft work of the city and its environs was carried out, as in the surrounding countryside, by Fälašas and Muslims. The Fälašas, some of whom were settled in a village by the Qäha river, played a major role in construction. Their chief employment, according to Salt, consisted in "building and thatching houses," and their skill in these fields was "most to be admired." Fälaša house-builders worked, according to Coffin, for one Maria Theresa thaler per six-day week, while a thatcher would complete a roof for a piece-rate of four thalers. The extent of Fälaša building activity was also emphasised by subsequent observers, such as Plowden who termed them "the best masons in the country," and Dufton who later went so far as to affirm that "all the builders and artisans" were Fälaša. The Fälašas of Gondär, as elsewhere, were likewise prominent as blacksmiths, and were so important as potters that Rüppell went so far as to assert that they were responsible for all the city's potting.

The Muslims were also much involved in craftsmanship. They provided most of the city's weavers, and were also active in embroidering women's shirts, as well as in making caps for the Muslim population.

Gondär also had a community of foreign craftsmen, consisting mainly of Egyptians and Greeks, some of whom were involved, according to Rüppell, in the repair of rifles. Because of the difficulty of obtaining new weapons their services were always in great demand. The city was also renowned for its parchments, carpets and tanned hides.

Some of the neighbouring Qemant, who had some cultural affinity to the Fälašas, and lived outside the city to the west, were also to the fore as craftsmen. They supplied the capital with most of its wood, and were said by Plowden to have been "skilful carpenters." Another group of craftsmen catering for the needs of the old metropolis were the stone-workers, many of whom lived on the island of Däq in Lake Ṭana, and produced well-fashioned stone grinding-mills.

The civil wars of the early nineteenth century, and the subsequent looting of the city by Emperor Téwodros in the 1860's, led to the decline of craftsmanship in and around Gondär. Flad reported in 1869 that "a great number" of Fälašas had fled to Bägémder, Bälässa and Lasta. Some had been "received by the King's command," and were "employed in his work," while "others earned a livelihood by their trades" -

presumably, as in the past, mainly as blacksmiths, weavers, potters and house-builders.[14]

Other Urban and Religious Centres

Though Gondär was in its day the country's most populous urban centre, and hence the location of the largest number of craftsmen, skilled workers also congregated at other provincial centres where their services were in demand by rulers and churchmen, as well as by the population at large. The majority of such handicraft-workers lived, according to Pearce, "most undisturbed" lives. Even if blacksmiths suffered, as we have seen, from many trials and tribulations, most other craftsmen were respected, and "considered the best Christians." Those who worked in gold, silver, or brass, or who followed the carpenters' trade, were in particular "esteemed as persons of rank." Many craftsmen, as in the old days of moving capitals, travelled extensively. Whenever the desire seized them they would thus leave their abode, and establish themselves, Arnauld d'Abbadie says, in another town. They might, alternatively, attach themselves to one of the great lords, and journey over the country in the wake of an itinerant army.[15]

Aksum

Aksum, the religious capital of Ethiopian Christendom and site of the great church of St. Mary of Şeyon, had numerous skilled craftsmen in the service of the Church. Many of the inhabitants of the city and its neighbourhood were "celebrated," Salt records, in the preparation and use of parchment, as was confirmed by such later writers as Combes and Tamisier who claim that Aksum parchment was the most highly regarded in the entire country.

Ecclesiastical craftsmanship was also produced at many smaller, lesser-known monasteries, for example in the early nineteenth century at Myolones in Šäwa, where the monks, according to Johnston, worked as blacksmiths while the nuns made earthenware vessels.[16]

Adwa

Adwa, at this time the principal political and commercial centre of the north, was a flourishing handicraft centre renowned for a wide range of goods. The "chief production," according to Salt, was cloth, the manufacture of which was so

---

[14]Combes and Tamisier (1838) IV, 85-6; Arnauld d'Abbadie (1868) 162, 164-5; Rüppell (1838-40) I, 367, II, 179-82; Ferret and Galinier (1847) II, 431; Lefebvre (1845-8) II, Part II, 45, III, 244, 246-9; Guèbrè Sellassié (1930-1) I, 72-3, 209-11; Valentia (1809) III, 67, 161; Salt (1814) 426; Pearce (1831) I, 244; GB House of Commons (1868) 110; Dufton (1867) 92; Krapf (1867) 461; Flad (1869), 10-1. The high status of the carpenters of Gondär is apparent from an engraving of one of them, Gäbrä Selassé, as depicted in Lefebvre's *Atlas*, Plate 30. See page 229. On the Qemant see Gamst (1969).

[15] Pearce (1831) II, 286; Arnauld d'Abbadie (1868) 165.

[16] Salt (1814) 426; Combes and Tamisier (1838) IV, 78; Johnston (1844) II, 320-2.

considerable that it created a "great demand for cotton" throughout the neighbouring lowlands. The coarse cloth of Adwa, which circulated throughout much of Tegré instead of money, was "considered unrivalled," while the finer weaves were thought "little inferior" to those of Gondär. Some, "worn by the principal men of the country," took several months to make, and sold for as much as 12 Maria Theresa thalers each. Christian weavers usually produced three in a year; Muslims more, but inferior in quality, and hence cheaper. The majority of the city's weavers, like those of Tegré as a whole, were Muslim.

Adwa also boasted a number of tailors. One of whom record remains was a Greek, Demetrius, better known as Sidi Pétros, who, according to Parkyns, had been "a long time" in the country, and was "well acquainted with its customs." There were also numerous tanners whose work was prized, Combes and Tamisier say, far and wide, as well as leather-workers who made shields, saddles and slippers.

The goldsmiths and silversmiths of the city also enjoyed a great reputation. Some of the most prominent were Greek and Armenian immigrants who in the passage of time were succeeded by their half-Ethiopian children and grand-children. Several of the city's jewellers, according to Parkyns (who knew them well) were, whether they liked it or not, "obliged to be rogues." They made "a tolerably good thing of their business," but did this by appropriating a large proportion of the gold and silver entrusted to them for their work. Given Maria Theresa thalers with a high silver content, they returned alloy "scarcely so good as a Turkish piastre," and one goldsmith received 30 Venetian sequins for a job on which he used only seven and a half. Remarking that it might seem "scarcely fair" to "tell tales out of school" as he had worked with these jewellers, and was therefore familiar with their "secret goings-on," Parkyns declares: "they are more to be pitied than blamed. They are considered almost in the light of slaves ... that is, they are not allowed to leave the country; and though treated with considerable kindness, and even some distinction, their supplies are neither over-plentiful nor very regularly paid."

The early nineteenth century jewellers of Adwa included two Greeks, Avostalla, who made crowns, crosses and church bells, and Mika'él, who had fled from Khartoum "with a quantity of silver which had been given to him to be worked," and an Armenian, Haji Yohannes, who was said to have once been an illegal coiner. There was in addition a jeweller of Ethio-Greek descent, Wäldä Giyorgis, who turned out highly prized silver drinking-cups.

The city also had a number of blacksmiths who as elsewhere were despised, and a group of armourers. Most of the latter were foreigners - Copts, Armenians and Greeks. One of them, the afore-mentioned Avostalla, constructed a cannon for Wäldä Gabre'él, a local governor of Tegré, who, to obtain the metal required, ordered the purchase of all the brass in the province. Three months later sufficient had been collected for the Greek to cast the weapon, under the direction of a Turkish soldier called Isma'él. Its carriage was built by an Ethiopian Muslim carpenter, Haji Nuro. The gun was duly tested in Adwa market, which greatly terrified many of the citizens. When fired with a small charge, the weapon performed admirably, but, on being subsequently more heavily loaded, exploded, seriously injuring poor Isma'él. Haji Nuro, who lived to tell the tale, later became head-carpenter to Ras Wäldä Sellasé, the subsequent ruler of Tegré. Other armourers of the time included an Armenian, Yohannes, and an Italian, Valieri, who on at least one occasion mended a cannon for

Däjazmač Webé. Though some armourers thus occasionally repaired or attempted to cast pieces of artillery, most were concerned exclusively with the maintenance of rifles.

Adwa, as the provincial capital of Tegré, also had many craftsmen working on the production of other military supplies of all kinds, including spears, swords and shields, as well as gunpowder and bullets, most of which were made either of iron or stone. The latter were often preferred as they were thought capable of penetrating any shield whereas those of iron were considered scarcely harder than lead.[17]

Other Towns of the North and North-West

Specialist craftsmen, though in smaller numbers, also forgathered at other provincial capitals of the north, among them Antalo, Addigrat and Čäläqot in Tegré, and Därita and Qoräta in Bägémder. Antalo, Ras Wäldä Sellasé's capital in the early years of the century, had several foreign skilled workers. One of them, Nasar 'Ali, a Macedonian, constructed a horse-drawn grinding-mill, which, according to Salt, "excited great admiration." The town was likewise renowned for its tanning and leatherwork. Čäläqot, where Ras Wäldä Sellasé also resided, likewise had a number of fine craftsmen. They included the Ras's "chief painter," who struck Salt as "a very ingenious man." Something of a philosopher he once said, "I am like a man blindfolded: I go muddling in the dark, until I produce something." Another worker of the town was an Armenian leatherworker called Nazaret. Addigrat too had a number of craftsmen, who included a lapsed German missionary carpenter by name Aichinger who designed an Ethiopian Orthodox church for the then ruler of Tegré Däjazmač Säbagades.

Därita, a commercial centre on the trade route south of Gondär, was particularly renowned for its leatherwork, which was finer, according to Combes and Tamisier, than cotton cloth. The craftsmen of the town also produced beautiful cords of silk which served as money throughout the neighbouring provinces. Qoräta likewise had a significant population of craftsmen who benefited from the town's status as a place of asylum. which enabled them to produce better crafts, Rüppell claims, - including brassware - than most parts of the country.

There were also a number of specialised craftsmen in Gojjam, many of them attached to the court of Däjazmač Berru Gošu. The latter was "fond of superintending his smiths and other workmen", in whose labours, Beke says, he seemed to take even more interest than did King Sahlä Sellasé of Šäwa, for he not only directed, but often actually took part in their work. No accounts of their activities are, unfortunately, preserved.[18]

---

[17] Valentia (1809) III, 78-9, 161; Salt (1814) 425; Holland and Hozier (1870) I, 398; Parkyns (1853) I, 241, II, 15, 36-7, 43, 45-7, 276; Combes and Tamisier (1839) IV, 66, 77; Pearce (1831) I, 257-8, II, 213, II, 15; Ferret and Galinier (1847) II, 40-3; Lefebvre (1845-8), I, 53-4, II, 195; Arnauld d'Abbadie (1868) 37, 211.

[18] Salt (1814) 361, 393-4; Combes and Tamisier (1838) II, 46, IV, 77; Isenberg and Krapf (1843) 503, 512-3; Lefebvre (1845-8) II, 55-6; Rüppell (1838-40) II, 225; Beke (1840-3) 416; Shepherd (1868) 73-5; Markham (1869) 199; Hozier (1869) 109; Holland and Hozier (1870) I, 342.

Ankobär and Angoläla

Numerous craftsmen, including several foreigners, congregated in the principal towns of Šäwa. One of the first was a Greek artist who travelled from Gondär to Šäwa where he entered the service of King Wäsän Sägäd (1808-1813). This painter, according to Rochet d'Héricourt, was asked by the monarch to decorate his tomb at Qundi with frescos of battles and royal hunts.

Many craftsmen, mostly Ethiopian, were later attached to King Sahlä Sellasé's palaces at the twin Šäwan capitals, Ankobär and Angoläla. The monarch, whose court, according to Combes and Tamisier, was "the most brilliant in the country," took a keen interest in handicraft work. "Though much absorbed in the cares of the war," he is said to have found time to "direct himself towards the industrial arts which he loved with passion," and insisted that "all handicraft work be carried out under his eyes." His love of such work was so great, the Frenchmen go so far as to claim, perhaps because of their Saint Simonian fervour, that "the principal personages of his court were workers whom he treated with the greatest consideration." Be that as it may, there can be no denying the travellers' report that Sahlä Sellasé's palaces were crowded with carpenters, masons and craftsmen engaged in making gunpowder, repairing rifles and producing intricate jewellery and other articles of gold, silver and ivory. Their workshop also turned out magnificent pieces of cloth which were said to rival those of Gondär, as well as shields, arm-bands and rifle-plates, razors, scissors and needles, ivory bracelets, drinking-horns, and chessmen, besides, Harris says, "all manner of curious amulets and devices." This picture is confirmed by Krapf who states that blacksmiths, weavers and other craftsmen were gathered together at the Ankobär and Angoläla palaces, and that the King frequently visited them to watch their work which had to be altered if not pleasing to him. No total estimate of the number of craftsmen gathered at the two towns is available, but Krapf believed that the King employed no less than 600 spinning-women, two hundred of whom produced fine cotton cloth which the monarch presented to his governors, favourites and family, while the remaining four hundred span ordinary cloth, mainly for the soldiers. A number of craftsmen were also lodged at another of Sahlä Sellasé's establishments, situated at Mähal Wänz, where Harris saw blacksmiths, armourers, jewellers and illuminators of manuscripts, all "plying their craft ... under the royal eye."

There was in addition a number of blacksmiths in royal employ working in an ironworks, outside Ankobär, at the village of Gureyon by the Čača river. Its blacksmiths, according to Harris, broke the ore into small pieces which were then roughly pulverized, mixed with a large proportion of charcoal, and placed in a clay furnace which resembled an ordinary smith's hearth, but was furnished with a sloping cavity below the level of the blast pipes. Four pairs of hard-worked bellows were then used to bring the ore to fusion point, whereupon the iron, together with the dross, sank to the bottom. The metal, on setting, was broken and re-fused, after which the dross flowed off, and the pure metal was discharged in lumps, or pigs, which by repeated heating and welding were wrought into bars. Owing to the "very rude and primitive apparatus" employed, ten hours of "unceasing toil" were, however, needed to produce a mere two pounds of "very inferior iron."

Prominent among the craftsmen of early nineteenth century Šäwa was Ato Čakol, Sahlä Sellasé's principal armourer - and one of the few Ethiopian craftsmen of this period whose name has been preserved. Trained by working with a Greek called Elias who was active in the 1820's, he was capable, according to Combes and Tamisier, even of making an entire rifle. There were also a number of foreign craftsmen. Besides the aforesaid Elias, they included two other Greeks, Demetrius and Johannes, who a decade or so later built the monarch's palace at Angoläla and a grinding-mill on the Ayrara river. Another craftsman at Ankobär was Stefanos, an Armenian silversmith who was active for a few years in the 1830's, but fled when accused of coining money. There was also a Greek or Armenian merchant called Pétros who is said to have introduced the art of dying leather red and green.

Specialised handicraft work also took place elsewhere in Šäwa. The inhabitants of the highlands, notably around Däbrä Berhan, produced tents and other articles of black wool, while to the east many of the Muslim Argobbas in the lowlands were employed in weaving, and, though using "very inferior" equipment, are said by Graham to have turned out cloth which was both "well made and cheap."

Ankobär, the most important of the above-mentioned Šäwan settlements, maintained its population of craftsmen for much of the nineteenth century. In the 1870's Cecchi reported that the inhabitants still included a large number of skilled workers, among them tanners, saddlers, blacksmiths, joiners, wood-cutters and carpenters, masons, stone-workers, many of them engaged in the manufacture of grinding-stones, dress-makers, sewers, goldsmiths, charcoal-makers, scribes, painters, and traditional-style physicians and surgeons.[19]

Jewellers

Jewellers who were to be found, as we have seen, exclusively in the principal political, commercial and religious centres, worked mainly in gold, silver and brass.

Gold jewellery was not in widespread use, for only members of the ruling family, as we have seen, were allowed to wear it. The precious metal, out of which the local jewellers fashioned their artifacts, came partly from local mines, and partly from Venetian sequins imported mainly by way of Massawa. This money was in such demand that coins worth 2.38 Maria Theresa thalers at the port fetched, according to the French Scientific Mission, almost three at Gondär.

Most of the silver jewellery was made from Maria Theresa dollars which were then being imported in the course of trade in increasing numbers, and were valued, according to Johnston, only as a means of enabling their owners to "adorn themselves or their women." All the coin entering the country, he believed, ultimately found its way into the crucible, except such as fell into the hands of the king, and were

---

[19] Rochet d'Hericourt (1841) 216, (1846) 244; Combes and Tamisier (1838) II, 349, III, 8-9, 23-4, IV, 67-9, 72, 84; Harris (1844) II, 31, 44-89, 100-1, 262, 389; Lefebvre (1845-8) III, 246; Isenberg and Krapf (1843) 57, 62, 120, 247; Krapf (1867) 23-4; Graham (1867) 33; Johnston (1844) II, 60; Burton (1894) II, 223, 231; Soleillet (1886) 131-2; Beke (1840-3) 201, 307; Barker (1906) 273, 288; Cecchi (1885-7) I, 292. On the Saint Simonian attitude to workers, which may have coloured their accounts of Sahlä Sellasé's craftsmen see Pankhurst (1969) 169-223.

deposited in the royal treasury. From these useful coins the jewellers of Ethiopia made a great variety of crosses of all shapes and sizes, for both religious and secular use, as well as hairpins, earrings, necklaces, lockets, bracelets, rings and anklets, earpicks, ornaments for shields, swords, spears and guns, and sundry paraphernalia for horses and mules.

Brassware, which in some areas, Combes and Tamisier believed, was less common than silverware, was used in the manufacture of a wide range of articles, among them incense-holders, sistra, small bells, bracelets, chains, jugs and bowls for washing purposes, shield, sword and scabbard ornaments, and sundry mule collar and harness decorations. The workers in brass were praised by several foreign observers, including Salt, who thought the best were found among the Oromos, and Rüppell, who stated that the craftsmen at Qoräta made finely worked and very attractive church ornaments and harness decorations.

Jewellery, as we will see in a later chapter, was extremely popular among Ethiopian women, causing the often critical Stern to observe that those who possessed the means carried their love of trinkets to "such an excess" that they often had "more than three pounds weight of silver bells, chains and little scent boxes dangling down their bosom", besides "other *et ceteras*, such as rosaries, bangles and an endless variety of charms."[20]

Horn- and Ivory-Workers

Horn-carving, which required some modest equipment, as well as skill, was carried out by specialised craftsmen. Many of them fashioned ox, buffalo, ibex and other horns into such articles as drinking-vessels and sword-handles. Some such artifacts were of considerable size as the horns of *sanga* cattle were often as much as two feet or two feet eight inches long and eight to ten inches wide at the base. Carvers in horn made use of a mould and a simple but efficient lathe which was based, Johnston says, of "two sticks placed in the ground, not more than three inches above the surface." From the centre of each end of the mould an arm projected about six inches long, which was armed with a bit of iron. These iron points were received in the short stick supports, and the mould, with the horn upon it, then revolved freely. The workman sat upon the ground, and with his feet pressed hard against a stick, supported it against two stones, placed at a convenient distance in front of his work. This formed a rest for his cutting instrument, which he held in his left hand, and pressed against the horn, whilst with his right he wheeled backwards and forwards the mould by a small catgut. The drinking horns were finished by a piece of round wood being fitted like a thin cork into the lower and smaller end. To make a drinking-vessel an ox-horn of the desired size would be selected, and cut to the required length, after which it would be softened with hot water, fixed on a conical wooden mould, and left on it for several days. When formed to the required shape the horn would be placed on the lathe to receive a series of circular cuts with which the outside was usually decorated.

---

[20] Lefebvre (1885-8) II, Part II, 81; Johnston (1844) II, 355-6; Combes and Tamisier (1838) IV, 79-81; Stern (1862) 315; Salt (1814) 426; Rüppell (1838-40) II, 225; Heuglin (1857) 52, (1868) 257. On jewellery see Duchesne-Fournet (1908-9) II, Plates XV, XVI; Moore (1969); Kobariewixz (1973) and Kamil (1975).

Hornware was produced in many parts of the country. Some of the best, according to Salt, came from Gojjam, but the craftsmen of Šäwa were said by Johnston to have also displayed "considerable ingenuity." Many of the most popular earrings of Šäwa were cut from the long black horns of the *sala*, a species of antelope common in Adäl and the neighbouring low countries. Describing this manufacture in detail, Johnston observes: "The solid extremities of the horns only are used, so that not more than two earrings can be made from one horn, which is at least two feet long. The earrings are large and clumsy, but, considering the simple means employed in making them, are not despicable works of art. Each is turned in two pieces, ... with small straight shafts projecting from the inside centres. These shafts are made so that one receives the other, and the earring thus formed looks like two small wheels connected by a small axle. To receive them into the ear a very large hole is required, and the axis of one of the halves being first introduced, the other is fixed upon it, and the lady then turns round, to ask how the ornament looks". Besides these horn earrings, which were sometimes ornamented with "an inlaid star of silver," the workers in hornware also made "neat little bottles", each about two inches long, and "turned in a very ingenious manner," which were used to hold *kohl* to decorate the eyelids.

Ivory, though exported in large quantities, was also used by local carvers, some of the finest of whom worked at Sahlä Sellasé's palaces, and, according to Combes and Tamisier, produced excellent bracelets and chessmen.[21]

Shoe-makers

Shoe-makers, though unknown in the country at large, were to be found, as we have seen, at Gondär and a few other urban centres. They plied their profession, according to the French Scientific Mission, with the aid of a pattern, a piece of ivory to mark out the desired shape, a curved knife for cutting the leather, two awls (one for making holes and the other for threading the cord), and a needle to stitch the border.[22]

---

[21] Combes and Tamisier (1838) IV, 83-4; Lefebvre (1845-8) III, 244; Parkyns (1853) I, 157; Johnston (1844) II, 333-5; Valentia (1809) III, 149; Isenberg and Krapf (1843). For examples of hornware see Duchesne-Fournet (1908-9) II, Plate XVIII.

[22] Lefebvre (1845-8) III, 248.

IX

SLAVES AND SERVANTS

The Extent of Slavery

Numerous slaves of both sexes in the early nineteenth century were in domestic service throughout the country. They were to be found, according to Rüppell, in the houses of most well-to-do families of the north - as well, as we shall see, further south. Chiefs, not surprisingly, had many more: Ras Wäldä Sellasé, for example, according to Pearce, always had "a great number" around him.

The number of women slaves, who were mainly employed in the carrying of water and fire-wood and the grinding of flour, may have exceeded that of men. Gobat believed that there were "relatively few" male slaves in the north, but that "all" who could afford it had female slaves, it being "a mark of comfortable circumstances and of benevolence to have several servants." The result was that everyone kept as many as they could feed, even though they might not give them much work.

There were also many slaves in Šäwa, where Harris claimed that "from the governor to the simplest peasant every house possessed slaves of both sexes, in proportion to the wealth of the proprietor." The greatest number were at the main capital, Ankobär, where King Sahlä Sellasé was said to have 300 grinding-women, an even larger number of girls fetching water, and several hundred more engaged in the brewing of beer and mead, besides a considerable number of males employed in transporting wood. A further fifty royal slaves served as wood-gatherers at nearby Däbrä Berhan.

Most slaves throughout this period came from the south and west of the country. The slave population of Tegré, as Salt noticed early in the century, consisted largely of Gallas, or Oromos, from the south, and Šanqellas from the west. The preponderance of both groups was later confirmed by Rüppell who stated that the slaves in the north in fact comprised three distinct categories: 1) free-born highland Christians taken prisoner in war or captured by brigands; 2) Šanqellas from lands north and north-west of Gondär seized in slave-raiding expeditions; and 3) Gallas from lands south of the Blue Nile who were regularly brought to market. Each of these groups had its own particular reputation in slave-owning circles. Those from the north were considered lazy and spendthrift liars; the Šanqellas were said to be loyal and obedient, while the Oromos, if treated with understanding, were held to be loyal and affectionate. The slaves of Šäwa also originated largely from the south and west, and consisted mainly, according to Krapf, of Guragés, Gallas and Šanqellas, but also included people from Jänjero, Enarya and Käfa.

Slaves taken from the south and west for service in the highlands in many cases changed hands on a number of occasions, for ever increasing prices, before reaching their final destination. Not untypical was the case of an eighteen-year-old youth called Dilbo, from Sabba in Enarya, whose story was recorded by Krapf. This youngster, who had been seized by slave-raiders in Nono, was taken to Migra, and thence to Agabja where he was sold for forty *amolés*, or salt pieces. Conveyed to Gona, in the Soddo area, he was then put on sale again, this time for sixty bars. He was then brought to the renowned Šäwan slave market of Rogé, where he fetched 80 pieces, before being brought to Golba in the district of Abeju where his price rose to 100. Taken next to the great Šäwan market of Aleyu Amba, he was for the first time valued in money, and sold for twelve Maria Theresa thalers. He was subsequently purchased by a rich widow for fourteen thalers, and at her death passed into the possession of her brother, who was, however, later disinherited, after which Dilbo became the property of King Sahlä Sellasé. Slave prices, as evident from this account, thus varied immensely from region to region.[1]

Conditions of the Slaves

Men, women and children captured in slave-raiding expeditions, or taken as slaves in war, suffered greatly from being uprooted from their native land, as well as from their separation from their families. The pathos of the slaves' situation is preserved in a song sung by two Šanqella youths from the Täkkäzé area recorded early in the century by Salt, which ran as follows:

"They come, and catch us by the waters of the Tacazze: they make us slaves,
"Our mothers with alarm flee to the mountains and leave us alone in strange hands."[2]

Despite their sadness at separation from families and friends the life of most slaves, if we can believe the reports of foreign travellers, was not too arduous. Henry Salt, who had spoken with a number of slaves in Tegré, claimed that "generally speaking" they were "very happy," and adds:

"several of those I have conversed with, who have been captured at an advanced period of life, preferred their latter mode of living to that which they had led in their native wilds .... The situation of slaves, indeed, is rather honourable than disgraceful ... and the difference between their state and that of western slaves in strikingly apparent. They have no long voyage to make, no violent change of habits to undergo, no out-door labour to perform, no 'white man's scorn' to endure, but, on the contrary, are frequently adopted, like children, into the family, and to make use of an Eastern expression, 'bask in the sunshine of their master's favour.'"[3]

A picture of contentment on the part of the slave, and benevolence on that of the master, is likewise presented by other observers. Pearce for example recalls that Ras Wäldä Sellasé kept a teacher for the education of his slaves, while Salt claims that they even had a voice in advising the chief when the latter played chess. Rüppell, writing more generally of the north, considered that slaves were contented and treated mildly, more or less as ordinary servants, and, though very exceptionally chained, were never severely punished, while Combes and Tamisier state that slaves were far from

---

[1] Rüppell (1838-40) II, 26-7, 193; Pearce I, 217; Valentia (1809) III, 48; Krapf (1867) 50-1. For slave prices in various parts of the country see Pankhurst (1968a) 84-7.

[2] Salt (1814) 381.

[3] Salt (1814) 381-2

unfortunate as they received abundant food, lived among people with customs not too different from their own, and were treated as "children of the house."

The situation in Šäwa was reportedly not dissimilar. Johnston claims that slaves were generally considered as "near relations, or rather, perhaps, as foster children" - though when their behaviour was "so very bad as to alienate the affection of their indulgent masters" they were "not infrequently dismissed," and on occasion sold to Muslim merchants for export to the coast. Beke likewise stated that the treatment slaves received was "on the whole mild," while Harris, though normally most critical of the Ethiopian scene, agreed that their condition was "with occasional, but rare exceptions, one of comfort and east." Later observers paint a similar picture: Waldmeier states that slaves in Bägémder during the time of Emperor Téwodros were "very kindly treated and regarded as members of the families," while Rassam observed that the Ethiopians were "generally ... very kind to servants, treating them as members of the family, especially on their marriage or death."

Slaves, young and old, exported to the coast or Sudan. Note chains, which seem in fact to have been only rarely used. From T. Waldmeier, *Autobiography of Ten Years in Abyssinia* (London and Leominster, 1886).

The slaves' own view of their situation - which may of course have differed considerably from that of foreign observers - is not, however, recorded.[4]

---

[4] Pearce (1831) I, 217-8; Johnston (1844) II, 176; Valentia (1809) III, 51; Rüppell (1838-40) II, 29; Combes and Tamisier (1838) IV, 95-6; Beke (1845) 28; Harris (1844) III, 309; Waldmeier (1886) 37; Rassam (1869) II, 256.

The Slave Trade

Besides the many slaves who remained in the country there were large numbers who were exported to foreign lands. Slave caravans, mainly from the south and west, were a frequent sight along the principal trade routes, as reported by a number of foreign observers, several of whom offered estimates of the extent of the slave trade in their day. Pearce for example reported that 2,000 prisoners of war, 700 young children and 160 eunuchs were taken through Adwa as slaves in 1812, while Beke in the 1840's estimated that 2,000 to 3,000 passed through Ankobär each year, and Krapf that 3,000 were seized annually in the Guragé country.

Slave exports via Tegré to Massawa are known to have been considerable. In the first decade of the century Salt put shipments from the port at 1,000 a year, while Rüppell in the 1830's wrote of double that number. In the following decade Degoutin, the French consul at Massawa, wrote of an annual export of 1,600 (composed of 1,000 slaves captured in war, 300 Galla girls, mainly twelve or thirteen years old, 200 Šanqellas, and 100 eunuchs), and later of 2,500 (made up of again 1,000 prisoners, besides 800 Galla girls, 300 Galla boys, 200 Šanqellas, 100 kidnapped Christian children, and 300 eunuchs). Ferret and Galinier at about the same time quoted an annual export of 1,500 to 2,000 slaves, while official Turkish figures, quoted by Plowden, reported that 1,100 had been exported in 1852. These and other estimates show an average annual export from Massawa in the first three-quarters of the century of about 1,750 slaves. Exports via Šäwa to the Gulf of Aden ports of Zäylä' and Täjurä were probably somewhat higher, for Harris claimed that no less than 3,000 slaves a year were shipped from the former port alone. Slave exports on the western trade route via Mätämma to Sudan were more difficult to obtain. Combes and Tamisier, however, estimated them at 2,000 per annum in the 1830's, but the Italian missionary Massaia put the figure in 1850 at no less than ten times that number.[5]

The condition of slaves on these trade routes, like those in the country itself, was said, by foreign writers, to have been not unbearable. Beke, describing a caravan bound for Massawa, for example declares:

> "The slaves go along without the least constraint, singing and chattering, and apparently perfectly happy. They are generally treated with attention, stopping frequently on the road to rest and feed. They are mostly well dressed ... The girls, almost without exception, have necklaces and beads. In fact, it is not to the interest of their owners, to treat them otherwise than well; for as more than one merchant said to me at Yejjubi, when asking for medicine for them, 'they are our property (*kabt*, literally cattle), and we cannot afford to lose them.'"[6]

---

[5] Pearce (1831) II, 207, 236; Beke (1844) 20-1, 27; Krapf (1867) 62; Valentia (1809) II, 70-1; Salt (1814) 426; Douin (1936-41) III, Part I, 262-3; Ferret and Galinier (1847) II, 429; GB House of Commons (1868) 73, 287; Combes and Tamisier (1838) IV, 95, 192; Massaia (1885-95) I, 103-4, 139. For estimates of slaves exported at this time see Pankhurst (1964a) 220-8 and (1968a) 82-4.

[6] Beke (1845) 20-1.

The women slaves, Beke admits, nevertheless suffered many hardships. "All the female slaves, without exception, whatever their number, and however tender their age - and many are children of eight or nine years at most - are concubines of their master and his servants during the journey, the same continuing through the various changes of ownership until are disposed of to their ultimate possessors." It was customary for slave merchants to "invest the best looking of their female slaves, in most cases a full-grown girl, with the title of wife during the journey." Treated in consequence with an "extra degree of attention and kindness," she would frequently be mounted on a mule, on arriving at a station for the night she would have a hut built for her (and her master!), and throughout the journey would receive "from the others the respect to which her temporary rank entitles her." This did not, however, "prevent her from being sold with the rest on reaching their place of destination."

A slave market at Galabat, on the eastern frontier, in the late 1870's. From A.E. De Cosson, *The Cradle of the Blue Nile* (London, 1877).

The trade to the Gulf of Aden ports was probably not dissimilar. Harris claims that the majority of slaves were too young to be aware of their subject status, while the adults, who were unfettered, were mainly "in good spirits, all being well fed and taken care of."[7] He adds:

---

[7] Beke (1845) 20-1;Harris (1844) III, 308.

"Although the majority were of tender years and many of them extremely pretty they did not excite that interest which might have been anticipated, for they very readily adopted themselves to the will of their new masters whose obvious interest was to keep them fat and in good spirits. With few exceptions all were merry and light-hearted. Recovered from the fatigues of the long march, there was nothing but dancing, singing, and romping; and although many wore an air of melancholy, which forms a national characteristic, the little victims of a traffic so opposed to every principle of humanity, might rather have been conjectured to be proceeding on a party of pleasure, than bending their steps for ever from their native land."[8]

Foreign travellers' accounts such as the above cannot, however, be accepted at fully face value. Their authors tended to be aloof from the slaves, with whom they had in the main little or no contact, and were unable to perceive, let alone to share, their feelings. The slaves' own perception of their condition, we may be sure, was far less favourable than the British envoy's report would suggest. This is evident for example in the Oromo slave children's correspondence referred to in a previous chapter, where the ex-slave boy Otsu, writing to Akafedé in fraternal terms, observes:

"My brother, did you say, 'I will be eaten by the *Bulgu* [i.e. cannibals] when you left your country?' I myself had water rubbing my stomach. Were you not seized with fear when you left your country? Were you not much afraid? I was very frightened because I thought I would be taken by the *Bulgu*."

Describing his experience in the slave caravan he continues:

"I left the country with many Gallas. Many of us left the country, and we were very frightened. ... Whenever we ate, our stomach burnt with fire, for we were full of longing; we could not sit and we could not sleep. The sand burnt our feet."

Akafedé likewise declared that many of his compatriots could "do nothing but grieve at the separation from their fathers and mothers," and Aga agreed, observing poignantly "we have endured separation from our country, our mothers, our fathers, our brothers and our sisters."

Revulsion at the trade is likewise apparent in the attitude of an Oromo slave-girl on the way to the coast in the 1840's, who, when shown a Maria Theresa dollar by the Saint Simonians Combes and Tamisier, is said to have exclaimed, "It is that then which serves to buy children and men!"

The journey westwards to the Sudan was, it was generally agreed, significantly more arduous than those to the Red Sea or Gulf of Aden ports. Slaves travelling from Gondär to Khartoum, along a route largely bereft of water, are said by Plowden to have undergone "great hardship," and perished in numbers, while Beke states that

---

[8] Harris (1844) I, 233-4.

Šanqellas conveyed to the Sudan were sometimes shackled at night, so that they could only move about by taking short jumps with both feet together.[9]

The principle of slavery, which received recognition, as we have seen, in the *Fethä Nägäst*, was generally accepted by Ethiopian society of this period. The missionary Samuel Gobat recalls that while teaching at Gondär in 1830 he declared "among other things, that the same God who created us created the *Shangalas* (negroes), and that they are children of Adam as well as well as we." On hearing this revelation one of his young disciples struck his breast, and exclaimed, "What! the *Shangalas* then are our brethren! And why do we make slaves of them?"[10]

Household Servants

Household servants were by all accounts far less numerous than slaves, and for the most part no better remunerated, for they received little more than their subsistence, an occasional gift of clothes, and a very small number of *amolés*. Servants in Tegré, according to Pearce, were thus paid in salt, but were given the equivalent of only three Maria Theresa dollars a year besides their upkeep. This, the Englishman felt, was indeed the maximum they could judiciously be given, for, he declares: "I have often observed, that if through their faithfulness and attention the master may think fit to make them an addition to their pay, or any present, they become immediately ungovernable and insolent, the least indulgence spoiling them for good servants." When not so indulged they were, he says, "very submissive", and "never received anything from their master's hand without bowing and kissing the article."

Pearce's was of course an employers view - what the servants themselves felt is not recorded.[11]

---

[9] Combes and Tamisier (1838) IV, 95, 192; Pankhurst (1976a) 98-110; GB House of Commons (1868) 119.

[10] Gobat (1834) 239.

[11] Pearce (1831) I, 342.

X

WOMEN AND GENDER RELATIONS

Ethiopian women played an important role in economic, social and cultural life. Upon them, Henry Salt declared, devolved "most of the laborious occupations", including the grinding of corn and the carrying of fire-wood and water, as well as much cultivation, especially in weeding, reaping and winnowing. The country's womenfolk, who were, in Gobat's view, "far more active and industrious" than members of the opposite sex, were in fact prominent in agriculture, trade and handicrafts, as well as in the domestic field in general. Women were also active, as already noted, as potters and weavers.

Agriculture

Women were not involved in ploughing, which was exclusively carried out by men, but were much involved, as we have seen, in weeding, reaping and winowing. They thus helped their husbands, in the fields, Arnauld d'Abbadie, states, as far as their strength permitted. Weeding was in fact a family occupation, in which all members participated, and, because of the "great number of weeds," was, according to Salt, "one of the most irksome of toils." Women sometimes played a leading rôle in weeding, as at Degsa, in Tegré, where when the ploughing was completed, they broke the clods with rude hooked instruments, after which they "most carefully" picked out all weeds. If any still remained men, women, and children later assembled, when the grain was half ripe, and, forming a line, plucked out the weeds with singing and merriment.[1] Pearce, a decade or so later, confirms that both sexes were usually involved in the work, and declares:

> "The Abyssinians always help each other to weed their corn, which is done with great ceremony; a chief will muster every soldier in his service and march at the head of them to his corn-fields, there they lay down their arms, form a line, join in chorus to sing, and, in general led by a female, march on plucking up the weeds. In this way they soon get through a number of fields, throwing the weeds down as they pluck them, and leaving the farming-men, boys and girls, to carry them to the borders of the field."[2]

Women were no less prominent in reaping. Many of them were engaged in this work, as noted by Salt who recalls that they "uniformly greeted" his party with a "shrill cry", and "a quick and somewhat tremulous application of the tongue to the palate, producing the sound heli li li li li li li."

Women's participation in animal husbandry varied considerably from region to region. In Tegré it was "not customary," Pearce reports, for members of the female

---

[1] Gobat (1850) 192; Arnauld d' Abbadie (1980) 152; Valentia (1809) II, 506-7, III, 232.

[2] Pearce (1831) I, 345-6.

A peasant woman from Agamé in Tegré. From T. Lefebvre and others, *Voyage en Abyssinie* (Paris, 1845-8).

sex to milk cows or goats, and "in most parts it would be considered a great disgrace for them to do so." Women in the "southernmost districts of Amhara," however, were sometimes engaged in milking, having apparently been taught this skill by their Galla, or Oromo, sisters who were said to "attend more to the cattle than the men." This statement is confirmed by Krapf who observes that, among Oromo agriculturalists, "the men plough, sow, and reap, while the women look after the oxen, cows, horses, sheep, and goats."[3]

Land-Ownership

Ethiopian noblewomen, as revealed in manuscript marginalia for the reign of the puppet Emperor Sahlu (1832-1844), continued to own land and be involved in land transactions. One of the documents of this time records for example that a certain Wäyzäro Mehrak purchased four pieces of land from a priest, Abba Nob, for six Maria Theresa dollars, while other texts tell of various transactions involving one Wäyzäro Tebläts whom we find buying land from her brother Lej Čuffa and an unspecified vendor, for one or two dollars, selling land to two clerics, Memher Wäldä Mika'él and Däbtära Wäldä Giyorgis, for three dollars and 18 bars of salt respectively, and acting as a guarantor in other purchases and sales.[4]

Spinning

Women played a major role in the production of clothing, which was based on a rigid sexual division of labour in which they responsible for the first stages of the operation (cleaning cotton and spinning), while men monopolised the later phases of the work (weaving and tailoring).

Spinning-women cleaned the cotton with the help of two implements: a twelve inch long iron rod one inch wide in the centre which tapered towards the extremities, and a flat stone slightly larger than a brick. The woman, holding the rod in her hands, would kneel in front of the stone, on the nearest extremity of which she would place a small quantity of cotton seeds. She would then roll the rod backwards and forwards over the stone to free the cotton fluff from the seeds which were at the same time gradually forced backwards off the stone. The fluff was then collected and placed on a hide, and cleaned of dust and other extraneous matter. The next operation was carried out with the aid of four other artifacts: a bow made of catgut, a gourd, a basket, and a leather bag. The spinner, still kneeling, held the bow in her left hand above the cotton in such a way that it just touched the topmost fibres, while with her right hand she held the curved neck of the gourd with which she twanged away at the bow. Each vibration of the string threw up some of the lighter filaments, while the heavier matter sank to the bottom. The fine cotton thus separated was then deposited in the basket, after which it was taken out, and twisted around the rod. The latter was subsequently withdrawn, leaving the cotton in twisted knots, six or seven of which were then folded together and put into the bag.

---

[3] Valentia (1809) III, 232; Pearce (1831) II, 8; Krapf (1867) 75.

[4] B.L. Orient 636; Or. 518, f. 171. See also Arnauld d' Abbadie (1868) 128.

A woman spinning. Note bobbin in her right hand. From S.F. Veitch, *Views in Central Abyssinia* (London, 1868).

The scene was thus set for the actual spinning operation which was carried out with a small reed, perhaps 20 cm. long, in many cases tipped with horn or ivory. The spinner, holding the cotton in her left hand, lifted it to its furthest extent, while with her right she rotated the reed on her bare thigh. The thickness of the thread depended on the speed with which the cotton was drawn out. A hard-working woman toiling full-time, might spin enough cotton in a month for a *šämma*, and could in this way earn, Rüppell learnt, about ten Maria Theresa dollars a year. A housewife, with other duties, would, however, spin much more slowly, the work probably taking three or four months. No woman moreover span all the time, and the operation, like most other work, was not carried out on the Sabbath as Gobat explains.

Spinning, though some might think tedious, was considered an honourable occupation. Well-to-do women, according to Arnauld d'Abbadie, would spend much of their time spinning the thread required for their husband or children's clothes, and "ladies of the higher class," Parkyns says, "seldom" employed themselves in any manual operation "except spinning." This tradition continued into the twentieth century when princesses and noble ladies considered spinning a pastime, and Empress Taytu was proud of her reputation as a spinner.[5]

Wood and Water-Carrying

Women were the principal gatherers, and carriers, of both fire-wood and water. Wood was collected by young girls, who would leave home at daylight, Pearce says, with a cake of bread as their sole sustenance, and return only at dark. Their work was not without its dangers. One evening after dark at Adwa the girls, he recalls, were just about to enter the town with their loads of wood, and were forming themselves into parties, to come back singing, when there was a great disturbance among them. Several were screaming violently, and, on running to see what was the matter, he found that the nose and eyes of the last girl in the line, who was scarcely more than a child, had been torn away by a hyena.

Many women, of all ages, were likewise engaged in the transportation of water which they carried on their backs in large earthenware jars. Pearce, who declared it "almost incredible what a weight of water" a woman could carry, reports: "A young girl, not more than twelve years of age, will carry to a great distance a jar of water, which a strong man could with difficulty lift from the ground." Explaining how this was done he continues, "They fill the jar on the bank of the river or spring, as the elevation enables them to get it more easily on the back; a leather strap passes from the neck of the jar round the breast and below the shoulders, and, stooping as they go, they will carry it, though at a slow pace, a long way even up steep roads."[6]

Trade

Men and women were both involved in trade, but there was some division of labour between them. Men, Gobat notes, thus "seldom" trafficked in cotton, or "women in meat." Moreover though there were market-vendors of both sexes, itinerant traders were exclusively male. Women, on the other hand, were the principal vendors of eggs, poultry, grain and other farm produce. Trade in these articles was a time-consuming, if not tedious, affair. Saleswomen at the great Šäwan market of Aleyu Amba for example would, as we have seen, sit "for the whole day," Johnston notes, beside "very limited stores" which they sought to exchange for grain. The goods they exposed for sale would consist of "a thimbleful" of *kohl*, or antimony for blackening the eyes, a "few lumps" of gum myrrh, a "handful" of frankincense, a few imported

[5] Johnston (1844) II, 29, 314; Combes and Tamisier (1838) III, 65; Parkyns (1853) II, 40-1: Gobat (1850) 192; Rüppell (1838-40) II, 224; Arnauld d' Abbadie (1980) 152; Mérab (1921-9) III, 407.

[6] Pearce (1831) II, 7, 206-7; Rüppell (1868-40) II, 194; Plowden (1868) 235, 373; Combes and Tamisier (1838) I, 260.

blue and red threads for weaving ornamental borders of *šämmas*, and sometimes "three or four lemons, or as many needles."

Women were no less in evidence at Adwa market where De Cosson later saw "a group of tawny maidens, with necklaces of blue beads, and leopard skins around their loins, sitting beside the large baskets of Indian corn, lentils, *téf*, and other kinds of grain," which they had carried in on their heads over-night.

Women made their way to market even during periods of political turmoil or warfare. The women of Jemma and Horro for example are said by Plowden to have attended the markets of Gudru without molestation even in times of conflict, and, when passing between inimical tribes, would send messages in advance to ensure that they were received in friendship.

In the markets of Tegré and the north women were also responsible, as in Alvares's day, for the measuring of grain, and employed servants with measuring containers for this purpose. For every basket they measured, Pearce reports, they collected about half a pint of corn called a *dergo*. Anyone in favour with the lady in office, on sending their servant to her, would have the grain they wished to buy measured in a larger container than that in general use. No one dared object to its use as it was called the government measure. One such woman official was a certain Wäyzäro Ṣegé who held sway at Adwa for "many" market days. "Persons going to market were likewise often subject to a tax exacted by the governor's cook, who, as at Gondär, was a woman of some power, for she collected "small duties on all butter, pepper, onions, wood etc. ... not according to a regular standard, but as she might think proper in her mercy towards the poor peasants."[7]

Grinding of Grain, Preparation of Alcoholic Drinks, Cooking and Banquets

Women had sole responsibility for working in the home. They ground the grain, prepared both *täj*, or mead, and *tälla*, or beer, collected herbs and spices for the daily repast, and, as Pearce says, did "all the cooking." Women's involvement in such activity was so culturally ingrained that men would starve, Plowden believed, "rather than do this work."

Women spent much time, and effort, as in the past, in grinding. This was often carried out on hand-mills which consisted, Johnston says, of "a large flat stone of cellula lava, two feet long and one foot broad, raised upon a rude pedestal of stones and mud, about one foot and half from the ground." The rough surface of this stone sloped gradually forwards into "a basin-like cavity," into which the flour fell as it was ground. A second stone, which weighed about three pounds, would be grasped in the hand of grinding-women who would move it up and down the inclined stone, thereby crushing the grain and gradually converting it into coarse flour. "Very few houses," and "those only of the poorest people," Johnston recalls, had but one such mill. Most families had two or more which stood side by side, and the numbers of mills a person had was often mentioned as a way of conveying an idea of his wealth, and the size of the retinue to be fed. Grinding, like spinning, was never conducted on the Sabbath.

---

[7] Gobat (1850) 476; Harris (1844) I, 383; Johnston (1844) II, 238; De Cosson (1877) I, 111; Plowden (1868) 310; Pearce (1838) II, 12, 17.

A woman's kitchen yard at Adwa. Note pestel and mortar, large pots, perhaps for containing *tālla*, a local beer, and some poultry. From M. Parkyns, *Life in Abyssinia* (London, 1853).

An important household institution over which women presided was the family granary, upon which the household depended throughout the greater part of the year. Often placed beside the grinding-mill it might occupy half the room. The contraption often consisted of a raised platform of stones and clay about two feet high on which stood what Johnston described as "a huge butt-like basket, smoothly plastered over inside and out with clay." This container was able to preserve the family's *téf*, wheat or other grain from the depredations of mice, "a thorough pest," throughout the year.

The major rôle of women in looking after the family's grain - and their difficulties with rodents - found expression in an Ethiopian folktale about a woman servant employed by a rich man to guard his grain - which she did with the help of a cat. The woman, dissatisfied with her pay, one day resigned, but when she handed over the grain entrusted to her care it transpired that fourteen *dawullas*, i.e. about 1,400 kilos, were missing. Her employer, angered, took her to the elders, and demanded that

A woman, with her baby tied to her back, grinds grain. Note storage vessels pots and baskets. From R. Acton, *The Abyssinian Expedition* (London; 1868).

she should return to him the full amount of grain. She replied that there was "no deficit," for the rats had eaten seven *dawulla*, and she had used the other seven to make soup for the cats. Her defence was, however, rejected by the elders who declared, in a famous judgement, "The moment that cats do not guard against rats one stops their food."

The kitchen, in which women spent much of the day, cooking and preparing food and drink, was either part of the main house, or, as often in Tegré, a small separate structure which, as Parkyns notes, was often full of smoke. The cooking women, who never stood up to do their work, "squatted as low as possible, either near the door or fire," while every article in the room became soot black.

Despite their important rôle in the preparation of food and drink women were often accorded an only subordinate position in State banquets. Such gatherings were often sexually segregated. Gobat states that in the houses of governors, and sometimes even in those of private families when numerous guests were invited, it was customary for "males and females to take their repast in separate apartments." Where this was not convenient, curtains would often be suspended between the sexes, "so as entirely to exclude them from the view of each other." As a result of this segregation women were excluded from many important State receptions. Plowden in the middle of the century went so far as to observe that women were "never admitted" as guests, and that their participation in feasts, as reported by Bruce a century earlier, was a thing of the past.

At ordinary meals, however, husband and wife "usually" sat "side by side," Gobat reports, and would introduce rolls of *enjära* and *wät* "reciprocally, and at the same time into each other's mouth." When this was not the case, and each served himself or herself, it was a sign that they were not on good terms.[8]

Clothes-Washing

Notwithstanding their overriding involvement in household chores women participated only to very limited extent in the washing of clothes, perhaps because this was generally carried out in streams or rivers often at some distance from the home. According to Pearce, they "never" undertook such work, which was considered "improper for them," and was therefore "appropriated by the men." The only exception, as noted by Gobat, arose in the case of women's own garments which they chose to wash for themselves.[9]

---

[8] Valentia (1809) II, 506; Pearce (1831) I, 347; Gobat (1850) 192, 474, 476; Isenberg and Krapf (1843) 188; Krapf (1867) 75; Rüppell (1838-40) II, 194; Johnston (1944) II, 27-8; Moreno (1948) 39-40; Parkyns (1853) I, 363; Plowden (1868) 185, 383. For other descriptions of banquets see Plowden 211-3, 241-2.

[9] Pearce (1831) II, 7; Gobat (1850) 476.

A finely-dressed noblewoman, reposing on her *alga*, or bed, and her more scantily clad slave-girl, with her hand on the large pot in which she perhaps carried the family's water. From T. Lefebvre and others, *Voyage en Abyssinie* (Paris, 1845-8).

Slaves, and Servants

Innumerable women served throughout the country as slaves or household servants. Slave-owning in the early nineteenth century was widespread, and most well-to-do families, according to Rüppell, would, as we have seen, have several slaves, male and female, engaged in household chores. Among the rich the mistress of the house would spend much of her time, Arnauld d'Abbadie notes, lying on an *alga*, or bed, and perhaps spinning, while she directed the work of her many servants or slaves.

Slave women were mainly employed in carrying water or fire-wood, and in the grinding of grain, for their mistress herself did most if not all the cooking. Slave women, however, also served the food and drink.

Many slave women were to be found at royal palaces. "Several hundreds of slaves, particularly females," Krapf records,were employed in each of Sahlä Sellasé's residences, at Ankobär, Angoläla, Däbrä Berhan and Qundi. The king's "household slaves, male and female," were said by Harris to have exceeded "eight thousand." Such women slaves were occupied in most of the duties which normally befell their sex, notably water-carrying, grinding of grain, the preparation of food and drink, and serving at table. Johnston judged that about two hundred slave women at Ankobär were engaged in supplying the king's household with water, and "at least" a hundred more in grinding flour, brewing alcoholic drinks, and making pepper sauce. Krapf's estimate of the size of the palace staff was substantially higher. The King's grinding-women, he wrote, were "three hundred in number," and the "water girls," who carried "all the necessary water for the King's household" and for foreigners maintained by the monarch, were "more than that in number." There were, he thought, also at least "two hundred" cooks, besides "some hundreds" of women preparing mead and beer, so that the total number of Sahlä Sellasé's "female-slaves" was in excess of a thousand.

The women slaves at Ankobär caught the attention of several foreign visitors. Johnston, who has left a vivid description of the drawers of water, tells of a "noisy crowd of chatting, romping girls, with large jars slung between their shoulders by a leather belt, or rope ... across the breast." These "water-girls", he explains: "were the slaves of the Negoos, and their chief employment consisted of this daily duty of carrying water from the stream to the palace at the summit of the hill ... they supply all water required for the use of the courtiers and guests, beside a body-guard of three hundred gunmen, all of whom are daily fed at the royal table."[10] "The slave women engaged in cooking, preparing alcoholic and non-alcoholic drinks and other domestic chores, were likewise described by the inimitable Captain Harris. Writing of the "daily labours" at Ankobär of "three thousand slaves" and their supervision by a palace eunuch, he observes:

"In one quarter are to be seen groups of busy females, engaged in the manufacture of bees [i.e. *berz*, an unfermented honey drink] and hydromel. Flat cakes of teff and wheat are preparing by the hundred under the next roof, and from the dark recesses of the building arises the plaintiff ditty of those who grind the corn by the sweat of their brow. Here caldrons of

---

[10] Arnauld d' Abbadie (1980) 152; Rüppell (1838-40) II, 194; Plowden (1868) 212; Isenberg and Krapf (1843) 120; Harris (1844) III, 306; Johnston (1844) II, 79.

red pepper soup yield up their potent steam; and in the adjacent compartment, long twisted strips of old cotton rag are being dipped into a sea of molten bees' wax. Throughout the female establishment the bloated and cross-grained eunuch presides; and his unsparing rod instructs his loquacious and giggling charge that they are not there to gaze at the passing stranger."[11]

There were also at the palace, it was said, numerous concubines: two hundred on Johnston's estimate, and three hundred on that of Harris. These women, according to the former observer, were "kept in the strictest seclusion," under the supervision of several eunuchs. Though described by foreign observers as "concubines" they had in fact other functions, for they were responsible, Johnston states, for spinning "the more elaborately-spun cotton thread ... used for the finer descriptions of cloths, which are presented by the Negoos to his greatest favourites and governors."

The spinning women at the palace were, as earlier noted, of two distinct categories. The first, who, according to Krapf, numbered two hundred, produced thread for the "finer cloth" which the King himself wore, or presented to his friends and favourites, while the second, about four hundred strong, turned out poorer quality thread for the clothing of the ordinary soldiers. Both categories of spinners, he believed, seemed in fact to be "free" women rather than slaves.

The palace of Sahlä Sellasé's mother, Zänäbä Wärq, resembled that of her son, but on a smaller scale, and, according to Krapf, likewise housed "a great number of female servants, mostly slave girls."[12]

Camp-Followers

Women in the early nineteenth century continued to play a by no means insignificant rôle in warfare. They often called their menfolk to arms, accompanied them to battle, and incited them to fight with valour. Women, who, as we have seen, had long constituted a larger proportion than men of the camp-followers of most armies, had in fact major duties and responsibilities in the camp and on the march, as well as in battle.

The encouragement given by women to the soldiers in the civil wars of the early nineteenth century is recalled by Pearce who states that Ras Wäldä Sellasé's camps in Tegré were "full" of Amhara women. Composed of "gangs" of girls in one, and grown women in the other, they sang to the sound of a drum, which a woman carried slung with a string about the neck, and beat at both ends. The ditty contained the following words: "Give the Badinsah [i.e. Ras Wäldä Sellasé] breeches, and he is a lion: where is the man that will dare to hold his shield to him?" The phrase "give him breeches" meant "get the chief up, dressed and ready," while the reference to the shield implied that "no one dared face him."

---

[11] Harris (1844) II, 261.

[12] Johnston (1844) II, 79-80; Isenberg and Krapf (1843) 120, 292, 295.

Testimony to women's involvement in mobilisation is provided by Gobat who reports for example that when the news of Ras Webé's advance to Anṭalo reached them in February 1831 the women of the nearby villages "collected together every evening, to cry, at the highest pitch of their voices, 'To arms! To arms! Oubea is coming to destroy us!' The soldiers," we are told, "immediately rallied." Some months later the women were again heard on all sides crying, "To arms! to arms!"

In some parts of the north, notably Hamasén, women are reported by Pearce to have actually to "intermixed" with the soldiers when in battle. The women on such occasions would cry out, *Sellasé, Sellasé*, i.e.. "Trinity, Trinity!," and keep up this chant in a "very dismal tone," until the engagement was over, after which, if victorious, they changed their song to one of "rude merriment."[13]

Female participation in various aspects of camp life elsewhere in the northern provinces is also noted by Pearce who observes:

"Women of the lower class frequently go to camp with the soldiers, chiefly for the purpose of carrying jars of maize [i.e. *mes*, mead] or *tsug* [i.e. *suqo*, an alcoholic drink]. The great people have also their cook and her servants, who carry the cooking utensils and different articles of provisions, such as butter, and barley-meal, called *bosso* [*bässo*]. They have also, according to their wealth, from fifty to a hundred women called *gumbones* [i.e. carriers of *gämbos*, or jars], who carry jars of maize or *sowa* [i.e. *sewa*, or beer]. It is surprising how these poor creatures endure their labour, having to pass over mountains - and the worst roads, where at times they are obliged to crawl on their hands and feet up steep precipices, with jars on their backs, yet they are seldom known to break the jars."[14]

These women "always" kept together "in gangs," behind the main army, but before its main rear-guard.

The important rôle played by women on the march was later confirmed by Plowden, who, also writing of the north, states that they carried most of the "earthen vessels, for cooking and bread-baking, gourds for water, and grindstones," etc.

Women were no less prominent in Šäwa. Sahlä Sellasé's army was thus accompanied, according to Harris, by a colourful band of "forty dames and damsels, professing the culinary art." Muffled in "crimson-striped robes of cotton," they had "elaborately-crisped bee-hive wigs, greased faces bedaubed with ochre, and arched blue eye-brows." This "demure assemblage" was "rigorously guarded on all sides by austere eunuchs armed with long white wands," and was accorded an honoured position in the line of march, immediately behind the fusiliers. The women cooks were so highly regarded that they were often the first to decide where the army should halt - and on which spot they should "pursue the important avocations of their calling." The Šäwan army also had "throngs of women carrying pitchers of beer and hydromel on their backs."

---

[13] Pearce (1831) I, 236, II, 6-7; Gobat (1850) 397, 417.

[14] Pearce (1831) II, 6.

Observers varied in their assessment of the camp-followers' lot. Combes and Tamisier wrote with admiration of these women who accompanied the soldiers, and who, despite the hard work to which they were condemned, "lived a happy life," often singing, without a worry about the dangers of war to which their male companions were exposed. The ever-critical Stern, on the other hand, argued that camp-followers, "burdened with heavy loads, and ready to drop from incessant fatigue," were "poor things", albeit, he concedes, "unconscious of their degradation and misery who "voluntarily chose" their "wretched existence" in preference to what he romantically describes as "the healthy lot of the peasant, and a quiet and virtuous life in the mountain-hut."

At the successful conclusion of a battle, women were once more to the fore. On hearing of the victory, or on catching a glimpse of their chief or leader, they would ululate, and sing loud traditional songs of praise.[15]

Prostitutes or Courtesans

Prostitutes or courtesans, whose profession was considered entirely natural, and suffered little or no disapprobrium, were to be found in most towns and military camps. Gondär, the capital, was described by Combes and Tamisier (who had an eye for such matters) as "a town of pleasures" which "abounded in courtesans." These women, according to Ferret and Galinier, displayed "distinction and elegance of manners," and were "not despised in the capital of Abyssinia like those in our countries of Europe," for "nothing shameful or degrading" was associated with their occupation.

Däbrä Tabor, the principal settlement in Bägémder, was likewise referred to, by Combes and Tamisier, as "a town of joy," whose population, composed largely of pleasure-seeking soldiers, attracted "a large concourse of dancers and courtesans" from near and far. "All adorned with jewels," their profession was "as lucrative for them" as it was "agreeable to others."

Däjazmač Webé's camp in Tegré was similarly inhabited by numerous courtesans who amazed Combes and Tamisier by their beauty, sumptuous clothing, and fine jewellery.[16]

Poets, and Minstrels

The country's minstrels, who roamed the land, included a fair number of women, some of whom acquired considerable reputations for their versification and their wit. Many women thus earned a living by making rhymes and attending funeral lamentations. Often travelling immense distances to attend one for a person of distinction, they would be rewarded, according to Pearce, by sizeable quantities of

---

[15] Plowden (1868) 215; Harris (1844) II, 168-70, 182; Combes and Tamisier (1838) I, 218; Stern (1862) 55; Pearce (1831) I, 264; Harris (1844) II, 205.

[16] Combes and Tamisier (1838) I, 236, II, 61-2, 119, III, 342; Ferret and Galinier (1847) II, 227-30, 241-2.

grain, cattle and cloth. The "best poet" in the country, in his day, was in fact a middle-aged woman called Wällätä Iyäsus. Born at Gondär, and the daughter of a man from Tegré, she had studied poetry from infancy, and, though in possession of a large estate, attended all mourning ceremonies at Adwa "for no other purpose than to distinguish herself." Many "great men" were said to have asked for her hand in marriage, but she could never be persuaded to accept any of their proposals.

Songs in praise of valour were also often composed by young women and girls who used them, Pearce says, to signal "their esteem or contempt for one person more than another." A chief and his soldiers would be "obliged to listen" to these compositions "without shewing their anger," for it would "only make matters worse to fall out with the women." The only way to put an end to such songs was to be generous and give a cow to each of them. "On all great holidays," Pearce explains, the women would "go to the premises of different chiefs there to sing in praise of each," until he "gave them a cow," but, if he did not, "the song would be changed to one of abuse or ridicule," and "if a chief had ever done anything to the prejudice of his character, such as shewing symptoms of cowardice," the women would "make it the subject of a song which they would sing over and over again," perhaps "for days on end." Should he have "no blemish on his character" they would nevertheless "criticise him for his stinginess," and he would be "obliged to bear it with patience," or "comply with their demands." If he paid them no attention they might, to the general derision, even stage a sham mourning ceremony for him. Although he might "order his soldiers to beat them away, that would only make things worse," as they would get their own back on the soldiers, by saying, "You can fight with women, but are afraid to meet your own sex." Very few chiefs therefore had the courage to deny the women their demands. Even in the case of an ordinary soldier who had killed a lion, elephant, wild buffalo or human enemy, the young girls of the town would plague his master until he perhaps gave them a cow.

The existence of such practices was later confirmed by Plowden who states that when at Fitawrari for example arrived in camp with the tusks of an elephant he had killed, the women were "thrown into an ecstasy of delight." The death of an enemy, or elephant, justified "a week's song and merry making," and the bearers of the *täj*, and the cooks, together comprising perhaps 150 women, obtained "no small profit, as well as pleasure," for the slayer, as well as all other men or rank, were obliged to "bestow on them bullocks, dollars, etc. under pain of a fearful castigation in their songs, and consequently becoming a laughing stock throughout the country." Songs adapted to passing events, and often "earthy and apt" were "dreaded as much as the lash of the chiefs." Singing for the killing of an elephant might be carried on by the women "night and day," while the men looked on, and jokes were "the order of the day."

Women singers were in many cases attached to a particular chief, and were well remunerated. This was particularly the case, Plowden says, in Wärra Himäno and Yäjju, where they were "exceedingly prized," as their praise or blame could make or mar a reputation. Female songsters were also prominent in Šäwa where Krapf describes them "singing hymns in praise of the King."

Women singers, and dancers, were much in evidence at the principal religious festivals. On Christmas day for example they made merry, Pearce recalls, "composing and singing silly verses," while at Easter Combes and Tamisier tell of "many dancing women" running through the roads of Däbrä Tabor, and stopping in front of important houses where they executed their pantomimes, and never left without receiving their wages in food or more often in drink. Songs were often sung by a woman to the accompaniment of a drum, while her companions, grouped in a circle around her, delivered a quickly repeated chorus, often longer than the song itself. They also clapped their hands, and uttered occasional shrill cries, while rhythmically swaying their bodies and jerking their necks to the beat of the music.[17]

Churches, and Church Ceremonial

Though barred from the priesthood, and from the vicinity of several monasteries which dated back to antiquity, women at times played a notable rôle in church ceremonial. Outside the church of Abba Gärima near Aksum, for example, Pearce saw "thousands of women" gathered to celebrate an annual festival. While the priests performed their rites, these women filled the air with their shouting, and "gangs of young girls" danced and sung energetically to the beat of a drum.[18]

Sorcerers, Prophets and Spirit Possession

Women, no less than men, in some instances acquired great reputations as sorcerers and prophets. In early nineteenth century Gondär for example the "queen of the boudas or sorcerers" was, according to Gobat, a Fälaša woman. The influence of a woman prophet at Adwa was noted at about the same time by Pearce who recalls that on one memorable occasion "all the townspeople" formed themselves into large parties, and posted themselves on the outskirts of the city where they called incessantly for Christ's forgiveness. The alarm had been created, it transpired by a "great poetess" and professed interpreter of dreams who claimed that she had dreamt that the town would be attacked by three chiefs, and that many people would die unless the whole population, great and small, prayed to God for three days.

Women, by all accounts, often suffered from various mental disturbances and epileptic fits. A typical case reported by Gobat was that of a young woman of his acquaintance who was "suddenly seized with a kind of spasms, or convulsion fits," as a result of which "she almost instantly lost her reason, and, besides the agitation that shook her limbs, she uttered frightful cries, which strikingly resembled the howlings of the hyena. This circumstance led the bystanders to conclude that she was under the influence of *boudas*, or sorcerers." Several other cases of spirit possession, real or supposed, were recorded in some clinical detail by Mansfield Parkyns. One related to a servant-woman at Rohabayta who complained of general languor and a heavy feeling about the head. This later seemed to increase, whereupon "she cried a little, but was perfectly reasonable, and excused herself by saying that it was only because she felt low and melancholy." Later, however, she "burst into hysterical laughter, and complained of a violent pain in the stomach and bowls." It was at that stage that people began to suspect that she was under the influence of a *buda*. She shortly

---

[17] Pearce (1831) I, 195, II, 224-5; Plowden (1868) 215-6, 407; Isenberg and Krapf (1843) 188, 212; Combes and Tamisier (1838) II, 19, 61.

[18] Pearce (1831) II, 243-4.

afterwards became quiet, and "by degrees sank into a state of lethargy, approaching to insensibility." Her companions tried to wake her by pinching her repeatedly, but "pinch as hard as we could," Parkyns recalls, "she never moved a muscle of her face, nor did she otherwise express the least sensation." His application of strong smelling salts was no less effective. All the time she held her thumbs tightly bent inside her hands. She did this because the thumbs were said to belong to the *buda* who would "allow no person to take them." Several people in consequence tried to open her hand to get at them, but she resisted with "wonderful strength for a girl," and bit their fingers till she in more than one instance drew blood. Parkyns later deluged her with bucketfuls of water, but "could not even elicit from her a start or a pant." At night she became restless, and spoke several times, both in a strange tone and in her normal voice. Later that night a hyena was heard howling nearby, whereupon, though tied hand and foot, she rose, freed herself from her bonds, and crept on all-fours towards the door, but, prevented from leaving, groaned for hours. On the morrow she appeared a little better, and talked more rationally, though still wildly, and would neither eat nor drink. The following day she consented to eat a little bread, but was immediately sick. A better night, however, did her some good, and by slow degrees she regained her health.

Though often afflicted from *budas* women, if we can extrapolate from later evidence, probably also played a major rôle in the treatment of persons deemed affected by such spirits, as well by the "evil eye" in general. A list of medical and other practitioners at Gondär completed in 1932 records the existence of no less than fourteen women claiming to treat persons so possessed. Reference is also made to a woman who carried out circumcision, and five others who dealt with such varied medical problems as difficult births, jaundice, neuralgia, fainting and poisonings.[19]

Marriage, Concubinage and Divorce

Marriages, like so many other practices, were subject to considerable regional variation. Weddings in the north generally took place, according to Pearce, when the bride was "incredibly young." Parkyns agrees that they were contracted "at a very early age," and states that he had seen brides no more than "eight or nine years old." Though rich Amharas thus often gave away their daughters in marriage before they were nubile, the Oromos, according to Arnauld d'Abbadie, by contrast married only at the age fixed by nature.

Most marriages were arranged by the couple's parents, largely for their own interest, with little or no attention to the future wife's - or in many cases even the future husband's - wishes. Chiefs or well-to-do farmers, when seeking to marry their daughters, would thus "look for some person's son of the same station as themselves," and "all great men" strove to increase their influence, Pearce says, "by giving their daughters to the sons of powerful chiefs, and engaging the daughters of other chiefs for their sons." A person of substance would moreover "never give two daughters to men of one district," but, on the contrary, preferred to enter into conjugal ties with those from districts furthest from their own, "for, if he were to give and take daughters from his neighbours only, he would have no more connections than he formerly had,

---

[19] Gobat (1850) 261, 329; Pearce (1831) II, 154; Parkyns (1853) I, 146-9; Antoine d'Abbadie (n.d.) 703; Rodinson (1967) 78-106.

as the true natives of every district consider themselves by birth attached to each other's cause."

To get their daughter-married it was common practice for Amhara and Tegré parents to "plait her hair very neat," blacken her eyes with *kohl*, or antimony, and dye her hands with a dark red dye. She would then be "placed constantly at the door" of the house, either spinning or cleaning corn, so that everyone who passed might behold her. She would be taught by her mother to turn up the whites of her eyes whenever young men or strangers passed, and to "put on a smiling look, between modesty and bravery when answering their questions." If any man took a liking to her, be he young or old, he would either go or send to the mother, or any other relation of the girl, and ask for her. To satisfy himself about her character and qualities he might also send a female acquaintance to inspect her. The mother would then demand a dowry, which might be a dress, consisting of a cotton skirt and a piece of cloth, together costing not more than five Maria Theresa dollars. The bride-to-be would at the same time agree to work in her husband's house, but, if the family could afford it, would be allowed a servant or slave to fetch wood and water, and do other drudgery.

An alternative scenario took place, Parkyns explains, when it was a lad who wished to marry. He would inquire for a suitable girl, preferably one who possessed "twice the number of oxen" he could muster, or their value. His proposals were then made to the girl's father, and: "unless there is some strong motive for rejecting him, he is accepted, and everything is arranged without consulting the lady's taste or asking her consent. They are usually betrothed three or four months before marriage, during which time the bridegroom frequently visits his father-in-law elect, and occasionally propitiates him with presents of honey, butter, a sheep, or a goat, but he is never allowed to see his intended wife for a moment, unless, by urgent entreaty or a handsome bribe, he induces some female friend of hers to arrange the matter, by procuring him a glance... For this purpose he conceals himself behind a door or other convenient hiding-place, while the lady, on some pretext or other, is led past it. Should she, however, suspect a trick, and discover him, she would make a great uproar, cover her face, and screaming, run away and hide herself, as though her sense of propriety were greatly offended by the intrusion; although previous to his making the offer she would have thought it no harm to romp with him, or any other male acquaintance, in the most free and easy manner. Even after she has been betrothed, she is at home to every-one except to him." When the wedding-day approached the bride-to-be would be "well-washed, her hair combed and tressed." She was thus "rendered in every way as agreeable as possible" to her husband.

Marriages were essentially secular, for, as Pearce observes: "No marriages are performed in churches, or by the interference of a priest. A man may have as many wives as he chooses, if he does not think it prudent to be attached to one, which is seldom the case." The result, Combes and Tamisier claim, was that "nothing" was "more simple" in Ethiopia than the union of the sexes.

Despite the Church's insistence on monogamy, concubinage among the higher aristocracy, was, according to Krapf, also "habitual and general." Sahlä Sellasé, he said, led the way with a "bad example," for "whenever a beautiful woman was pointed out to him he sent for her." The daughters of many grandees were likewise used "to effect political alliances," and the King for a time "even wished for an English princess to consolidate his alliance with Great Britain." Though the idea may have raised eyebrows among the good missionary's readers in England the King was perhaps not unaware that their monarch, Queen Victoria, was in fact arranging dynastic marriages for her family throughout Christian Europe.

Marriages, in the nineteenth century, as earlier, were for one reason or another, often unstable. One of many causes of marital break-down arose from the reappointment, or transfer, Pearce notes, of provincial officials. An officer, when dismissed, was often "obliged to fly to another district for refuge, leaving his wife and children, if he has any, in her native place." The result was that she would "soon get another husband," while her last, if he prospered, would "marry another wife."

Such practices were, however, opposed by the Church - so much so indeed that Gobat goes so far as to claim that Ethiopians "after a third divorce" could neither "contract a regular marriage" nor "partake of the symbols of the sacramental supper" unless they consented to "embrace the life, and perform the duties of monks". The above observations are echoed by Combes and Tamisier who assert that men or women were permitted to divorce "up to three times", but could not do so more than that "on pain of being excluded from Communion." A man who had divorced his third wife, and wished to obtain "the privileges of holy communion," might therefore reconcile himself with one of his former wives, Gobat says, after which the reunited couple would "live together for the remainder of their days." None of these statements are confirmed by later writers, but, in view of the missionary's by no means superficial knowledge of the Ethiopian scene, cannot fully be discounted.

Despite the prevalence of divorce it was also not uncommon for elderly couples who had been together for many years to enter into indissoluble bonds: "When a man and woman imagine they can be content with each other, and live together a religious life," Pearce explains: "they agree in the presence of the elders of the town, or district, called *shummergildas* [i.e. *šemagellé*, or elders] to put whatever property they may have together, which property is considered to belong to them both, and the one cannot dispose of any part of it without the approbation of the other. Then they swear, in the presence of the *shummergildas*, to be mutually faithful, and to take the holy sacrament together frequently and on holy days; after which they go to church, to make a confession, and the sacrament is administered to them for the first time."

Though such marriages were supposed to be permanent Pearce claims that adultery, or suspected adultery, was not uncommon. In such cases the accused party was taken before the elders who, if the crime was proved, consulted together and passed what sentence they thought fit, according to the nature of the offence. If, after that, the couple wished to remain together - which was often the case - the offender was obliged to part with his or her property which was given to the offended party as a penalty, to be at his or her disposal. If, on the other hand, the complainant insisted on being parted, the offender had to forfeit half his or her property. If they had children these were divided, according to the sentence of the elders. When there was a boy and a girl the former was in general taken by the father, and the latter by the mother. On one occasion he saw there was a dispute about the custody of a girl, and the parents drew lots. The elders presented the contestants with two sticks which a stranger then rolled in his hand, and finally threw one down, saying, "In the name of

God this is the owner" - whereupon the parent thanked God, and the successful one took away the child.[20]

Childbirth, Ritualistic Impurity, and Motherhood

Before giving birth an expectant mother would grind grain into flour to make a kind of porridge which she would eat in the period after her delivery. Later, in the last stages of her pregnancy, she would be attended by all her female friends and neighbours. Men at this time were rigidly excluded, in part because their presence at that time was considered improper, and in part "because the room, and everything in it" was "considered utterly unclean." A man who entered at that time, Parkyns says, would indeed be "refused admittance to the church for forty days."

Immediately prior to giving birth the woman would seat herself nearly upright on two stones a little separated from each other. A female friend then supported her, holding her shoulders, and constantly calling on the Holy Virgin to provide her assistance. The patient's feet were propped up on a chair or table, and held there by another woman who occasionally rubbed her feet and the calves of her legs which she placed an angle of about eighty degrees with her body. As soon as the shoulders of the child appeared the delivery was assisted by the women, and the infant was received into a flat wicker basket filled with flour. The infant was then at once washed in cold water and perfumed, after which a woman moulded the head and its various features were shaped by pressing them with her fingers, while a man poked a lance into his mouth, if a boy, to make him courageous. This was done through a window, to avoid entering the supposedly poluted chamber. It was also customary at this time for a young boy to cut the throat of a fowl in front of the new-born babe, while the womenfolk filled the air ritually with exultation, repeating their cries twelve times if the infant was male, or three times if female. The women then rushed forth, singing and dancing their jubilation.

Three days after the birth the mother's clothes were carried to a nearby river or stream to be washed, and on the eighth day the child, whether a boy or a girl, was circumcised. Some days later the house was visited, as we have seen, by priests with crosses and incense, who sprinkled it with holy water, thereby purifying it and all its inmates.

Women, in Christian societies, were not allowed to enter a church for forty days after childbirth. This bar was even more pronounced in the case of Fälašas and Qemants, both of whom kept special houses in which the women of their communities after giving birth were segregated.[21]

Women, it goes without saying, also devoted much of their time to child-bearing and motherhood - and would often be seen carrying children on their backs.[22]

---

[20] Pearce (1831) I, 283, 307-10, 314-6, II, 21; Parkyns (1853) II, 41-2; Antoine d'Abbadie (n.d.) 756; Arnauld d'Abbadie (1980) 147, 153; Krapf (1867) 41; Isenberg and Krapf (1843) 315; Gobat (1850) 451-2; Combes and Tamisier (1838) II, 105-6; Hyatt (1928), 224; Flad (1869) 55; Gamst (1969) 100.

[21] Parkyns (1831) II, 34-8.

[22] Valentia (1809) II, 506; Pankhurst and Ingrams (1988) 78, 111.

Social Life, Coquetry and Seclusion

Women's social life, like that of the menfolk, was enlivened by the activities they shared in associations, or *mähabärs*, which normally met, as we have seen, once a month on a particular Saint's day. These clubs generally consisted of twelve persons, but were sometimes more numerous. Women normally had their own *mähabärs*, entirely separate from the men's, though when a member of either sex could not attend a gathering a spouse might attend instead.[23]

Female coquetry, according to Pearce, was not uncommon. "Women of superior rank," he declares, were "fond of shewing themselves off." They might do so:

"either in attending church, or in paying or returning visits, on which occasions they are mounted on a mule, with a soldier on each side to steady them, and a whole train of spearsmen following behind, and a great number of their female attendants running in front. Whether the lady can read or not, she has two or three books carried before her, which are generally tied round the necks of young boys or girls smartly dressed. ... The ladies, when on their excursions, always keep the head and part of the face covered with the cloth they wear; when in church, their book is opened before them, and some one in favour turns over the leaves, as they pretend to read. Their eyes roll about on all sides, viewing those about them, though they never stare anyone in the face who looks at them. Whether going or coming, they take as roundabout and as public a way as possible, that everyone may see their grandeur. If on foot, their pace is very slow; indeed it would be scandalous to see a lady walk quick."[24]

Notwithstanding such practices Salt states that married women in Tegré, so far from enjoying the "free intercourse with males" earlier asserted by the at times not too reliable Bruce, were actually "watched with some caution by their husbands, and even occasionally secluded from male society." The existence of this latter practice was confirmed by Arnauld d'Abbadie who says that married women were "more or less rigidly" secluded. "Every lady of rank, after her marriage," Stern claims, was thus "closely watched by stern janitors when at home," and, when she rode outside her house was "enveloped and swathed in a suffocating quantity of white shamas and cotton belts." This sequestration, d'Abbadie believed, was not, however, resented by the women, who on the contrary regarded it as "a mark of honour and solicitude rather than of jealousy." As a proof of her affection for her husband a woman might in fact declare that there was no value in her being seen by the birds of the sky, nor even by the rays of the sun, but only by her spouse. Circumstances which allowed a married woman to appear in public with her face uncovered would be when there were mourning lamentations, above all for her husband, but also for her father, mother or very close relative.[25]

---

[23] Pearce (1831) II, 19.

[24] Pearce (1894) II, 194.

[25] Arnauld d' Abbadie (1980) 152; Stern (1852) 85; Girard (1873) 201-2.

Jewellery

Jewellery of one kind or another was worn by a large section of the femal population. The use of articles of gold was highly restricted, for the metal, as we hav seen, was the "exclusive privilege of royalty," and was forbidden to the population a large. Jewellery of silver (produced by the melting down of Maria Theresa dollars which were then coming into increasing circulation), brass and tin, as well as horn and ivory, was, however, widely worn.

Women in the north, according to Mansfield Parkyns, wore "a profusion of silver, in the shape of chains, bracelets, etc." A "well-dressed lady" thus often hung three or four sets of amulets around her neck, besides her blue cord, symbol of Christianity, and a "large flat silver case (purporting to contain a talisman, but more often some scented cotton) ornamented with a lot of little bells hanging to the bottom edge of it, ... the whole suspended by four chains of the same metal." Three pairs of "massive silver and gilt bracelets" often adorned her wrists, and a similar number of bangles her ankles, while over her insteps and heels were placed "a great quantity of little silver ornaments, strung like beads on a silk cord." Her fingers, and even their upper joints, might also be "covered with plain rings, often alternately of silver and silver-guilt," while a silver hair-pin would complete her decoration. This prevalence of jewellery was confirmed by Antoine d'Abbadie, one of whose women acquaintances wore three rings on each of her fingers, and two on both her thumbs. Women of the poorer class were also not without their jewellery, and, often, Parkyns says, wore "ivory or wooden pins neatly carved in various patterns, and stained red with henna-leaves." Such decorations were also worn on ordinary days by their more prosperous sisters. The women of Šäwa were likewise "exceedingly fond of silver ornaments," which, according to Johnston, often "constituted all their riches." Some silver earrings weighed as much as two or three ounces each, and almost invariably took the form of three large beads surmounted by a fourth, like a bunch of grapes.

Another ornament of silver which women of Šäwa often wore, upon their breasts, hanging from the neck by a chain of silver, was in the form of a clasp, three or four inches long, and one inch broad, upon the front surface of which a simple design in waving lines was not infrequently engraved. Bracelets of silver, according to Johnston, were also "sometimes seen." Those of Muslim women were "invariably of that metal," but Christian women generally wore plain ones, made of pewter, with anklets to match. The "silver bracelets of Islam" were different from those of the Christians in that they consisted of "two or three thick silver wires, twisted upon each other, and finished at each extremity by a beaten square bead." This artifact was "looped round the wrist" where it remained until required as a security for loans which, Johnston believed, was "the most important use" of silver articles amongst persons of both religious denominations.

Such Christian women as could afford to, also wore "large necklaces of beads," which were generally made of "a succession of hoops, consisting of seven or eight threads of different coloured seed beads, collected at certain lengths into one string, through a large angular-cut piece of amber. Eight or ten of these loops formed a long negligee, which, ornamented with a large tassel of small beads, was a present suited even for the acceptance of royalty." The Muslim women, on the other hand, wore a string of beads "formed of a hundred large and differently coloured beads," among which "bright red ones" seem to be preferred. They were "divided into lengths by the interposition of pieces of amber at least twice as long" as those worn by the Christians.

Horn earrings, in some instances ornamented with an inlaid star of silver, were also widely worn, particularly in Šäwa, the jewellery of which also included large tin bracelets, which were worn in pairs, as well as necklaces of glass beads. Many women, particularly in the northern highlands, also wore imported beads which, according to Salt, were used to decorate both their necks and their arms.

Ethiopian women, like those of many countries of the East, also often darkened their eyelids, as we have seen, with antimony, and also stained their hands and feet with henna. Some women likewise had themselves tatooed, but in Tegré, this was not common outside Adwa, and was, in Parkyns's opinion, "a fashion imported from Amhara." It was also not uncommon among noblewomen in some areas to allow the nails on their left hand to grow to a "great length", after which these were protected, Salt reports, by leather cases in some instances several inches long.[26]

Education, and Literacy

Church education, the only type of schooling traditionally available in the country, was largely closed to women, who were therefore for the most part illiterate. Not a few women nonetheless played an important rôle in state affairs - and a few seem to have succeeded to learn to read. Gobat tells of a "female of distinction" whom he met at Gondär, while Stern writes of a young "lettered female" of Bägémder, who "took an active part in the conversation".[27]

---

[26] Harris (1844) III, 33; Johnston (1844), II, 334-7; Parkyns (1853) II, 26-7, 29; Arnauld d'Abbadie (1980) 236; Antoine d'Abbadie (n.d.) 454; Rochet d'Hericourt (1841) 271; Valentia (1809) II, 506.

[27] Stern (1862) 245; Gobat (1850) 196.

PART FOUR

SOCIAL CHANGE AND ATTEMPTED REFORM

The church of St. Mary of Seyon at Aksum. From G. Valentia, *Voyages and Travels* (London, 1809).

I

SOME CHANGING FEATURES OF SOCIAL LIFE

Despite the elements of continuity in the half millennium or so covered by the present volume it would be a mistake to assume, as some have done, that the Ethiopian social scene was in some inexplicable manner fossilised, or that the country resembled a museum of unchanging old-time customs. It is on the contrary evident from the foregoing pages that the Ethiopian world was far from static. Changes in some areas, particularly those connected with the State, government and war, were so dramatic that they were obvious alike to contemporary observers and later historians. Change in other fields, on the other hand, was in some cases so gradual that it was often not apparent to any single generation, and was therefore scarcely, if at all, mentioned in chronicles or other contemporary writings. Some developments can in fact only be seen by examining the unfolding of events over a span of several centuries. To illustrate some of the long-term changes that were occurring throughout this period it may be convenient to recall the fluctuations that took place in the powers of the monarchy, and then focus attention on several less apparent areas of change, namely three developments originating from within the society itself, i.e. population growth, urbanisation and deforestation, three connected with the imports from abroad, i.e. the coming of fire-arms, Maria Theresa dollars, and foreign medicines, and three customs on which the Church had much to say, i.e. Sabbath observance, smoking and snuffing, and the drinking of coffee.

Changes in Monarchical Power

Reference has been made, in earlier chapters, to the changes in the power and prestige of the monarchy which varied greatly over the period, but for the most part declined. The principle of the Divine Right of Kings, annunciated in the thirteenth century *Fethä Nägäst*, found its highest expression perhaps during the reign of Emperor Zär'ä Ya'qob (1434-1468) when, according to his chronicle, "everyone trembled" before the "power of the king." Little over half a century later, however, his great-grandson Lebnä Dengel (1508-1540), was defeated by the Muslim warrior Ahmäd Grañ, and reduced to the status of a hunted fugitive fleeing from one mountain fortress to another. Though Grañ's ascendancy lasted no more than a decade, the monarchy never fully recovered from the blow it had suffered.

Later in the century Lebnä Dengel's grandson Särsä Dengel (1563-1597) nevertheless won many notable victories which once more strengthened the monarchy, and served as a prelude early in the following century to the rise of the Gondarine state. Founded by Fasilädäs (1632-1667) this polity reached its apogee only three generations subsequently, during the reign of his grandson Iyasu I, also known as Iyasu the Great (1682-1706), the closing years of which, however, marked the beginning of another period of political decline. His son Bäkaffa (1721-1730), according to Bruce, "cut off the greatest part of the ancient nobility" in the Gondär area, and thus "saved his country from aristocratical or democratical usurpation." This achievement was, however, short-lived, for the death of his grandson Iyasu II (1730-1755), sometimes called Iyasu the Little, only a few decades later coincided with the beginning of the era of the *mäsafent* or judges, a period of disunity and civil war during which the monarchs were scarcely more than puppets in the hands of the feudal lords. It was of this time, as we have seen, that a chronicler bemoaned that the kingdom had become "contemptible to striplings and slaves," and a "laughing stock to the uncircumcised."

The difficulties of the late eighteenth century, which marked the dissolution of the traditional monarchy, coincided with the decline of Gondär, the growing independence of several of the provinces, notably Tegré, Bägémder, Gojjam and Šäwa, and the rise of a Yäjju dynasty in Wällo. The first half of the nineteenth century continued to be characterised by disunity, and civil war, but was followed only a few years later by the meteoric rise of Emperor Téwodros (1855 - 1868) whose attempts to restore the powers of the monarchy, important as they were, endured scarcely more than a decade.

The unfolding of these events, which involved innumerable wars and civil disturbances, as well as major changes in the system of government and taxation, had far-reaching effects, not only on the court, but also on many aspects of social life - and left a vivid impression on Ethiopian historical consciousness. It was not surprising that the royal chronicles, which were largely written in sycophantic vein to praise the reigning monarch, should have tended to identify the state of the nation with the fortunes - and indeed the character - of the ruler. A chronicle of the era of the *mäsafent* thus quoted a "king among kings," asking "a wise man among wise men," how the "goodness of a time" should be reckoned, whereupon the latter is supposed to have replied, "The times are indeed as art thou. If thou art evil the times are evil, and if thou art good the times are good." Reiterating this view the text cited the Biblical saying, "As is the ruler, so is the land," and concluded, "The destruction of a city is by the wickedness of her ruler and the life (prosperity) of a city is in the goodness of her ruler."[1]

Population Growth

Documentation on the Ethiopian demographic history of the period is virtually non-existent, but it would seem probable that the five centuries covered by these pages were characterised, as in the corresponding period in many other countries, by significant population growth. Pressure on the land was therefore almost certainly increasing - and was doubtless a major cause of deforestation, which, as we shall see, was then in progress.

The ratio of people to livestock was probably also increasing. Support for this admittedly tentative view may be found in accounts by Alvares of vast herds seen in the country in the early sixteenth century, as well as in the practice, reported by Lobo in the following century, whereby cattle-owners counted their livestock by the thousand, and held ritual baths each time that figure was reached. This custom was not reported in the post-Jesuit era, by which time it may well have fallen into disuse. The herds described by later observers moreover would appear to have been significantly smaller than those of the past.

---

[1] Perruchon (1893) 16; Basset (1909) 343, 347-8, 359, 363-5, 370, 453; Bruce (1790) II, 607; Weld Blundell (1922) 417, 471-2, 549. On "turning-points" in Ethiopian history see Tubiana (1966) 162-3.

Urbanisation

Though the country throughout the period under review remained a land of small villages and isolated homesteads major changes occurred in the field of urbanisation. The Middle Ages, as we have seen, were characterised by the existence of large royal camps which were commanded and presided over by monarchs who were constantly on the move, as the chronicle of Emperor Gälawdéwos states, until they reached their "last resting place," the place of their "eternal repose." Composed of immense agglomerations of population their camps consisted not only of courtiers and warriors, but also of numerous non-combatants, among them wives, servants and slaves, armourers, tent-carriers, muleteers, priests, traders, prostitutes, beggars, and even not a few children, some of whom had perhaps been born on an expedition.

The late sixteenth and early seventeenth centuries by contrast witnessed the rise of a, succession of more static capitals, largely associated with the construction of stone castles, the first of which were probably of foreign inspiration, erected with the aid of Indian or Portuguese craftsmen, though later ones, as earlier noted, seem to have been of entirely native origin. Foremost among such early settlements were Emfraz (or Guzara) and 'Ayba, established during the reign of Emperor Särsä Dengel, and Gorgora and Dänqäz in that of Susneyos.

The development of castle-based camps culminated in the emergence, in the late-1630's, of the city of Gondär which became a great political, religious, and commercial centre. By far the most extensive urban centre in the land, it had a population in its heyday, on Bruce's evidence, of perhaps 60,000 inhabitants. The capital in consequence developed an urban civilisation, with a specialisation of labour - and development of commerce and handicrafts - unparalleled in the realm at large.

The dissolution of the empire in the second half of the eighteenth century, and the rise of virtually independent provincial rulers, subsequently led to the decline of Gondär, and the growth of a number of local capitals, among them Adwa, Antalo, Čälaqöt and Addigrat in Tegré, Säqota in Wag, Däbrä Tabor in Bägémder, Bičäna and Dima in Gojjam, and Ankobär, Angoläla and Däbrä Berhan in Šäwa. These settlements to a greater or lesser extent all developed urban characteristics, with specialised craftsmen in the service of State or Church scarcely seen elsewhere in the country.[2]

Deforestation

Deforestation, which resulted from both population growth and the development of agriculture and pasturage, seems to have taken place throughout Ethiopian history. It is quite possible, as the modern forestry expert, Dr. H.F. Mooney, has argued, that Ethiopia was "a densely wooded country in ancient, and not so remote times." It is, however, no less apparent that Ethiopian trees were slow-growing, and that forests were easily depleted in areas of human habitation, particularly in the vicinity of settlements. The picture of Ethiopia half a millennium ago as presented by Alvares

---

[2] Pankhurst (1982) 317-21; Conzelman (1895) 149-50.

was already one of grass-lands, with some cultivated fields, rather than of extensive forests. The extent of deforestation was later apparent to Almeida who in the seventeenth century expressly stated that the country had "not much woodland." The shortage of trees, he explained, was "not the soil's fault," "but the inhabitants," for the latter cut down trees "every day" for the construction of houses, and firewood - but "none of them" had "the energy or the will to replant a single one."

Deforestation was most apparent in the most densely populated areas, and those longest inhabited - such as much of Tegré, as well as in the neighbourhood of towns. After the establishment of Gondär in 1636 for example the lands in its vicinity were soon depleted of whatever trees had earlier grown there. The citizens of the capital, Bruce reports, had thus "everywhere extirpated" available supplies of wood, and in consequence laboured "under a great scarcity of fuel."

By the early nineteenth century the principal areas of settlement, as evident from foreign writings - and engravings - were all largely denuded of trees. In the north the Asmära plain was described by Arnauld d'Abbadie as treeless with very little bush, while the area around Adwa was said by Lejean to be suffering from an acute shortage of timber. The whole of Tegré, a region of settlement for thousands of years, was, according to Girard, likewise extensively deforested. Evidence of this could be seen at the time of the British expedition against Téwodros. The construction by the British of a military telegraph line in the Sän'afé area was reported by Hozier to be "much impaired" by "want of poles," while Henty wrote: "Not a single tree is to be met which could be used for telegraph poles; the engineers were completely at a non plus." At Addigrat the British commander was therefore obliged to offer one Maria Theresa dollar for six poles, and the population was "so eager to obtain the prized coin that many pulled timbers out of their houses."

The more important areas of settlement in Šäwa were by this time also largely deforested. The province as a whole was described by Harris as a "timberless realm," and the land around Däbrä Berhan as "barren of trees", while in the area between it and Ankobär there was "not a tree, nor even a shrub higher than the Abyssinian thistle". The vicinity of Angoläla, site of one of Sahlä Sellasé's capitals, was similarly denuded. The French Scientific Mission reported that trees were "rare" and that "none but mimosas" were to be seen. Many neighbouring areas were also greatly denuded. Johnston described the "high tableland of Abyssinia" as "but poorly wooded," while the French Scientific Mission noted that the stretch of country between Angoläla and Finfini (the site of present-day Addis Ababa) was "completely clear of trees."

Deforestation had a significant impact on economic and social life, as well as on the ecology, leading to drought, often followed in turn by famine and epidemics. Besides making possible extended agricultural and pastoral activity, the cutting down of trees also contributed significantly to the decline in wild life, which, as we shall see, had implications for the population at large. The steady elimination of trees from areas of settlement also affected the social life of the people at large, particularly of women who were traditionally responsible for the carrying of fire-wood, and were obliged to travel further and further afield in search of trees and bushes. Shortage of fire-wood became in many places so acute that people were obliged to make do with dung for burning, a practice which in the long run led to significant impoverishment of the soil.[3]

The Coming and Increasing Diffusion of Fire-arms

The advent, and increasing diffusion of fire-arms, which was of crucial military importance throughout the period, also had widespread political and social ramifications.

(i) The Middle Ages

Fire-arms, which reached Ethiopia early in the fifteenth century, were at first the exclusive possession of emperors who employed a small - but steadily increasing - number of riflemen. Weapons, however, were later more and more diffused, particularly in Tegré where they greatly enhanced the political power of the province, and were acquired by numerous chiefs and even some of the peasantry, thereby significantly modifying the texture of social life.

The first Ethiopian ruler with access to fire-arms was probably Emperor Yeshaq I (1414-1429), one of the rulers of Šäwa, who is reported by Maqrizi to have made use of the services of a certain Tabunga Muqrif, a former Turkish governor of upper Egypt, to train his men in their operation. Despite this initiative the difficulty of importing such weapons into the interior was so great that few were acquired by the rulers of Ethiopia for almost a century. In the 1520's Emperor Lebnä Dengel was thus reported, by Alvares, to have had only two swivel guns - and fourteen muskets then recently purchased from the Turks. The scarcity of fire-arms at this time was so great that those which were imported were probably all in the possession of the monarch, whose power vis-à-vis his subjects was thereby enhanced. Fire-arms were moreover so scarce that there were still only a small number of riflemen in the country, almost all of them in royal employ.

The Ethiopian soldiers of this period were for the most part unfamiliar with fire-arms, and above all with cannons. Lebnä Dengel and his forces were therefore at a serious disadvantage when Ahmäd Grañ, a Muslim ruler in the east of the country, rebelled and began his military incursions into the highlands in 1527. Grañ, who enjoyed easy access to the Gulf of Aden port of Zäylä', was able to import substantial numbers of guns which were to prove of major strategic importance. The military inexperience of Lebnä Dengel's soldiers was vividly displayed at the battle of Antukyah which began - and virtually ended - when Grañ's men opened fire with their artillery. One of the first shells crashed into Christian army, where it cut an olive tree in two; the Empèror's soldiers are said to have been so terrified by this that they "tumbled the one on the other," and fled.

---

[3] Mooney (1955) 15; Beckingham and Huntingford (1961) I, 188, 264 et passim, (1954) 48, 188; Bruce (1790) III, 192; Arnauld d' Abbadie (1868) 108; Lejean (1872) 48; Girard (1873) 54; Hozier (1868) 113; Holland and Hozier (1870) II, 139; Shepherd (1868) 204; Henty (1868) 231; Harris (1844) II, 13, 48-9, 52; Lefebvre (1845-8) II, 223, 236; Johnston (1844) II, 226. For illustrations of forests in this period see Pankhurst and Ingrams (1988).

Lebnä Dengel, however, later acquired a number of cannons of his own, and during subsequent fighting in the Awaš area the imperial army was reported by Arab-Faqih to have been obliged to abandon eight pieces of artillery, while the insurgents were said to have been using six cannons captured from their enemies. It is, however, doubtful whether many Ethiopians had yet been trained as cannoneers. The Christian artillery, according to Šihab al-Din, was then in fact operated by two individuals called Hasän al-Basri and ʿAbd Asfar Turki who would appear to have been renegade Arabs, and, to judge by their names, came respectively from Basra and Turkey.

Though the Emperor's soldiers in Šäwa were thus for the most part ignorant of fire-arms, a significant number of these weapons were at this time finding their way into the north of the country. This was particularly the case in Tegré, whose inhabitants could obtain them relatively easily through the port of Massawa. Such fire-arms came into the possession, not just of the ruler, as was the case in the interior, but also of a wider section of the population. The first evidence of this development is found in the statement by Šihab al-Din in 1533 that people of the province had "cannons and muskets."

The struggle with Ahmäd Gran meanwhile entered a new phase when the Portuguese, responding to an Ethiopian appeal for help, landed a well-armed expeditionary force led by Vasco da Gama, son of the famous Vasco, at Massawa in 1541. The presence of the Portuguese, who had no less than 400 rifles, transformed the military balance of power, for the musket, as one of da Gama's men observed at the time, was then still a weapon that "the Abyssinian does not understand." The advent of the Portuguese, with their near-monopoly of fire-arms, thus played a decisive role in Grañ's defeat and death in battle in 1543.

The importance of fire-arms was by then so obvious that Lebnä Dengel's son and successor Emperor Gälawdéwos deemed it desirable to retain the services of some 170 Portuguese soldiers who had assisted in Grañ's defeat. He rewarded them, Telles says, with "considerable Lands, on which they liv'd plentifully, after the Country Fashion, most of them having Horses, Mules and Servants to attend them both in Peace and War." Friction between the Emperor and the Portuguese, however, soon developed. The latter's arrogance - and their attempt to impose Catholicism on the country - led to conflict, and, in due course, to their banishment to the provinces.

Fighting with the Muslims to the east was not long afterwards resumed, for Grañ's nephew, Nur ibn al-Wäzir Mujahid, who, like his uncle, had ready easy access to fire-arms, determined on a war of revenge. Gälawdéwos, though confronted, like his father before him, by a far-better armed enemy, was reported to have had a hundred musketeers - six times more than his father only a generation or so earlier. Gälawdéwos also had the services of some the Portuguese who had earlier fought against the common enemy: eighteen of them were reported to have been with him when he was later fatally wounded by one of the enemy's bullets.

The number of Ethiopian riflemen continued to increase in the following decades. Emperor Särsä Dengel, faced by a Turkish advance inland from Massawa in 1578, is said to have on one occasion reinforced his army with 150 musketeers. Since it is unlikely that he began the battle without any others it is probable that his total force of riflemen must have been at least a couple of hundred strong. He soon afterwards defeated the Turks in a series of engagements which culminated in his capture of their fort at Debarwa. In the course of these battles he seized many prisoners, as well as an immense booty, including many rifles and all the enemy's cannon. The debâcle of the Turks was so great that many of their riflemen surrendered and entered Ethiopian service. They are thereafter mentioned in the chronicles as *Nar*, the Arabic word for "fire." These or other Turks also served as riflemen during the reign of Särsä Dengel's son Ya'qob, who, however, also employed a number of Portuguese musketeers. The latter were described by Bruce as the "remnants" of Christovão da Gama's expeditionary force, who had by then "multiplied exceedingly," the children having been "trained by their parents in the use of fire-arms." The force consisted, according to Telles, of "about 200 Men, able to bear Arms."

The descendants of the Portuguese continued to play an important role during the reign of Emperor Susneyos (1607-1632), who, according to Almeida and Telles, employed "many" of them in his army and rewarded them with the gift of a number of good estates. These foreign riflemen were, however, made subordinate to a trusted Ethiopian courtier called Yolyos who was accorded the Arabic title of *baša* which had earlier been used by the chief of the Turkish and Arabic musketeers. Susenyos also attempted to obtain further arms, and musketeers, from Portugal, and to that end went so far as to adopt the Catholic religion.

Despite the manifest military importance of such foreigners there were by this time also a sizeable number of Ethiopian riflemen. Almeida estimated that there were "more than 1,500 muskets" in the country. The riflemen who handled them thus constituted a sizeable force, though "no more than 400 or 500" of them, he believed, ever participated in any single expedition. They were moreover still poorly trained, for "most of them" had "so little skill" that they could not "fire more than once in any action." This was scarcely surprising for gunpowder and bullets were "so scarce" that there were "not many" men with "enough" bullets "to practice four shots at a target now and then in the year." Some of the grandees were able to fire their guns from time to time, but they did so only from a stand or rest which they had no time to use in actual battle, so that what they learnt was of "little use to them." Underlining the Ethiopian soldier's then inability to make effective use of fire-arms Almeida adds: "guns have not been much used hitherto, they handle them so badly that they do not fight much with them." Even limited use of fire-arms nevertheless terrified opposing armies unaccustomed to such weapons - which explains Ludolf's observation that in the fighting of that time the Gallas "might easily be vanquish'd" by the Emperor's armies, if the latter only knew "the use of Muskets."

The fire-arms situation in the north meanwhile continued to be appreciably different from that in the rest of the country. In the later 1580's a peasant of Hamasén, called Wäldä Ezum, defeated a Turkish force armed with "many rifles" which he succeeded in capturing, and as a result became so well-armed that he rebelled against Emperor Särsä Dengel, but was later defeated. Further conflicts with the Turks occurred in the following century, during which time the latter suffered more reverses, and lost a significant number of arms to the Ethiopians. In one incident, in 1616, sixty muskets changed hands, and in another two hundred, while on a third occasion the Ethiopians actually attacked a Turkish fort at the small Red Sea port of Dafalo, and captured five cannon. Though discouraged by the Ottoman rulers at Massawa the local rulers of Tegré, according to Barradas, also received fire-arms by secret purchase, and as gifts. The result was that muskets, he reports, could be found over the entire province. All the local aristocrats had many good guns, and invariably carried them when travelling or going to war. Musketry skill, as elsewhere in the country, was, however, still fairly low. The inhabitants of the province carried their weapons mainly for bravado, and in general used them "little and badly" because they were unable to practice with them. Skilled riflemen were nevertheless "now and then" found. One man, however, told him that though he always carried a musket he had never fired it as he had never thought fit to provide himself with ammunition.

The existence at court of a force of indigenous musketeers, and the reduced need to depend on foreigners, meanwhile enabled Susenyos's son and successor Emperor Fasilädäs to break the military power of the Ethio-Portuguese riflemen, by banishing them to the provinces. This was in its way a daring decision for they were by then very numerous. One of the Jesuits, Antonio da Virgoletta, estimated them in 1639 at no less than 3,000 strong. Going so far as to claim that they were not allowed to leave the realm "because without them" the Emperor could "not make war," he claimed that they were the country's "musketeers and bombardeers," for no one else used such arms or knew "how to make war." Their final political elimination was, however, later successfully accomplished by Fasilädäs's son Yohannes I whose church council of 1668 which decreed that all *Färänj,* or foreigners, should embrace the Ethiopian faith or leave the country. Most of the riflemen of Portuguese descent seem to have chosen the second alternative, and, before leaving, were obliged to surrender their weapons, which included "a large quantity of muskets."[4]

(ii) The Gondär Monarchy

The influx of fire-arms continued throughout the period of the Gondär monarchy. Its rulers, situated far away from the coast, were less able than the inhabitants of Tegré to import fire-arms, but nevertheless succeeded in obtaining sizeable numbers. Emperor Yohannes I, who was trained as a musketeer in his youth, thus obtained weapons from various sources, including the Dutch East India Company which presented him with an ornamented cannon in 1675. His son Iyasu I while of tender years likewise learnt how to fire a musket "which sounded like the thunder of the rainy season," "burnt rapidly like lighting," and "dispersed like dust all the forces of the enemy."

Despite the increasing number of fire-arms - and the resultant emergence of an expanding class of native riflemen - use continued to be made of foreigners. Some came from various parts of the Arab world, and served under the command of an Ethiopian official with the long-established Arabic title of *baša.* Iyasu's troops thus included a number of Turkish musketeers, and a contingent of black troops - probably Sudanese - who were dressed in Ottoman style and carried muskets. Iyasu's great-grandson Iyo'as (1755-1769), on the other hand, made use of a number of Greek fusiliers. Besides such elite units there were by then also sizeable contingents of Ethiopian riflemen, who, according to his chronicle, possessed "innumerable rifles".

---

[4] Beckingham and Huntingford (1961) II, 516, (1954) 77-8, 186; Basset (1909) 185-6, 218, 240-1, 407; Whiteway (1902) 194; Tellez (1710) 131-2, 141, 171; Cozelman (1895) 175-6: Ludolf (1684) 174, 218; Conti Rossini (1907) 77, 82, 84-5, 117-22, 146, 152, 170; Esteves Pereira (1900) 71, 130, 185; Bruce (1790) II, 243; Beccari (1903-17) I, 347-9, 378, IV, 155-60, 471; Jesuits (1626) 5-7, 65; Guidi (1903) 8.

The number of rifles - and riflemen - in Tegré meanwhile was still expanding. The influx of weapons greatly increased the political importance of the province, the premier status of which was recognised in 1690, when Iyasu I laid down that its ruler had precedence over all other provincial rulers. Confirmation of the vast number of fire-arms in the province is found in the chronicle of Iyasu II which noted that when the latter visited it in 1730 he was greeted by the inhabitants with "many muskets." The riflemen of Tegré were by then so highly regarded that many of them entered the service of Emperor Iyo'as, who was reputed to have employed no less than five hundred of them. The abundance of fire-arms - and riflemen - in the province later contributed greatly to the rise of one of its most remarkable rulers, Ras Mika'él Sehul, who succeeded in overcoming Turkish opposition to the import of weapons via Massawa, and early in his career won the favour of his overlord, Emperor Iyasu II, by supplying him with a "large" annual tribute, which included "many rifles."

The possession of fire-arms by this time was, however, no longer restricted to the Emperor's army and the inhabitants of Tegré, but was spreading to soldiers in other parts of the north, notably to the chiefs of the Amhara provinces, the sound of whose firing was likened in Iyo'as's chronicle to the thunder heard during the rainy season. Fire-arms, the control of which had earlier strengthened the central power of the emperor, thus began to contribute towards disunity by facilitating provincial rebellions against the government at Gondär.

By far the largest number of fire-arms was, however, controlled by Ras Mika'él, who, according to a contemporary chronicle, left his capital, Adwa, in 1767 with "thousands of musketeers," and, travelling across Tegré, received extensive tribute, including, significantly, "many rifles." Iyo'as, faced by insubordination in other parts of the realm, had little option but to ask Mika'él to come to the capital in the following year . The ruler of Tegré accordingly rode to Gondär with a "large number of musketeers" and other soldiers, the entire force equal, a chronicler claims, to "the stars in the sky or the sand of the sea." The large number of riflemen deployed was later confirmed by Bruce, who, arriving in the country a year or so later, noted that Mika'él had "26,000 men, all the best soldiers in Abyssinia, about 10,000 of whom were armed with fire-locks", i.e. perhaps six hundred times more than had existed in the country at the time of Lebnä Dengel two and a half centuries earlier. It was to these weapons, the chief's nephew was quoted as saying, that the Ras "owed all his victories." Bruce, who accepted this view, estimated at about this time that in the whole country there were about 7,000 muskets, all but 1,000 of which were in the possession of the soldiers of Tegré who were moreover "very expert in the management of them," and therefore the best in the empire.

Musketry techniques in the realm as a whole seem, however, to have advanced little since the time of the Jesuits a century and a half earlier. Most Ethiopian soldiers thus did not rest their guns on their hands, but placed them on rests, a practice which had been abandoned in Europe a century earlier. Such stands, which were made of long sticks of wood about four feet long with hooks or rests on each side at alternate intervals, were issued, Bruce states, to all musketeers, and at the outset of any engagement would be stuck in the ground. The musketeer would then place his weapon upon the rest best suited to the height of the object at which he wished to fire. This procedure was, however, so time-consuming that it precluded fast shooting of any kind. Another difficulty confronted by most Ethiopian musketeers was that they were still chronically short of ammunition with which to practice, and usually had to make do with locally-made iron bullets, sometimes even with stones. The local Greeks, Greek half-castes and such Muslims as had been in Arabia, India or Egypt -or had contacts therewith - were in this respect at a marked advantage in that they used lead bullets which fitted better into their guns.

Despite their deficiencies the fire-arms in use, according to Bruce, were still of tremendous psychological importance. The mere fixing of the gun-sticks into the ground, a process which made a greater noise than the cocking of muskets, produced "a fatal and most unreasonable" fear on the part of the enemy. On hearing this sound soldiers unused to fire-arms would "halt immediately," even if about to charge, and thus give opportunity to their enemies to take aim, and after "suffering from a well-directed fire," would usually "fall into confusion, and run, leaving the musquetry time to re-charge." The influence of such fire-arms depended in fact more on the fear with which they were regarded than on their actual efficiency. It was as if the soldiers without guns, Bruce observes, had "voluntarily" agreed to their own "destruction," for if the cavalry, on hearing the infantry fixing their sticks in the ground, or after the latter had discharged their guns, decided to gallop at the musketeers the latter would have been "cut to pieces every time they were attacked." This, the Scotsman comments, however, never in fact happened until late in the eighteenth century.

A major turning-point in the fire-arms story came in 1771 when Ras Mika'él, then in possession of "nearly 7,000 musqueteers," was confronted by a rival provincial chief, Bäwändwässän of Bägémder. The latter's soldiers had by then acquired a few hundred rifles, and, more important, having "been trained and disciplined" with the troops of Tegré, had seen "the effect of fire-arms, which they no longer feared as formerly." Unknowingly following Bruce's above quoted prescription for success, they "boldly rushed in upon the musqueteers, sometimes without giving them time to fire, or at least before they had time to charge again." Three battles were fought. In the first the ruler of Tegré, thanks to his overwhelming superiority in fire-power, was victorious, and in the second his rifles threw the enemy into the "utmost confusion." In the third engagement, however, the small Bägémder force of riflemen succeeded in capturing one of Mika'él's most strategic positions, after which 300 riflemen from Lasta turned against the old Ras who was in consequence obliged to flee the field.

The confrontation between Mika'él and his enemies was of major importance in the history of fire-arms, for the Tegré army, far away from its home base, was obliged to surrender its weapons which thus fell into the hands of the men of Bägémder and other Amhara provinces who in this manner for the first time came into possession of large numbers of guns. The significance of this development was not lost on the French traveller Arnauld d'Abbadie, who, visiting the country half a century later, learnt that the fire-arms which Ras Mika'él had brought to Gondär gradually spread all over the north-western provinces as far as Gojjam. This diffusion of weapons, which for the first time brought vast populations to the south of Tegré into intimate touch with fire-arms, also had important strategic implications in that it increased the power of their new Amhara owners *vis-à-vis* the Oromos south of the

Blue Nile. The latter had long held the military initiative, but, being virtually without fire-arms, were thereafter placed very definitely on the defensive.[5]

(iii) The Early Nineteenth Century

The import of fire-arms in the early nineteenth century was, as in the past, discouraged - but far from prevented - by the Ottoman administration at Massawa. Many weapons continued to find their way into the country, the majority, as previously, being retained in Tegré. The soldiers of that province thus remained the best armed - and most skilled - riflemen in the country. In 1809 Nathaniel Pearce reported that Ras Wäldä Sellasé, the then ruler of the province, had 5,500 matchlocks, and his chiefs a further 3,400, i.e. a total of 8,900, as compared with only 500 in Gojjam, 450 at Gondär and 100 in Lasta. The figure for Tegré, which was almost twenty times greater than that for Gondär, the capital, was later corroborated by Henry Salt who shortly afterwards wrote that Wäldä Sellasé commanded "upwards of eight thousand soldiers armed with matchlocks". This imbalance between the number of weapons in Tegré and the rest of the country continued in the decades which followed. In the 1830's Plowden estimated that Tegré had 8,000 rifles while Rüppell put those in Gondär at no more than about 400, i.e. one-twentieth of those in the northern province. Later again, around the middle of the century, d'Abbadie stated that Däjazmac Webé of Tegré had some 16,000 rifles in his army, and 12,000 in his stores, or a total of 28,000, whereas his nominal overlord, Ras Ali Alula, had scarcely 4,000, or a seventh of that number. Limited numbers of fire-arms by this time were, however, being imported into several provinces south of Tegré. They had been introduced, Plowden believed, into Yäjju, Wärrä Himano and Wällo. The ruler of the latter region possessed about a thousand rifles, according to Krapf, while the chief of Wag, because of his contact with Massawa, was thought to have several times as many.

The riflemen of Tegré, on account of their familiarity with fire-arms, nevertheless remained the best in the land. Combes and Tamisier in the 1830s considered them the "most skilled", while Plowden a decade or so later stated that because Amharas were still "little acquainted with guns," the "most expert" riflemen in Šäwa and Wällo were of Tegré origin, the "most skilful" of all being those of Agamé. Tegré riflemen in fact retained their reputation throughout our period, at the end of which Markham observed that the men of Addigrat in Agamé were renowned for their "excellence as musketeers," while Girard declared that those of Teltäl had great renown. Among the "few" riflemen in the Amhara country there were, however, also some Šanqellas slaves, who, according to Plowden, were generally the "best shots", as they were strong and most ready to learn, though their shooting, he felt, was, by then European standards, still "very ordinary indeed."

Šäwa, because of its rulers' ability to import fire-arms through the Gulf of Aden ports, was also moderately well supplied with rifles. The province, in the opinion of both Krapf and Johnston, had about a thousand, i.e. the same number as Wällo, or little more than a thirtieth of that of Tegré. These weapons, as in the past, seem to

---

[5] Ludolf (1681) 261; Guidi (1903) 7, 61, 103, 130-1, 152-3, 197, 223-4, 234, (1912) 22,102-4, 181, 185-8, 191-2, 197-9, 204-6, 214, 216-7, 226, 235, 248, 308-9 Conti Rossini (1942) 101; Basset (1882) 144, 161-2, 170; Bruce (1790) II, 703, 706, III, 233, 549, IV, 9, 63, 199-200, 202, 210, 232, 253-6; Antoine d' Abbadie (n.d.) 753, 770-1; Arnauld d' Abbadie (1868) 269.

have been kept almost entirely in the possession of the monarch, so that whereas the soldiers of the north tended to have their own fire-arms, those of Šäwa were held in the ruler's possession, and even the king's guards usually handed them in before leaving the palace. The degree of the soldiers' dependence on the monarch in the two regions thus varied immensely.

Despite the steady influx of fire-arms, and the increase of riflemen, actual armament was slow to change. Around the middle of the century two basic types of rifle were in use: the old match-lock or wick-gun, called *qwad* in Amharic, and the more modern flint-lock, known as *bulad*. The former was fired, as its name suggests, with the aid of a match which was used to light a wick serving as a fuse, which burned until it reached, and ignited, the gunpowder, and thereby discharged the bullet. The flint-lock by contrast made use of a trigger mechanism which struck a flint, thereby producing a spark which set fire to the powder. Guns embodying this latter device were technically more efficient in that they could be fired more or less exactly when required, whereas with the older type of weapon there was an inevitable, and somewhat unpredictable, delay between the lighting of the fuse and the actual shooting of the bullet. Despite the manifest advantage of the flint-lock, with its faster shooting and therefore more accurate marksmanship, this weapon was generally disliked in Ethiopia as its firing mechanism easily went out of order, and, in the absence of skilled mechanics, could not easily be repaired. Flint-locks were therefore "little valued," Plowden says, except in Tegré where, because of longer familiarity with fire-arms, maintenance facilities, it may be presumed, were more easily available. Wick-locks on the other hand were in universal demand.

Prices of fire-arms at this time varied greatly. In Tegré the cheapest could be obtained for as little as four or five dollars, and those of better quality for from 15 to 18, but, if decorated with a little gold or silver, fetched 20 to 30, while fine ones with elaborate ornament might cost as much as 200. Prices further inland, however, were considerably higher, and weapons could sometimes be scarcely obtained at any price.

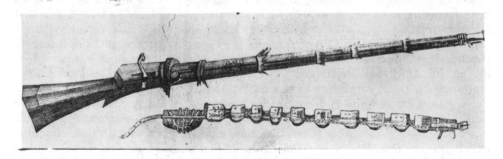

An old-fashioned Ethiopian rifle and cartridge-belt as seen in Šäwa by the Italian geographical mission of the 1880's. From A. Cecchi, *Da Zeila alle frontiere del Caffa* (Rome, 1885-7).

Because of the difficulty of importing fire-arms, and their consequent expense, many old, and indeed obsolete, weapons were retained long after they had ceased to be efficient. Not a few old models, according to Combes and Tamisier, had inordinately long - and hence unwieldy - barrels. Each gun, Johnston recalls, moreover required "three or four individuals" to hold it, while another ran up with a lighted stick to discharge it, after which those who stood behind found it "desirable to get out of the way," for the recoil threw it "several yards out of the hands of the gunmen." Guns in service around the middle of the century are said by Arnauld d'Abbadie to have included Indian, Persian, Turkish or Kurdish carbines of considerable antiquity, many of which were so badly equilibrated that they no longer shot straight.

Little improvement had likewise taken place in the bullets used in this period. Because of import difficulties, and non-availability of lead, the only projectiles generally available, even in Tegré, were stone pebbles or crude locally made pieces of iron. Such "bullets", which seldom fitted the gun-barrels, often damaged the latter, and rendered accurate shooting difficult if not impossible. The use of stones was particularly common in Šäwa, where King Sahlä Sellasé, according to Johnston, "never" issued his men with "more than five or seven" iron bullets each. His men therefore had little opportunity of gaining much practice.

The gunpowder in general use was also scarcely any better than that of medieval times. The soldiers for the most part made their own supplies, out of local sulphur, saltpetre and charcoal. The resultant mixture was often lumpy, Combes and Tamisier explain, and the exact proportions of its components sometimes varied considerably, thereby leaving much to be desired. Local saltpetre moreover sometimes contained extraneous salts, above all sodium nitrate. The latter, "not decomposing by explosion," left "a residuum of globules" which, Johnston says, "besides fouling the barrels of the guns, deteriorates, considerably, the exploding effects of the powder; so much so, that an ordinary charge for a common musket, is two or three large handsful, and it is nothing unusual to see the ram-rod, after loading, projecting twelve, or even eighteen inches beyond the muzzzle." Most locally-made gun-powder was at this time, in the Englishman's opinion, therefore "very bad."[6]

The difficulties associated with such antiquated weapons, bullets and powder were graphically described by Parkyns who observed that most Ethiopians of his day were "exceedingly clumsy" in the use of guns, for, they:

"prefer large, heavy, matchlocks to load which is a labour of some minutes. They carry their powder in hollow canes, and having no fixed charge pour out at hazard a small quantity with the hand. This they measure with the eye, occasionally putting back a little if it appears too much, or adding a little if it seems not enough. After this operation has been performed two or three times, till they are well satisfied as to its quantity, it is pounded into the barrel. The proper charge is now tested by the insertion of the ramrod. Lastly, when all is settled, some rag and a small bar or ball of roughly-wrought iron are rammed down. This last operation (with the exception that the ramrod often sticks in the rag for half an hour) is not

[6] B.L., MS. 19, 347 f. 68; Salt (1814) 288-9; Plowden (1868) 70, 76, 376; Rüppell (1838-40) II, 180-1; GB House of Commons (1868) 122, (1868F) 105; Isenberg and Krapf (1843) 348, 487; Combes and Tamisier (1838) I, 215-6; Plowden (1868) 67; Markham (1869) 229; Girard (1873) 104, 111; Krapf (1867) 36; Johnston (1844) II, 75-6, 261, 264, 400-2; Ferret and Galinier (1847) II, 401, 431; Arnauld d' Abbadie (1868) 249; Rüppell (1838-40) II, 180-1.

difficult, as the ball is made about a quarter of an inch less diameter than the bore of the piece for which it is intended."[7]

Shooting, under such circumstances, was still both slow and inaccurate!

Change by the middle of the nineteenth century was, however, in the air, most noticeably in Šäwa, where the King's riflemen seem to have been particularly well organised and armed. In the 1820's a Greek called Elias is said to have rendered King Sahlä Sellasé the "great service" of teaching the riflemen to shoot in groups of three. One man would kneel down, the second placed the rifle on the latter's shoulder, and the third lit the wick. The old, and, as we have seen, highly inefficient, use of wooden gun-rests was thus abandoned. The Šäwan riflemen's weapons were likewise improved at this time, or a little later, by an unknown foreigner, who shortened the barrels of many old weapons, thus, Johnston says, producing "something like portable guns." The coming of percussion guns, which seem to have first arrived in Šäwa in the 1840's, doubtless by way of the Gulf of Aden ports, marked, however, a far greater technological break-through, for these weapons, which were to gain increasing popularity in the decades which followed, for the first time made possible fast and accurate shooting.

Sahlä Sellasé's policy of monopolising weapons entering his country nevertheless militated against their diffusion in Šäwan society. This was apparent to Captain Graham of the British diplomatic mission. Conceding that the use of fire-arms in the early 1840s was "partially known and fully appreciated," and that the King's company of fusiliers was "gradually increasing," he notes that because of the monarch's "habitual suspicions" guns were "always deposited within the walls of the palace, except during the actual period of the expedition," and that this prevented the natives of the province from becoming "thoroughly acquainted with the use of fire-arms."

Despite their manifest advantage percussion guns remained rare for many years, and the country continued to rely heavily on antiquated muskets to the very end of our period. Early in his career Emperor Téwodros's soldiers, according to his chronicle, were thus armed "mainly with matchlocks," *qwad,* and "a few flintlocks," *bulad.*[8]

(iv) Emperor Téwodros's Innovations

Téwodros, whose modernising interests centred largely, as we shall see, on matters military, captured a significant number of weapons from the provincial rulers he conquered, including 7,000 rifles and two cannon from Däjazmač Webé of Tegré and three cannon from Sahlä Sellasé's son and successor King Haylä Mälakot of Šäwa. The reforming monarch also obtained four cannon and 100 rifles from Said Pasha of Egypt, and attempted to import no less than 20,000 muskets through Yohannes Kotzika, a Greek trader in Sudan. Deeply conscious of the need to conserve and marshal his weapons, Téwodros guarded his fire-arms jealously, and assigned them to responsible officers, Heuglin states, who issued them exclusively to worthy soldiers,

---

[7] Parkyns (1853) II, 23-4.

[8] Graham (1843) 640; Fusella (1954-5) 72, 75.

thereby helping to establish greater military discipline in his army than had formerly existed, at least in the northern provinces.

Dragging one of Téwodros's mortars, called "Sebastapol" after the battle in the Crimean war, from Däbrä Tabor to Mäqdäla. From H. Rassam, *Narrative of the British Mission to Theodore* (London, 1869).

Notwithstanding this policy Téwodros suffered throughout his brief but heroic career from the fact that he was based, like the rulers of Gondär before him, in the north-west of the country, far away from the ports. He was therefore less able than the rulers of Tegré - and perhaps even Šäwa - to obtain the fire-arms he so desperately desired. Small-arms, it is true, could always be smuggled to him across hostile territory, but the import of cannons of any size - which could not be transported inland without the prior construction of special roads for them - was virtually impossible. It was this overriding factor of geography, and the resultant acute shortage of fire-arms, which lay behind his remarkable efforts, discussed in the following chapter, to cast cannons: a project for which he will ever be remembered. The British assault on Téwodros's mountain fortress at Mäqdäla in April 1868, which brought an end to his reign, was in itself another turning-point in the history of fire-arms in Ethiopia, for the invading army was equipped *inter alia* with breech-loading rifles. These fast-firing weapons, which were used at Mäqdäla for the first time in war - **and** were later to be imported into the country in sizeable quantities - were destined to play an increasingly decisive role in the decades which followed.[9]

(v) Armourers

The coming of increasing numbers of fire-arms had implications in many fields of Ethiopian life. One of these was the emergence in the more important early nineteenth century towns of a number of armourers specialising in the repair of rifles and other weapons. Some of these craftsmen, who were originally taught, according to Combes and Tamisier, by Egyptian Copts, Armenians or Greeks, were said to be extremely skilled, and capable of repairing any guns, as well as effectively soldering broken cannon.

The population of Gondär in the first decades of the century thus included a number of gunstock-makers and gun-menders, mainly foreigners from Greece or Egypt, some of whom had the reputation, according to Rüppell, of cheating by soldering over weapons instead of mending them properly. This sometimes produced accidents, particularly if the gun was loaded with more than its proper charge of powder. A class of gunsmiths also emerged in Šäwa where the afore-mentioned Greek, Elias, is said to have introduced the craft in the 1820's to several Ethiopians. Before long King Sahlä Sellasé had a number of such workers, as well as other craftsmen at his palaces at Ankobär and Angoläla, one of whom, according to Combes and Tamisier, had actually made a complete rifle plate.

Emperor Téwodros later also had his armourers whose ranks - and sophistication - were greatly swollen when he embarked, as we shall see, on his ambitious programme of casting cannons and mortars.[10]

Hunting and the Destruction of Wild Life

The coming, and increasing diffusion, of fire-arms also contributed to another significant development in the period under review, namely a substantial decrease in wild life, the numbers of which were to be further greatly reduced in the next half century or so.

Though hunting had doubtless taken place since time immemorial, Ethiopia in the medieval period is said to have still abounded in wild animals which carried out many depredations. In the sixteenth century Alvares reported that the country was inhabited by "many animals of various kinds," including lions and "tigers" (by which he probably meant panthers or other members of the greater cat family), as well as elephants, foxes, jackals and other beasts. The multitude of such beasts was not

[9] Herbert (1867) 142; Heuglin (1857) 107-8, (1868) 358; Krapf (1867) 440; Dufton (1867) 131; Stern (1862) 69, 75, (1868) 221; Moreno (1942) 161, 175; Beke (1867) 161; Lejean (1865) 19; Stanley (1974) 273; GB House of Commons (1868) 188-9, 192-3; Methodios of Aksum (1970) 55; Pankhurst (1972b) 91-2

[10] Rüppell (1838-40) II, 118; Combes and Tamisier (1838) I, 216, III, 9-10, 23-4, IV, 98-9; Lefebvre (1845-8) III, 246; Beke (1840-3) 306; Krapf (1867) 23-4.

surprising, he observes, for the people did not know how to kill them, and had "no devices" for the purpose. Virtually the only wild creatures hunted were therefore partridges, which were killed, he says, with bows and arrows - and was still the sport, it will be recalled, of some of the early nineteenth century children whose lives were described in a previous chapter. The result was that game bred extensively, and, being "not pursued," was "almost tame."

A serious consequence of this abundance of wild life was that the people - and livestock - of this time suffered greatly from the ravages of lions, "tigers" and other animal predators which Alvares describes as "very pestilent". In one not untypical incident, which took place in a village near Debarwa, a man was sleeping with his little son at the door of his enclosure guarding his cows, when a lion entered, killed and seriously mauled the father, but mercifully spared the child. In a second incident, in another village, "tigers" broke into the settlement and carried off a boy, after which they attacked a large farm, where Alvares was himself residing. A mule and a donkey were so frightened that they broke out of the compound, and one of them was immediately devoured by predators.

People in this period were indeed so terrified of attack by wild animals that they did not dare to go out of their houses at night "for fear of the wild beasts." Domestic animals, notably cattle, sheep, mules and donkeys, were in many cases shut up every night. At Debarwa for example the inhabitants of a group of ten to fifteen houses would keep all their livestock in a closed yard with a gate which they kept "well fastened." They then lit a "great fire," and appointed watchmen to guard against the wild animals that roamed about the town all night. Without such precautions, Alvares believed, "nothing alive would remain which they would not devour," and even as it was they often broke into the enclosures to "kill the cows, mules and asses at night." The Portuguese author wrote from personal experience. On one occasion he and his companions spent the night in fear that they were going to be eaten by "tigers," while on another they tied their mules together to prevent them from panicking, after which his companions guarded them with drawn swords. Fierce battles with wild animals often occurred, and the Portuguese, we are told, once "spent the whole night thrusting their lances at tigers," which attacked them so "vigorously" that they could not sleep all night.

The coming of fire-arms in the next few centuries brought about a major change in the relationship between man and beast, for it led to the extensive destruction of wild animals, as well as to a great expansion in the export of ivory and animal skins.

(i) Royal Hunts

One of the most spectacular - and best documented - results of the acquisition of fire-arms was the institution, during the hey-day of the Gondarine monarchy in the late seventeenth and early eighteenth centuries, of great royal hunts which became a notable feature of court life.

Perhaps the first monarch to undertake such an expedition was Emperor Iyasu I, who was referred to in his chronicle as a skilled rifleman, and by Poncet as "the best marksman in his dominions". In 1683, the chronicle reports, Iyasu and his courtiers went down to the Blue Nile valley in search of wild animals, and killed two buffaloes.

Three years later he undertook a much greater hunt to the Šanqella country, where he killed "many elephants, in number 200", while countless other animals were hunted down by his guards. Later in the same year he bagged an elephant, and in 1687 a buffalo and hippopotamus. In 1691 he enjoyed three days' relaxation in the Takkäzé gorge where he once more hunted wild animals, and killed a large elephant, while his followers successfully hunted others. The kill in 1693 likewise included "many" elephant and buffalo. Iyasu went off to hunt again in 1696, in 1697 when he killed "a powerful animal called *awraris*," i.e. a rhinoceros, in 1698 when he ventured into the lowlands of Wägära, and in 1700 when he killed an "innumerable quantity" of beasts. On these expeditions he was often accompanied by his son Fasilädas, who, the chronicler claims, did battle with elephants, rhinoceroses, buffaloes and other wild animals. Though not admitted in the official records, such hunting was not always successful, for on at least one occasion the monarch is reported, by Poncet, to have commanded a cannon to be fired against hippopotami on the shores of lake Ṭana, but the soldiers "not being nimble enough in shooting, the animals dived into the water and disappeared." Iyasu was, however, remembered as a notable hunter, and after his death was referred to as "the mighty elephant killer."

Royal hunts were carried out by most of the later Gondarine rulers. Emperor Täkla Haymanot (1706-1708) for example is reported to have killed a buffalo, while Yostos (1708-1711) carried out at least three great hunts. In the first he killed various unspecified wild animals; in the second he wrought "immense carnage"; and in the third he slaughtered an unstated number of elephants and buffaloes. Emperor Bäkaffa continued the hunting tradition. He and one of his courtiers both killed a rhinoceros in 1726, albeit with a lance, and in 1728 is reputed to have hunted down many animals.

Iyasu II later also led many notable hunts. In 1728, while still of tender years, he captured a herd of monkeys which he brought back to Gondär, the capital. Subsequently, on reaching maturity, he asked permission from his mother, in 1741, to carry out a more serious hunt. She at first refused, but later consented, whereupon, according to Bruce, he proclaimed a "general hunt" as a declaration of his "near approach to manhood," and duly killed two elephants and a hippopotamus, whereupon the nobles, "seeing his bravery," were "astonished, and admired greatly." In the following year he slaughtered another elephant, a rhinoceros, and a giraffe, while his kill in 1743 included four buffaloes on which occasion his courtiers struck down a fifth buffalo, three elephants, two rhinoceroses and a giraffe. A much larger hunt took place towards the end of the reign, and resulted in the shooting by the king's guards in 1754 of a huge lion, two leopards, "numerous buffaloes" and a twenty cubit long snake, while one nobleman and his followers killed fourteen elephants, and another no less than ninety buffaloes. Other lords slaughtered "innumerable elephants," besides smaller numbers of rhinoceros and buffalo.

Bruce, writing of this period, recalls that it was the "constant practice" of the rulers "to make a public hunting-match the first expedition of their reign". On such occasions the monarch, attended by "all the great officers of state", reviewed his young nobility, who all appeared "to the best advantage as to arms, horses, and equipage, with the greatest number of servants and attendants". The "scene of hunting" was always the *qolla*, [or lowlands], which were "crowded with an immense number of the largest and fiercest wild beasts, elephants, rhinoceros, lions, leopards, panthers, and buffaloes fiercer than all, wild boars, wild asses, and many varieties of the deer kind."

Subsequent hunts took place during the era of the *mäsafent*, or judges, by which time the provincial nobles had, as already stated, usurped most of the powers hitherto wielded by the sovereign - and thus also emerged as great hunters. In 1767 for example Ras Mika'él Sehul, ruler of Tegré, is said to have attacked "elephants without number," while later in the year his overlord, Emperor Iyasu II, also went chasing and killing wild beasts. Other hunts, by a variety of nobles, are also referred to in later chronicles.

(ii) Professional Elephant Hunters

The increased diffusion of fire-arms, which took place, as we have seen, first in Tegré, and later in other northern provinces, was accompanied in the late eighteenth or early nineteenth century, by the emergence of bands of professional elephant hunters. Most of them made use of wick-guns, which, according to the French Scientific Mission of the 1840's, were, however, far from satisfactory for they took so long to fire that the elephants often smelt the burning fuse and therefore made good their escape before the bullet left the barrel.

Hunting was later greatly facilitated by the import into the northern provinces of a new type of rifle which fired heavy bullets weighing a quarter of a pound, and cost 15 to 28 Maria Theresa dollars. These weapons were, however, clumsy, and often broke, especially if overloaded; their blast moreover was so violent that the hunter was sometimes knocked over by the recoil. A much improved type of elephant gun was nevertheless introduced in the later 1850's, mainly through the good offices of Walter Plowden, then British Consul at Massawa. This weapon was light to carry, and, being based on the percussion principle, for the first time made possible rapid, and infinitely more efficient, firing. Most hunters, however, continued for many years to use more antiquated weapons.

The advent of large numbers of fire-arms of varying efficiency led to a vast expansion of hunting, at first in the northern provinces and later in the country south of the Blue Nile. The most important hunts in the 1840's were in such areas as Wälqayt, Širé and Wajerat in Tegré, Särayé and the Teltäl country in the north, Ras al-Fil in the west, and the lands south of the Blue Nile. Such expeditions, though carried out by private hunters, were often encouraged or provoked by merchants who, according to the French Scientific Mission, in many instances actually purchased the ivory in advance. Hunts were mainly carried out in January, February and March when the animals, who were then short of water and tormented by flies, left the relatively inaccessible lowlands for cooler plateau districts. Hunting required the permission of local rulers, but this was in most cases easily obtained in return for a present or due. Elephants were killed almost entirely for their ivory, as the carcase had no other value, except for its skin which was sometimes used in the manufacture of shields.

The early nineteenth century also witnessed a great expansion in the ivory trade. Twelve caravans, according to the Scientific Mission, thus passed through Adwa in 1841 with no less than 800 mules laden with tusks bound for Massawa, while two other caravans with 20 loads went by way of Anṭalo, and another 20 through Särayé. A further 300 mule loads were said to have passed that year through Aleyu Amba. There was also a not insignificant export of tusks via Galabat to Sudan. Ivory by the end of our period was moreover on sale at all the principal markets of the country, notably Gondär, Adwa, Däbrä Abbay, Antalo, and, further south, at Aleyu Amba in Šäwa. The result, Parkyns notes, was that elephant-hunting was "one of the best speculations". A man who had capital enough to invest in a few guns of sufficient calibre" had "only to intrust these to men of some respectability and skill in hunting", and would "possibly in a short time obtain a (comparatively speaking) large fortune." He himself knew "many instances of this.[11]

Hunting, which had thus been steadily increasing for some three and a half centuries, led throughout this period to a gradual decline in the country's population of wild life, particularly in the northern provinces. The relationship between man and wild-animals had begun to tilt significantly in the former's favour. People were less frightened than formerly of wild animals - which within only a few more decades would be entirely eliminated in many areas.

Fire-arms in Social Ritual

Contacts with the Portuguese in the sixteenth century, and with the Turks in the seventeenth, showed that fire-arms were not only invaluable in war, and hunting, but could also have a by no means insignificant ceremonial role.

(i) Fusillades for Royalty

One of the first occasions when this was seen was in 1541, during the fighting with Ahmäd Grañ, when the men of Christovão da Gama's expeditionary force invited Queen Säblä Wängél to visit them. They received her, Bermudes recalls, "with trumpets and the firing of artillery, with which she was much astonished, for it is not their custom," i.e. that of the Ethiopians. The Turkish troops in the north followed a similar practice, as later reported in the chronicle of Emperor Särṣä Dengel (1563-1596), which states that it was their habit to fire cannons and rifles whenever their commander returned to his fort at Debarwa. Särṣä Dengel, as we have seen, later succeeded in defeating the Turks, after which the garrison surrendered, and honoured him with a fusillade similar to that which they fired for their own leader.

The victorious monarch, who was much taken by this salute, and had, as already noted, recruited a number of Turkish musketeers, was perhaps the first ruler to introduce fusillades into the Ethiopian coronation ceremony. The role played by the new weapons is colourfully depicted in his chronicle which relates that "the muskets and cannon were fired, and the noise was like that of thunder." The procedures instituted by Särṣä Dengel soon became firmly established. They were followed almost exactly by Emperor Susneyos who was crowned at Aksum in 1609, on which occasion the formalities once again included the firing of fusillades. A contemporary account by Baltazar Telles states that "the air resounded with Acclamations of joy, Vollies of

---

[11] Beckingham and Huntingford (1961) I, 67, 92, 113, 117, 172, 174, 182-3, 186, 251; Foster (1849) 127, 136; Guidi (1903) 64, 76, 98-9, 103, 107-9, 118, 120-1, 160, 173, 185, 196, 202; Basset (1882) 62-3, 67-8, 174, 180-1; Guidi (1912) 92, 108, 170-2, 232-3; Weld Blundell (1922) 36, 67, 70-3, 92, 117-8, 120-1, 353, 305-5; Bruce (1790) II, 451, 629; Pankhurst (1972a) 52; Lefebvre (1845-8) II, Part II, 31-3, 46; Salt (1814) 425; Ferret and Galinier (1847) II, 426; Guillain (1856-7) II, Part II, 530-9; Parkyns (1853) I, 268.

small Shot," as well as "the Noise of Trumpets, Kettle Drums, weights and all other Musical Instruments."

Such fusillades subsequently captured the imagination of the rulers of Gondär whose supplies of fire-arms, as we have seen, increased considerably in the second half of the seventeenth century. Riflemen, the chronicles reveal, began to participate more and more in court ceremonial. The first state occasion on which they are reported to have made their appearance was in 1686 when Emperor Iyasu I held a military review at which the firing of cannon and rifles is said to have sounded like thunder. Their presence at court is confirmed by an illustration in a *Tä'amrä Maryam*, or Miracles of Mary, housed in the Institute of Ethiopian Studies in Addis Ababa, which depicts the monarch preceded by a contingent of musketeers. Not long afterwards, in 1697, a chronicle notes that one of the Emperor's commanders, Blattengéta Baselyos, had his men discharge a "large number of rifles" to impress a visiting Amir who was in consequence "very frightened."

Fire-arms at about the same time also began to be seen, and heard, at religious festivals. The first such occasion recorded was the feast of the Assumption of the Virgin at Gondär in 1699. Poncet, who left a vivid description, recalls that the Emperor walked to church with his courtiers followed by "musqueteers, in their closebody's coats of different colours," and that on the monarch's entry and departure "they discharged two pieces of cannon." The Easter celebrations of 1704 were likewise the occasion, according to the chronicler, of shooting which had already been adopted for Epiphany. The Emperor ordered his soldiers and servants armed with rifles to discharge all their rifles together, so that the "entire land of Gibé trembled." The importance of fire-arms in the thinking of this period is further apparent in the prominence given to them in contemporary paintings: one, which gained considerable popularity, depicts the armies of the Pharaoh attempting to cross the Red Sea anachronistically with guns in their hands.

Fusillades continued to form an essential part of coronation ritual throughout the eighteenth century. During the ceremonies for the accession of Iyasu II at Gondär in 1730, for example, his chronicler claims that "the earth trembled" because of the noise, which included the "thundering of rifles which were heard from far off." Such displays were also adopted on royal marches. Iyasu is said have been preceded in 1746 by soldiers whose guns "resounded like thunder" so that the earth once more "trembled." Iyasu's death, and the accession of his son Iyo'as in 1755, likewise witnessed several impressive fusillades. On the first day the archers at Gondär discharged their arrows, and the riflemen their guns, while on the next morning the rifles once again resounded far and wide. Volleys of this kind are said to have been most impressive, but sometimes created no small fear among persons unused to the noise, and were probably not without some danger to bystanders. At a reception given by Emperor Täklä Giyorgis in 1781 it is reported for example that the soldiers brought "guns without number" whereupon the people "covered their faces and feet ... that they might be saved from the fire that flew from the hands of the riflemen."

(ii) Fusillades for the Nobility

The growing supply of fire-arms in the late eighteenth century, as well as the rising power of the nobility, led to an increase in the number of persons honoured by the firing of fusillades, which began to be discharged in honour of the more important lords, especially in Tegré. A chronicle, describing the fusillade fired on Iyasu II's death in 1755, states that such shooting was by then the custom of the people of Tegré. A decade or so later, in 1766, Ras Mika'él Sehul is said to have been welcomed in Bägémder by his Tegré troops, not only with singing and music, but also with the noise of rifles which resembled the thunder of *keremt* [i.e. the rainy season], and could be heard a day's journey away. The people of Bägémder and Dawent were so "astonished" by this uproar, the chronicler declares, that it seemed to them that they were witnessing nothing less than the coming of Christ. Mika'él' Sehul's arrival in Gondär in 1767 was likewise celebrated by both the beating of drums and the firing of guns which is again likened to thunder. The custom of firing fusillades for members of the nobility later spread to other parts of the country. A chronicle reports that when one of the chieftains of Gondär, Haylu Ešäté, marched into Wägära, he was received "with salutes of guns" according to the custom of that country.

Fusillades by the late eighteenth century were also fired throughout the northern provinces to announce the death of members of the nobility. A chronicle for 1782 for example indicates that a discharge of guns informed the people of the death of Däjazmač Bäqatu, one of the governors of Amhara, while Pearce, describing the funeral at Antalo in 1807 of Däbäb, brother of Ras Waldä Sellasé, the ruler of Tegré, states that on the appearance of the cortège, "numbers of soldiers in front began firing their matchlocks."

(iii) Fusillades for the Common People

The import of increasing numbers of fire-arms into Tegré and other areas of the north in the early nineteenth century led to a further significant widening in the class of persons whose funerals were honoured by fusillades. By the 1840's the firing of rifles had thus become common at many funerals in and around Adwa, where Mansfield Parkyns reported that "those who have guns discharge them in the air." The use of funeral fusillades was also reported at about the same time in Bägémder where Antoine d'Abbadie noted that rifle shots were customarily fired over the grave.

By this time fire-arms also played a prominent rôle, at an increasingly popular level, in Tegré wedding festivities. Pearce notes that the dowry of many a chief's son would include "a certain number of matchlocks," besides Maria Theresa dollars, and such traditional items as swords, cattle, cloth and *amolé*, or salt bars. A generation or so later Parkyns indicated that the better-to-do farmers in the Adwa area were by then also in possession of fire-arms which accordingly formed part of many dowries. Such gifts, depending on the wealth and generosity of the family, usually consisted of "a gun or two," in addition to "a two-edged sword mounted in silver," a rug, some brass utensils, such as a ewer and basin, and several articles of furniture. Poorer farmers, though in most cases not yet possessing their own fire-arms, were likewise accompanied to their weddings by "a considerable number of men carrying guns," which would, however, be "all borrowed." The bridegroom nevertheless carried himself as gallantly as possible, and looked "as proud as if the gunners, shield-bearers, mules, finery, and all really belonged to him; though perhaps only the day before he was toiling and cracking his whip behind his plough oxen."

Rustic weddings in Tegré, as a result of the diffusion of fire-arms, were thus by then accompanied by fusillades reminiscent of the royal ceremonies of old. On the wedding day the bridegroom and his party setting out for the house of his betrothed would by then take a number of fire-arms with them. On reaching their destination the bridal party would "commence galloping around," whereupon, Parkyns states, the gunners fired off their match-locks, and lancers dashed here and there, enacting a sort of sham-fight. Another prominent feature at many weddings in Tegré was the *deball*, or war dance, which was performed by men "armed with shields and lances," who, "with bounds, feints and springs", attacked others armed with guns, so as "to approach them, and at the same time avoid their fire", while the gunners made "similar demonstrations", and at last fired off their guns "either in the air or into the earth".

Fusillades by this time were so common in the northern provinces that they were also employed at church festivals in the more important towns. At Däbrä Tabor the feast of St. John was thus celebrated in 1834, Combes and Tamisier state, with such old-style features as music and dancing, to which was added, by way of novelty, the firing of rifles. At Adwa the celebration of Mäsqäl, or Feast of the Cross, likewise began, Parkyns records, with "a discharge of fire-arms at sunset, from all the principal houses."

Fusillades, which little more than a century earlier had been the exclusive prerogative of emperors, had thus by the early nineteenth century entered the life of the common people.[12]

The Advent of Money and its Consequences

Though money had been coined in the Aksumite kingdom for close on a millennium, the Ethiopian economy throughout most of the period covered by this volume was based on barter or on exchange employing such items of "primitive money" as bars of salt or iron or pieces of cloth. Foreign currency, which was to have a significant impact on economic, social and cultural life in a number of directions, nevertheless made its appearance in medieval times, and expanded greatly in circulation in the late eighteenth and early nineteenth centuries.

(i) Foreign Medieval Coins

Coins, which were imported into Ethiopia in the course of trade, seem to have first arrived in the country in the early medieval epoch. In the fourteenth century Egyptian *dinars* and *drams*, according to Ibn Fadl Allah, had some currency in the eastern provinces, notably Ifat, while a century later the Ethiopian monk Brother Antonio of Lalibäla told Zorzi that Hungarian and Venetian ducats and the "silver coins of the Moors" were employed in purchasing consignments of imported goods at the major trading centre of Gendebelu in eastern Šäwa. The circulation of such coins

---

[12] Whiteway (1902) 148; Conti Rossini (1907) 77; Esteves Pereira (1900) 95-6; Tellez (1710) 184; Pankhurst (1972a) 53, 56; Guidi (1903) 100, 187, 246-7, (1912), 43, 136, 181, 219-20, 226; Foster (1949) 117-8; Weld Blundell (1922) 258, 262; **Pearce (1831)** I, 193, 316; Parkyns (1853) II, 53, 55, 63, 83; Antoine d' Abbadie (n.d.) 44.

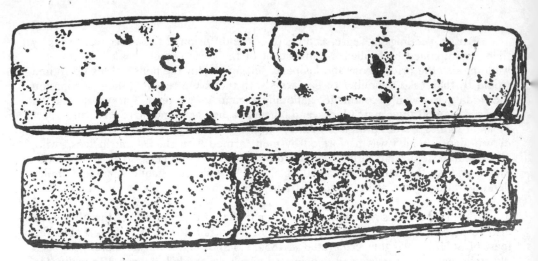

Amolé, or bars of salt, traditionally used as currency, but by the mid-nineteenth century beginning to be replaced by the Maria Theresa dollar. From A.H. Quiggin, *A Survey of Primitive Money* (London, 1949).

was, however, limited, and trade, continued to be based in the main on barter, or "primitive money."[13]

(ii) The Maria Theresa Dollar

Foreign currency made its appearance on a larger scale towards the end of the eighteenth century, when the Maria Theresa dollar, or thaler, began to be brought into Ethiopia by foreign merchants. The coin, which was first struck in Vienna in 1751, and soon gained popularity throughout the Middle East, owed its circulation in Ethiopia to the fact that the value of the country's exports, through Massawa and other ports and trade routes, was greater than that of non-monetary imports, the difference being made up by the import of currency.

Maria Theresa dollars, like fire-arms, were imported along the main trade routes, and therefore found their way first to the ports and principal commercial centres inland, and later to the country at large. Tegré, because of its relative proximity to Massawa, was one of the provinces in which the coin first arrived in substantial quantities. Supplies in the early days were, however, far from plentiful. In the opening decade of the nineteenth century Henry Salt reported that he had been unable to obtain any coins either at the great market town of Adwa or at Antalo, Ras Wäldä Sellasé's capital, where the chief told him that it was a town of "cattle, bread, and honey," and added, "Why do you want money? There is none to be had here." Money, Salt commented, was "an extremely scarce article", and its shortage "a most serious inconvenience". Stocks, however, seem to have later increased fairly rapidly, for when the old Ras died in 1816 his treasurer, Gäbrä Maryam, revealed that his master had amassed no less than 75,000 Maria Theresa dollars. Imports into Šäwa by way of the Gulf of Aden ports, and into the Gondär area from Sudan, were also considerable. In the 1830's Rüppell estimated that almost 100,000 coins were in circulation in the northern provinces, while in the following decades there were

---

[13] Gaudefroy-Demombynes (1927) 14; Crawford (1958) 173.

reports, as we shall see, of even larger numbers entering Šäwa. Testimony to the advent of money is found in Bägémder land sales of this period, many of which are recorded in *berr*, literally silver, the term used for Maria Theresa dollars, rather than in *wäqét*, or ounces, of gold, as was customary in earlier records.

The Maria Theresa thaler, or dollar, first imported into Ethiopia in the late eighteenth century and the main coin in circulation in the nineteenth. From G. Bianchi, *Alla terra dei Galla* (Milan, 1886).

The new currency, despite its obvious advantage over barter and "primitive money," was not easily accepted. Many people, particularly in the central or southern provinces, were thus reluctant to use or receive coins. The Gallas, or Oromos, at Bollo Wärqé market near Angoläla in Šäwa were for example said by Krapf to have had "a great aversion to money." Harris likewise recalls that during the preparation for one of Sahlä Sellasé's expeditions a chief called Abägaz Marä᷅c offered his horse for sale. "Two hundred pieces of salt was the price fixed upon," but "as this small change was not procurable within thirty miles, and moreover would have formed the load of two jack-asses," ten Maria Theresa dollars "were forwarded in lieu thereof." The chief, far from pleased, replied, "I have kept your silver because you have sent it; but in future when I sell you a horse, I shall expect you to pay me in salt."

The peasants, who had formerly scrutinised bars of salt and other items of "primitive money" (the size and quality of which was highly variable) with great care before accepting them, subjected the new currency to a similar critical inspection. Coins, Rüppell reports, were accepted only after careful examination. Vendors when offered a dollar might insist for example that Maria Theresa's diadem should have seven clearly marked pearls, that her face be free from any veil, that the star on her shoulder be of the right size and be surrounded by a distinctly visible row of pearls. Suspicious persons would even look out to ascertain that the minters' initials "S.F." were visible under the queen's head. Thalers of Emperor Franz Josef of Austria, though of the same size and silver content as the Maria Theresa dollar, were likewise accepted only with difficulty, and at a discount of at least ten or fifteen per cent, while Spanish piastres and other silver coins, though in use in many parts of the Middle East, were entirely rejected. A merchant who arrived at Gondär from Sennar in ignorance of this fact was reported to have been obliged to change his Spanish coins for Maria Theresa dollars at an exchange rate of three to two before he could do business. Coins other than the Maria Theresa dollar, though rejected by the peasants and the public at large, nevertheless had non-monetary value, as they could be handed over to silversmiths for melting down into jewellery - or be disposed of to traders travelling outside the country.

The situation in Šäwa was not dissimilar. Maria Theresa dollars were invariably treated with the most careful scrutiny, and to be acceptable, Krapf says, had not only to have the seven points and the initials "S.F.", but should be "spick and span", for it was widely suspected that a dirty coin might have had filth applied to it to conceal the fact that it was a forgery. Coins bearing the effigy of Maria Theresa were often spoken of as *sét berr*, or "woman dollars," to distinguish them from those Franz Josef, referred to as *wänd berr*, or "man dollars," which had as much as a quarter less purchasing power.[14]

(iii) Increasing Taxation

Despite much popular opposition to the new currency, the coming of substantial quantities of coins was important in that it provided Ethiopian society with a new and in many ways much more convenient form of wealth than had previously existed This was particularly useful to rulers and governors who used the newly introduced money both for immediate purchases, especially of fire-arms, and as a means of saving, mainly for the future acquisition of weapons.

As long as taxes had been collected in kind, in such articles as grain, cattle, salt, honey, butter, etc., the amount that a chief could effectively use - or store - was fairly restricted, but with the advent of money there was no such limitation. The revenue he desired, and sought to obtain, was thus greatly expanded, with the result that the exactions on the peasantry, traders, and common people in general were correspondingly much increased.

The coming of money thus resulted in a significant increase in taxation. A first, and apparently substantial, augmentation appears to have taken place in Tegré in the middle of the eighteenth century during the time of Ras Mika'él Sehul, whose great wealth is evident from the chronicle of Iyasu II (1730-1755) and that of the latter's son and successor Iyo'as I. These annals ecstatically report the tribute which the Ras received in gold, "silver"- almost certainly Maria Theresa dollars - carpets and other objects, much of which he later gave to his dependants or passed on to his nominal overlords at Gondär. Mika'él was "violent in the pursuit of riches... in his own province", Bruce wrote, and "spared no means nor man to procure them," but, on coming to Gondär, was "lavish of his money to the extreme; and indeed ... set no value upon it farther than it served to corrupt men to his end," with the result that "all Gondär were his friends." The importance of such taxes was not lost on Iyo'as's chronicler, who quotes Biblical sanction for it in the words, "Render ... unto Caesar the things that are Caesar's; and unto God the things that are God's."

Memories of what must have been a considerable rise in taxation were still alive in the early nineteenth century when Henry Salt visited Tegré, and was told by an

---

[14] Valentia (1809) III, 63, 154; Pearce (1831) II, 95-6; Rüppell (1838-40) II, 18-9, 332; Harris (1844) II, 171, III, 28; Pankhurst (1968a) 468; Isenberg and Krapf (1843) 275, 365; Combes and Tamisier (1838) IV, 108-9; Lefebvre (1845-8) II, Part II, 81; Johnston (1844) II, 234.

old man that during the reign of Iyasu I (1682-1706) his district had "paid only three hundred pieces of cloth," but that Ras Mika'él had "raised it to three thousand." Further evidence of an increase in taxes is afforded by oral tradition, recorded by Perini, which states that during the reign of Emperor Iyasu II a levy of a Maria Theresa dollar per animal on peasants ploughing with beasts of burden, and half a dollar on persons cultivating by hand, was introduced in the districts of Hamasén, Särayé and Akkälä Guzay.

A subsequent increase, and apparent monetarisation, of taxes took place in the late eighteenth and early nineteenth centuries during the governorship of Ras Wäldä Sellasé, the very time when large quantities of the new currency were being imported. The imposition of taxes in this period is recalled in the oral traditions of Şä'azzäga and Hazzäga, as recorded by Kolmodin: referring to an earlier codification of taxes carried out by Iyasu I in 1698, these relate that Wäldä Sellasé called important chiefs to the market town of Kodofälassi, where he asked each of them, "How much do you pay, according to the tax of the King of Kings Iyasu?" The people of Kärnešem, who were dishonest, replied, "Our tribute is three hundred and fifty dollars," but Käntiba Zär'ay, a nobleman who wished to win the Ras's favour, intervened, saying, "That is a lie! Your tribute is five thousand!" The men of Kärnešem, realising that their statement was disbelieved, then changed their tune, and remarked to the other representatives there assembled, "Then you can pay as much as us, and you must also do so!", a suggestion which Wäldä Sellasé of course promptly accepted. The inhabitants of nearby Däqätäšem then assembled, presumably on their master's orders, to decide on their taxes, although, significantly enough, they had never paid anything at all in the time of Iyasu.

Wäldä Sellasé's taxes were also levied on the merchants, and in particular on those engaged in export-import business who had easiest access to money, and other imported commodities. From such traders the ruler of Tegré extracted a share of their wares, among them "dollars", as well as "cloths, matchlocks, carpets, velvets, silks, and other articles." The right of tax collection was granted, or farmed out, to special officials, often bearing the title, as we have seen, of nägadras, or chief of the traders, who held "the office of collector" and paid "a certain sum yearly for it, whether trade be slack or brisk." Income from such taxes amounted at Adwa to 110 ounces of gold, or the equivalent of 1,760 dollars per year, besides two-thirds of all duties upon foreign goods brought up from the coast, as well as on slaves, ivory, and civet from the interior. Receipts at Antalo were somewhat smaller: 55.ounces of gold in addition to a third of the duty on slaves, horses, mules, and ivory, and all those on salt. Special taxes, levied partially in cash, were also on occasion ordered, notably in 1815 when Wälda Sellasé proclaimed, as we have seen, by the beat of the drum that every village chief should "collect from his tenants two dollars each in hard money, cloth, or salt, and the larger towns from ten to twenty each, as a subscription to pay the expenses of bringing a patriarch from Egypt."

The collection of taxes in Maria Theresa dollars appears to have been further stepped up in the second and third decades of the century. In Akkälä Guzay, one of the few areas for which information is available, the nominal yearly tribute was one carpet and a rifle until the time of Däjazmac Säbagades (1817-1824), who introduced a tax of 1,000 Maria Theresa dollars, albeit payable in either silver or cattle, as Antoine d'Abbadie asserts. This was subsequently increased by Däjazmač Webé (1825-1855) who, according to traditions collected by Perini, established an annual tax of

5,000 dollars, for which reason the Italian considered him the real initiator of the district's taxes. It was not, however, long, d'Abbadie states, before the tax was augmented to 11,000 or 12,000 dollars. A similar expansion in monetary taxes occurred in neighbouring Hamasén and Särayé, which, according to Combes and Tamisier, together provided Webé in the 1830's with an annual revenue of 30,000 dollars.

Rulers of the country were by then so interested in obtaining revenues in cash that, spurning their subjects' prejudice against all but the most perfect of dollars, they often gave orders to the merchants, Combes and Tamisier report, to "accept any kind of dollars." Despite his injunction, the traders, doubtless reflecting the more conservative attitudes of the populace, "always refused" to use any but Maria Theresa dollars.

Taxation towards the middle of the century reached considerable proportions. Webé, after his defeat by Ras Ali in 1842, levied a special tax on Adwa to make good his losses, and, according to Isenberg, collected 2,400 dollars which worked out at about a dollar per citizen. Peasants throughout Tegré and other northern provinces were by this time also subjected to a significant amount of taxation in cash, as well as in kind. "Numerous imposts" on land - as opposed to trade, where cash payments had been common somewhat earlier - thus, according to Consul Plowden, "sometimes took the form of a regular tax in money." The burden of the common people moreover was not confined to taxes, but also included all sorts of fines, which, Parkyns observes, were "frequently converted by bad men - especially in troubled times, when the throne is unstable, and men do as they please - into a means of cruel extortion."

Efforts were also made to augment the monetary revenues from trade. Though the records on the subject are imprecise, and difficult to correlate, the evidence tends to suggest that the number of *kella*, or internal customs posts at which merchants were obliged to pay dues, was increased. The proportion of dues collected in money seems likewise to have risen. Merchants passing through Anṭalo early in the century paid mostly in imported cloth and *berellé*, or glass bottles, as Salt records, but by the 1830's Rüppell and Blondeel both record heavy monetary exactions, while Combes and Tamisier exclaimed that the tolls, notably at Adwa, had "above all in recent times" become "revolting." The proportion of taxes actually collected in cash varied, however, greatly from place to place, and depended largely on the uneven penetration of money. At the smaller tolls it was still normal practice in the 1840's, Ferret and Galinier affirm, for dues to be levied in cloth, salt and even tobacco, and only "rarely" in money, but at an important place like Adwa they were largely paid in currency. Webé, according to a British naval officer, Commander Nott, thus collected a dollar on every slave passing through the town, and two dollars on every ivory tusk, while Plowden reported in 1852 that dues there and at Däbareq "generally" amounted to "about 1 dollar per mule-load."

While Wälda Sellasé was introducing new taxes in Tegré, the system of tribute was likewise being reorganized in Šäwa, where significant quantities of money were then also beginning to arrive. The new dues were imposed by the local ruler Märedazmač Asfä Wässän (1775-1808), who, according to Rochet d'Héricourt, for the first time levied "a light tax on each village," and thereby "created an annual revenue not enjoyed by his predecessors." Taxes in Šäwa, as in Tegré, fell heavily on trade. By the early 1840's Aleyu Amba market was said by Barker to have yielded an annual revenue of not less than 3,000 dollars in cash as against only 2,000 in kind. The monetization of taxation by this time was thus well advanced.

Changes in the tax structure also took taken place in Bägémder around the turn of the century or a little later when Ras Gugsa Mersa (1799-1825) appropriated lands from the nobility, and, according to Arnauld d'Abbadie, "increased his revenues by a considerable figure." Taxes in this province, as elsewhere, were largely levied on trade. Such dues in early nineteenth-century Gondär were estimated by Pearce at 520 ounces of gold, or the equivalent of 8,320 dollars per annum, while the city's chief customs officer, Nägadras Ašaber, later told Gobat in 1830 that he paid the provincial ruler "five thousand dollars yearly." The revenues of Däbareq were likewise considerable, and provided 3,000 dollars to the governor of Sämén, and the same amount again to the *nägadras*, or chief of customs, whom the people accused of being a "tyrant."

The coming of large numbers of coins had thus by the middle of the century substantially increased the revenues of the rulers, as well as the tax burden on the common people throughout the country.[15]

(iv) Capital Accumulation and Money-Lending

The advent of money, and the related augumentation of taxes, greatly facilitated the accumulation of capital by the few. Several rulers succeeded in filling their treasuries with coin, much of which, as above noted, was from time to time dispensed in the purchase of fire-arms, while a number of churches and monasteries receiving dues in money also acquired small fortunes. A group of merchants engaged in export-import trade likewise obtained much wealth in cash. Usury, a practice earlier banned at Gondär, and hitherto virtually unknown in the country at large, thereupon began to flourish.

In Tegré Ras Wäldä Sellasé amassed considerable wealth. At the time of his death in 1816, he was, as we have seen, reported to have been in possession of no less than 75,000 silver dollars, as against 50 ounces i.e. 800 dollar's worth, of gold. His successor, Däjazmač Säbagades (1818-1831) similarly possessed a considerable amount of cash which enabled him on one occasion to give his British aide Coffin 2,000 dollars for the purchase of fire-arms, and the chief's sons were later reported to be buying percussion rifles for over 50 dollars each. Several of the more important religious establishments of Tegré likewise acquired extensive stocks of silver, in part because, unlike the rulers, they had no need to spend their money on arms. A monastery in the "wilderness" of Tämbén was thought by Pearce to have thus come into possession of no less than 5,000 dollars.

The rulers of Sämén also followed an acquisitive policy. Ras Gäbré and his successor Däjazmač Haylä Maryam are stated by Parkyns to have both accumulated

---

[15] Pankhurst (1979-80) 43-4; Bruce (1790) II, 650, III, 107, 112, 118; Guidi (1903) 125-6, 132, 156, 206-7, 214, 220, 222, 224, 226-30, 264-5; Kolmodin (1912-5) 97-8; Pearce (1931) I, 340-1, II, 11-5, 51, (1920), 47; Perini (1905) 75-6; Antoine d'Abbadie (n.d.) 352-3, 562; Parkyns (1853) II, 231; Lefebvre (1845-8) I, xliii; Plowden (1868) 137; Valentia (1809) III, 213-5; Combes and Tamisier (1831) IV, 124-5; Tamisier and Combes (1837) 33; Ferret and Galinier (1847) II, 411-2; Rüppell (1838-40) I, 249,310, 327, 337, 355, 358, 360, 371, 375-6, 391, 394-5; Blondeel (1838-42), 42-4; Isenberg (1843) 17 June; Rochet d'Hericourt (1841) 212, (1846) 243; Cecchi (1885-7) I, 240; Gobat (1834) 76, 233; Barker (1906) 289.

"much wealth." The latter's famous son, Däjazmač Webé, subsequently paid his nominal overlord, the Emperor at Gondär, what Plowden describes as the "small yearly tribute" of 5,000 to 10,000 Maria Theresa dollars, while retaining the greater part of his revenues at his mountain fortress of Amba Hay. When captured by Emperor Téwodros in 1855, his treasury there was found to contain, according to Stern, 40,000 dollars, besides "a great quantity of gold and silver plate," "a vast quantity of copper, and a countless number of coloured Venetian bottles." The figure of 40,000 dollars was also quoted by other travellers, among them Lejean and Dufton.

A not dissimilar horde of wealth was collected in Bägémder where Empress Mänän, mother of Ras Ali Alula, is said to have held in her treasury 30,000 dollars which she was later obliged to hand over to Téwodros, as Flad asserts. Several monasteries in the province also acquired considerable stocks of cash, among them that at Qoräta, whose members were reputed by Gobat to have been "very rich." Despite earlier clerical opposition to usury, they are reputed, as we have seen, to have exacted 240% interest per annum as against the more usual 10% per month, or 120% per year.

The merchants of Bägémder, and above all of Gondär, were also able to accumulate sizeable amounts of cash. One of the most prosperous, in the 1830's and 1840's, was Nägadras Kidanä Maryam, described as "a rich merchant" and "one of the wealthiest" men in the country, who supplied cash to Gobat and Combes and Tamisier, normally at a rate of interest of 10% per month. Another wealthy merchant was Wäldä Kidanä Maryam, possibly the son of the latter, who was said by Flad to have been worth 60,000 dollars. On his deathbed in 1858 he bequeathed five dollars to each of Gondär's forty-four churches, and fifteen dollars to each of his 40 slaves whom he then manumitted.

The rulers of Šäwa similarly obtained substantial monetary revenues which probably reached their peak during the reign of King Sahlä Sellasé, whose annual income, Harris asserts, amounted to 80,000 or 90,000 dollars a year, accrued chiefly from duties on foreign merchandise, slaves and salt, whereas state expenditure did not exceed 10,000 dollars.

Sahlä Sellasé, who, because of his relative isolation had less need than the rulers of the north to purchase extensive quantities of fire-arms, probably indeed saved a considerable proportion of his income. A "large part" of the coins entering the realm, according to Rochet, thus ended up in the royal treasury, with the result that "very few" remained in circulation. Johnston agreed that "all the coin" coming to the country, if not melted down to produce jewellery, fell "into the hands of the King." This picture is confirmed by Harris who declared it "probable" that the monarch, during his long reign of nearly thirty years, "must have amassed considerable treasure" which was "carefully deposited underground and not lightly estimated by its possessor."

Rochet, who claims, perhaps truthfully, to have been allowed to see Sahlä Sellasé' treasury, asserts that it was situated at Qundi, north of Ankobär, and consisted of a cave ten metres long by three wide and two high in which the coins were kept in two rows of closely packed jars with a narrow passage of only two or three feet between them. There could have been, he claimed, almost three hundred jars, each containing 5,000 to 6,000 dollars, i.e. a total of 1,500,000 to 1,800,000 coins - which must, however, be reckoned an improbably high figure. Hitherto, he was told, the king had followed his predecessors' example in having the coins melted down, but later, "realising that the principal advantage of money" was its "mobility," contented himself with keeping it in sacks. Reference to this treasury was, interestingly enough, also made by Johnston who states that the money was "securely packed in jars, and deposited in caves." The hill of Qundi, he adds, was "pierced by numerous subterranean passages, in which are hidden in this manner immense treasures in gold and silver. They are kept closed by heavy doors of iron, and the whole hill, which is surmounted by a church, dedicated to the Virgin, is under the care of a vast number of priests."

Sahlä Sellasé's interest in money is also evident from the fact that he went so far as to ask the missionaries Krapf and Isenberg, in 1843, whether they "understood" how to stamp dollars," and, when asked what he needed from Europe, replied that he "wished for nothing, except a coining apparatus." The monarch's wealth, and that of his son and heir King Haylä Mäläkot, were legendary. One probably apocryphal story, recorded in the early twentieth century by British Consul Walker, has it that when the latter ruler realised that his death was near "he caused to be written a paper of declaration telling of all the money he had. Fearing lest his boy [i.e. Menilek] in his ignorance might not gather together all the wealth, he made a list of all - not omitting one broken needle - and had the writing sewn up in a leather case. And this was strung upon the long neck-cord of Menilik. But, before the boy had grown to manhood and knowledge, there came an enemy, the Emperor Theodore, who seized him and asked where was his father's money. And Menilik replied, 'My father gave me nothing - only this which I carry round my neck.' Then Theodore broke the stitches and found where the money was buried."

The advent of coins in early nineteenth century Šäwa led, as in the northern provinces, to a fair amount of money-lending, which was based on a rate of interest of one bar of salt per dollar, or the equivalent of between 5% and 10% per month, or 60 to 120% per annum. Some of the province's peasants seem also to have realized the advantages of hoarding money. The people of Yefat were thus reported by Krapf in the 1840's to be storing their wealth in cash, a far easier commodity in which to do this than in primitive money.[16]

(v) Emperor Téwodros's Wealth

The rise of Emperor Téwodros led, as we have seen, to his seizure of considerable quantities of coin, including 40,000 dollars in Sämén, 30,000 in Bägémder, and an undefined amount in Šäwa. Though thus gaining access to unparalleled quantities of wealth, Téwodros never had sufficient to meet his needs, and in 1866 complained bitterly to Rassam of his compatriots' niggardliness, declaring, "The people of my country would sooner bury their money in the ground than trade with it or pay me a percentage out of it."

---

[16] Rochet d' Héricourt gave a much higher estimate of Šawän revenues, which, he claimed, were running at 250,000 to 300,000 dollars a year, an "enormous sum in a country where money is excessively rare, and almost never employed in individual transactions," while the king's expenses, he agrees, were "insignificant". This revenue figure must, however, be regarded with suspicion, particularly when it is realised that average annual mintings of Maria Theresa dollars in Vienna in the 1840s totalled scarcely over 250,000 coins - which were exported not only to Ethiopia, but also throughout the Middle East.

Téwodros's revenues, which fluctuated with his military fortunes, were extracted from the various provinces under his sway. In 1859, for example, he obtained 10,000 dollars from Šäwa, as noted by the chronicler Zänäb. The Emperor's subsequent conquest of Tegré was important in that it made possible the collection of taxes in that province, as well as in the districts north of the Märäb river which were of great fiscal significance because of their relative proximity to the coast through which Maria Theresa dollars were imported. The prevalence of currency in the Hamasén area in this period is illustrated by a tradition which tells of a local chief, Bahr Nägaš Asgädom of Säfe'a, offering a bet of no less than ten thousand dollars.

Téwodros's annual revenues in the early 1860's, as indicated in tax records, ran at some 240,000 Maria Theresa dollars, of which 190,000, or about 80%, came from Tegré. Of that amount 32,000 dollars were collected from the lands "beyond the Märäb" river, i.e. Hamasén and Särayé, 15,000 from the area beyond Širé, 15,000 from Akkälä Guzay, 10,000 from the Teltäl nomads to the east, and 25,000 dollars in caravan dues. The magnitude of the taxes levied on the highland areas nearest the coast is confirmed by Egyptian records which state that Hamasén was supposed to pay 62,000 dollars a year, though it ceased to do so after 1861.

Bägémder and the country to the west, which obtained their currency as a result of trade through Sudan, also contributed significantly to the Emperor's coffers. One of Téwodros's tax documents indicates that the province yielded about 47,000 dollars, or about 20% of the total recorded revenue.[17]

Supplies of cash were also obtained by Téwodros though not on a regular basis - from punitive confiscations and fines. Abunä Sälama was said by Flad to have been obliged to surrender 20,000 dollars in 1863 for insulting the monarch, while two rich merchants of Qoräta were made to part with 20,000 and 10,000 each in 1865, and the rich Muslim merchants at Därita were reported by Massaia to have on one occasion provided 15,000 dollars. Gondär, whose inhabitants "refused to pay the usual taxes," Rassam notes, was sacked in 1864 and 1866 when the soldiers, according to Blanc, "searched every house" and "plundered every building," after which the monarch returned to his camp, Flad's wife Pauline reports, "laden with gold and valuables" which he showered on his European favourites, Mrs. Flad herself receiving 50 dollars. Some coins, including a cache of 590 dollars found at Gondär, were also melted down, together with sundry copper vessels, chronicler Wäldä Maryam relates, for the casting of one of the Emperor's most highly prized cannons.

Téwodros's monetary revenues which, taken together, must have been by no means inconsiderable, enabled him to spend large, but unfortunately not recorded, sums of cash on the import of arms, as well as to attempt the introduction of monetary payments to the troops. He also rewarded sundry European gunsmiths with

---

[17] Much higher figures were, however, quoted by Téwodros's European captives. Blanc (1868, 310) believed that the taxes of Bägémder amounted to 300,000 dollars a year, while Rassam (1869, II, 16) wrote of 350,000. Both figures should perhaps be treated with caution. Much of the taxes collected in Bägémder came from trade, Rassam claiming that Celga, one of the main customs posts on the western trade route, yielded 100,00 dollars per annum.

sums of 1,000 or 500 dollars each, and displayed unprecedented largesse, presenting Rassam, for example, with two gifts each of 5,000 dollars.[18]

(vi) The Dollar as a Unit of Weight

The arrival of the Maria Theresa dollar also had notable non-monetary consequences, one of which was to provide the society with its first accurate measure of weight. The Ethiopians had long possessed scales, and had used a number of conceptual units of wealth, the most popular of which were the *wäqét*, or ounce, and the *rotl*, or pound, both borrowed from the Arabs, as well as several Biblical measurements which are mentioned in literary texts. Actual weights with which to weigh were, however, for practical purposes non-existent, though there are indications that foreign coins had sometimes been made to serve the purpose, as recorded by Alvares who states that in the sixteenth century the Portuguese *crusado* was so used. The widespread diffusion of Maria ` Theresa dollars, however, greatly facilitated weighing, for it became customary, as Beke noted in 1852, for these coins to be "placed in the scale as a weight." The dollar was equated with the *wäqét*, while a dozen or more coins - actually anything between 12 and 19 - were taken as equal to the *rotl*.

Though grain and other such provisions were usually measured in locally-made baskets or other units of capacity, the dollar, or *wäqet*, became the principal measurement used in the weighing of precious goods, principally gold, silver and civet, while the *rotl* was much used for ivory and other export articles, among them coffee, wax, civet and cardamom. The Maria Theresa coin thus played an important rôle in introducing a more accurate system of measurement than in pre-monetary times.[19]

(vii) Marriage and Funeral Ceremonies

After their appearance Maria Theresa dollars, like fire-arms, soon became a familiar feature in the social life of the commercially more advanced areas of the country. Early in the nineteenth century it was thus customary in Tegré, when a chief's son or daughter was married, for the dowry to include "hard money" and matchlocks besides such traditional gifts, Pearce says, as swords, cattle, cloth and salt. A similar state of affairs was reported in Šäwa, a decade or so later, where Graham stated that it was by then not unusual, when concluding a marriage contract, for "a mule, an ass, a dollar, a shield and some spears" to be "noted against the lady's stock of wheat, cotton and bed-steads."

---

[18] Pearce (1831) II, 95; Rüppell (1838-40) I, 327; Combes and Tamisier (1838) III, 347, IV, 110; GB House of Commons (1868) 67-8; Parkyns (1853) II, 115; Lejean (1864) 218; Dufton (1867) 131; Gobat (1834) 87, 167-8, 242, 303; Veitch (1860) 59; Harris (1844) II, 96, III, 28; Rochet d' Héricourt (1841) 286-7, 301; Johnston (1844) II, 235-6; Isenberg and Krapf (1843) 137, 306; Walker (1933) 32; Rassam (1869) I, 35, 305, II, 7, , 45, 131; Moreno (1942) 174; Kolmodin (1912-5) 146; Pankhurst and Germa-Sellassie Asfaw (1979) 7-8; Douin (1936-41) III, Part I, 333; Flad (1922) 141, 143, 163, 177; Massaia (1885-95) IX, 27; Mondon-Vidailhet (1905) 177.

[19] Beckingham and Huntingford (1961) I, 123-4; Beke (1852) p. 18; Parkyns (1853) I, 406, 408-21; Lefebvre (1845-8) II, Part II, 31, 34. For the measures cited see Pankhurst (1970) 58 et passim.

On the death of a man of substance it likewise became the practice in Tegré, according to Parkyns, for the "price of forty days' masses" to amount to "from six to twelve dollars, or more, according to the wealth of the family."

Fines and "blood money" by this time were also paid in cash. A murderer at Däbareq, Gobat reports, was thus condemned to pay 200 dollars, and in consequence took his stand in the market, begging for charity, until he had the wherewithal to pay. This was no unusual case, for the governors often proposed that the death penalty be commuted to a money payment, often as much as 250 dollars.[20]

(viii) A Source of Silver

The coming of the Maria Theresa dollar was also important in overcoming the country's hitherto acute shortage of silver, a deficiency that was the more acute in that the use of gold, as we have seen, was traditionally restricted to royalty, and therefore not available for the population at large. By the 1830's vast numbers of coins, Combes and Tamisier suggest, were already being melted down for the manufacture of jewellery, an operation which, Parkyns noted a decade or so later, yielded handsome profits to the jewellers of Tegré. Artifacts of silver, which had been little known until this time, also gained great popularity in Šäwa where the womenfolk, Johnston recalls, were, as earlier noted, "exceedingly fond of silver ornaments," so much so indeed that almost "all their riches" consisted of "such stores."

The Maria Theresa dollar thus came to constitute in the words of the subsequent Georgian physician Dr. Mérab, "the silver mine of the Ethiopians," and thereby provided the society with the metal out of which a large proportion of its jewellery was fashioned - and it was in the nineteenth century that the personal name Berru, literally "The silver" or "His silver", seems to have first become popular.[21]

The Coming of Modern Medicine

There was a great yearning throughout this period for foreign medicines and medical treatments which, like fire-arms and coins, made headway at first in royal and princely circles, and later gained currency among the nobility, and more generally, among the population of capitals and other centres of political power.

(i) Medieval Times

Interest in foreign medicine can be traced back at least to the early sixteenth century when Emperor Lebnä Dengel wrote in 1521 to King João of Portugal, asking the latter to supply him with "men who make medicines and physicians and surgeons to cure illnesses." This request evoked no response, but João Bermudes, a barber-surgeon attached to the Portuguese mission of that time, was considered so valuable

---

[20] Pearce (1831) 316; Great Britain, India Office, Political and Secret Letters 5/ 420, para 2; Parkyns (1853) II, 65; Gobat (1850) 443-4.

[21] Parkyns (1853) II, 15-6; Johnston (1844) II, 335; Mérab (1921-9) III, 401.

that he was retained in the country for over a decade during which time he is believed to have introduced the monarch's court to European medical treatment.[22]

(ii) The Gondär Period

Shortly after the founding of Gondär in 1636 a German Lutheran missionary, Peter Heyling, carried out a number of European-style cures in that city. A favourite of Emperor Fasilädäs he was given a "delightful Apartment", Ludolf says, together with a large revenue. The metropolis, because of its foreign contacts, was probably the site of other medical innovations. One such was the use of steam-baths for the sudorific treatment of syphilis. A number of such bath-houses - which had then recently become popular in Europe - were constructed in the vicinity of the great castle of Fasilädäs, the palace of Empress Mentewwab, and other imperial structures.

Considerable interest in foreign medicine was later displayed by Emperor Iyasu I who sent one of his trade agents, Haji Ali, to Cairo in 1698 to procure medical assistance for himself and his son, both of whom were afflicted by a troublesome skin complaint. In response to this request a French physician, Charles Poncet, duly travelled to Gondär where he arrived in July 1699, and at once began treating the royal patients, who, he claims, were soon "perfectly cur'd."[23] Iyasu is said to have been deeply interested in the Frenchman's medical knowledge, for, Poncet reports:

"I had carried with me into Aethiopia a little chest of chemical medicines, which had cost me the labour of six or seven years. The Emperor inform'd himself exactly after what manner those remedies were prepar'd, and how they were applied: what effects they produc'd: for what distempers they were proper. He was not satisfied with only a verbal account of things, but he order'd it to be taken in writing. But what I most admir'd (i.e. wondered at) was that he seem'd to be extremely pleas'd with the physical reasons I gave him of everything."[24]

The Frenchman also taught Iyasu how to make a "bezoar," or cure, for "intermitting fevers," from which the monarch and two of his sons were later suffering, and treated Iyasu's consort, Queen Mäläkatawit, for some other unidentified illness. Before leaving, Poncet left the Emperor a box of medicines, as well as some familiarity with European treatment - but no doctor.

Determined to remedy this latter deficiency Iyasu wrote in September 1701 to the French Consul in Cairo, M. de Maillet, for a good doctor or surgeon. Nothing came of the request, but the Emperor shortly afterwards took into his service a Greek physician named Demetrius. The Greek medical presence in Gondär thus initiated may well have continued for many years, for Bruce in 1770 found a Greek there called Abba Christophorus who acted as a physician as well as a priest. The Scotsman, for his part, also practiced medicine, first at Adwa, where he claims to have "saved many

---

[22] Beckingham and Huntingford (1961) I, 61, 72, 390, II, 505; Rey (1929) 127-8;

[23] Ludolf (1684) xxxv; Foster (1949) xxiv, 115-7; Pankhurst (1975a) 209-10;

[24] Foster (1949) 131-2.

young peoples' lives" during a smallpox epidemic, and later at Gondär where he treated other smallpox patients, among them several royal princes and some children in the Muslim quarter of the city. He subsequently also effected a number of cures in other parts of the country.[25]

The Early Nineteenth Century

The impact of Western medicine increased substantially in the early nineteenth century, as a result of growing contacts between Ethiopia and the outside world. In the 1830's Combes and Tamisier discovered that King Sahlä Sellasé was already in possession of a "mass of European medicines which he had received from India by way of Zeila." One of the foreign medicines which gained considerable popularity at this time was sarsaparilla, a cure for syphilis then widely used in Europe as well as the Arab world. This medicine became known in Ethiopia as *wešeba*, a term reported early in the century by Pearce. Confirmation of the use of this drug is provided by Combes and Tamisier who stated a generation later that it was used in particular by Ethiopians who travelled down to the port of Massawa. Sarsaparilla was also employed in Šäwa where it was, however, almost prohibitively expensive, a complete cure in the early 1840's costing no less than twenty Maria Theresa dollars.[26]

Growing Ethiopian awareness of foreign medicine owed much to the increasing numbers of foreign travellers who arrived at this time. Most of them, like those of former times, practiced medicine to a greater or lesser extent, and seem indeed to have been constantly asked to provide such assistance. "Everyone," Combes and Tamisier recall:

> "was perfectly persuaded that as whites we must be profoundly versed in the study of medical sciences; also each person is anxious to consult us, to ask for remedies or amulets with the conviction that we could achieve the cure of the ill with which they were afflicted. ... Important men appealed to us to give them aphrodisiacs and sterile women thought we could procure for them the means of becoming fertile. A priest came to present to us his son who was afflicted by a disease considered in Europe as incurable."[27]

The extent to which Ethiopians of this time had resort to foreigners for medical treatment is confirmed by other travellers, among them Gobat, who, while in Gondär in 1830, noted in his diary on May 4 that he could "hardly get across the city," for "everybody stops me, begging me to go to see the sick. The more I tell them I am not a physician, the more they are persuaded that what I advise is the best remedy." On May 25 he likewise wrote, "today I had to deal only with sick people," while on May 27 he added, "passed the forenoon in visiting the sick," and on the following day that "from sun-rise, till ten o'clock" his house was "full of people" seeking treatment. Other

---

[25] Foster (1949) xxiv, 115-7, 120, 131-2; Beccari (1903-17) XIV, 178, 348-9, 486; Bruce (1790) III, 200, 210, 245, III, 209-12.

[26] Combes and Tamisier (1838) I, 279, II, 17-8, 34, 351; Pearce (1831) I, 301-2; Kirk (1843) 21.

[27] Combes and Tamisier (1838) II, 8-9.

foreigners practicing medicine at this time included Arnauld d'Abbadie, who visited many parts of the north, and was reported to be treating people with "considerable success;" the Protestant missionary Krapf, who travelled across the country, and found calomel, or choloride of mercury, "very useful" in the treatment of venereal diseases; and Mansfield Parkyns who used the same specific in Tegré to cure "many" cases with "much success." Several foreign visitors also practiced medicine in Šäwa, among them Rochet d'Héricourt, who treated King Sahlä Sellasé for rheumatism, and his consort, Queen Bäzabeš, for toothache; and one of the first medical practioners, the British ship's captain, Charles Johnston, who supplied undefined "professional services" at Ankobär, Angoläla and Aleyu Amba.

The French scientific mission of 1839-43 and the British diplomatic mission of 1841-2 were both also involved in medicine. The former included two physicians, Petit and Quartin-Dillon, who treated many sick people and carried out numerous inoculations, mainly in Tegré, but also in Šäwa. The British embassy, which also included two medical practitioners, Kirk and Impey, handled 2,000 to 3,000 patients, in and around Ankobär. Sahlä Sellasé is said to have taken a keen interest in the medicaments brought in by his British visitors. Harris thus reported, on May 8, 1942: "The King's attention would appear to be now solely engrossed in amassing medicines. Finding that the stock of calomel had been nearly exhausted in the cure of fifteen hundred syphilitic patients he has sent constantly during the last fortnight to request supplies of every drug contained in the stores, with explicit directions for use." Reverting to the matter in a subsequent report of June 20, the envoy noted, "The royal stock of medicines was again brought down to be labeled, although very ample directions relative to their properties had previously been given in Arabic writing at Debra Berhan."

Besides visiting physicians there were a number of resident foreign practitioners of sorts. They included an Armenian called Gorgorius who lived in Tegré and administered corrosive sublimate in the cure of venereal diseases, a Turkish veterinary assistant who had deserted from the Egyptian army and provided treatment in Gondär, and an Ottoman bashibazouk at Massawa who made use of foreign medicines acquired from various foreign travellers.

The cumulative effect of the coming, and residence in the country, of these and other foreigners, as well as of the import of foreign medicines in the course of trade, had far-reaching implications. Though the majority of the Ethiopian population continued to depend on local, or traditional, medicines - based for the most part on a wide range of local plants, the period under review witnessed a significant increase in the use of foreign medicines, many of them chemicals, imported from abroad. This development, which affected mainly the court and aristocracy, prominent traders with access to the ports, and the better-to-do sections of the urban population, was particularly noticeable in the treatment of venereal diseases, the medical field in which the Ethiopian public was perhaps most responsive to change.[28]

---

[28] Gobat (1834) 194-5; Arnauld d' Abbadie (1868) 159; Parkyns (1853) II, 274; Rochet d' Héricourt (1841) 22-3, (1846) 125; Johnston (1844) II, 256; Lefebvre (1845-8) II, 355-66; India Office, Bombay Secret Proceedings, 159/ 1486B, Krapf December 2, 1841, 185/ 1440 Barker, January 7, 1842, 189/2040, Harris, March 3, 1842, 193/2918A, Harris, May 8, 1842, 193/2919, June 2 and 12, 1842, 193/2919A, Harris, May 8, 1842; Blanc (1868) 71-2, (1887) 361.

Sabbath Observance

Besides the above changes, connected with population growth, urbanisation, deforestation and the advent of fire-arms, currency and foreign medicine, there were other developments which no less directly affected the life of the Ethiopian people.

One such area of change, or proposed change, was that of Sabbath observance which was the subject of controversy throughout much of the period under review. The practice of observing Saturday as well as Sunday as the Sabbath dates back to antiquity, and can be traced, according to Taddese Tamrat, to as early as the eleventh century. Despite its antiquity Sabbath observance was vigorously opposed by the Coptic Abuns from Egypt. These prelates, who constituted the apex of the Ethiopian Church hierarchy, condemned it as a Jewish heresy, and gradually won over the Ethiopian monarchy to their views. How far they succeeded in changing actual behaviour in the countryside cannot be determined. It is, however, clear that many of the Ethiopian clergy were unwilling to yield to anti-Sabbatarian pressure from officials of either Church or State.

The arguments of the Coptic hierarchy were challenged in the fourteenth century by the Ethiopian monk Ewostatéwos who was persecuted for his opposition to its attempt at Sabbath reform. His followers, however, soon became so powerful that the reigning monarch, Emperor Dawit I, was obliged to call off attacks on the Ewostatéwosians, and went so far in 1404 as to grant them his protection. The views of the pro-Sabbath partly thereupon rapidly gained ground, even within the court. Emperor Zär'ä Ya'qob, who came to the throne in 1434, was in particular a supporter of the Ewostatéwosian theses, and convened a church council in 1450 which ruled that God had revealed the duty of the faithful to observe the two Sabbaths. This view was likewise proclaimed in his *Mäshafä Berhan*.

Coptic intransigence nevertheless continued, and gained ground in the late fifteenth century during the reign of Eskender (1478-1494) who issued a doubtless unpopular decree ordering that Saturday observance should be abandoned. Whether this was followed must again be a matter for speculation. Alvares, who learnt of the dispute a generation or so later from the Coptic Patriarch of his day, Abunä Marqos, states, however, that the anti-Sabbath position collapsed when two foreigners, the Venetian artist Brancaleone and the Portuguese Pero de Covilhão, arrived, and began to observe the Sabbath like the Ethiopian population. Some of the priests then approached the Emperor, and, criticising the Coptic position, declared: "What thing is this? These Franks who have come from Frankland, each one from his own Kingdom, and they keep our ancient customs, how is it that this Abima [Abun], who has come from Alexandria, orders things to be done which are not written in the books?" It was as a result of this initiative, Alvares was informed, that the Emperor gave orders that the country should return its "former usages."

Sabbath observance, which had been challenged for so long by the Coptic Abuns, later came under even fiercer attack from Roman Catholics, missionaries and others. The first assault took place in the immediate aftermath of Ahmäd Grañ's defeat in 1543 when the Portuguese, hoping to profit from Ethiopian gratitude for the help they had rendered in the late war, tried to persuade Emperor Gälawdéwos to accept the tenets of Catholicism. The monarch, however, refused to listen to the blandishments of his erstwhile allies, and wrote his famous tract, the *Confession of Faith*, to rebut the contentions of the *Färänj*. One section of the work dealt specifically with the Sabbath, and, rejecting the Catholic argument that his compatriots had not freed themselves from the ideas of the Jews, cleverly, if disingenuously, emphasised the difference between Ethiopian and Jewish ideas and practices. The *Confession*, referring to the Sabbath, thus observed: "We do not celebrate it after the manner of the Jews, who crucified Christ, saying, 'His blood be on us and our children.' (Matthew xxvii, 25). For the Jews do not draw water, or light a fire, or cook a dish of food, or bake bread, or go from one house to another. But we celebrate the Sabbath as the day in which we offer up the offering (i.e. the Sacrament), and we make feasts thereupon, even as our Fathers the Apostles commanded. We do not celebrate the Sabbath as the first day of the week, but as a new day, whereof David said, 'This is the day which the Lord hath made, let us rejoice and be glad in it.' (Psalm cxviii, 24). For on the Sabbath our Lord Jesus Christ rose from the dead, and on it the Holy Spirit descended upon the Apostles in the upper room of Zion, and on it the Incarnation took place in the womb of Saint Mary, the perpetual Virgin, and on it [Christ] will come again to reward the just and to punish sinners."

A further, and even more violent, confrontation over Sabbath observance began some fifty or more years later when the Jesuits arrived, and in due course succeeded in converting Emperor Susenyos to Catholicism in 1626. Not long after this the Jesuit Patriarch, Affonso Mendes, a man of extreme bigotry, attacked the celebration of the Sabbath and other Ethiopian festivals, which, Ludolf later noted, had no specifically religious basis, but "depended meerly" on Ethiopian custom. The prelate proceeded to order the newly converted monarch to punish employers who failed to make people work on Saturdays. Susenyos therefore issued a proclamation, which, according to Bruce, stated that "all outdoor work, such as ploughing and sowing, should be publicly followed by the husbandman on the Saturday, under penalty of paying a web of cotton cloth, for the first omission, ... the second offence was to be punished by a confiscation of movables, and the crimes were not to be pardoned for seven years." This edict was, however, short-lived, for popular opposition to this, and other Jesuit policies, led to so many rebellions that Susneyos was obliged to issue a new proclamation, in 1632, restoring to the people "the faith of your fathers." The observance of the Sabbath, which, despite the decree, had probably continued in most of the Christian regions, was thus officially restored, and was doubtless strengthened when Susenyos's son Fasilädäs, a firm supporter of the Orthodox faith, shortly afterwards succeeded to his father's throne.

The traditional Ethiopian practice of twin Sabbath observance, as we have seen in earlier chapters, was thus in force throughout the rest of the period covered in these pages."[29] Gobat reported, that on the Saturday Sabbath, Ethiopian men and women generally abstained from all their main occupations, though the womenfolk as a rule continued with their spinning, while Harris, writing of Šäwa, declared:

---

[29] Taddesse Tamrat (1972) 209, 213, 216-7, 219, 222, 226, 230; Beckingham and Huntingford (1961) II, 354, 358; Ludolf (1684) 357-8; Bruce (1790) II, 338; Gobat (1850) 192; Budge (1928b), II, 354. See also Hammerschmidt (1965) 5-11; Ullendorff (1968) 109-13.

"The Jewish Sabbath is strictly observed throughout the Kingdom. The ox and the ass are at rest. Agricultural pursuits are suspended. Household avocations must be laid aside, and the spirit of idleness reigns throughout the day, and when, a few years ago, one daring spirit presumed, in advance of the age, to burst the fetters, His Majesty the King of Shoa, stimulated by the advice of besotted monks, issued a proclamation that those who violated the Jewish Sabbath should forfeit his property to the royal treasury and be consigned to the state dungeon."[30]

Sabbath observance was if anything stronger in Gojjam where Plowden observes:

"The Saturday... is held of equal sanctity with the Sunday, so that water cannot be drawn, nor wood hewn, from Friday evening to Monday morning."[31]

Smoking and Snuffing

Though most of the dictates of the Church, including fasting, food prohibitions and celebration of the twin Sabbath, continued throughout the period, some changes in connection with smoking, taking snuff and the drinking of coffee were beginning to take place.

Smoking, a practice which is said to have originated among the Muslims, and later gained popularity with other non-Christian sections of the population, for that reason incurred the animosity of the Ethiopian Orthodox Church. The custom, according to a tradition recorded in a nineteenth century *Amharic History of Gran and the Gallas* of uncertain historical accuracy, was introduced into the Ethiopian realm in the sixteenth century, during the reign of Lebnä Dengel (1508-1540). The text claims that smoking was brought in by the Oromos, and later adopted by the Emperor and his Christian subjects who as a result were consumed by the sins of pride, debauchery and idolatry. The Eč̣ägé, or chief of the monks, it is said, was deeply concerned at the introduction of smoking, but a group of Egyptian and other foreign Christians told the Emperor that the practice was permitted in their own countries. He therefore prevented the clergy from condemning the custom, after which "all the priests began to smoke." The practice gained such popularity that a monk at Däbrä Metmäq is said to have taken tobacco while celebrating Mass, but was reputedly struck down as a punishment for this offence.

Opposition to smoking was expressed in even stronger terms in the *Dersanä Ragu'él*, or "Homily in honour of the Archangel Ragu'él," a work of about the same period, which refers to tobacco by the mysterious term "plant of Setätira," and declares that it was "poisoned by the devil," and "more impure than hyena's flesh." The text focuses on the supposed coming of tobacco during the reign of Lebnä Dengel, and claims that Ragu'él warned the monarch against smoking, prophesying that if they smoked the monarch's soldiers would be defeated, for God would "cut them to pieces"

---

[30] Harris (1844) III 150-1.

[31] Plowden (1868) 90.

by placing "the sword of malediction" in the hand of their enemies," and the country's priests would be "exterminated in war and famine." Support for the belief that tobacco gained acceptance during the reign of Lebnä Dengel is found in the writings of the Ethiopian historian Aläqa Aṣmä Giyorgis, as well as in the chronicle of Menilek II which asserts, on what evidence it does not state, that the sixteenth century monarch smoked tobacco and smeared his horse with blood after the fashion of the Gallas.

A very different traditional explanation for the rejection of tobacco was subsequently recorded by Pearce. It states that use of the plant had been banned on account of a priest called Zär'ä Beruk who had been accustomed to smoke, and, running out of tobacco, while on a pilgrimage to Däbrä Libanos, had replenished his supply by selling his silver cross to a "pagan" Galla. The smoker subsequently confessed his sin to the Ečägé at Gondär who "instantly" issued an order forbidding Christians from making any use of the plant.

The Ethiopian Church at this time waged a strong, though by no means fully effective, war against tobacco. In the north of the country Pearce in the first decades of the century reported that "the priests and clergy abhor the smoking of tobacco, and no one is allowed to enter a church who has previously been smoking, though numbers of them take snuff. Indeed, the smoking of tobacco is forbidden by the priests to all classes, yet many are addicted to the habit, for which they are answerable to their father-confessor, it being accorded a sin." The priests of Šäwa were likewise strongly opposed to smoking. One of their arguments against it, according to Harris, was that it was stated in Biblical writ that "what cometh out of the mouth of man defileth him."

The intensity of clerical dislike of tobacco - and of coffee, with which, as we shall see, it was often popularly associated - doubtless owed much to the fact that both addictives were used in "pagan" or "animist" ceremonies. One such was the *wädaja* of Wällo in which the "chief men", according to Krapf, met early on Thursday and Friday mornings for prayer, at which time they smoked tobacco, drank coffee, and chewed the narcotic *čat*. At such gatherings it was believed that the Oromo religious leaders received "spiritual revelations in reference to military expeditions and other matters," and the populace prayed that they might be "blessed with increase of cows, clothes, etc.," and that Allah would "bestow gold and silver on their chief, and increase his power and dominion." The Gallan Gallas were likewise said to make annual sacrifice to their God, Waq, at which time they alluded to the weed, saying, "O Wake, give us tobacco, cows, sheep and oxen, and help us kill our enemies."

Evidence of the extent of Church opposition to the "unChristian practices" of smoking, and coffee drinking is evident from the statement by Harris that the British diplomatic mission to Šäwa when attempting to enter the church of Maryam at Ankobär, received what he termed the "insolent reply" that "since the English were in the habit of drinking coffee and smoking tobacco, both of which were Mohammadan abominations interdicted in Shoa upon religious grounds, they could not be admitted within the precincts of the hallowed edifice as it would be polluted by the foot of a Gyptzi [i.e. European]." Confirmation of this account is provided by Graham who recalls that he and his compatriots were considered as Muslims, because they were known to smoke, and drink coffee, and "only escaped excommunication by a timely present of money to the priests." Hostility to smoking was expressed also by Fälašas, who, according to Flad, were likewise "strictly forbidden" from smoking, and, like the

Christians whom they resembled in so many ways, were not allowed to enter their places of worship if they took snuff.

Despite such widespread opposition to tobacco, snuffing towards the end of our period seems to have been gaining popularity. Around the middle of the century Arnauld d'Abbadie reported that "many" Ethiopians, both men and women, were by then taking snuff. European-style snuff-boxes were, however, rare, most people making use instead of such local substitutes as a hollow cane or a cow's horn. A generation or so later the Armenian traveller Dimothéos was even more emphatic, observing that by Téwodros's time "all the Abyssinians, without exception of age or sex, took tobacco to snuff." Smoking, however, was still "entirely unknown," and foreigners seen smoking were on occasion loudly criticised for this unChristian habit.[32]

Coffee-Drinking

Coffee-drinking, which was unknown at the beginning of our period, was another custom which, as we have seen, was often condemned by the Church whose opposition, however, later somewhat diminished.

The coffee plant, though native to south-western Ethiopia, does not seem to have been introduced into other parts of the country until around the latter part of the sixteenth century, at the time of the great northward movement of the Oromos, who, Bruce believed, had actually "transplanted" it to some parts of the north. One of the first such places where its presence is recorded, by Almeida in the early seventeenth century, was in the Azäzo area immediately north of Lake Ṭana.

Coffee-drinking in the northern provinces at least gained popularity, however, only slowly. At the end of the seventeenth century, Poncet found that people did not "esteem" coffee "much," made "no use" of it, and cultivated it "only as a curiosity." Bruce, three-quarters of a century later, seems to confirm that coffee was still of little significance in the Christian highlands, for he reports its use only at the port of Massawa, and among some of the Gallas of the south-west. The latter did not drink it, but roasted and pulverised the beans which they then mixed with butter to form balls, about the size of billiard-balls, which, they claimed, kept them "in strength and spirits during a whole day's fatigue, better than a loaf of bread, or a meal of meat."

Coffee cultivation seems to have expanded in the years which followed, and by the early nineteenth century was fairly extensive in several parts of the north-west. The bush grew, according to Pearce, in Agäwmeder and "most of the Galla districts," while Rüppell a few decades later reported that it was cultivated in several areas around Lake Ṭana, notably at the largely Muslim town of Qoräta, on the eastern shore, where almost every dwelling had a group of coffee trees, as later observers also testify. Coffee by this time was also grown in some parts of Wällo, and southern Šäwa, particularly on river banks.

---

[32] Caquot (1957a) 141-2, (1957b) 94, 113, 116; Pearce (1831) I, 335-6; Bairu Tafla (1987) 97, 181; Guèbrè Sellassié (1930-1) I, 31; Harris (1844) II, 20, III, 176; Krapf (1867) 83; Isenberg and Krapf (1843) 151; Graham (1867) 14; Krapf (1867) 83; Isenberg and Krapf (1843) 151; Graham (1867) 14; Flad (1869) 58; Arnauld d' Abbadie (1868) 527; Dimothéos (1771) II, 37.

Opposition to coffee-drinking in this period was, however, still widespread throughout the Christian areas of the country. The Christians of the north had "a prejudice" against it, according to Pearce, because it was "used so frequently by the Mahomedans." Rüppell, a generation later, agreed that the practice was "customary only with Muslims" - but added that "all Christians occasionally drunk it with pleasure." The Church was, nevertheless, still strongly opposed to the bean, and had "forbidden" its use by the Christian population, as Ferret and Galinier note.

Coffee-drinking was particularly strongly opposed by the priests of Šäwa, in part, according to Krapf, because of their "opposition to the Mahomedans" who liked it "very much," and in part because it was seen to be connected with "pagan" Galla worship. The extent of clerical opposition to coffee is confirmed by Harris who states that, thought the plant flourished wild in many areas, coffee-drinking was "at all times strictly forbidden on pain of exclusion from the church." The extent of the popular prejudice against coffee is evident from the fact, noted by Krapf, that he and his travelling companions "could never prevail on Christians" to let them make coffee in their houses, "as they instantly took us for Mahomedans and sent us out of their houses, nor would they by any means give us a vessel for making coffee because it would make the vessel unclean." Despite such dislike of coffee, it is interesting to note that no restriction seems to have been placed either on its sale within the country, or to its export, which took place both via Massawa and Zäylä', as well as along the trade route to Sudan.

The Ethiopian Church's condemnation of coffee was attacked over the years by several European missionaries. Krapf in particular held many disputations, in which he claims to have "proved" - at least to his own satisfaction - that "everything created by God" was "clean, good," and, if received with thanksgiving, "not to be refused." The Almighty, he declared, had made coffee grow "as well as other things for the use of man," and anyone who forbade its use was therefore "in opposition to the Creator." Besides such theological arguments he offered more practical considerations, telling his Ethiopian audiences, with reason, that their country could produce "plenty of coffee" which they could sell abroad for their "temporal welfare." It is doubtful, however, whether such preaching had much influence on the population at large.

Opposition to coffee, as to tobacco, was nevertheless perhaps beginning to wane. Though earlier foreign travellers had noted strong rejection of coffee those of Téwodros's time, such as Rassam and Stern, report that when on their travels they offered people coffee it was warmly accepted, but only in private. A decade or so later coffee-drinking, according to the great Ethiopian Church scholar Aläqa Lämma Haylu, was still only drunk in secret, and did not become popular among Christian Ethiopians until after the founding of Addis Ababa in the late 1880s.[33]

* * * * * *

---

[33] Rüppell (1838-40) I, 368, II, 225-6; Bruce (1790) II, 226, III, 13, V, 37; Beccari (1903-17) VI, 387; Foster (1949) 106, 155; Pearce (1831) II, 13, GB House of Commons (1868) 98; Waldmeier (1896) 126; Ferret and Galinier (1847) II, 401; Isenberg and Krapf (1843) [33], 190-1, 237, 429, 445-6; Bairu Tafla (1987) 91; Graham (1867) 12; Harris (1844) III, 176; Rassam (1869) II, 205, 309;'Pankhurst (1962) 114; Stern (1862) 240,(1868) 230; Mängestu Lämma (1959) 91-3.

The period under discussion thus witnessed a number of significant changes in social life, some of which foreshadowed even more substantial development in the decades which followed.

II

THE ATTEMPTED REFORMS OF EMPEROR TEWODROS II

The attempted reforms of Emperor Téwodros II (1855-1868), though only partially implemented and in the event largely unsuccessful, provide a convenient point of termination for this volume in that they serve to underline some of the more important problems facing Ethiopian society in the closing years of our period - and suggest at least one possible scenario by which they might have been tackled if not solved. These issues, the resolution of which were to take many decades, included the need for the reunification of the war-torn land, the erosion of feudalism, the curtailment of the soldiers' exactions on the peasantry, land reform, particularly in relation to what many considered excessive Church holdings, the reduction in the number of internal customs posts, the replacement of Ge'ez by Amharic as the country's principal written language, the despatch of students for study abroad, the introduction of written messages and commands, the abandonment of Gondär as the imperial capital, road-building, some measure of industrialisation, abolition of the slave trade, and the modernisation of many aspects of the economy, society and government.

Unification, and the Curtailment of Feudal Power

Téwodros rose to power by overthrowing the principal feudal leadership in the north of the country. It was thus only by crushing Ras Ali Alula and the latter's mother Empress Mänän in Bägémder, and later Däjazmač Webé of Sämén and Tegré that Téwodros could proclaim himself King of Kings, and begin the work of reunification so generally associated with his name. His objective, as his British admirer Consul Plowden reported, was to integrate the country by placing "the soldiers of the different provinces under the command of his own trusty followers" to whom he gave "high titles," but "no power to judge or punish," thus in fact creating "generals in place of feudal chieftains more proud of their own birth than of their monarch." In this way he started "organising a new nobility, a legion of honour dependent on himself, and chosen specially for their daring and fidelity," and thus began "the arduous task of breaking the power of the great feudal chiefs - a task achieved in Europe only during the reign of many consecutive Kings."[1]

Military Reorganisation, and Limitation of Looting by the Soldiery

The battles which Téwodros waged at the beginning of his career against the technically more advanced armies of the Egyptians on Ethiopia's western frontier showed him the military advantages of a modern army, as well as the difficulties created by his country's traditional unpaid soldiers who, as we have seen, were constantly ravaging the countryside in search of provisions. As early as 1853, two years before his coronation, he was reported, by Plowden, to have "in a degree disciplined his army," and, a year later the Consul went so far as to declare that the chief, having

---

[1] GB House of Commons (1868) 150. See also Beke (1868) 36.

"taught his soldiers some discipline," was able to make war without baggage or camp followers. Later, in June 1855, Plowden explained that Téwodros, who had been crowned four months earlier, had "adopted the practice of giving his soldiers sums of money from time to time, thereby accustoming them to his intention of establishing a regular pay," and was himself drilling his matchlockmen who had been placed under officers commanding from 100 to 1,000. "In the common soldiers," he added, "he has effected a great reform, by paying them, and ordering them to purchase their food, but in no way to harass and plunder the peasant as before." To implement this policy granaries for the troops were set up, according to Heuglin, at several places, most notably at Däbrä Tabor, Mäqdäla and Zebit.

Anxious to establish a "regular standing army armed with muskets only" Téwodros also wished, according to Dufton, to adopt "European discipline." To this end he placed some 1,000 men under the command of a British adviser, John Bell, who had instructions to train them. The men, however, do not seem to have taken kindly to the marching, saluting and such-like discipline expected of them, and the scheme had therefore soon to be abandoned. Undeterred the Emperor himself carried out much of the training. Two or three Frenchmen are, however, said to have also served for a time as drill-masters.

Téwodros's projected reforms were, however, difficult to effect and enforce. Zänäb's chronicle of this time records, for example, that the Emperor, apparently conceding the need for at least some appropriation of supplies by the troops, told the latter when they were in Dälanta in 1856 that they could take what they needed to eat, i.e. presumably grain, but insisted that they should touch neither the inhabitants' cattle nor their clothing. The men nevertheless seized, and slaughtered, all the livestock they could find, whereupon Téwodros is said to have cursed them, declaring, "Soldiers, as you have killed that which belongs to the poor, so God will do unto you!"

Despite his attempted reforms the movement of his troops, like those of Ethiopian rulers throughout the country's recorded history, seems to have often occasioned grave disquiet among the peasantry. Stern, who accompanied Téwodros's army, was a bigoted critic, but may not be altogether exaggerating when he claims that the Emperor's soldiers, though much "admired" when ravaging enemy country, were "to judge from the anxious looks and terrified countenances which greeted our arrival not much courted when they approached one of their own native settlements. The poor peasants, who dreaded to receive a dozen of these hungry heroes for guests, were in an ecstasy of delight when they saw them saluting their chief, and cantering across the plain towards the neighbouring villages." The "fear of an impending famine, which a night's sojourn of our troops might have brought upon the small settlement, had thus been averted."

Testimony to Téwodros's enduring desire to eradicate the abuses of looting, is, however, afforded by other observers, notably Rassam, a fairer observer, who recalled, as late as 1866, that it was "cheering to see how well his Majesty protects the crops of his faithful subjects," by "sending parties commanded by officers to guard the corn-fields and villages against the ravages of the soldiery." Téwodros was, however, by no means always able to afford the peasantry such protection, and the chronicles and other Ethiopian sources, like the memoirs of foreign travellers, are unfortunately replete with descriptions of the ravages effected by his men.

King of Kings Téwodros II (1855-1868) inspecting his men cross a ravine. From H. Rassam, *Narrative of the British Mission to Theodore King of Abyssinia* (London, 1869).

The extensive fighting of Téwodros's reign was all in all characterised by extensive warfare no less detrimental than that of the period of the *mäsafent* which preceded it. Many accounts of pillage are to be found in the writings of the Ethiopian chroniclers Wäldä Maryam and Zänäb, as well as in the contemporary Amharic letters of Däbtära Assäggahañ. Some of the worst destruction occurred in Bägémder, while the renowned coffee plantations of Zägé were hacked to the ground, and the towns of Gondär and Ifag both ravaged. One of the results was that a famine broke out at the capital where, Däbtära Assäggahañ states, "many people died of hunger," while Wäldä Maryam confirms that "the people suffered much."

The depredations of the period are also described in some detail by foreign writers. Stern, describing Téwodros's expedition to Wällo in 1856, states that "the villages were burnt, the fields laid waste, and men, women and children unsparingly butchered, or dragged into irredeemable captivity." Later expeditions were no less destructive. Rassam, writing of Dämbeya in 1866, observed, "only two years before this district was in a most flourishing condition, every foot of it was under cultivation, and a succession of villages dotted the length and breadth of the plain." Since that time, however, the area had become "almost a desert owing to the King's continued oppression of the poor inhabitants ... only a field here and there appeared to be under tillage, and the villages - small groups of miserable huts - were few and far between, while the bulk of the inhabitants were said to have died of hunger or disease." Notwithstanding all that it had suffered the area was soon afterwards again raided, the "whole district" being "completely despoiled of everything which the rapacious soldiery could lay hands on." Téwodros's missionary craftsman Martin Flad agrees that many villages were repeatedly plundered, many people being burnt to death in their houses, and that in a region which had once abounded in cattle not a single cow could then be seen. On one occasion, he believed, over 80,000 head of livestock were slaughtered, large numbers being left for the hyenas, and on another no less than 1,000,000 were killed in a fortnight, and "no one was allowed to keep a cow."

Considerable destruction was likewise noted in other areas. At Méčča, for example, Rassam reported in 1866 that Téwodros's soldiers had been "engaged in laying waste every village and cultivated spot within reach; the former were generally set fire to; and the latter plundered of the standing crops." On reaching Bifata, the Emperor, we are told, learnt that all the inhabitants had fled, whereupon he "ordered all the villages to be burned, and all the standing crops to be appropriated by the soldiery - an order no sooner issued than it was eagerly carried into execution - volumes of smoke almost immediately rising up in all directions, darkening the atmosphere for miles around." At Zägé the ravages were so great that the locality, Stern claimed, would "for years not recover from the horrors of its King's latest visit." The ills of this period were later summed up by the Italian missionary Massaia who observed that many regions were reduced to acute poverty, with plough oxen and cattle slaughtered, granaries despoiled, people killed or mutilated, and youths taken away to fight.[2]

---

[2] GB House of Commons (1868) 76, 119, 150; Heuglin (1868) 306, 313, 326; Dufton (1867) 183-4; Dye (1880) 472; Beke (1867) 36; Moreno (1942) 160-1, 169, 172-3, 179; Stern (1862) 34, 86-7, 212, 286; Weld Blundell (1906-7) 492; Mondon-Vidailhet (1905) 25, 27, 29, 41-3, 46, 48-9, 54; Fusella (1954-5) 68-9, 79, 106-7, 109; Conti Rossini (1935) 455-6; Rassam (1969) I, 215; Flad (1922) 201, 206; Massaia (1885-95) VIII, 10.

Pacification, and Opening of Trade Routes

Though involved throughout his reign in frequent fighting, Téwodros appears to have been well aware of the country's need of pacification. Early in his reign he issued a decree at Amba Čara, in August 1855, stating, according to French consul Guillaume Lejean, that "everyone should return to his lawful avocation, the merchant to his store, and the farmer to his plough." This edict was intended, Plowden states, as "a reassurance to the country, till then so distracted by civil war, that the primary aim of its ruler was imperatively directed towards the establishment of peace and prosperity throughout the realm."

These aspirations, however, Téwodros failed to achieve, and there is no evidence that his reign witnessed any amelioration of the heavy and often arbitrary burdens imposed on the peasantry which were intensified by the needs of the war. In 1866 for example we find him levying a tax in Bägémder, Rassam states, of no less than one-fifth of all cattle, and sheep - less no doubt than a ravenous army left to itself might exact, but almost certainly more than the taxes operative in earlier, more peaceful, times.

Téwodros nevertheless took resolute action to uproot banditry, and, according to Lejean, did so with "draconian severity." The people of Tisba, who were incorrigible bandits, once came to the ruler's presence, armed to the teeth, asking him to confirm their right, which they claimed had been recognised by Emperor Dawit (conceivably the early eighteenth century ruler of that name) to be allowed to exercise the profession of their fathers. "What is this profession?", asked Téwodros without suspicion. "Highway robbery," they insolently replied. "Listen," he declared, "your profession is dangerous, and agriculture is more profitable. Go down to the plain and cultivate it. It is the most beautiful in the empire. I will myself give you oxen and ploughs." The men of Tisba proving obdurate he dismissed them, giving them a later appointment at which they were suddenly, and without warning, put to death. Such severity, according to Lejean, achieved its result. The roads then blood-stained by brigandage and civil war, became as safe as those of France or Germany. "An inhabitant of Jenda said to me ... that before Theodore this village did not count a single market-day which was not followed by a murder: under the new reign not a single murder had taken place in the village or its surroundings." This picture is corroborated by the British traveller Henry Dufton who observed that Téwodros did his best to open the caravan routes which had been closed by war, and "dealt very mercilessly with the bandits and highway-robbers, whose ravages ... had tended to make the roads unsafe."

Further to assist trade Téwodros also "put an end" to the vexatious number of internal customs posts that had hampered commerce, and ordered, as Plowden noted in June 1855, that duties should be levied "at only three places in his dominions." This is confirmed by Dufton who observed that the monarch "simplified the regulations regarding commerce and customs dues". The reform was however, short-lived, and, as E.A. De Cosson, a subsequent British traveller, discovered, was "discontinued at Theodorus's death."[3]

---

[3] Lejean 1865) 63-4; GB House of Commons (1868) 151; Dufton (1867) 137; De Cosson (1877) I, 220.

Innovations at Gafat

Téwodros's ambition to strengthen and modernise his army had implications in the field of technology. His awareness of the need for mechanical and other innovations in the military field caused him to accept with enthusiasm an offer by the former Protestant missionary Samuel Gobat, by then the Anglican Bishop of Jerusalem, to provide him with missionary craftsmen. These artisans, who were Swiss-Germans trained at the Pilgrim's Mission at St. Chrischona, near Basle in Switzerland, consisted of Messrs. Bender, Kienzlen, and Mayer who arrived in 1855, and were joined three years later by two colleagues, Waldmeier and Saalmüller.

Gafat soon became the site of a royal workshop and arsenal, and was described by Waldmeier as "quite a colony of Europeans." No less important, "large numbers" of Ethiopians soon joined them, and not long afterwards the missionaries opened a school at which they taught handicrafts, in addition to reading, writing and religion.

Several technically-minded foreigners, who had come to Ethiopia independently to seek their fortune, were also settled at Gafat. They included Moritz Hall, a Polish Jew who was said to have deserted from the Russian army, Bourgeaud, a French gunsmith who had previously lived in Egypt, his compatriot Jacquin, a metal worker, and the enterprising German scientist Dr. Schimper, a renowned botanist who incidentally devised a way of producing local champagne. At Gafat these and other foreigners worked together fairly harmoniously. They served, Heuglin notes, as smiths, carpenters, engineers, saddlers, carriage-builders, and even armourers and manufacturers of cannon. They were hard-working, and, Waldmeier asserts, before long erected "a powerful water wheel" to power different kinds of machinery. The workshops at Gafat thus outclassed those of earlier rulers such as Däjazmač Berru Gošu or Negus Sahlä Sellasé.

Téwodros, an innovator in this as in other matters, "also contemplated" sending a batch of Ethiopians to England and France "for the purpose of learning useful trades," as Dufton reports. No such project seems to have ever been envisaged by earlier nineteenth century rulers of the country.[4]

The Gafat Foundry

The foundry at Gafat, which deserves an honourable place in the history of Ethiopian technology, made use, according to Waldmeier, of three feet high furnaces, which were operated with the help of traditional skin bellows worked by hand, and produced a temperature of 700 degrees centigrade. The coal for the foundry came from Čelga and the right bank of the Gälila river where there were six seams, according to Beke, of "very good quality" coal three miles long and ten inches deep, while the lime was obtained from Däbrä Tabor and Dälanta. Though produced by unskilled missionaries and their largely untrained Ethiopian assistants the metal obtained at Gafat, Stern was told, "needed only more skilful preparation to equal the best English pig-iron."

---

[4] Dufton (1867) 72-92, 167; Stern (1862) 77-9; Blanc (1868) 169-70; Waldmeier (1886) 63-9, (1896) 9, 46; Heuglin (1868) 304-5.

The foreigners at Gafat were not allowed to leave the country, but were well treated by their royal master, who, whenever in the neighbourhood, paid frequent visits to inspect the progress of their labours. The monarch, Rassam noted in June 1866, "used to go down almost every day to see his artisans at work." Thanks to his encouragement, and the craftsmen's efforts, Gafat was "transformed," Flad observes, "into a large arsenal and factory where gunpowder, carriages, cannons, and bombs were manufactured and brʰken flintlocks were repaired." In addition to the Europeans close on a thousand Ethiopians worked at Gafat. "All the clever men of Abyssinia," Waldmeier claims, were "brought thither by order of the king." The labour force is said to have comprised 200 Christian Amharas, 300 Gallas, and 200 Fälašas, some of whom the proselytising missionaries succeeded in converting.

The establishment at Gafat made a deep impression on the local Ethiopian population. The foreign artisans built a "fine town," a contemporary chronicler observed, with running water inside and outside the compound, a water-mill capable of cutting wood and grinding and sieving gunpowder, and a "fine house" with glass doors and windows. The entire compound was protected by a strong wall guarded by four cannon. The remains of these buildings and the surrounding wall can still be seen. Abbäbäw Yégzaw, an Ethiopian scholar from the area who revisited it in 1971-2, claimed that amid the ruins he was able to discern the manner in which water had been made to flow into four successive compartments. "What is astounding," he wrote, "is that the remains of iron and glass are still found. The elders of the area know what each compartment was used for. This is where the charcoal was prepared; here was the area for smelting, etc."[5]

Cannon-Making

The highlight of the craftsmen's presence at Gafat was the manufacture of cannon, which was the most remarkable technological event of the reign. Téwodros, whose power base lay in the north-west of Ethiopia, where it was extremely difficult to import cannon, was deeply conscious of the need to manufacture such weapons in the country. He seized the opportunity of attempting to do so in 1861 when a French metal-caster called Jacquin declared his willingness to make a mortar if assisted by the other craftsmen at Gafat. The result, as the Swiss missionary Theophilus Waldmeier later reported, was that "the King wrote us a letter ordering us to stand by Jacquin in every way, to support him with advice and action, and to serve him as translators. We made no objection to this for we had been recommended as people who possessed technical skill and who were ready to help with anything required. The work was therefore undertaken, and a blast furnace was built and a bellows installed. The iron was carried on the back of loyal servants from far away. After much time and many efforts the day for pouring arrived. A great crowd stood around the furnace awaiting the happy result while the others worked the bellows with great speed hoping for a great reward from the King. ... M. Jacquin soon noticed that the work had failed, for the furnace, which was made out of poor material, had melted before the iron reached melting-point. The Frenchman began to lament and weep; he went half-mad, cried wildly, and finally asked the King's permission to leave."

---

[5] Waldmeier (1886) 19, 46, 73, (1896) 127-8; Beke (1867) 319-20; Stern (1862) 320; Rassam (1869) II, 148; Flad (1869) 55; Fusella (1954-5) 105-6; Abbäbaw Yegzaw (1965 E.C.)

Not long after the Frenchman's departure Téwodros, Waldmeier continues, "came to Gafat and swore by his death that we should not abandon Jacquin's work, but go on trying. We replied, 'Your Majesty, we have neither knowledge nor experience in this matter, and are quite ignorant of it, and we are afraid to undertake what is above our strength.' 'That does not matter,' answered the King, 'If you are my friends, try. If God allows it to succeed, it will be well; if not, it will be well.'" To underline his insistence on the missionaries' cooperation, however, he arrested the latters' servants.

Waldmeier and his colleagues, however, continued to argue that they were "incapable of establishing a blast furnace," but were "willing to undertake any other work to which they were equal." Téwodros, who showed himself much displeased at this, replied by asking the visitors to make a cart, but later, in an effort to overcome the royal displeasure, Waldmeier made a gunstock, whereupon the monarch expressed himself delighted, and at once released the missionaries' imprisoned servants. He then asked their masters to devote their attention to making a blast-furnace for the manufacture of guns. At about this time the enterprising Polish Jew, Moritz Hall, succeeded in casting a small mortar and some bullets. "When the King saw this," Waldmeier reports, "he jumped with happiness and thanked God, but he was not fully satisfied, for the mortar was too small for him, so he gave Moritz orders to cast a bigger one. ... Herr Moritz said, 'I am unable to undertake such a work, but if the Europeans at Gafat help me I hope to be able to oblige your Majesty.' 'Good,' replied the King, 'Waldmeier and all the Europeans shall be at your disposal.'"

Téwodros then ordered Waldmeier and his comrades to help the project in every way. "I could not oppose this," the missionary recalls, "for I had good reason not to arouse the King's wrath." The missionaries accordingly set to work, but, Waldmeier continues, "Herr Moritz, the caster, was at a loss what to do, and the work made us unhappy. We were in great difficulty and were helpless *vis-à-vis* the moody King who sent us letter after letter asking us whether our work had succeeded. Time and time again we were obliged to give a negative answer, but the King's patience was greater than ours; he comforted us and sent us word: 'Begin again from the beginning.' This we did, but in vain."

The workers at Gafat nevertheless continued to persevere. "After unspeakable effort," reports Waldmeier, "we made a final despairing attempt ... and, behold, for the first time we were successful. All the Abyssinians of the area, who had for a long time laughed at our work, came to share our joy and to congratulate us. We ourselves, together with our new brothers, were glad, for we, as well as they, could now count on a good reception on the part of the King. ... The King was pleased beyond all measure with our little piece of metal, kissed it and cried, 'Now I am convinced that it is possible to make everything in Habbesh. Now the art has been discovered God has at last revealed Himself. Praise and thanks be to Him for it.' The King ... then asked us what, apart from his crown and the throne, would we like to have from him. 'Your Majesty,' we answered, we wish for nothing but to remain in constant possession of your love and friendship.' He replied, 'I will give you my love and friendship, and, in addition, each one of you shall have 1,000 dollars and provisions for your household.'" Soon afterwards he asked the missionaries to make a larger gun, and, Waldmeier duly notes: "We cast a bigger mortar with which all the Abyssinians were very pleased."

Gun-making then proceeded apace, and when Dufton visited the country in 1862-3 he found that the Europeans were engaged in the manufacture of cannon and mortars, while their Ethiopian assistants and trainees were "beginning to profit" from the work. The craftsmen, he adds, soon afterwards "produced a small mortar, which, considering the manner in which it was made, was a marvel. The metal was melted in some thirty crucibles, on fires in the ground, blown by hand-bellows of the most primitive description - consisting of a leather bag, the mouth of which is opened on being drawn up for the receipt of air, and closed again when the air is to be driven by pressure through the clay tube conducting to the fire ... every encouragement is given by the king to his people in their endeavours to perfect themselves in the manufacture of these implements, for he is fully aware that this is the best way for him to secure his independence of other nations."

Téwodros made extensive use of missionary craftsmen, it should be noted, because he had scarcely any other source of skilled manpower. He was, however, like many of his predecessors over the last four centuries, constantly trying to import other workers, as well as fire-arms, from abroad. In October 1862 for example he spoke to British Consul Cameron of his desire to purchase weapons from England, and Cameron subsequently reported to London that the most acceptable presents for the monarch would include mortars, rockets, small cannon, grenades, fire-arms and ammunition. Such hints were, however, largely ignored by the British Foreign Office. The ruler later, in January 1864, sent Flad to England, in an unsuccessful attempt to engage gun-smiths and other artisans. Later again - at the height of his quarrel with the British Government - we find Téwodros attempting to obtain skilled workers through the assistance of the British envoy Hormuzd Rassam who recorded, in April 1866, that the Emperor had sent him a note declaring, "My desire is that you should send to her Majesty, the Queen, and obtain for me a man who can make cannons and muskets, and one who can smelt iron; also an instructor of artillery. I want these people to come here with their implements and everything necessary for their work, and then they shall teach us and return." The Ethiopian ruler's tragedy resulted in large measure from the fact that the British Government failed to heed these requests.

Téwodros meanwhile was redoubling his efforts, and demands, for the local manufacture of weapons. In 1863 Moritz Hall and the missionaries cast a large mortar which, however, Waldmeier reports, only whetted the royal appetite for more. The labours of the gunsmiths were therefore again intensified. Writing of 1866 the missionary observes: "We had to work like slaves night and day under the orders of the King who had set up his camp at Gafat. The King wanted work from us which was beyond our skill and power. He wanted us to cast 30 pounders, 7 feet long. We could not oppose the constantly irritated King, for the least thing drove him to such fury that he could easily have attacked us.... We undertook the work trembling, but after the second attempt we succeeded."

Waldmeier, whose relations with the monarch had then seriously deteriorated, records, with venom, that toward the end of the year the latter "ordered us to cast a mortar from which a 1,000 pound cannon-ball could be fired. We were afraid to refuse and were afraid to obey, but God did not abandon us in this hour of need. ... The Lord helped us by letting our work succeed. ... The king wanted to put us all in chains and throw us into prison, but because we were busy making this great gun he was prevented from doing us harm, for he wished to satisfy his boundless pride through this colossal work for which he needed white slaves."

The making of guns strained the Emperor's' resources to the utmost. Brass was collected, chronicler Wäldä Maryam recalls, from all parts of the country to be melted down, together with 30 vases from Mäqdäla, after which "the Negus manufactured a cannon, which they called *Bomba*, of such a size as had never been seen in Ethiopia before. A man could get into it and come out again the other end." This weapon, which was later christened Sebastapol after the famous battle in the Crimean war, is said to have weighed seven tons, and, required as many as 500 people, Rassam says, to pull it uphill. "It was unquestionably a wonderful piece of ordnance for its size," the envoy commented, "and more wonderful still as the workmanship of his Majesty's European artisans who had no experience of casting cannon." Téwodros later declared that the day of its casting was one of the happiest of his life.

By such means Téwodros succeeded in building up the first significant arsenal of artillery in Ethiopian history. At Mäqdäla the Ethiopian ruler, Clements Markham, the British geographer-cum-historian reports, had twenty-four brass cannon, four cannon and nine brass mortars, the latter all made in Ethiopia, "some with neat inscriptions in Amharic."[6]

First Steps in Road-building

Téwodros can be seen as an innovator also in the field of road-building which until his time had been rare in Ethiopia. His motivation, like that of great road-builders in other lands, was primarily military, and sprang from his need to move his troops - and cannon - quickly from one part of the country to another. An early glimpse of his activity as a road-builder is afforded by Consul Plowden, who, in a report of March 1859, noted that the Ethiopian ruler was then employing some Europeans in road-making, and paid them "handsomely' for their work as he said that he "could only succeed in conquering all his foes by making wide roads, that he may pass with his army rapidly from one point to another." By working at the roads with his own hands Téwodros, the consul adds, overcame his men's traditional dislike of manual labour, and showed himself "delighted with the operation of blasting." Not long after this Téwodros, with the help of the Protestant workmen's mission, began the construction of the country's first embryonic road network, to link Däbrä Tabor with Gondär, Gojjam and Mäqdäla. The craftsmen, with Téwodros's approval, at about this time also constructed a carriage to travel on these roads - one of the first such vehicles ever seen in the land.

Téwodros's courage and determination as a road-builder in the last months of his reign, when he was engaged in transporting his cannon from Däbrä Tabor to the mountain citadel of Mäqdäla, was later described by Henry Blanc, who though one of the Emperor's British captives, wrote with admiration that "from early dawn to late at night Theodore was himself at work; with his own hand he removed stones, levelled the ground, or helped to fill up small ravines. No one could leave so long as he was there himself; no one would think of eating, drinking, or of rest, while the Emperor showed the example and shared the hardships." Describing the country traversed by

---

[6] Waldmeier (1886) 7-9, 11-2, 47, 55-8, 60-7; Dufton (1867) 84-6, 166-7; GB House of Commons (1868) 219, 467, 486, 570; Rassam (1869) II, 101-3, 303-4, 306; Weld Blundell (1906-7) 26-7, 33; Markham (1969) 367.

the road in the vicinity of Mäqdäla, Blanc adds: "the work now before him would have driven any other man to despair. ... He went, however, steadily to work. Little by little he made a road, creditable even to a European engineer."

The immensity of the work likewise later impressed members of the British expeditionary force despatched against the reforming Ethiopian ruler. Captain H.M. Hozier described Téwodros's road to Mäqdäla as "a grand feat of rude engineering," and adds: "rocks had been hurled aside or blasted through, at an immense expense of labour and of time." Markham agrees that the road was "a most remarkable work - a monument of dogged and unconquerable resolution. Rocks were blasted, trees sawn down, revetment walls of loose stones mixed with earth and branches built up, and everywhere a strengthening hedge of branches at the outer sides, to prevent the earthwork from slipping. The details of blasting and revetting were of course done under the direction of his German [in fact Swiss!] artisans; but the King himself was the chief engineer, who selected the trace and organised the labour. At one or two points several trial traces were marked out, before the final one was adopted. ... From early dawn until dark the Europeans were obliged to be in attendance on this extraordinary man, whose resolute determination to overcome all obstacles never failed him. ... Well might Mr. Flad exclaim 'He has indeed an iron perseverance!'" Alexander Shepherd, a reporter for the *Times of India*, took a similar view, observing that the road "bore witness to the perseverance and pains-taking efforts of its maker," for though the gradient was sometimes too steep, the road was "altogether a kingly structure; its august engineer had scorned to adopt the little devices in vogue among the profession for overcoming or avoiding whatever difficulties unkind nature had placed in his way. If rocks could be rolled aside bodily, they had been so rolled aside; if otherwise, they had been cut asunder at an immense sacrifice of time, labour, and powder; but in no instance had they been allowed to interfere with the symmetry of the King's highway. So with the hills and every other species of let or hindrance.[7]

A Boat on Lake Tana

Téwodros's innovative mind also found expression, albeit abortive, in an attempt to establish a fleet on Lake Tana. Blanc, who describes this remarkable initiative, comments that "there was no doubt that his Majesty had made up his mind to have a small navy." To this end he asked the European craftsmen at his court to start boat-building, but they replied, as they had done in the question of casting the cannon, that they lacked the necessary skill though they were willing to learn under experts. Notwithstanding this refusal Waldmeier and his missionary colleague, Saalmüller, subsequently made a raft. Téwodros also asked Rassam about boat-building, but the latter, according to Stern, "shirked the question" by pleading ignorance.

Téwodros was, however, not to be dissuaded by such replies. "Seeing that everybody seemed reluctant to help him," writes Blanc, "he went to work himself; he made an immense flat-bottomed bulrush boat of great thickness, and to propel it made two large wheels worked by hand: in fact he had invented a paddle steamer, only the locomotive agent was deficient." Rassam, who has also left an account of this attempt at boat-building, states that for nearly a month, in April 1866, Téwodros was "engaged

---

[7] Dufton (1867) 137-8; GB House of Commons (1868) 189-90; Waldmeier (1886) 73; Stern (1862) 103; Blanc (1868) 342-4; Hozier (1869) 178; Markham (1869) 294-7; Shepherd (1868) 217, 222.

in building what he called an imitation of a steamer. Two large boats, sixty feet long and twenty feet wide midships, with wooden decks, and a couple of wheels affixed to the sides of each, to be turned by a handle like that attached to a common grindstone, were accordingly constructed; but although nearly a hundred men were taken on board, the wheels were only immersed about four inches. The day they were launched, he invited the members of the [British diplomatic] Mission to witness the experiment, and the vessel in which he had embarked moved so rapidly after the bulrushes had got well soaked, which made it subside deeper into the water, that he seemed frantic with joy, whilst the natives looked on with admiring wonder.... He proceeded to try how the vessel would behave against the wind, and on rounding the peninsula encountered a strong breeze, which soon convinced him of the futility of the attempt. The incongruous material of which the boat was constructed, one elastic and the other the opposite - no effort having been made to ensure an equal pressure upon them from without - began to give way after a little tossing, and his Majesty deemed it prudent to return as speedily as possible to the smooth water of the bay." This, Rassam notes, was the end of Téwodros's attempt at building a navy - which was scarcely surprising as he was soon to face a major land invasion which was to lead to his death.[8]

Attempted Suppression of the Slave Trade

Téwodros differed from earlier rulers - Emperor Susenyos perhaps alone excepted - in that he was a strong opponent of the slave trade. In November 1854 - some three months before his coronation - he wrote to Plowden, stating that he had forbidden the export of slaves on pain of severe punishment. On coming to power the reforming monarch again declared the trade illegal - but, like later rulers who followed in his foot-steps, was in no position to enforce his anti-slavery decrees. Realising the impossibility of achieving complete abolition he permitted existing slaves to be sold to Christians, provided that they purchased them for charity, and himself set the example by paying the Muslim dealers for slaves which he then had baptised. Later, however, he seems to have had second thoughts as to the wisdom of this policy, and informed Consul Cameron of his intention to "stop the trade effectively - not as a concession to us, but because he hated it himself." The Emperor subsequently ordered the amputation of the right hand and left food of anyone found guilty of selling Christian slaves. The sincerity of his anti-slavery credentials was fully accepted by Waldmeier who recalls that Téwodros wrote to him, saying, "Teach these young boys arts and religion, ... and I will pay all their expenses." His opposition to the enslavement, and sale of slaves, was based on the *Fethä Nägäst*, or traditional Ethiopian code of law, and was therefore concerned primarily with Christians - moreover it did not prevent his men while on campaign from capturing many "pagans" as slaves.[9]

---

[8] Blanc (1868) 147, 164; Stern (1868) 251; Rassam (1869) II, 120.

[9] Methodios of Aksum (1970) 51; GB House of Commons (1868) 221; Beke (1867) 255; Waldmeier (1886) 71-2; Moreno (1942) 175, 177; Blanc (1868) 2; Stern (1862) 129, 146.

Attempted Land Reform

Téwodros was also a would-be land reformer. On gaining control of Šäwa he at once endeavoured to reform its land system by strengthening rights of tenure. He accordingly issued a proclamation, chronicler Wäldä Maryam states, designed to institute private property in the province. He decreed that land should belong to those whose fathers had already held it as fiefs, and that persons without such claims should look to him as their father. Though this edict was at first universally acclaimed it is said that after its promulgation there was no one in Šäwa who did not claim land or pretend that this or that property belonged to his father. There were in consequence so many disputes that Téwodros was obliged to issue a new decree reinstating the old institutions.

Some of the priests also clamoured for a share in the land distribution proclaimed in Šäwa. In September 1857 they are said by Däbtära Zänäb to have been asked to be allowed the lands they had possessed prior to the period of the *mäsafent*, but the monarch, who felt that the Church was already over-endowed with landed property, was unsympathetic. "What shall I eat and give to my soldiers?," he is supposed to have said. "You have taken all the lands, calling them 'Lands of the Cross!' [i.e. Church lands]". In the ensuing dispute a priest insolently declared that Téwodros should follow the time-honoured practice of marching from place to place in order to spread the burden of his court and army over the whole empire. "Remain four months," he said, and eat up Armäččäho, Sägädé, Wälqayt and Tegré, then establish yourself at Aringo, and eat up Bägémder, Lasta, Yäjju, Mécca, Agäw[meder], Damot and Gojjam as was done in the past." Téwodros, however, was not amused, and cried out, "You effeminate one, if you found me alone, you would kill me with your muslin turban as was done to Emperor Iyasu!" A fierce quarrel then broke out between the Emperor and his soldiers, on the one side, and the Abun and the priests on the other. Téwodros likewise made some changes in land tenure elsewhere in the country, notably in the north where he restored certain lands in Akkälä Guzay which had earlier been given, by Däjazmač Webé, to personalities in Särayé, and also established hereditary ownership of land in the former district.

Perhaps the most important of Téwodros's proposed land reforms, however, was in relation to Church property. His efforts in this field were described by Stern, who, though himself a critic of the Church's extensive ownership of land, was even more critical of Téwodros for trying to reduce it. The extent of Church land-holding was, as he put it, "a great eyesore" to the monarch who, "anxious to appropriate these extensive possessions for his own use ... artfully promised to provide for the wants of the clergy, while depriving them of their land." This proposal was, predictably, opposed by the clergy, whose objections so angered him that, the missionary claims, "he would probably have evoked the sword to decide the quarrel, but his faithful followers reminded him that the troops and the nation were with the priests, and that serious consequences might ensue". The result was that "the storm abated," and Téwodros, "convinced of the unreasonableness of a conflict that might, at the very outset of his reign, convulse the whole realm to its very centre, yielded to the dissuasions of his friends, and the church spoliation plan was suspended till 1860, when it was carried into effect." Blanc, who tells the story with somewhat different emphasis, declares that Téwodros "could not tolerate any power in the State but his own," and that when he judged the time favourable he "confiscated all the Church lands and revenues," including some of the Abun's own property. All land belonging to ecclesiastical establishments, an anonymous Amharic document of the time confirms, was accordingly seized, and the number of priests attached to a church was limited to five, or seven in the case of the more important ones. Téwodros, the text claims, disliked monks and above all *däbtäras*, complaining that they "wore turbans on their heads and neither fought nor paid taxes," preferring to "live in cities with prostitutes or other people's wives."

Téwodros's attack on Church property not surprisingly produced much discontent on the part of the clergy. Stern, writing, it will be recalled, as a critic, states that the latter were "not so easily gulled" by the Emperor's offer to look after their material needs while taking their lands, and "all unanimously declared that they would not be slaves dependent on royal bounty." The Abun's anger at this time, Blanc says, "knew no bounds", while Dufton says that the Emperor's action "aroused the inveterate enmity of the sacerdotal caste." His kindness to poor priests, however, "proved that he was not conspiring against the religion of the land, and justified the act of spoliation in the eyes of the people", while the increased revenues thus obtained "helped him to support his numerous soldiery, and to carry out those other measures for the improvement of the country which he had instituted, he himself living in the simplest and most unkingly manner possible."

Opposition from the priesthood nonetheless seems to have contributed significantly to Téwodros's troubles and ultimate fall. His defeat by the British, and subsequent suicide, brought an end to these attempted reforms, for Wagšum Gobazé (later King of Kings Täklä Giyorgis), the ruler of Amhara, proved his zeal for the Orthodox faith, according to the French historian Georges Douin, by at once declaring the restoration to the Church of its former lands.[10]

Abandonment of Gondär

One of the most important decisions taken by Téwodros, at the very beginning of his reign, was his decision to establish himself at Ras Ali Alula's capital, Däbrä Tabor (which he subsequently abandoned in favour of the mountain fortress of Mäqdäla). Téwodros's successive use of these two capitals - and his armed attacks on the city of Gondär on two separate occasions in 1864 and 1866 - finally sealed the fate of the old metropolis, which, unable to survive the collapse of centralised imperial power, had been declining for a little over a century. Gondär, which in Téwodros's time thus forfeited its status as a empire-wide capital, thereby lost most of what was left of its old political, commercial and religious importance, and was abandoned by many of its churchmen - including the Abuna, as well as not a few of the traders and craftsmen whose work and activities have been described in these pages.[11]

---

[10] Mondon-Vidailhet (1905) 17-8; Moreno (1942) 166-7; Perini (1905) 107; Fusella (1954-5) 90-1; Stern (1868) 24-5; Blanc (1868) 281; Dufton (1867) 140-1; Douin (1936-41) III, Part II, 293.

[11] Pankhurst (1985) 41-88.

Marriage and Dress Reform, Letter-Writing and the Use of Amharic

Despite his conflict with the Church, Téwodros was a keep protagonist of Christian values, particularly in relation to marriage. Opposed to the lax sexual mores of his day, he was, according to Plowden, "married himself at the altar and strictly continent," and "ordered or persuaded all who love him to follow his example." He also "forbade the maintenance of concubines," Kotzika, a Greek merchant, states; and insisted, the consul says, on "the greatest decency of manners and conversation."

Another of his attempted reforms related to dress, where he insisted, according to Plowden that "all about his person" should wear "loose flowing trowsers," instead of the "half-naked costume" which had by then introduced by the Oromos. On the other hand he criticized the old sumptuary laws, which had prevented all but the nobility from wearing shirts, as a "childish custom," and decreed that all Ethiopians, Rassam states, "might wear a cotton shirt, which, however, was not to descend below the knees." At the same time he used dress to distinguish his officers from his other subjects "by raising the silk shirt into an Order of distinction, retaining its investiture as a prerogative of the Sovereign, and decreed that all those on whom it had not been conferred, and who held offices under the State, were to wear their cotton shirts below the knees."

Téwodros also took steps early in his career "to substitute letters", as Plowden reports, "for verbal messages." Most of these written communications have disappeared with the passage of time, and many were doubtless destroyed by the British in 1868 when they looted Mäqdäla and later burnt it to the ground. Sufficient are, however, extant to show that their author was familiarising his courtiers and officials with a more literate, efficient and structured system of administration than had existed in former times.

Doubtless aware of the country's cultural decline, to which reference has been made in an earlier chapter, he likewise took steps to collect a great library of Ethiopian manuscripts - the finest such collection ever assembled. These works were housed in the compound of the church of Mädhané 'Aläm at Mäqdäla which Téwodros had earlier erected, but were subsequently looted by the British who took some four hundred volumes, the best in the collection, to London in 1868.

The innovating ruler seems also to have appreciated the need to promote Amharic in place of the classical language Ge'ez. It was in this connection significant that he had a volume of the Gospels of Matthew and Mark in Amharic written for himself, and that the chronicles of his reign, unlike those of previous centuries, were written in that language which was thereafter to remain the country's administrative and literary language.[12]

Most of Téwodros's efforts, however, were rendered futile by the debacle of Mäqdäla. They were, however, historically important, for they indicate the direction in which the reforming ruler had hoped to steer his country's destiny. His attempted reforms for the most part were not substantially implemented during his lifetime, but for that very reason remained in a sense blue-prints for the rest of the century.

---

[12] GB House of Commons (1868) 150-1; Methodios of Aksum (1970) 51; Rassam (1869), I, 199, II, 5, 6, 11; Heuglin (1868) 347; R.J. Pankhurst (1973) 15-42; B.L. Orient 733; Wright (1878) 34.

A turning-point in Ethiopia's 19th century history: The destruction of Téwodros's capital, Mäqdäla, by British sappers, seen below. From R. Acton *The Abyssinian Expedition* (London, 1868).

BIBLIOGRAPHY

House in Čäläqot, Tegré, where Nathaniel Pearce, one of the most interesting foreign residents in early 19th century Ethiopia, resided. From H. Salt, *A Voyage to Abyssinia* **(London, 1814)**

BIBLIOGRAPHY

Abbäbaw Yegzaw (1964) "Gäfat yä'asé Téwodros yä-berät fabrika," Ya-zareytu Ityopya 25 Ter 1956 E.C = February 4, 1964.

Abbadie, Antoine d' (1868) L'Abyssinie et le roi Théodore, Paris.

Abbadie, Antoine d' (1881) Dictionnaire de la langue amariñña, Paris.

Abbadie, Antoine d' (1898) Géographie de l'Ethiopie, Paris.

Abbadie, Antoine d' (n.d.) Journal et mélanges, France, Bibliothèque Nationale, France, Nouvelle Acquisition MS. 21,300.

Abbadie, Arnauld d' (1868), Douze ans de séjour dans la Haute-Ethiopie, Vol I, Paris.

Abbadie, Arnauld d' (1980, 1983), Douze ans de séjour dans la Haute-Ethiopie, Vols II and III, Città del Vaticano.

Abir, M. (1965) "Brokerage and Brokers in Ethiopia in the First Half of the 19th. Century," Journal of Ethiopian Studies, III, No. 1, 1-5.

Abir, M. (1968) Ethiopia: The Era of the Princes The Challenge of Islam and the Reunification of the Christian Empire 1769 to 1855, London.

Abir, M. (1966) "Salt, Trade and Politics in Ethiopia in the 'Zämänä Mäsafent,' Journal of Ethiopian Studies, IV, No. 2, 1-10.

Acton, R. (1872) The Abyssinian Expedition and the Life and Reign of King Theodore, London.

Akalou Wolde Michael (1966) "The Impermanency of Royal Capitals in Ethiopia," Yearbook of the Association of Pacific Coast Geographers, Cornvallis, Oregon, 147-56.

Aleme Eshete (1971) "Une ambassade du Ras Ali en Egypte: 1852," Journal of Ethiopian Studies, IX, No. 1, 1-8.

Aleme Eshete (1973) "The Rôle and Position of Foreign-educated Interpreters in Ethiopia (1800-1889)," Journal of Ethiopian Sudies, XI, No. 1, 17-27.

Annesley, G.: see Valentia, Lord.

Appleyard, D.L., Irvine, A.K. and Pankhurst, R. (1985) Letters from Ethiopian Rulers (Early and Mid-Nineteenth Century), London.

Arén, G. (1978) Evangelical Pioneers in Ethiopia: Origins of the Evangelical Church Mekane Yesus, Uppsala.

Asfa-Wossen Asserate, (1980) *Die Geschichte von Šawa (Äthiopien) 1765. Nach dem Tārika Nagaśt des Belatten Géta Heruy Walda Selasse*, Wiesbaden.

Aymro Wondmagegnehu and Motovu, J. (1970) *The Ethiopian Orthodox Church*, Addis Ababa.

Bairu Tafla (1987) *Aṣma Giyorgis and his Work*, Stuttgart.

Bairu Tafla (1977) *A Chronicle of Emperor Yohannes IV (1972-89)*, Wiesbaden.

Bairu Tafla (1973) "Education of the Ethiopian Makwenent in the Nineteenth Century," *Ethiopian Journal of Education*, VI, No. 1, 18-27.

Baratti, G. (1670) *The Late Travels of S. Giacomo Baratti into the Remote Country of the Abissins*, London.

Barker, W.C. (1906) "Narrative of a Journey to Shoa," in Forrest, G.W., *Selections from the Travels and Journals preserved in the Bombay Secretariat*, Bombay.

Bartnicki, A. and Mantel-Niecko, J. (1969-70) "The Role and Significance of Religious Conflicts in the Political Life of Ethiopia in the Seventeenth and Eighteenth Centuries", *Rassegna di Studi Etiopici*, XXIV, 5-39.

Basset, R. (1882) *Etudes sur l'histoire d'Ethiopie*, Paris.

Basset, R. (1909) *Histoire de l'Abyssinie (XVIe siècle) par Chihab El-Din Ahmed Ben 'Abd el-Qâder surnomé Arab-Faqih*, Paris.

Beccari, C. (1903-17) *Rerum Aethiopicarum Scriptores Occidentales. inediti a saeculo XVI ad XIX*, Roma.

Beccari, C. (1909) *Il Tigrè descritto da un missionario gesuita del secolo XVII*, Roma.

Beckingham, C.F. (1966) "The Travels of Jerónimo Lobo," *Journal of Ethiopian Studies*, IV, No. 1, 1-4.

Beckingham, C.F. and Huntingford, G.W.B. (1961) *The Prester John of the Indies*, Cambridge.

Beckingham, C.F. and Huntingford, G.W.B. (1954) *Some Records of Ethiopia, 1593-1646*, London.

Béguinot, F. (1901) *La cronaca abbreviata d'Abissinia*, Roma.

Beke, C.T. (!844) "Abyssinia - being a Continuation of Routes in that Country," *Journal of the Royal Geographical Society*, XIV, 1-76.

Beke, C.T. (1867) *The British Captives in Abyssinia*, London.

Beke, C.T. (1842) "Communication respecting the Geography of Southern Abyssinia", *Journal of the Royal Geographical Society*, XII, 84-101.

Beke, C.T. (1840-3) *A Diary written during a Journey in Abessinia in the Years 1840, 1841, 1842 and 1843*, British Library MS. 50,250A.

Beke, C.T. (1852) *Letters on the Commerce of Abyssinia and Other Parts of Africa*, London.

Beke, C.T. (1845) *A Statement of Facts relative to the Transactions between the Writer and the late British Politicʔl Mission to the Court of Shoa*, London.

Bell, J. (1842) "Extracts from a Journal of Travels in Abyssinia," *Miscallanea Aegyptica*, I, 9-25.

Bernatz, J.M. (1852) *Scenes in Ethiopia*, London.

Berry, LeVerle (1976) *The Solomonic Monarchy at Gonder 1630-1755: An Institutional Kingdom of Ethiopia*, Boston University Ph.D. thesis.

Blanc, H. (1868) *A Narrative of Captivity in Abyssinia*, London.

Blanc, H. (1874) "Notes médicales recueillies durant une mission diplomatique en Abyssinie," *Gazette Hebdomadaire de Médecine et de Chirugie*, XI, 129-33, 146-54, 193-200, 225-33, 241-9, 281-90, 297-305, 329-34, 345-52, 361-5.

Blondeel van Cuelebroeck, E. (1838-42) *Rapport générale de Blondeel sur son expédition en Abyssinie*, Bruxelles.

Bruce, J. (1790) *Travels to Discover the Source of the Nile*, 1st ed., Edinburgh

Bruce, J. (1813) *Travels to Discover the Source of the Nile*, 3rd ed., Edinburgh.

Budge, E.A. Wallis (1928a) *The Book of the Saints of the Ethiopian Church*, Cambridge.

Budge, E.A. Wallis (1928b) *History of Ethiopia, Nubia and Abyssinia*, London.

Budge, E.A. Wallis (1906) *The Life of Takla Haymanot*, London.

Burton, R.F. (1894) *First Footsteps in East Africa*, London.

Buxton, D.R. (1970) *The Abyssinians*, London.

Buxton, D.R. (1949) *Travels in Ethiopia*, London.

Caquot, A. (1957a) "Histoire amharique de Grāñ et des Gallas," *Annales d'Ethiopie*, II, 123-43.

Caquot, A. (1957b) "L'Homélie en honeur de l'Archange Raguel *Dersāna Rāgu'ēl*," *Annales d' Ethiopie*, II, 91-122.

Caraman, P. (1985) *The Lost Empire. The Story of the Jesuits in Ethiopia*, London.

337

Caulk, R. (1972a) "Firearms and Princely Power in Ethiopia in the Nineteenth Century," *Journal of African History*, XIII, 609-30.

Caulk, R. (1972b) "Religion and the State in Nineteenth Century Ethiopia," *Journal of Ethiopian Studies*, X, No. 1, 23-41."

Cecchi, A. (1885-7) *Da Zeila alle frontiere del Caffa*, Roma.

Cerulli, E. (1943-7) *Etiopi in Palestina; storia della comunita etiopica di Gerusa*lemme, Roma.

Cerulli, E. (1943) "L'Etiopia medievale in alcuni brani di scrittori arabi," *Rassegna di Studi Etiopici*, III, 272-94.

Cerulli, E. (1922) *The Folk-Literature of the Galla*, Cambridge, Mass.

Cheesman, R.E. (1936) *Lake Tana and the Blue Nile*, London.

Chojnacki, S. (1983) *Major Themes in Ethiopian Painting. Indigenous Developments, the Influence of Foreign Models and their Adaptation from the 13th to the 19th century*, Weisbaden.

Chojnacki, S. (1964) "Short Introduction to Ethiopian Painting," *Journal of Ethiopian Studies*, V, No. 2, pp. 1-11.

Combes, E. and Tamisier, M. (1838) *Voyage en Abyssinie, dans le pays des Gallas, de Choa et d'Ifat*, Paris.

Conti Rossini, E. (1916) "La cronaca reale abissina dall' anno 1800 all' 1840" *Rendiconti della Accademia Nazionale dei Lincei, Classe di scienze morali, storiche e filologiche*, II, 779-992.

Conti Rossini, C. (1935) "La fine di re Teodoro in un documento abissino," *Nuova Antologia*, 16 October 1935, pp. 453-58.

Conti Rossini, C. (1907) *Historia Regis Sarsa Dengel (Malak Sagad)*, Lonvain.

Conti Rossini, C. (1942), "Iyasu I, re d'Etiopia e martire," *Rivista di Studi Orientale*, XX, 65-128.

Conti Rossini, C. (1947) "Nuovi documenti per la storia d'Abissinia nel secolo XIX," *Rendiconti della Accademia Nazionale dei Lincei, classe di scienze morali, storiche e filologiche*, II, 357-416.

Conzelman, W.E. (1895) *Chronique de Galāwdēwos (Claudius), Roi d'Ethiopie*, Paris.

Cooke, A.C. (1867) *Routes in Abyssinia*, London.

Cozzika, J. (1867) *Question d' Abyssinie. Au peuple de la Grande Bretagne* (1867) Constantinople.

Crawford, O.G.S. (1958) *Ethiopian Itineraries, circa 1400-1524*, Cambridge.

Crummey, D. (1983) "Ethiopian Plow Agriculture in the Nineteenth Century," *Journal of Ethiopian Studies*, XVI, 1-23.

Crummey, D. (1972) *Priests and Politicians. Protestant and Catholic Missionaries in Orthodox Ethiopia 1830-1868*, Oxford.

Crummey, D, (1981a) "State and Society: 19th. Century Ethiopia," in D. Crummey and C.C. Stewart, *Modes of Production in Africa. The Precolonial Era*, Beverley Hills and London.

Crummey, D. (1969) "Tewodros as Reformer and Moderniser," *Journal of African History*, X, 457-69.

Crummey, D. (1971) "The Violence of Tewodros," *Journal of Ethiopian Studies*, IX, No. 2, 107-25.

Crummey, D. (1981b) "Women and Landed Property in Gondarine Ethiopia," *International Journal of African Historical Studies, XIV*, 445-65.

Crummey, D. (1918c) "Women, Property and Litigation among the Bagemder Amhara, 1750s to 1850s", in M.J. Hay and M. Wright, *African Women and the Law: Historical Perspectives*, Boston.

Dames, M.L. (1918-21) *The Book of Duarte Barbosa*, London.

De Cosson, E.A. (1877) *The Cradle of the Blue Nile. A Visit to the Court of King John of Ethiopia*, London.

Dimothéos Saprichian (1871) *Deux ans de séjour en Abyssinie ou vie morale, politique et religieuse des Abyssiniens*, Jerusalem.

Donzel, E.J. van (1979) *Foreign Relations of Ethiopia 1642-1700. Documents relating to the Journeys of Khodja Murad*, Istanbul.

Donzel, E.J. van (1986) *A Yemenite Embassy to Ethiopia 1647-1649. Al-Haymi's Sirat al Habasha*, Stuttgart.

Doresse, J. (1957) *L' empire du Prête-Jean*, Paris.

Douin, G. (1936-41) *Histoire du règne de Khédive Ismail*, Le Caire.

Duchesne-Fournet, J. (1908-9) *Mission en Ethiopie (1901-1903)*, Paris.

Dufton, H. (1867) *Narrative of a Journey Through Abyssinia in 1862-63*, London.

Dye, W. McE. (1880) *Moslem Egypt and Christian Abyssinia*, New York.

Ege, S. (1978) "Chiefs and Peasants: The Socio-Political Structure of the Kingdom of Shäwa in about 1840", *Horedoppgavi i Historie*, Bergen.

Esteves Pereira, F.M. (1900) *Chronica de Susenyos Rei de Ethiopia*, Lisboa.

Esteves Pereira, F.M. (1888) *Histoire de Minās, 'Ademas Saged, rei de Ethiopia*, Lisboa.

Faïtlovitch, J. (1905) *Notes d' un voyage chez les Falachas (Juifs d'Abssinie)*, Paris.

Faïtlovitch, J. (1907) *Proverbes abyssins*, Paris.

Ferret, P.V.A. and Galinier, J.G. (18478) *Voyage en Abyssinie, dans le provinces du Tigré, Samen et de l'Amhara*, Paris.

Ferry, C. (1961) "Quelques hypothèses sur les origines des conquêtes mussulmanes en Abyssinie au XVI siècle," *Cahiers d' Etudes Africaines*, II, 24-36.

Flad, F.M. (1869) *The Falashas (Jews) of Abyssinia*, London.

Flad, J.M. (1922) *60 Jahre in der Mission unter den Falaschas in Abessinien*, Basel.

Flad, J.M. (1869) *Zwölf Jahre in Abessinien, oder Geschichte des Königs Theodorus, und der Mission unter seiner Regierung*, Basel.

Flemming, J. (1890) "Hiob Ludolf," *Beiträge zur Assyriologie und Verleichende Semitische Sprachwissen*, I, 537-82.

Foster, W. (1949) *The Red Sea and Adjacent Countries at the Close of the Seventeenth Century*, London.

Foti, C. (1941) "La cronaca abbreviata dei re d'Abissinia in un manoscritto di Dabra Berhān di Gondar," *Rassegna di Studi Etiopici*, I, 87-118.

Fraenken, J.L.M. and Cope di Valromita, E. (1936) "L'Abissinia in alcune inchieste di funzionari olandesi del sec. XVII", *Rivista Storica Italiana*, I, 49-88.

Fusella, L. (1954-5) "La cronaca dell' Imperatore Teodoro II di Etiopia in un manoscritto amarico," *Annali dell' Istituto Universitario Orientale di Napoli*, VI, 61-121.

Fusella, L. (1953-4) "Le lettere del dabtarā Assaggākhañ," *Rassegna di Studi Etiopici*, XII, 80-95, XIII, 20-30.

Gamst, F.C. (1970) "Peasants and Elites without Urbanism; The Civilization of Ethiopia," *Comparative Studies in Society and History*, XII, 373-92.

Gamst, F.C. (1969) *The Qemant: A Pagan-Hebraic Peasantry of Ethiopia*, New York.

Gaudefroy-Demombynes, M. (1927), *Ibn Fadl Allah, al 'Umari, Masālik al abṣar el amṣar*, Paris.

G.B. House of Commons (1868) *Correspondence respecting Abyssinia 1846-1868*, London.

G.B. House of Commons (1868F) *Further Correspondence respecting Abyssinia*, 1868.

Gedamu Abraha (1967) "Wax and Gold", *Ethiopia Observer, XI, 226-43.*

Ghiorgis Mellessa (1969) "Gondar Yesterday and Today, " *Ethiopia Observer*, XII, 164-76.

Girard, S. (1873) *Souvenir d'un voyage en Abyssinie* (1868-69), Cairo.

Gobat, S. (1834) *Journal of a Three Years' Residence in Abyssinia... to which is prefixed A Brief History of the Church of Abyssinia by the Rev Professor Lee*, London.

Gobat, S. (1850) *Journal of a Three Years' Residence in Abyssinia... Preceded by an Introduction Geographical and Historical, on Abyssinia*, New York

Graham, D. (1867) *Glimpses of Abyssinia, or Extracts from Letters written while on a Mission from the Government of India to the King of Abyssinia in the Years 1841, 1842 and 1843*, London.

Graham, D. (1844) "Report on the Agriculture and Produce of Shoa," India Office, Bombay Secret Proceedings, Vol. 204, No. 1216D.

Graham, D. (1843) "Report on the Manners, Customs and Superstitions of the People of Shoa and on the History of the Abyssinian Church," *Journal of the Asiatic Society of Bengal*, XII, 625-728.

Guèbrè Sellassié (1930-1) *Chronique du règne de Ménélik II, rois de rois d'Ethiopie* Paris.

Guidi, I. (1903) *Annales Iohannis I, 'Iyāsu I et Bakāffā*, Lonvain.

Guidi, I. (1912) *Annales Regum 'Iyāsu II et 'Iyo'as*, Louvain.

Guidi, I. (1899) *Il "Fetha Nagast" o "Legislazione dei re"*, Napoli.

Guidi, I. (1901) *Vocabolario amarico-italiano*, Roma.

Guillain, M. (1856-7) *Documents sur l'histoire, la géographie et le commerce de l'Afrique orientale*, Paris.

Haile Gabriel Dagné (1971a) *Quran School System in Ethiopia*, Addis Ababa (mimeo).

Haile Gabriel Dagné (1971b) "The Traditional Ethiopian Curriculum," *Ethiopian Journal of Education*, IV, No. 2, 79-80.

Haile Michael Mesghinna (1966) "Salt Mining in Enderta," *Journal of Ethiopian Studies*, IV, No. 2, 127-35.

Halévy, J. (1877) *Travels in Abyssinia*, London.

Halls, J.J. (1834) *The Life and Correspondence of Henry Salt*, London.

Hammerschmidt, E. (1965) "Jewish Elements in the Cult of the Ethiopian Church", *Journal of Ethiopian Studies*, III, No.2, pp.1-12.

Harris, W.C. (1844) *The Highlands of Aethiopia*, London.

Henty, G.A. (1868) *The March to Magdala*, London.

Henze, R.L. (1977) *Ethiopian Jouneys. Travels in Ethiopia 1969-72*, London.

Herbert, M.E. (1867) *Abyssinia and its Apostle*, London.

Hess, R.L. (1969-70) "An Outline of Falasha History," *Proceedings of the Third International Conference of Ethiopian Studies*, I, 99-112, Addis Ababa.

Heuglin, T. (1868) *Reise nach Abessinien*, Jena.

Heuglin, T. (1857) *Reisen in Nord-Ost Afrika*, Gotha.

Historiale description d' Ethiopie (1558), Anvers.

Holland, T.J. and Hozier, H.M. (1870) *Record of the Expedition to Abyssinia*, London.

Houtsma, M.T. (1883) *Qui dicitur Al-Ta'qubi Ibn-Wadnih, Historiae*, Leiden.

Hozier, H.M. (1869) *The British Expedition to Abyssinia*, London.

Huntingford, G.W.B. (1965a) *The Glorious Victories of 'Amda Ṣeyon King of Ethiopia*, Oxford.

Huntingford, G.W.B. (1989) *The Historical Geography of Ethiopia, From the First Century AD to 1704*, London.

Huntingford, G.W.B. (1969) "Indices to Five Ethiopian Chronicles published in the Corpus Scriptorum Christianorum Orientalium, volumes 20-25," *Annali del' Istituto Orientale di Napoli*, XX, 281-316.

Huntingford, G.W.B. (1965b) *The Land Charters of Northern Ethiopia*, Addis Ababa.

Hussein Ahmed (1985) *Clerics, Traders and Chiefs: A Historical Study of Islam in Wallo (Ethiopia), with Special Reference to the Nineteenth Century*, Birmingham University Ph.D. thesis.

Hussein Ahmed (1988) "Traditional Muslim Education in Wallo", *Proceedings of the Ninth International Congress of Ethiopian Studies*, III, 94-106, Moscow.

Hyatt, H.M. (1928) *The Church of Abyssinia*, London.

Imbakom Kalewold (1970) *Traditional Ethiopian Church Education*, New York.

Isenberg, C.W. (1843) "Journal," Church Missionary Society, CA5/D13.

Isenberg, C.W. and Krapf, J.L. (1843) *Journal of the Rev. Messers. Isenberg and Krapf*. London.

Italy, Guida d' Italia della Consociazione Touristica Italiana, (1938) *Africa Orientale Italiana*, Milano

Jäger, O.A. and Pearce, I. (1974) *Antiquities of North Ethiopia*, Stuttgart.

Jesuits (1628) *Lettere annue di Ethiopia. Del 1624, 1625, e 1626*, Roma.

Johnston, C. (1844) *Travels in Southern Abyssinia. Through the Country of Adal to the Kingdom of Shoa*. London.

Jones, W. (1788) "Conversations with Abram, an Abyssinian, concerning the City of Gwender and the Sources of the Nile," *Asiatic Researches,* I, 383-88.

Kamil, M. (1975) "Die äthiopischen Prozessions - und Anghängekreuse," *Ethnologische Zeitschrift Zuerich*, I, 69-108.

Kammerer, A. (1936) *Le routier de Dom Joam de Castro*, Paris.

Katte, A. (1838) *Reise in Abyssinien*, Stuttgart.

Kinefe-Rigb Zelleke (1975) "Bibliography of Ethiopic Hagiographical Traditions", *Journal of Ethiopian Studies*, XIII, No. 2, 57-102.

Kirk, R. (1843) "Medical Report on the Kingdom of Shoa," *Transactions of the Medical and Physical Society of Bombay*, VII, 3-31.

Kobariewicz, W. (1973) *The Ethiopian Cross*, Addis Ababa.

Kolmodin, J. (1912-15) *Traditions de Tsazzega et Hazzega*, Roma and Upsal.

Krapf, J.L. (1867) *Travels, Researches and Missionary Labours*, London.

Lefebvre, T. (1845-8) *Voyage en Abyssinie*, Paris.

Legrand, J. (1728) *Voyage historique d' Abyssinie*, Paris.

Leiris, M. (1934) *L' Afrique fantôme*, Paris.

Leiris, M. (1934b) "Le culte de zars à Gondar", *Aethiopica*, II, 96-103, 125-6.

Lejean, G. (1864) "Théodore II et le nouvel empire d' Abyssinie," *Revue des Deux Mondes*, LIV, 200-35, 599-627.

Lejean, G. (1865) *Théodore II et le nouvel empire d' Abyssinie*, Paris.

Lejean, G. (1872) *Voyage en Abyssinie executé de 1862 à 1864*, Paris.

Levine, D.N. (1974) *Greater Ethiopia. The Evolution of a Multiethnic Society*, Chicago.

Levine, D. (1965) *Wax and Gold. Tradition and Innovation in Ethiopian Culture*, Chicago.

Lockhart, D.M. (1984) *The Itinerário of Jerónimo Lobo*, London.

Longhena, M. (1929) *Viaggi in Persia, India e Giava di Nicolo de' Conti*, Milano.

Ludolf, H. (1681) *Historia Aethiopica*, Frankfurt.

Ludolf, H. (1684) *A New History of Ethiopia*, London.

Ludolf, H. (1691) *Ad suam Historiam Aethiopicam antehac editam Commentarius*, Frankfurt.

Malécot (1972) *Les voyageurs français et les relations entre la France et l' Abyssinie de 1835 à 1870*, Paris.

Mängestu Lämma (1959E.C. = 1966-7) *Mäshäfä tezeta za Aläqa Lämma Haylu*, Addis Ababa.

Marco Polo (1954) *The Travels of Marco Polo*, London.

Markham, C. (1869) *A History of the Abyssinian Expedition*, London.

Massaia, G. (1885-95) *I miei trentacinque anni di missione nell' alta Etiopia*, Roma.

Mathew, D. (1947) *Ethiopia. The Study of a Polity 1540-1935*, London.

McCann, J. (1979) "The Ethiopian Chronicles: an African Documentary Tradition," *NorthEast African Studies*, I, 47-61.

Mendez, A. (1633) *Relation du revendissime patriche d' Ethiopie*, Lille.

Mérab, P. (1921-9) *Impressions d' Ethiopie. L' Abyssinie sous Ménélik II*, Paris.

Merid Wolde Aregay (1974) "Political Geography of Ethiopia at the Beginning of the Sixteenth Century," Accademia Nazionale di Lincei, *Problemi Attuali di Scienze e di Cultura*, I, 613-31.

Merid Wolde Aregay (1980) "A Reapprisal of the Impact of Firearms in the History of Warfare in Ethiopia (c. 1500-1800)," *Journal of Ethiopian Studies*, XIV, 98-121.

Merid Wolde Aregay (1984) "Society and Technology in Ethiopia 1500-1800," *Journal of Ethiopian Studies*, XVII, 127-47.

Mertens, R. (1949) *Eduard Rüppell. Leben und Werk eins Forschungsreisenden*, Frankfurt.

Messing, S.D. (1957) *The Highland-Plateau Amhara of Ethiopia*, University of Pennsylvania Ph.D thesis.

Methodios of Aksum [Fouyas] (1970) "An Unpublished Document edited and translated into English," *Abba Salama*, I, 15-64.

Mondon-Vidailhet, F.M.C. (1905) *Chronique de Théodoros II, roi des rois d' Ethiopie*, Paris.

Monti della Corte, A.A. (1938) *I castelli di Gondar*, Roma.

Mooney, H.F. (1955) *The Need for Forestry in Ethiopia*, Addis Ababa.

Moore, E. (1969) *Ethiopian Processional Crosses*, Addis Ababa.

Moreno, M.M. (1948) *Cent fables amhariques*, Paris.

Moreno, M.M. (1942) "La cronaca di re Teodoro attribuita al dabtarā 'Zaneb,'" *Rassegna di Studi Etiopici*, II, 143-90.

Morgan, M. (1969) "Continuities and Traditions in Ethiopian History. An Investigation of the Reign of Tewodros," *Ethiopia Observer*, XII, 244-69.

Munzinger, W. (1858) "Les contrés limitrophes de l'Habesch du coté du nord-est," *Nouvelles Annales des Voyages*, 6 série, IV, II, 5-55.

Natsoulas, T. (1977) "The Hellenic Presence in Ethiopia. A Study of a European Minority in Africa (1740-1936)," *Abba Salama*, VIII, 5-239.

Natsoulas, T. (1984) "Prologue to Modern Ties between Greece and Ethiopia: the Efforts of Ioannis Kotzikas during the Era of Tewodoros, 1845-1868," *NorthEast African Studies*, VI, Nos. 1-2, 147-70.

Nersessian, V. and Pankhurst (1982) "The Visit to Ethiopia of Yohannes Tovmačean, an Armenian Jeweller," *Journal of Ethiopian Studies*, XV, 79-104.

O' Mahoney, K. (1970) "The Salt Trail," *Journal of Ethiopian Studies*, VIII, No.2, 147-74.

Orhonlu, C. (1974) *Osmanli Imparatorlugu'nun Güneuy Siyaseti*, Istanbul.

Pakenham, T. (1959) *The Mountains of Rasselas*, London.

Pankhurst, E.S. (1955) *Ethiopia. A Cultural History*, Woodford Green.

Pankhurst, R. (1972a) "The Advent of Fire-arms in Ethiopian Ecclesiastical Manuscripts," *Ethiopia Observer*, XV, 51-62.

Pankhurst, R. (1979-80) "The Advent of the Maria Theresa Dollar in Ethiopia, its Effect on Taxation and Wealth Accumulation, and Other Economic, Political and Social Implications," *Northeast African Studies*, I, No.3, 19-48.

Pankhurst, R. (1984a) "Amharic Documents on Marriage and Adoption, Land Sales and Gifts and Disputes", *Quaderni di Studi Etiopici*, V, 98-107.

Pankhurst, R. (1968a) *Economic History of Ethiopia (1800-1935)*, Addis Ababa.

Pankhurst, R. (1984b) "Ethiopian Manuscript Illumination," *Azania*, XIX, 105-12.

Pankhurst, R. (1976a) "Ethiopian Slave Reminiscences of the Nineteenth Century," *Transafrican Journal of History*, V, No. 1, 98-110.

Pankhurst, R. (1964a) "The Ethiopian Slave Trade in the Nineteenth and Early Twentieth Century: A Statistical Inquiry," *Journal of Semitic Studies*, IX, 220-8.

Pankhurst, R. (1985-7) "Fear God, Honor the King. The Use of Biblical Allusion in Ethiopian Historical Literature," *Northeast African Studies*, VIII, 11-30, IX, 25-88.

Pankhurst, R (1962) "The Foundations of Education, Printing, Newspapers, Book Production, Libraries and Literacy in Ethiopia," *Ethiopia Observer*, VI, 241-90.

Pankhurst, R. (1971a) "Gabata and Related Board-Games of Ethiopia and the Horn of Africa", *Ethiopia Observer*, XIV, 154-206.

Pankhurst, R. (1981) "Hamasén and the Gondarine Monarchy: A Reapprisal of Oral Traditions," *N.E.A. Journal of Research on North East Africa*, I, No. 1, 32-50.

Pankhurst, R. (1971b) "The History and Principles of Ethiopian Chess", *Journal of Ethiopian Studies*, IX, No.2, pp. 149-72.

Pankhurst, R. (1976b) "The History of Bareya, Šanqella and Other Ethiopian Slaves from the Borderlands of Sudan," Paper presented to the Conference on Ethiopian Feudalism, Addis Ababa.

Pankhurst, R. (1977-9) "The History of Ethiopian-Armenian Relations," *Revue des Etudes Arméniens*, XII, 273-345, XIII, 259-312.

Pankhurst, R. (1982) *History of Ethiopian Towns from the Middle Ages to the Early Nineteenth Century*, Wiesbaden.

Pankhurst, R. (1985) *History of Ethiopian Towns from the Mid-Nineteenth Century to 1935*, Stuttgart.

Pankhurst, R. (1968b) "The History of Fire-arms in Ethiopia prior to to the Nineteenth Century," *Ethiopia Observer*, XI, 202-25.

Pankhurst, R. (1984c) "The History of Leprosy in Ethiopia to 1935", *Medieval History*, XXVIII, 57-72.

Pankhurst, R. (1974) "The History of Prostitution in Ethiopia," *Journal of Ethiopian Studies*, XII, No. 2, 159-78.

Pankhurst, R. (1961) *An Introduction to the Economic History of Ethiopia*, London.

Pankhurst, R. (1979) "The Kwer'ata Re'esu: the History of an Ethiopian Icon," *Abba Salama*, X, 169-87.

Pankhurst, R. (1964b) "Misoneism and Innovation in Ethiopian History," *Ethiopia Observer*, VII, 287-317.

Pankhurst, R. (1988) "Muslim Commercial Towns, Villages and Markets of Christian Ethiopia prior to the Rise of Téwodros," in S. Uhlig and Bairu Tafla, *Collectanea Aethiopica* (Stuttgart) 111-30.

Pankhurst, R. (1975a) "Old Time Ethiopian Cures for Syphilis, Seventeenth to Twentieth Centuries", *Journal of the History of Medicine and Allied Sciences*, XXIV, 119-216.

Pankhurst, R. (1969-70) "A Preliminary History of Ethiopian Measures, Weights and Values (Part III)," *Journal of Ethiopian Studies*, VII, No.1, 31-54, No.2, 99-164, VIII, No. 1, 45-85.

Pankhurst, R. (1971c) "The Rôle of Fire-arms in Ethiopian Culture (16th. to 20th. Centuries," *Journal des Africanistes*, XLVIII, No. 2, 131-44.

Pankhurst, R. (1969) "The Saint Simonians in Ethiopia," *Proceedings of the Third International Conference of Ethiopian Studies*, I, 169-223.

Pankhurst, R. (1975b) "Some Notes on the Historical and Economic Geography of the Meṣewa area (1520-1885)," *Journal of Ethiopian Studies*, XIII, No. 1, 49-91.

Pankhurst, R. (1983) "The Tents of the Ethiopian Court"," *Azania*, XVIII, 181-95.

Pankhurst, R. (1964) "The Trade of Northern Ethiopia in the Nineteenth and Early Twentieth Century," *Journal of Ethiopian Studies*, II, No. 1, 49-159.

Pankhurst, R. (1965) "The Trade of the Gulf of Aden Ports of Africa in the Nineteenth and Early Twentieth Century," *Journal of Ethiopian Studies*, III, No. 1, 39-81.

Pankhurst, R. (1972b) "Yohannes Kotzika, the Greeks and British Intervention against Emperor Tewodros," *Abba Salama*, III, 87-117.

Pankhurst, R. and Adi Huka (1975) "Early Nineteenth Century Oromo Childhood Reminiscences," *Ethiopian Journal of Education*, II, 39-47.

Pankhurst, R. and Germa-Selassie Asfaw (1979) *Tax Records and Inventories of Emperor Tewodros of Ethiopia 1855-1868*, London.

Pankhurst, R. and Ingrams, L. (1988) *Ethiopia Engraved*, London.

Pankhurst, R.J. (1973) "The Library of Emperor Tewodros II at Mäqdäla (Magdala)," *Bulletin of the School of Oriental and African Studies, University of London*, XXXVI, 15-42.

Pankhurst, R.J. and R.K. (1979) "Ethiopian Ear-picks", *Abbay*, X, 101-10.

Parkyns, M. (1853), *Life in Abyssinia*, London.

Paulos Tsadua (1968) *The Fetha Nagast. The Law of the Kings*, Addis Ababa.

Pearce, N. (1831) *The Life and Adventures of Nathaniel Pearce*, London.

Pearce, N. (1820) "A Small but True Account of the Ways and Manners of the Abyssinians," *Transactions of the Literary Society of Bombay*, II, 15-60.

Peiser, F.E. (1898) *Zur Geschichte Abessiniens im 17 Jahrhundert: Der Gesandtschaftsbericht des Hasan ben Ahmed El-Haimi*, Berlin.

Perini, R. (1905) *Di qua del Maréb*, Firenze.

Perruchon, J. (1893) *Les chroniques de Zar'a Ya'eqôb et de Ba'eda Mâryâm*, Paris.

Perruchon, J. (1894) "Histoire d' Eskender, d' 'Amda Syon II, et de Nā'od," *Journal Asiatique*, 9 sér., III, 319-66.

Perruchon, J. (1889) *Histoire des guerres d' 'Amda-Seyon, roi d' Ethiopie*, Paris.

Plant, R. (1985) *Architecture of Tigre, Ethiopia*, Worcester.

Plowden, W.C. (1868) *Travels in Abyssinia and the Galla Country, with an Account of a Mission to Ras Ali in 1848*, London.

Pollera, A. (1926) *Lo Stato etiopico e la sua Chiesa*, Roma and Milano.

Pollera, A. (1936) *Storie, leggende e favole del paese dei Negus*, Firenze.

Quirin, J.A. (1977) *The Beta Israel (Felasha) in Ethiopian History: Caste Formation and Culture and Change*, University of Minnesota Ph.D. thesis.

Rassam, H. (1869) *Narrative of the British Mission to Theodore, King of Abyssinia*, London.

Rey, C.F. (1929) *The Romance of the Portuguese in Abyssinia*, London.

Reybaud, L. (1841) "Voyage dans l' Abyssinie méridionale," *Revue des Deux Mondes*, XXVII, 59-93.

Rochet d' Héricourt, C.F.X. (1851) "Rapport sur le troisième voyage en Abyssinie", *Comptes rendus Hebdomadaires des Séances de l'Académie des Sciences*, XXXII, 215-41.

Rochet d' Héricourt, C.F.X. (1846) *Second voyage sur les deux rives de la Mer Rouge, dans le pays des Adels et le royaume de Choa*, Paris.

Rochet d' Héricourt, C.F.X. (1841) *Voyage sur la côte orientale de la Mer Rouge, dans le pays d' Adel et le royaume de Choa*, Paris.

Rodinson, M. (1967) *Magie, médecine et possession à Gondar*, Paris and La Haye

Rohlfs, G. (1885) *L' Abissinia*, Milano.

Rohlfs, G. (1883) *Meine Mission nach Abessinien*, Leipzig.

Rosen, F. (1907) *Eine deutsche Gesandtschaft in Abessinien*, Leipzig.

Rosenfeld, C.P. (1980) "Subject and Author Index, *Ethiopia Observer* (E.O.) (1967-1974) and *Journal of Ethiopian Studies* (JES) (1963-1975)", *NorthEast African Studies*, II, 1, pp.81-112.

Rubenson, S. (1987) *Acta Aethiopica I. Correspondence and Treaties 1800-1854*, Evanston, Illinois and Addis Ababa.

Rubenson, S. (1966) *King of Kings Tewodros of Ethiopia*, Addis Ababa.

Rubenson, S. (1977) *The Survival of Ethiopian Independence*, London.

Rüppell, W.P.S.E. (1838-40) *Reise in Abyssinien*, Frankfurt.

Saineanu, M. (1892) *L' Abyssinie dans la seconde moitié du XVIe siècle ou la règne de Sarsa-Dengel (Malak-Sagad) (1563-1594)*, Leipzig and Bucharest.

Salt, H. (1814) *A Voyage to Abyssinia*, London.

Shelemay, K.K. (1986) *Music, Ritual and Falasha History*, East Lansing, Michigan.

Shepherd, A.J. (1868) *The Campaign in Abyssinia*, Bombay.

Simone, E (1975) "The Amhara Military Expeditions against the Showa Galla (1800-1855): A Reappraisal", *Proceedings of the First United States Conference on Ethiopian Studies*, pp.135-41, East Lansing, Mass.

Soleillet, P. (1886) *Voyages en Ethiopie (janvier 1882 - octobre 1884)*, Rouen.

Spencer, D. (1974) "Travels in Gojjam: St. Luke ikons and Brancaleon re-discovered", *Journal of Ethiopian Studies*, XII, No. 2, 201-20.

Stanley, H.M. (1874) *Coomassie and Magdala; the Story of Two British Campaigns in Africa*, London.

Stern, H.A. (1868) *The Captive Missionary*, London.

Stern, H. A. (1862) *Wanderings among the Falashas in Abyssinia*, London.

Stitz, V. (1975) "The Amhara Resettlement of Northern Shoa during the 18th and 19th Centuries", *Proceedings of the First United States Conference on Ethiopian Studies*, pp.70-81, East Lansing, Mass.

Stitz, V. (1975) "Distribution and Foundation of Churches in Ethiopia," *Journal of Ethiopian Studies*, XIII, No. 1, 11-38.

Stitz, V. (1974) *Studien zur Kulturgeographie Zentraläthiopiens*, Bonner Geographische Abhandlungen, LI.

Taddesse Tamrat (1970a) "The Abbots of Däbrä-Hayq 1248-1538," *Journal of Ethiopian Studies*, VIII, No. 1, 67-117.

Taddesse Tamrat (1972) *Church and State in Ethiopia 1270-1527*, Oxford.

Taddesse Tamrat (1970b) *Education in Fifteenth Century Ethiopia: a Brief Note*", Addis Ababa (mimeo).

Taddesse Tamrat (1984) "Feudalism in Heaven and on Earth. Ideology and Political Structure in Medieval Ethiopia," *Proceedings of the Seventh International Conference of Ethiopian Studies*, Addis Ababa.

Taddesse Tamrat (1974) "Problems of Succession in Fifteenth Century Ethiopia: A Presentation of Documents," Accademia Nazionale dei Lincei, *Problemi di Scienze e di Cultura*, No. 191, 501-535.

Taddesse Tamrat (1966) "Some Notes on the Fifteenth Century Stephanite 'Heresy' in the Ethiopian Church," *Rassegna di Studi Etiopici*, XXII, 103-15.

Tamisier, M and Combes, E. (1837) "Extrait de la relation du voyage de MM. Maurice Tamisier et Edmond Combes en Abyssinie pendant 1835 et 1836," *Bulletin de la Société de Géographie*, VII.

Tedeschi, S. (1966) "Poncet et son voyage en Ethiopie," *Journal of Ethiopian Studies*, IV, No. 2, 99-126.

Tekle-Tsadik Mekouria (1968), *Les noms propres, les noms de bâptème et l'étude généalogique des rois d'Ethiopie (XIII-XX⁰ siècles) à travers leurs noms patronymiques*, Belgrade.

Tellez, B. (1710) *The Travels of the Jesuits in Ethiopia*, London.

Thomas, H. (1938) *The Discovery of Abyssinia by the Portuguese in 1520*, London.

Trimingham, J.S. (1952) *Islam in Ethiopia*, London.

Tsehai Berhane Selassie (1981) *The Political and Military Traditions of the Ethiopian Peasantry (1800-1941)* Oxford University D.Phil. thesis.

Tubiana, J. (1966) "Turning points' in Ethiopian History," *Rassegna di Studi Etiopici*, XXI, 162-6.

Ullendorff, E. (1973) *The Ethiopians. An Introduction to Country and People*, London.

Ullendorff, E. (1968) *Ethiopia and the Bible*, London.

Valentia, G. (1809) *Voyages and Travels to India, Ceylon, the Red Sea, Abyssinia and Egypt*, London.

Veitch, S.F.F. (1860) *Notes from the Journal of J.M. Flad*, London.

Veitch, S.F.F. (1868) *Views of Central Abyssinia*, London.

Wainwright, G.A. (1942) "Early Records of Iron in Abyssinia," *Man*, XLII, 84-8.

Waldmeier, T. (1886) *The Autobiography of Theophilus Waldmeier*, London and Leominster.

Waldmeier, T. (1896) *Erlebnisse in Abessinien*, Basel.

Walker, C.H. (1933) *The Abyssinian at Home*, London.

Weld Blundell, H. (1906-7) "History of King Theodore," *Journal of the African Society*, VI, 12-42.

Weld Blundell, H. (1922) *The Royal Chronicle of Abyssinia 1769-1840*, Cambridge.

Whiteway, R.S. (1902) *The Portuguese Expedition to Abyssinia*, London.

Wolff, J. (1839) *Journal of the Rev. Joseph Wolff*, London.

Wolde Michael Kelecha (1987) *A Glossary of Ethiopian Plant Names*, Addis Ababa.

Wright, W. (1878) *Catalogue of the Ethiopic Manuscripts in the British Museum*, London.

INDEX

Index

357

363

mead 46, 60, 68, 148, 150, 175, 193, 241, 253, 258
meat 8, 43, 50, 54, 55, 142, 148, 150, 174, 205, 206, 211, 252, 314
Mecca 20, 55, 102, 214, 224
Mécca 320
medicines 63, 179, 188, 213, 244, 273, 306-310
Mendes, Alfonso 311
mendicants 176 see also: beggars
Menilek I, son of Queen of Sheba 29
Menilek II, Emperor 84, 127, 232, 313
menstruation 71
Mentewwab, Queen 84, 95, 106, 109, 115, 117, 307
Mérab, P., Dr 252, 306
merchandise 46, 50, 55-57, 103, 126, 207, 209, 217, 302
merchants 47, 49-57, 65, 66, 69, 79, 100-104, 113, 125, 181, 183, 207-214, 216-220, 238, 243, 244, 245, 291, 296, 297, 299-302, 304, 321, 331
mercury 233, 309
mes 198, 260
messengers 5, 24, 94, 156, 168, 176
Metical Aga, merchant 102, 103
mice 10, 137, 254
Migra 241
Mika'él, Archangel 193
Mika'él, Greek jeweller 235
Mika'él Sehul, Ras 79, 81, 87, 88, 99, 102, 116, 176, 281, 291, 294, 298, 299
Milan 121, 124, 160, 171, 225, 297
milk 7, 43, 85, 142, 143, 147, 204, 216, 228, 229, 250
milking 135, 138, 250
millers 232
millet 10, 33, 42, 138, 139, 190
mimosas 276
mines 19, 51, 60, 238, 306
minstrels 174, 261
mirrors 106, 213, 216, 233
missionaries 11, 45, 59, 70, 117, 125, 128, 131, 178, 180, 182, 183, 186, 204, 205, 206, 224, 236, 244, 247, 266, 303, 307, 309, 310, 315, 320, 322-325, 327, 329
mobilisation 13, 83, 153, 154, 260
Mogadishu 56
monarchs 3, 7, 8, 13, 14, 15, 18, 20-28, 31, 36, 38, 41, 49, 54, 63, 68, 79-81, 83, 84, 86, 89, 90, 92-94, 98, 103, 112, 114, 118, 141, 153, 162, 164, 165, 169, 170, 173, 174, 176, 187, 202, 219, 237, 238, 258, 266, 274, 275, 277, 284, 286, 289, 290, 292, 293, 302-304, 307, 310-313, 317, 321, 323, 324, 325, 328, 329 see also individual rulers by name
monarchy 18, 27, 75, 79, 83, 86, 88, 89, 92, 93, 162, 169, 170, 273, 274, 280, 289, 310
monasteries 3, 8, 29, 32-34, 35, 42, 44, 57, 62, 71, 94, 126, 128, 178, 187, 188, 199, 217, 234, 263, 301, 302
money 19, 34, 49, 50, 53, 56, 84, 104, 106, 141, 156, 170, 172, 179, 181, 186, 212, 216, 217, 219, 235, 236, 238, 242, 295-301, 303, 305, 306, 313, 318
money-lending 104, 301, 303
monkeys 145, 146, 290

monks 6, 8, 29, 32-39, 41-44, 47, 51, 60, 61, 62, 64, 93, 94, 96, 97, 126, 128, 130, 176, 177, 178, 180-183, 186-189, 202, 204, 234, 266, 295, 310, 312, 330
monogamy 26, 265
Mooney, H.F. 275, 277
Moors 47, 53, 55, 56, 57, 81, 83, 295 see also: Muslims
moqimoqo 118
Morat 224, 229
Morocco 56
mortar 105
mortars (artillery) 105, 287, 288, 323-326, 326
mortars (grain) 190, 229, 254
mortification of the flesh 44
Moses 23
mosques 102
Mota 214
motherhood 267
mountains 6, 17, 27, 29, 44, 51, 52, 77, 79, 91, 123, 135, 146, 152, 169, 178, 188, 220, 260, 261, 273, 287, 302, 326, 330
mourners 46
mourning 46, 97, 98, 190, 196, 198, 262, 268
moving capitals 25, 50, 54, 58, 63, 93, 234
Muhammäd Ali, Pasha 182
Muhämmäd, Nägadras 101
Muhammäd Ibrahim, merchant 214
mules 21, 17, 19, 21, 34, 35, 37, 38, 49, 50, 52, 70, 71, 72, 83, 84, 106, 116, 118, 137, 141, 144, 152, 168, 183, 187, 199, 190, 198, 207, 209, 210, 211, 213, 214, 218, 219, 220, 222, 232, 239, 245, 268, 278, 289, 291, 294, 299, 300, 305
muleteers 17, 275
Munnai river 144
Münzinger, W. 159
Murad, Armenian merchant 79, 103, 104
murder 186, 200, 321
music 130, 263, 294, 295
musicians 28
musketeers 16, 28, 150, 154, 278-283, 292, 293
muskets 16, 81, 198, 199, 277-282, 285, 286, 292, 318, 325
Muslims 13-15, 26, 43, 42, 45, 47-50, 53, 54, 56, 57, 60, 62, 63, 64, 65-67, 89, 100-104, 106, 111, 168, 182, 200, 204, 205, 207, 212, 214, 217-219, 224, 227, 233, 235, 238, 243, 269, 273, 277, 278, 282, 304, 308, 312, 313, 314, 315, 328 see also: Moors
myrrh 50, 55, 101, 217, 252
Na'ibs 204
nägadras 50, 101, 212, 219, 299, 301, 302
Nägassi, Abéto 88
nails 71, 98, 118, 213, 222, 270
Na'od, Emperor 26
Nar 279
Nasar 'Ali, craftsmen 236
Nayzgi, Däjazmač 79
Nazaret, Armenian leather-worker 236
Neburä Ed 199
necklaces 46, 239, 244, 253, 269, 270
needles 58, 101, 213, 216, 217, 222, 237, 240, 253, 303
Negusä Nägäst 169
neuralgia 264

prelates 29, 34-36, 70, 93, 99, 181-183, 200, 310, 311 see also: clergy
Prester John 21, 27, 36, 56
priests 3, 10, 19, 27-29, 32-42, 44-47, 54, 64, 65, 70, 71, 93, 96, 97, 114, 127, 128, 130, 131, 132, 141, 148, 176, 178-183, 186-189, 190, 191, 193-196, 198-203, 204, 205, 206, 232, 250, 263, 265, 267, 275, 303, 307, 308, 310, 312, 313, 315, 329, 330 see also: clergy, priests
primitive money 49, 212, 295-297, 303
primogeniture 27
princes 27, 46, 86, 90, 91, 98, 113, 102, 176, 308
prisoners 65, 91, 112, 156, 241, 244, 279
proclamations 22, 46, 83, 84, 153, 163, 181, 311, 312, 329
prophecies 94, 187, 202
prophets 224, 263
prostitutes 261, 275, 330 see also: courtesans
Protestants 59, 125, 131, 182, 183, 204-206, 309, 322, 326
provisions 10, 11, 13, 34, 50, 54, 55, 83, 84, 87, 100, 104, 116, 142, 143, 148, 153, 154, 159, 161, 198, 209, 260, 305, 317, 324
Psalms 2, 3, 5, 30, 38, 41, 96, 97, 126, 128, 130-1, 185, 311
pupils 3, 127-129, 131 see also: students
Qäha river 83, 100, 101, 212, 233
Qälämsis, Abba, librarian 188
Qañazmac 155
qäy 112
qeddastä qedusan 38
Qeddusan mäsähaft 130
Qemants x, 233, 267
qené 37, 130
qennaj 112
Qérellos, Abunä 181, 186, 201
Qoran 204
Qoräta 181, 207, 212, 214, 236, 239, 302, 304, 314
Qundi 237, 258, 302, 303
qwad 284, 286
qwalqwal 230
Qwara 59, 187, 214
qwerban 38
Qwesqwam 109
rafts 51, 327
Ragu'él, Archangel 312
rains 15, 25, 51, 79, 122, 128, 138, 146, 147, 209, 212
raisins 33
Ras al-Fil 291
Rassam, Hormuzd 167, 213, 243, 287, 303-305, 315, 318-321, 323, 325-328, 331
rate of interest 302, 303
rats 10, 137, 256
razors 46, 71, 213, 216, 222, 237
reading 3, 5, 66, 128, 130, 131, 196, 322
rebellions 12, 13, 22, 150, 165, 172, 176, 220, 281, 311
refuge 200, 223, 266 see also: asylum
Regeb Bär, Gondär 100
revenues 32, 33, 34, 91, 94, 99, 103, 148, 162, 164, 167, 169, 172, 179, 181, 219, 298, 300-304, 307, 329, 330
rheumatism 309

rhinoceroses 168, 213, 232, 290
ribbons 219
riding 3-5, 62, 90, 92, 93, 172, 187
Rif 42
rifle-butts 229, 232
riflemen 80, 156, 183, 277-284, 286, 289, 293
rifles 5, 92, 126, 149, 150, 152, 207, 222, 223, 229, 232, 233, 236, 237, 238, 278-284, 286-288, 291-295, 299, 301
rings 83, 222, 232, 239, 269
rivers 15, 17, 41, 51, 57, 83, 88, 97, 100, 101, 138, 144, 145, 154, 191, 193, 202, 212, 214, 233, 237, 238, 252, 256, 267, 304, 314, 322
roads 10, 11, 32, 51, 101, 153, 155, 183, 205, 218, 219, 244, 252, 260, 263, 287, 317, 321, 326, 327
road-building 317, 326
robbers 207, 321
robes 37, 60, 183, 260
Rochet d'Héricourt, C.F.X. 171, 175-177, 217, 218, 222, 226, 237, 238, 270, 300-303, 305, 309
Rogé, market 218, 242
Rohabayta 145, 263
Rohlfs, G. 128, 130
Roman Catholics 33, 36, 70, 206, 279, 310-1 see also: Catholicism, Jesuits
Romanä Wärq, Princess 36, 70
Rome 47, 53, 105, 121, 124, 160, 171, 202, 206, 225, 284
royalty 70, 72, 162, 169, 269, 292, 306
Rufa'él, Brother 62, 100
Rufa'él stream, Gondär 100
rugs 294
rulers 4, 7, 13, 18-20, 21-24, 26, 27, 28, 33, 46, 47, 53, 54, 58, 65, 68, 81, 86-89, 92, 94, 96, 98, 102, 103, 106, 109, 111, 142, 144, 145, 148, 150, 152, 153, 155, 157, 159, 162-165, 169-176, 179, 182, 186, 187, 202, 204, 219, 234, 235, 236, 274, 275, 277, 278, 279, 280, 281-284, 291, 292, 293, 294, 298, 299-302, 303, 318, 321, 325-327, 328, 330, 331
running 125, 146, 168, 172, 173, 229, 252, 263, 268, 303, 313, 323
Rüppell, W.P.S.E. 58, 84, 135, 137-139, 141, 144-147, 159, 161, 171, 207, 211-214, 216, 217, 219, 220, 222, 224, 226, 227, 229, 232-234, 236, 239, 241, 242, 243, 244, 251, 252, 256, 258, 283, 285, 288, 296-298, 300, 301, 305, 314, 315
Sä'azzäga 299
Säbagades, Däjazmac 156, 157, 170, 181, 186, 236, 299, 301
Sabbath 40, 131, 251, 253, 273, 310-312
Säblä Wängél, Queen 19, 26, 72, 292
sacks 128, 207, 216, 228, 303
Sacrament 39, 184, 189, 193, 200, 266, 311 see also: Mass
Sädäqä Nesrani, builder 105
saddles 21, 62, 83, 202, 217, 218, 227, 232, 235
Säfe'a 304
sähafä lam 7
Sähay, Wäyzäro 120
Sahlä Sellasé, Negus 128, 141, 145, 150, 154, 165, 169, 171, 173-176, 186, 187, 195, 203, 204,

soil 6-7, 9, 41, 78, 135, 137-138, 144, 173, 276, 277
soldiers 5, 11, 13, 15-17, 19, 33, 50, 57, 62, 63, 64, 66, 68, 79-81, 83, 84, 86, 99, 112, 116, 126, 135, 139-141, 143-145, 148-157, 159, 161, 163, 167, 168, 182, 183, 189, 193, 200, 202, 223, 224, 235, 237, 248, 259-262, 268, 277-279, 281-286, 290, 293, 294, 304, 312, 317, 318, 320, 329
Solomon, King of Israel 2, 26, 162
Somalis 217
songs 15, 93, 98, 130, 135, 159, 189, 242, 260, 261-263
soothsayers 202
sorcerers 59, 223, 263
sorcery 223, 224
sorghum 123, 139
sowing 6, 33, 42, 138, 164, 311
Spanish 105, 297
spears 4, 5, 16, 58, 59, 62, 83, 92, 116, 125, 126, 149, 151, 152, 158, 161, 167, 183, 198, 207, 210, 218, 222, 223, 224, 229, 232, 236, 239, 305 see also: lances
spearsmen 168, 268
Spencer, Diana 62
spices 47, 49, 55, 57, 103, 211, 213, 216, 253
spikenard 213
spinning 58, 127, 237, 250-253, 258, 259, 265, 311
spinning-women 237, 250
spirit possession 263
springs 125, 201, 295
stables 176, 193
standard of living 147
Stefanos, Armenian silversmith 238
Stella, Giovanni, Father 204
Stern, H.A. 131, 132, 146, 165, 171, 177, 180, 182, 201, 211-213, 223, 224, 226, 230, 239, 261, 268, 270, 288, 302, 315, 318, 320, 322, 323, 327-330
stibium 101, 213
stirrups 58, 81, 83, 85, 92, 109, 222, 225
stone 4, 38, 41, 71, 105, 146, 184, 187, 222, 228, 233, 236, 238, 250, 253, 275, 285
stone-masons 105
stones 19, 44, 53, 67, 68, 105, 133, 135, 146, 187, 209, 222, 228, 230, 238, 239, 253, 254, 267, 282, 285, 326, 327
straw 133
students 3, 5, 126-131, 177, 178, 317 see also: pupils
Suakin 42
succession 6, 23, 25, 27, 34, 54, 105, 173, 187, 211, 269, 275, 320
Sudan 49, 55, 56, 102, 103, 111, 212, 213, 243, 244, 246, 247, 286, 291, 296, 304, 315
Sudanese 213, 280
sugar 216
sulphur 213, 285
Šum 163, 164, 166
sumptuary laws 25, 26
superstitions 206, 223
suqo 260
Surat 101, 104, 219
surgeons 63, 71, 238, 306, 307
Suriano, Francesco 13

Susneyos, Emperor 3, 15, 25, 26, 33, 66, 105, 275, 279, 292, 311
Swiss 117, 159, 322, 323, 327
Switzerland 162, 206, 322
swords 2, 16, 24, 28, 46, 62, 63, 151, 152, 158, 161, 166, 167, 172, 183, 207, 210, 213, 216, 218, 222, 232, 236, 239, 289, 294, 305, 313, 329
Synaxarium 27
tables 60, 69, 142, 152, 230, 258, 267
tabots 38, 42, 92, 96, 186, 188, 189, 193, 194
Taddesse Tamrat 13, 27, 28, 49, 53, 54, 57, 311
taffeta 25, 86
tailors 59, 62, 63, 232, 235
täj 68, 167, 175, 253, 258, 262 see also: mead
Tajura 217-8
Täkkäzé river 88, 144, 212, 214, 216, 242
Täklä Giyorgis I, Emperor 114, 293
Täklä Giyorgis II, Emperor 330
Täklä Giyorgis I, governor 11
Täklä Haymanot, Emperor 79, 84, 90, 114
Täklä Haymanot, Saint 3
talismans 173, 269
tälla 68, 253, 254
Tämbén 24, 301
Tamisier, M. 109, 117, 125, 126, 138, 139, 141, 144, 145, 147, 172, 181, 188, 211, 213, 214, 216-219, 222-224, 226, 227, 229, 230, 232, 234-240, 242, 243, 244, 246, 247, 252, 261-263, 265-267, 283-285, 288, 295, 298, 300-302, 305, 306, 308
Tana, lake 7, 55, 61, 62, 77, 101, 102, 109, 145, 212, 214, 233, 290, 314, 327
Tanguri 101
tanners 227, 235, 238
tanning 227, 228, 236
tapsters 68
Taranta 182
Täsfä Haylu, merchant 207
tatooed 270
taxation 7, 13, 102, 133, 139, 140, 142, 170, 189, 220, 274, 298, 300, 301
taxed 165, 221
taxes 8, 19, 34, 51, 57, 79, 102, 104, 125, 139, 141, 142, 144, 148, 163, 164, 165, 166, 170, 204, 207, 219-221, 253, 298-301, 304, 321, 330
Taytu, Queen 252
Te'elmar, Wäyzäro 114
teachers 3, 128, 129, 131, 242
Tebläts, Wäyzäro 250
téf 10, 133, 135, 138, 139, 253, 254
Tegré 6, 7, 9, 10, 15, 21, 24, 28, 29, 33, 34, 37, 42, 43, 50, 51, 67, 68, 72, 77-79, 81, 84, 86-88, 94, 99, 102, 104, 118, 131, 136-138, 141, 142, 144, 150, 152, 154, 162-164, 166-168, 170-173, 176, 183, 184, 186, 187, 192, 196, 198, 200, 202, 204, 206, 213, 218-220, 223, 224, 235, 236, 241, 242, 244, 247-249, 253, 256, 259, 261, 262, 265, 268, 270, 274-287, 291, 294-296, 298-301, 304-306, 309, 317, 329
Telles, Baltazar 66, 105, 278, 279, 292
Telq 13
Teltäl 156, 283, 291, 304
Temmenon, a farmer 141
temperature 138, 322
Temqät 41, 96, 154, 193, 194

369

371